I0885510

POLITICAL VIOLENCE AND THE INTERNATIONAL COMMUNITY: DEVELOPMENTS IN INTERNATIONAL LAW AND POLICY

Kirsti Samuels

MARTINUS NIJHOFF PUBLISHERS
LEIDEN / BOSTON

Cover photo by Kirsti Samuels, Somalia, March 2006.

Library of Congress Cataloging-in-Publication Data

Samuels, Kirsti.
Political violence and the international community : developments in international law and policy / Kirsti Samuels.
p. cm.
Includes bibliographical references and index.
ISBN 978-1-57105-374-9
1. Intervention (International law) 2. War (International law) 3. Sovereignty. 4. Political violence. 5. Coups d'état. 6. Humanitarian assistance. 7. United Nations. Security Council. I. Title.
KZ6368.S26 2007
341.5'84—dc22

2007027869

Koninklijke Brill NV incorporates the imprints Brill, Hotei Publishers, IDC Publishers, Martinus Nijhoff Publishers, and VSP.

Manufactured in the United States of America

TABLE OF CONTENTS

ABOUT THE AUTHOR

Dr. Kirsti Samuels is the Senior Programme Manager of the Constitution-Building Processes program at International IDEA, an inter-governmental organization that supports sustainable democracy worldwide. In 2006, she worked in Somalia and Kenya as the lead legal consultant to UNDP on a constitution-building process for Somalia and with the interim government for Somalia and later the Constitutional Commission in developing and implementing an inclusive and participatory process.

Dr. Samuels has consulted to the World Bank on Rule of Law reform in post-conflict countries and the Clinton Global Initiative on state-building policy and civil conflict. During 2003–2005, she headed the state-building program at the International Peace Academy, focusing on the challenges faced and the lessons learned from previous state-building experiences. She has taught Law at University College Oxford (2000–2002), clerked on the Australian constitutional court and final court of appeal for the Hon. Justice Michael McHugh (1998–1999), and worked with the Australian Delegation to UNESCO in Paris, on the Underwater Cultural Heritage Treaty Negotiation and the campaign for Director General (2000).

Dr. Samuels holds a Law Degree and Science Degree from the University of Sydney, and a Masters in Laws and a Doctorate from Oxford University.

Recent publications include: RULE OF LAW REFORM IN POST-CONFLICT COUNTRIES: OPERATIONAL INITIATIVES AND LESSONS LEARNED (World Bank Social Development Papers Series, Oct. 2006); *Post-Conflict Peace-Building and Constitution-Making*, 6(2) CHICAGO JOURNAL OF INTERNATIONAL LAW (Winter 2006); CONSTITUTION BUILDING PROCESSES AND DEMOCRATIZATION: A DISCUSSION OF TWELVE CASE STUDIES (International IDEA, 2006); CONSTITUTIONAL ENGINEERING AFTER CONFLICT: THE CONSEQUENCES OF GOVERNANCE CHOICES IN POST-CONFLICT CONSTITUTIONS (IPA, 2006); *Sustainability and Peace-Building: A Key Challenge*," 15(6) JOURNAL OF DEVELOPMENT IN PRACTICE (Nov. 2005); *State-Building and the Political Transition after Conflict*, PROCEEDINGS OF THE AMERICAN SOCIETY OF INTERNATIONAL LAW ANNUAL CONFERENCE (2005).

ACKNOWLEDGMENTS

I am infinitely grateful to Professor Sir Frank Berman QC, advisor and friend, for his challenging and insightful supervision of the Dphil thesis that developed into this book. For friendship beyond the call of duty and dedicated reading and discussion of drafts, I gratefully thank Drew Evans. Thanks to my sister, Saffron, for extraordinarily patient proof-reading, and to my father, Dr. Rob Samuels, whose intellectual curiosity and vitality inspired me to start the doctoral work, and whose trust and patient reading sustained me to its completion.

Thank you to Magdalen College and its members that were my home and my Oxford family during the years of writing the thesis. I am grateful for financial support through a Senior Mackinnon Scholarship and a Herbert Warren Benefaction from Magdalen, and to the Sir Robert Menzies Memorial Trust for a Scholarship in Law.

Finally, I want to thank my mentor and friend Justice Michael McHugh of the Australian High Court, whose intellectual rigor and integrity, and lifelong dedication to justice, will always remain an inspiration and example to me.

LIST OF ABBREVIATIONS

AFRC	Armed Forces Ruling Council (Sierra Leone)
ASEAN	Association of Southeast Asian Nations
A.U.	African Union
DRC	Democratic Republic of the Congo
ECOMOG	Economic Community of West African States Monitoring Group
ECOWAS	Economic Community of West African States
EU	European Union
FIS	Islamic Salvation Front
FRY	Federal Republic of Yugoslavia
ICRC	International Committee for the Red Cross
KLA	Kosovo Liberation Army
LURD	Liberations United for Reconciliation and Democracy
MINUCI	U.N. Mission in Côte d'Ivoire
MODEL	Movement for Democracy in Liberia
MPCI	Patriotic Movement of Côte d'Ivoire
OAU	Organization for African Unity
OSCE	Organization for Security and Cooperation in Europe
RUF	Revolutionary United Front (Sierra Leone)
SLA	Sierra Leone Army
U.N.	United Nations
U.N. OCHA	U.N. Office for the Coordination of Humanitarian Affairs
UNAMIR	U.N. Assistance Mission for Rwanda
UNAMSIL	U.N. Mission in Sierra Leone
UNAVEM	U.N. Angola Verification Mission
UNITA	Uniao Nacional Para a Independencia Total de Angola (United Front for the Total Liberation of Angola)
UNMIL	U.N. Mission in Liberia
UNOMSIL	U.N. Observer Mission in Sierra Leone
UNOSOM	U.N. Operation in Somalia
UNPROFOR	U.N. Protection Force in Croatia
UNTAET	U.N. Transitional Administration in East Timor

CHAPTER 1
INTRODUCTION

Political violence within a state can take the form of a range of violent struggles aiming to capture or retain political power in a state, including civil conflict, coup d'état, terrorist actions, as well as riots or violent demonstrations and the violent repression of such movements. While questions surrounding terrorism and the protection of political speech and other human rights have been widely debated and form an important aspect of international legal and policy discourse, the response of the international community[1] to civil conflicts and coups d'état has not been subject to systematic analysis in the international law or policy arena.[2] However, violence in the domestic context, particularly civil war and coup d'état, is proving itself to be a particularly intractable and complex issue currently facing the international community. Civil war has become the dominant type of war in number[3] and

1 I use the term "international community" as a shorthand to encapsulate a variety of different actors on the international plane that are relevant to a discussion of emerging international norms: states, regional organizations, and U.N. bodies, particularly the General Assembly, the Security Council, and the Secretary-General.

2 The study of civil conflict has largely focused on the legality of intervention in civil war by third parties (*see, e.g.*, Richard Falk, *Introduction, in* 1 THE INTERNATIONAL LAW OF CIVIL WAR 1 (Richard Falk ed., 1971); LAW AND CIVIL WAR IN THE MODERN WORLD (John Norton Moore ed., 1974); or CHRISTINE GRAY, INTERNATIONAL LAW AND THE USE OF FORCE (2000)) and the application of humanitarian laws of war (*see, e.g.*, LINDSAY MOIR, THE LAW OF INTERNAL ARMED CONFLICT (2002)). One exception to this trend is HEATHER A. WILSON, INTERNATIONAL LAW AND THE USE OF FORCE BY NATIONAL LIBERATION MOVEMENTS (1988), which considered the legality of the use of force by rebels in wars of national liberation and concluded that despite a trend toward the extension of the authority to use force to national liberation movements, the resort to force in such wars "remained a matter of self-help beyond the purview of international law" (*Id.* at 28). Another is Ruth Wedgwood, *The Use of Force in Civil Disputes*, 26 ISR. Y.B. HUM. RTS. 239 (1996), which suggests, albeit in an introductory and tentative manner, that contemporary international practice implies that the prohibition on the use of force "may be extended to bar large-scale military force in pursuit of domestic political objectives" (*Id.* at 239).

3 *E.g.*, Sierra Leone, the Democratic Republic of Congo, Angola, Sudan, Rwanda, Burundi, Western Sahara, Colombia, East Timor, Sri Lanka, Kashmir, Nepal, West Papua, Laos, Afghanistan, the Former Yugoslavia, Kosovo, and Chechnya represent a few of the more prominent. Evan Luard, *Civil Conflicts in Modern International Relations*, *in* THE INTERNATIONAL REGULATION OF CIVIL WARS 7 (Evan Luard ed., 1972), contrasts seven international conflicts with at least 34 civil wars during 1945–70. The vast

severity.[4] It has caused humanitarian devastation on a vast scale, as well as serious disruption of regional and international peace and security.[5]

The purpose of this work is to collate and analyze a broad range of international community practice with respect to civil conflicts and coups d'état and to investigate how this practice, which has undergone substantial change in the last 15 years, is shaping international law and policy. "International policy" is used to describe norms that have widespread acceptance within the international community from a moral or rational perspective, whereas "international law," in particular customary law, is used to describe those norms that satisfy the formal requirements for the emergence of international legal norms within the legal discourse.

Since the end of World War II and particularly in the last decade, states, regional organizations, and the United Nations have become increasingly involved in situations of civil conflicts and coups d'état. They condemn them, call on parties to cease fighting and to resolve their disputes by peaceful means, and frequently impose sanctions or intervene forcefully. The international community has also formulated a series of rationales for its actions, ranging from rejecting violence against civilians to rejecting the use of force against democratic governments.

For many years, such responses to civil conflicts and coups d'état took place in the Cold War context, and they were largely governed by geopolitical ideology and superpower motives rather than international

---

majority of the 30 wars in Africa since 1970 have been civil wars. *See* The Secretary-General, *Report of the Secretary-General into the Causes of Conflict and the Promotion of Durable Peace and Sustainable Development in Africa, delivered to the Security Council,* U.N. Doc. A/52/871, S/1998/318 (Apr. 16, 1998), *available at* http://www.un.org/ecosocdev/geninfo/afrec/sgreport/index.html. Of the 11 U.N. peace-keeping operations established between 1992 and 1995, 82 percent dealt with internal conflicts. *See* The Secretary-General, *Report of the Secretary-General on the Work of the Organization: Supplement to an Agenda for Peace,* U.N. Doc. A/50/60*, S/1995/1* (Jan. 25, 1995).

[4] These wars have been frequently characterized by intense and deliberate assault of the civilian population, ruthless terror tactics, tribal or ethnic conflict, massive violations of human rights, and often a complete or partial breakdown of the state concerned. According to the Fund for Peace, more civilians have died from internal wars than from inter-state wars and terrorism combined, and civilian fatalities have grown to represent 90 percent of war-related deaths in the 1990s as compared to 5 percent at the turn of the century. FUND FOR PEACE, CONFLICT PREVENTION AND RECOVERY PROGRAM (2000).

[5] Consider, *e.g.*, the impact of the conflicts in the former Yugoslavia and Kosovo, Rwanda, Somalia, Sierra Leone, or Afghanistan.

policy or legal norms. Security Council involvement was sporadic—the Council generally only intervened once the parties had come to accept the need for a negotiated peace agreement.

However, since the end of the Cold War, the international community, and particularly the Council, has begun intervening frequently and consistently in such conflicts. These interventions are not easily explicable on the basis of geopolitical ideology and strategic interests. A large amount of new practice is accumulating, which raises the question of how international policy and legal norms are being shaped by this practice. This introduction reviews the existing international law and policy that addresses civil conflict and coup d'etat before turning to the recent practice.

A. A SHIFTING UNDERSTANDING OF SOVEREIGNTY

The context for the discussion undertaken includes a broad shift in the approach of the international community to matters of state sovereignty. The content of the concept of sovereignty provides the basis for interpretation of the scope of obligations of states and the international community, as well as of the rights of the international community vis-à-vis states, and a number of matters that used to be considered to fall within the exclusive jurisdiction, or sovereignty, of a state—including human rights, humanitarian intervention, and civil conflicts—are increasingly viewed as matters of international concern. For instance, a number of U.N. Secretaries-General have emphasized that sovereignty cannot be ascribed a meaning that shelters states from their responsibilities when serious human rights abuses are taking place. Most recently, Kofi Annan asserted, "State sovereignty, in its most basic sense, is being redefined—not least by the forces of globalization and international co-operation. States are now widely understood to be instruments at the service of their peoples, and not vice versa."[6] This statement takes up and expands on a statement by Secretary-General Javier Perez de Cuellar: "It is now increasingly felt that the principle of non-interference with the essential domestic jurisdiction of States cannot be regarded as a protective barrier behind which human rights could be massively or systematically violated with impunity."[7] And, Secretary-General Boutros Boutros-

---

6 Kofi Annan, *Two Concepts of Sovereignty*, ECONOMIST, Sept. 18, 1999, at 49.

7 The Secretary-General, *Annual Report of the Secretary-General on the Work of the Organization*, at 10–11, U.N. Doc. A/46/1 (Sept. 16, 1991).

Ghali has said: "The time of absolute and exclusive sovereignty, however, has passed; its theory was never matched by reality."[8]

The extensive and heated debate surrounding humanitarian intervention is another example of this trend.[9] The reformulation of that debate by the International Commission on Intervention and State Sovereignty as a question of the responsibility of states to protect their people[10] has resulted in a watershed decision by the General Assembly to adopt the responsibility to protect populations from genocide, war crimes, ethnic cleansing, and crimes against humanity. They stated that they "accept that responsibility and will act in accordance with it" and went on to hold that they were prepared to take collective action through the Security Council under Chapter VII of the U.N. Charter, "should peaceful means be inadequate and national authorities are manifestly

---

[8] The Secretary-General, *An Agenda for Peace: Preventive Diplomacy, Peacemaking and Peace-Keeping*, U.N. Doc. A/47/277, S/24111, ¶ 17 (June 17, 1992). *See also* American Society of International Law, *The End of Sovereignty?*, 88 PROC. ANN. MEETING OF ASIL (1995); Annan, *supra* note 6; Nico Schrijver, *The Changing Nature of State Sovereignty*, 70 BRIT. Y.B. INT'L L. 65 (1999). The debate continues, however. *See* Derek Bowett, *The Interrelation of Theories of Intervention and Self-Defense, in* LAW AND CIVIL WAR IN THE MODERN WORLD, *supra* note 2, at 38; INTERVENTION IN WORLD POLITICS (Hedley Bull ed., 1984); W. Michael Reisman, *Sovereignty and Human Rights in Contemporary International Law*, 84 AM. J. INT'L L. 866 (1990); Louis Henkin, *The Mythology of Sovereignty*, 21 PROC. ANN. CONF. OF CAN. COUNCIL INT'L L. 5 (1992); American Society of International Law, *The End of Sovereignty?*, 88 PROC. ANN. MEETING OF ASIL (1995); Thomas F. Franck, *Multiple Tiers of Sovereignty: The Future of International Governance*, 88 PROC. ANN. MEETING OF ASIL 51 (1994); MORTIMER SELLERS, THE NEW WORLD ORDER: SOVEREIGNTY, HUMAN RIGHTS, AND THE SELF-DETERMINATION OF PEOPLES (1996); NEIL MACCORMICK, QUESTIONING SOVEREIGNTY: LAW, STATE, AND NATION IN THE EUROPEAN COMMONWEALTH (1999).

[9] *See, e.g.*, Wolfgang Friedmann, *Intervention, Civil War and the Role of International Law*, 59 PROC. ANN. MEETING OF ASIL 67 (1965); Tom J. Farer, *Intervention in Civil Wars: A Modest Proposal*, 67 COLUM. L. REV. 266 (1967); John Norton Moore, *Toward an Applied Theory for the Regulation of Intervention, in* LAW AND CIVIL WAR IN THE MODERN WORLD 1, *supra* note 2; LORI F. DAMROSCH, ENFORCING RESTRAINT: COLLECTIVE INTERVENTION IN INTERNAL CONFLICTS (1993); Anthony Chukwuka Ofodile, *The Legality of ECOWAS Intervention in Liberia*, 32 COLUM. J. TRANSNT'L L. 381 (1994); JAMES MAYALL, THE NEW INTERVENTIONISM 1991–1994: UNITED NATIONS EXPERIENCE IN CAMBODIA, FORMER YUGOSLAVIA AND SOMALIA (1996); THEODOR MERON, HUMAN RIGHTS AND HUMANITARIAN NORMS AS CUSTOMARY LAW (1989); Lois E. Fielding, *Taking the Next Step in the Development of New Human Rights: The Emerging Right of Humanitarian Assistance to Restore Democracy*, 5 DUKE J. COMP. & INT'L L. 329 (1995); FERNANDO R. TESÓN, HUMANITARIAN INTERVENTION: AN INQUIRY INTO LAW AND MORALITY (2d ed. 1997); SIMON CHESTERMAN, JUST WAR OR JUST PEACE?: HUMANITARIAN INTERVENTION AND INTERNATIONAL LAW (2001).

[10] INTERNATIONAL COMMISSION ON INTERVENTION AND STATE SOVEREIGNTY, RESPONSIBILITY TO PROTECT 2.24 (2001).

failing to protect their populations from genocide, war crimes, ethnic cleansing and crimes against humanity."[11]

The way civil conflicts are perceived has also undergone dramatic change. The basic legal framework for the analysis of conflict remains the division of wars into civil and international,[12] and the most common legal formulation considers that civil conflicts are matters within the domestic jurisdiction of states.[13] However, it is widely accepted that subject matters are not irrevocably fixed within this reserved domain[14] and that such jurisdiction may be controlled and limited by international duties through treaty or custom or whenever a matter requires enforcement in relation to another state.[15] The practice of the international community reviewed in this book suggests that such conflicts are increasingly recognized as matters that are appropriate for international scrutiny and involvement.[16] Moreover, the Council has maintained that many civil con-

---

11 *2005 World Summit Outcome: Final Document*, U.N. Doc. A/60/L.1 (Sept. 20, 2005).

12 Civil wars involve conflicts primarily fought between factions internal to a sovereign state, and international wars, conflicts between two or more sovereign states. Richard Falk, *Preface, in* 1 THE INTERNATIONAL LAW OF CIVIL WAR, *supra* note 2, at xi. *See also* Rosalyn Higgins, *Internal War and International Law, in* 3 THE FUTURE OF THE INTERNATIONAL LEGAL ORDER: CONFLICT MANAGEMENT 81, 85 (Cyril E. Black and Richard A. Falk eds., 1969), pointing out that identification of a conflict as civil or international is "essential to the correct application of the relevant legal norms" but also that is it often difficult to appraise a conflict as simply internal.

13 Domestic matters are considered to be matters "where the jurisdiction of the state is not bound by international law." IAN BROWNLIE, PRINCIPLES OF PUBLIC INTERNATIONAL LAW (5th ed. 1998). See the discussion of the traditional approach in FALK, *supra* note 2, at 11–16; GRAY, *supra* note 2, at 51.

14 BROWNLIE, *supra* note 13, at 293; ROSALYN HIGGINS, THE DEVELOPMENT OF INTERNATIONAL LAW THROUGH THE POLITICAL ORGANS OF THE UNITED NATIONS 58–130, esp. 63 (1963); MALCOLM N. SHAW, INTERNATIONAL LAW (4th ed. 1997). The notion that domestic jurisdiction is relative is also expounded in Nationality Decrees Issued in Tunis and Morocco (French Zone) on November 8, 1921, Advisory Opinion, 1923 P.C.I.J. (ser. B) No. 4 (Feb. 7) [hereinafter *Nationality Decrees Case*].

15 BROWNLIE, *supra* note 13, at 293; Satvinder Juss, *Nationality Law, Sovereignty, and the Doctrine of Exclusive Domestic Jurisdiction*, 9 FLA. J. INT'L L. 219, 228–29 (1994). This view of domestic jurisdiction finds support in the *Nationality Decrees Case*, 1923 P.C.I.J. (ser. B) No. 4, at 24, and is consistent with the exemption for Chapter VII enforcement measures.

16 NIGEL D. WHITE, KEEPING THE PEACE: THE UNITED NATIONS AND THE MAINTENANCE OF INTERNATIONAL PEACE AND SECURITY (2d ed. 1997), *quoting Report of the Conference held at San Francisco by the Rt Hon Frazer*, NZ Dept. of External Affairs Publication, No. 11, 28, argued that Article 2(7) should be read to permit intervention where it is "proper in the interests of peace and justice, and in the preservation of human rights to interfere in the internal affairs of Member states." *Cf.* D.R. Gilmour, *The*

flicts represent a threat to international peace and security. Goodrich et al. point out that any situation that amounts to a threat to international peace and security is "patently a matter of international concern."[17] Falk's predicted "growth of a community willingness to remove internal wars from the sanctuary of 'domestic jurisdiction'"[18] has crystallized in the actual practice of states and the international community. The extent to which international law and policy has developed to reflect such changes is investigated in greater detail in Chapter 5.

B. INTERNATIONAL NORMS, LAW, AND POLICY

The term "international policy" is used to describe norms that have widespread acceptance within the international community from a moral or rational perspective, whereas international law, and, in particular, customary law, is used to describe those norms that satisfy the formal requirements for the emergence of international legal norms within the legal discourse.

In essence, this book considers international law to be a sub-system of international politics, whereby, since both are in a state of continual evolution, as new issues arise in international politics, so international policy is formulated and international law is slowly crystallized, and each reinforces the other. The real importance of international law may not be so much in its coercive power, since it is weak, but rather in the normative standards it sets, which play a role in shaping international politics and policy. These, like international law, are supported through normative influence and moral and diplomatic pressure.

The emergence and relevance of international law is a highly contested area of analysis both within international relations discourse and within legal jurisprudence. Commentators influenced by realpolitik conclude that only power and interest shape international norms, and any compliance with international law by states is merely a coincidence of

---

Meaning of Intervene Within Article 2(7) of the United Nations Charter, 16 INT'L & COMP. L.Q. 330, 349 (1967), who maintains that it excludes anything internal.

17 LELAND M. GOODRICH ET AL., CHARTER OF THE UNITED NATIONS: COMMENTARY AND DOCUMENTS 292 (3d ed. 1969). *See* Lois E. Fielding, *Taking a Closer Look at Threats to Peace: The Power of the Security Council to Address Humanitarian Crises*, 73 U. DET. MERCY L. REV. 551 (1996). White agrees: "[A]ny finding under Article 39, whether or not combined with enforcement measures, is sufficient to internationalise the situation and to escape the grasp of Article 2(7)." WHITE, *supra* note 16, at 56.

18 Richard Falk, *Janus Tormented: The International Law of Internal Law*, *in* INTERNATIONAL ASPECTS OF CIVIL STRIFE 185, 208 (James Rosenau ed., 1964).

interests. Because international law does not have enforcement capability and is largely based on consent, it has little relevance in an international order dominated by power.[19] However, others argue that international law does impact on the conduct of states and moreover plays a symbolic and standard-setting role in the international sphere.[20]

The chasm between these positions is exacerbated by widely divergent jurisprudential approaches to international law. Legal positivism, the most conservative approach to international law, focuses on legal rules with little interest in the political considerations and practical realities.[21] The feature "which characterizes all, or at least all traditional, Positivistic theories is that these are not concerned with values and ideals"[22] and hence divorce law from morality or values. Natural law theories, in contrast, see moral values as inextricably linked to policy choices and consider it possible to arrive at commonly agreed norms based on moral reasoning.[23] Renewed natural law theories have moved beyond reliance entirely on morality or natural law and seek to integrate an analytical approach to the identification of laws while still taking into

---

19 For a discussion of the Realist school and why it considers international law to be of little relevance to international politics, *see* Kenneth W. Abbott, *Modern International Relations Theory: A Prospectus for International Lawyers*, 14 YALE J. INT'L L. 338 (1989); ROBERT O. KEOHANE, NEOREALISM AND ITS CRITICS 7 (1986); Francis A. Boyle, *The Irrelevance of International Law: The Schism Between International Law and International Politics*, 10 CAL. W. INT'L L.J. 198 (1980); Robert G. Gilpin, *The Richness of the Tradition of Political Realism*, 38 INT'L ORG. 290 (1984). Keohane highlighted three assumptions: that states are the key units of action; that they seek power, either as an end in itself or as a means to other ends; and that they behave in ways that are essentially rational. KEOHANE, *supra*, at 6.

20 For an introduction to aspects of the debate from the international law perspective, *see* MARTIN DIXON AND ROBERT MCCORQUODALE, CASES AND MATERIALS ON INTERNATIONAL LAW ch. 3 (3d ed. 2000); INTERNATIONAL LAW, CASES AND MATERIALS ch. 1 (Louis Henkin and Wolfgang Friedmann eds., 1980); IAN BROWNLIE, THE RULE OF LAW IN INTERNATIONAL AFFAIRS (1998); MARTTI KOSKENNIEMI, FROM APOLOGY TO UTOPIA (1989).

21 Colin Warbrick, *The Theory of International Law: Is There an English Contribution?*, *in* THE UNITED NATIONS AND THE PRINCIPLES OF INTERNATIONAL LAW: ESSAYS IN MEMORY OF MICHAEL AKEHURST 49, 61 (Vaughan Lowe and Colin Warbrick eds., 1994); for an alternative approach, *see* PHILIP ALLOTT ET AL., THEORY AND INTERNATIONAL LAW: AN INTRODUCTION (1991).

22 G.J.H. VAN HOOF, RETHINKING THE SOURCES OF INTERNATIONAL LAW 34 (1983).

23 Colin Warbrick, *Brownlie's Principles of Public International Law: An Assessment*, 11 EUR. J. INT'L L. 621, 627 (2000). *See* Stephen Hall, *The Persistent Spectre: Natural Law, International Order and the Limits of Legal Positivism*, 12 EUR. J. INT'L L. 269 (2001), for a discussion of the ongoing role of natural law in international law.

account the role values can play in shaping the law.[24] Finnis, for instance, argues that the aim is not to "minimise the range and determinacy of positive law or the general sufficiency of positive sources as solvents of legal problems," but rather to show that the act of stating a legal rule "is an act which can and should be guided by 'moral' principles and rules; and that those moral norms are a matter of objective reasonableness, not whim, convention, or mere 'decision.'"[25] Thus, the aim of the natural law tradition becomes to "determine what the requirements of practical reasonableness really are, so as to afford a rational basis for the activities of legislators, judges, and citizens."[26]

In contrast, the policy and sociological approaches to international law seek to replace "the fictitious legalism of traditional jurisprudence with a conception nearer to the realities of the law."[27] They reject the certainty and clarity of the analytical approach, which they perceive as misleading and simplistic, since it does not reflect the complexity of reality, which includes power, economic rationales, and other influences on state conduct.[28] A common theme in many of the approaches is the recognition that international behavior arises from complex interactions between rules and political, social, and cultural factors.[29]

---

[24] *See* esp. JOHN FINNIS, NATURAL LAW AND NATURAL RIGHTS (1980); *see* M.D.A. FREEMAN, LLOYD'S INTRODUCTION TO JURISPRUDENCE 132 (7th ed. 2001).

[25] FINNIS, *supra* note 24, at 290.

[26] *Id. See also* RONALD DWORKIN, LAW'S EMPIRE 245 (1998). Dworkin's approach rejects the positivist separation between law and morals and argues that law constitutes rules and "non-rule standards"—moral and political standards—on which courts can draw in order to reach a decision in hard cases.

[27] Hans Morgenthau, *Positivism, Functionalism, and International Law, in* THE NATURE OF INTERNATIONAL LAW 159, 172 (Gerry Simpson ed., 2001).

[28] *See e.g.* Myres S. McDougal, *International Law, Power and Policy: A Contemporary Conception*, 82 RECUEIL DES COURS 133 (1953); MYRES S. MCDOUGAL AND W. MICHAEL REISMAN, INTERNATIONAL LAW ESSAYS: A SUPPLEMENT TO INTERNATIONAL LAW IN CONTEMPORARY PERSPECTIVE (1981); Jack L. Goldsmith and Eric A. Posner, *A Theory of Customary International Law*, 66 U. CHI. L. REV. 1113 (1999). For an interesting review of some of these theories, *see* MICHAEL BYERS, CUSTOM, POWER AND THE POWER OF RULES: INTERNATIONAL RELATIONS AND CUSTOMARY INTERNATIONAL LAW 125 (1999); and Morgenthau, *supra* note 27, at 172.

[29] ORIOL CASANOVAS, UNITY AND PLURALISM IN PUBLIC INTERNATIONAL LAW 85 (2001); OSCAR SCHACHTER, INTERNATIONAL LAW IN THEORY AND PRACTICE 27–28 (1991).

Some commentators argue that such emphasis on social reality undermines the ability of law to provide certainty and predictability and results in law acting as apology for power dynamics.[30] Indeed, some within this school side with those international relations scholars who discount international law and maintain that states comply with norms only because of self-interest and not out of "a sense of moral or legal obligation."[31] However, others consider that the policy approach can ground international law in reality, while at the same time maintaining its normative value. Higgins adopts a "law as process" approach that she argues "encourages interpretation and choice that is more compatible with values we seek to promote and objectives we seek to achieve."[32] In her analysis, formulating law is not a mechanistic process but a rational one, which involves choices between options, taking into account the political and social context to make decisions that best reflect community interests and promote common values. International law, in her analysis, is composed of norms that states believe to be necessary to guide their relations with one another.[33]

This book considers that both international law and international politics are relevant to the shaping of perceived reality. In the *practice* of international law and international relations, it is difficult to disentangle law from politics and power. Consider, for instance, how political and ideological perspective affected the degree to which the international intervention in Iraq was considered legal. As Scott aptly observes, "Power is not a consideration distinct from international law. It appears that the idea of international law is an important form of power in international politics."[34] Even from a legal perspective, Higgins points out that there is a close relationship between law and politics:

> Policy considerations, although they differ from "rules," are an integral part of that decision making process which we call international law; the assessment of so-called extralegal considerations is part of legal process, just as is reference to the accumulation of

---

30 *See, e.g.*, VAN HOOF, *supra* note 22, at 26.

31 Goldsmith and Posner, *supra* note 28, at 1114.

32 ROSALYN HIGGINS, PROBLEMS AND PROCESS: INTERNATIONAL LAW AND HOW WE USE IT 10 (1994).

33 *Id.* at 18, 95, 8–9.

34 Shirley V. Scott, *International Law as Ideology: Theorizing the Relationship Between International Law and International Politics*, 5 EUR. J. INT'L L. 313 (1994).

> past decisions and current norms. . . . There is no avoiding the essential relationship between law and politics.[35]

On the question of how to deal with a field of international law where practice no longer accords with traditional norms, this book is sympathetic to the view put forward by scholars such as Reisman, Franck, and Falk that international law must sufficiently mirror international reality to be able to influence and shape it. The conservative view has been to uphold the validity of the extant norms and discount inconsistent practice.[36]

However, increasingly, commentators support an approach that emphasizes the importance of descriptive accuracy, where laws are assumed to correspond to reality. Roberts argues:

> Descriptive accuracy (which focuses on what the practice *has been*) is valuable in justifying the content of international law because laws should correspond to reality. Laws must bear some relation to practice if they are to regulate conduct effectively, because laws that set unrealistic standards are likely to be disobeyed and ultimately forgotten. This consideration particularly applies to decentralized systems of law, such as international law, where traditional enforcement mechanisms are unavailable or underdeveloped. Descriptive accuracy is also essential to predictive power because a theory that accurately describes practice enables more reliable predictions of future state behavior.[37]

Similarly, Reisman rejects the approach of those international experts who "respond to the appearance of a discrepancy between existing and emerging legal arrangements by heatedly rejecting the new," without taking into account whether the traditional arrangements are appropriately attaining their goal, particularly in contexts different from those they

---

[35] Higgins, *supra* note 32, at 5, *quoting her position in* Rosalyn Higgins, *Integration of Authority and Control: Trends in the Literature of International Law and International Relations, in* TOWARD WORLD ORDER AND HUMAN DIGNITY 80 (W. Michael Reisman and Burns Weston eds., 1976).

[36] This approach is particularly prevalent with commentators who reject the emergence of new norms permitting humanitarian and pro-democratic intervention, and any other exceptions to the prohibition on intervention, and the crystallization of human rights customary law.

[37] Elizabeth A. Roberts, *Traditional and Modern Approaches to Customary International Law: A Reconciliation,* 95 AM. J. INT'L L. 757, 762 (2001).

were originally established to address.[38] Franck also supports attempts to reformulate the law to better reflect reality; otherwise "international law, like law dealing with drug addiction, cannot hope to influence the situation so long as the law itself induces everyone to pretend that the problem does not exist."[39]

Rules that are unenforced and do not represent the actual practice of states should be carefully scrutinized. Falk argues: "A legal norm that operates in such a climate of contradiction is bound to function as mere rhetoric and to erode generally arguments urging for international law."[40] "It is better explicitly to disregard particular rules of international law that have become obsolete than to make the entire legal system appear obsolete by disregard of rules in practice."[41] While rejecting the natural law-influenced approach where certain rules, such as rules against aggression and self-defense, have "higher normativity,"[42] Higgins maintains that the reason certain norms, such as the prohibition on torture, retain their status, despite breaches, is that the *opinio juris* in favor of such norms is not withdrawn.[43] But she also acknowledges that it is only by looking "behind the legal rhetoric to the reality" that "a more realistic legal order can be built."[44]

In essence, it is important to move beyond a formalistic approach that undermines the respect due to international law by rendering it an academic and theoretical field irrelevant to the circumstances and events in the real world. Such an approach hinders the development of principles that can guide the practice of the international community in relation to civil conflicts, as it masks the failure of the traditional rules. The

---

38 W. Michael Reisman, *Editorial Comment: Assessing Claims to Revise the Laws of War,* 97 AM. J. INT'L L. 82, 83 (2003).

39 Thomas M. Franck and Nigel Rodley, *Legitimacy and Legal Rights of Revolutionary Movements with Special Reference to the People's Revolutionary Government of South Viet Nam, in* THE VIETNAM WAR AND INTERNATIONAL LAW 723, 732 (Richard Falk ed., 1972).

40 FALK, *supra* note 2.

41 Falk, *supra* note 18, at 216.

42 Oscar Schachter, *Entangled Treaty and Custom, in* INTERNATIONAL LAW AT A TIME OF PERPLEXITY: ESSAYS IN HONOUR OF SHABTAI ROSENNE 717, 734 (Yoram Dinstein ed., 1989).

43 HIGGINS, *supra* note 14, at 22.

44 Rosalyn Higgins, *International Law and Civil Conflict, in* THE INTERNATIONAL REGULATION OF CIVIL WARS, *supra* note 3, at 169.

issue will be most difficult when real-world practice violates basic moral principles, but, even then, when a so-called norm becomes no more than empty rhetoric, its existence serves less to protect than to render complacent those who ought to be lobbying for a more effective law. It is vital that international law evolve better to approximate real-world practice and thereby reflect the changing perspective of the international community, providing guidance in the new situations that arise.

C. CIVIL CONFLICT AND COUP D'ÉTAT UNDER INTERNATIONAL LAW

Despite the growing general perception that civil conflict is no longer a matter within the exclusive jurisdiction of states, the conventional international legal approach to civil conflicts remains very limited. This section provides an overview of what law and policy has developed so far and sets the context for the remainder of the discussion.

Little has changed in the legal literature since Falk set out the scope of international law with respect to civil conflict as being restricted to (1) "a process for designating the degree of formal acknowledgment by third states of the claims made on behalf of the anti-government faction" (through the rules dealing with belligerency); (2) "a rhetoric for claiming and contesting various forms of external participation in internal wars"; (3) "a system for regulating the scope of hostilities by the application of the rules of war"; and (4) "limited control over the outcome of internal wars whenever the community consensus can be effectively mobilized in support of one faction" (where such wars are deemed a threat to international peace and security).[45]

The traditional position remains that civil conflict is largely beyond the reach of international law and neither legal nor illegal.[46] Accordingly, there is no restriction on the use of violence to initiate a civil conflict, whereas initiating an international conflict—the unilateral use of force by states against the territorial integrity or political independence of any other state—is outlawed, subject to the right of self-defense.[47] Borrowing

---

[45] Falk, *supra* note 18, at 194.

[46] WILSON, *supra* note 2.

[47] U.N. Charter Article 2, paragraph 4, provides: "All Members shall refrain in their international relations from the threat or use of force against the territorial integrity or political independence of any State, or in any other manner inconsistent with the Purposes of the United Nations." The prohibition has also crystallized as a general norm of international law, according to the decision in Military and Paramilitary Activities in and Against Nicaragua (Nicar. v. U.S.), Merits, 1986 I.C.J. 14 (June 27) [hereinafter *Nicaragua,* Merits]. The right to self-defense is preserved in U.N. Charter Article 51.

terminology from the international war context, no *jus ad bellum internum* norms prohibit civil conflict.[48]

As More points out,

> [t]he normative standards for differentiating permissible from impermissible resort to force have, like the other principal strands in the international law of conflict management, largely evolved in response to conventional warfare across national boundaries. Thus, for the most part, they provide only minimal guidance, if any, to normative judgment concerning conflicts purely within national boundaries.[49]

Perhaps unsurprisingly, given the view that civil conflicts were domestic matters, there has been little discussion or analysis of the legality of civil conflict under international law. In 1963, Lauterpacht stated without further discussion, "the Law of Nations does not treat civil war as illegal."[50] Similarly, Akehurst states: "There is no rule in international law against civil wars. Article 2(4) of the U.N. Charter prohibits the use or threat of force in *international* relations only.[51] It is possible that each side will regard the other side as traitors from the point of view of municipal law, but neither the insurgents nor the established authorities are guilty of any breach of international law."[52] This line of thought is reflected in Starke's comment, "It is trite law that civil wars are not prohibited by any international legal rules."[53] The assumption that there is no international

---

48 The terminology of "*jus ad bellum internum,*" "recourse to force," and "recourse to violence" in internal conflicts as used here must be distinguished from similar terminology and concepts used in international conflicts. In the international context, *jus ad bellum* governs the legitimacy of direct use of force against the sovereignty and territorial integrity of a state and possibly extends to indirect violence through support for subversive or terrorist armed activities within another state.

49 John Norton Moore, *Introduction, in* LAW AND CIVIL WAR IN THE MODERN WORLD, *supra* note 2, at xiii, xiii.

50 2 L. OPPENHEIM, INTERNATIONAL LAW, DISPUTES, WAR AND NEUTRALITY (Hersch Lauterpacht ed., 7th ed. 1963). Note that later editions did not update the volume of Oppenheim addressing this issue.

51 The San Francisco debates on the U.N. Charter do not discuss how to address civil conflicts. These were apparently not considered to be a threat to international peace and security at the time.

52 MICHAEL AKEHURST, A MODERN INTRODUCTION TO INTERNATIONAL LAW 281–82 (6th ed. 1992).

53 JOSEPH G. STARKE, INTRODUCTION TO INTERNATIONAL LAW (10th ed. 1989),

law addressing recourse to force is also consistent with a general lack of detailed discussion of the issue in many major texts.[54] One exception to this trend is a short but noteworthy article by Wedgwood that raised the question of whether international law should extend *jus ad bellum* to "bar large-scale military force in the pursuit of domestic political objectives," and concluded that irrespective of the many theoretical and moral difficulties arising from such a notion, "an international norm against use of force in questions of ethnic secession is worthy of debate."[55]

1. Civil Conflict and Coup d'État Defined

The terms "civil conflict" and "coup d'état" do not yet have an accepted specialized meaning in international law. Civil conflict requires more elaboration. Some commentators have used the term "civil wars," others refer to "internal wars," "non-international wars," "guerrilla wars," "revolutions," "belligerencies," "rebel wars," or "wars of self-determination." "Civil conflict" has been adopted here to refer to non-international violent conflict involving a government and one or more non-state actors that reaches a level of intensity of insurgency or belligerency.

Traditionally, international law dealt with civil wars according to their level of intensity and the extent of territorial control by rebels. The terminology of "rebellion," "insurgency," and "belligerency" was initially used to categorize different levels of civil strife for the purposes of international law. These constituted the basis of the original rules governing intervention discussed in Section C.2.

The lowest intensity category of civil disruption, a rebellion, defined as involving temporary or sporadic acts of violence, was the exclusive domestic concern of the state against which it was fought. Insurgency fell between rebellion and belligerency. It arose when it was not yet appropriate for third-party states to treat rebels as "having the full rights and

---

which also appears in the latter edition by Ivan Shearer; IVAN A. SHEARER, STARKE'S INTERNATIONAL LAW 489 (11th ed. 1994).

[54] *See e.g.* the reasoning in FALK, *supra* note 2, at 11; GRAY, *supra* note 2 (other than in the context of self-determination); MOIR, *supra* note 2, at 1. Similarly, in the report on law in civil conflicts, undertaken by the American Society of International Law, the discussion focused on the right to intervene in civil conflicts and did not consider the legality of waging the conflict. LAW AND CIVIL WAR IN THE MODERN WORLD, *supra* note 2, at 1.

[55] Wedgwood, *supra* note 2, at 239, 251.

obligations of a belligerent, or to regard third states as subject to the obligations of neutrality."[56] However, the conflict "may have such scope, and be accompanied by a sufficient degree of organisation on the part of the rebels, that they can no longer be treated as private individuals committing unlawful acts."[57] At a minimum, therefore, insurgency requires rebel control over territory and "sufficient military might for the interests of foreign States to be affected."[58] Belligerency, the state of civil disorder closest to international war, arises, according to Lauterpacht, when rebel forces occupy territory, have a measure of orderly administration, observe the rules of warfare, and there is a practical necessity for third-party states to define their attitude to the war.[59] Once a party is recognized as a belligerent, all the rules of international law with respect to warfare apply to it.[60]

This terminology has been criticized for being self-referential and discretionary, derived from practical necessity for a third-party state to define its attitude to the rebels,[61] and the practice of explicit recognition of belligerency has largely fallen into disuse—although Oppenheim suggests that a recognition of belligerency in ways other than by formal declaration is permissible and not an infrequent occurrence.[62] This division of civil conflicts has been termed "more theoretical than real," and not a single recognition of belligerency has occurred since World War II.[63] Nonetheless, for better or worse, important international law has been written in the language of this terminology, so it is necessary to engage with it.

---

[56] ROBERT JENNINGS AND ARTHUR WATTS, OPPENHEIM'S INTERNATIONAL LAW 165–66 (9th ed. 1992).

[57] *Id.* at 165–66.

[58] WILSON, *supra* note 2, at 24; FALK, *supra* note 2, at 11; Higgins, *supra* note 12.

[59] OPPENHEIM, *supra* note 50, ¶ 76.

[60] *Id.* at 249. *See also* JENNINGS AND WATTS, *supra* note 56, at 165, cross-referencing OPPENHEIM, *supra* note 50, paras. 55, 76, 76a; WILSON, *supra* note 2, at 24.

[61] Franck and Rodley, *supra* note 39, at 724. ANTONIO CASSESE, INTERNATIONAL LAW 67 (2001), calls the rules "rather confused and rudimentary." *See also* FALK, *supra* note 2, at 11, rejecting the view that an improper recognition would amount to an illegal interference in the affairs of a state.

[62] OPPENHEIM, *supra* note 50, at 250–51.

[63] WILSON, *supra* note 2, at 27.

The Additional Protocol II to the Geneva Conventions essentially adopted the standard of belligerency when it defined the conflicts that it applies to as being non-international armed conflicts involving armed forces of organized groups under responsible command and exercising control over a part of the territory.[64] However, the present discussion adopts the terminology of "civil conflict" to include both belligerency and insurgency, as there seems to be little distinction in the practice between the response of the international community to one or the other. This certainly implies a degree of violence greater than "merely limited local unrest,"[65] and the conflict must be of a sufficient scale and degree of intensity to differentiate it from riots and sporadic violence.[66]

Nonetheless, the term "civil conflict" is not intended to incorporate the somewhat dated and complex rules developed to deal with the legal recognition of the existence of a state of "war" between nations, according to which civil war only occurs once recognition of belligerency is made, which gives international recognition to the non-state party.[67]

The term "rebel" is used generically to refer to a non-governmental party involved in civil conflict. The term is not intended to impart any judgment, such as the notion that rebels "unjustly" take up arms, as de Vattel uses the term.[68]

It should be noted that the line between strictly internal and international conflicts is becoming increasingly blurred. Civil wars often evolve from strictly internal affairs to internationalized conflicts directly or indirectly involving other states. Moreover, under international law, certain categories of conflicts are taking on quasi-interna-

---

64 *See* Protocol Additional to the Geneva Conventions of 12 August 1949, Relating to the Protection of Victims of Non-International Armed Conflicts, art. 1, para. 1, 16 I.L.M. 1442 (1977) [hereinafter Additional Protocol II].

65 GRAY, *supra* note 2, at 58.

66 *See* discussion of different levels of conflict in WILSON, *supra* note 2, at 23; GRAY, *supra* note 2, at 58.

67 *See* OPPENHEIM, *supra* note 50, at 209; William T. Burke, *The Legal Regulation of Minor International Coercion: A Framework of Inquiry, in* THE VIETNAM WAR AND INTERNATIONAL LAW, *supra* note 39, at 79, 80, emphasizing the confusion and complexity of the terminology. INGRID DETTER, THE LAW OF WAR 3–25 (2d ed. 2000).

68 Emerich de Vattel, *The Law of Nations or the Principles of Natural Law, Originally Printed in 1758, in* THE VIETNAM WAR AND INTERNATIONAL LAW, *supra* note 39, at 1, 17.

tional status.[69] Wars of self-determination are one example of this trend. Internal conflicts are another example where third-party states have intervened.[70] Certain separatist conflicts have also been recategorized as international through the recognition of breakaway territories as new states (as occurred in the break-up of Yugoslavia for instance). This phenomenon of internationalization is an integral aspect of the current investigation, and hence such wars are included within the term "civil conflict."

Civil conflicts encompass a wide spectrum of conflicts and involve armed groups with different aims and approaches. Part of the complexity that confronts the analysis of such conflicts arises from the very diversity of contexts in which they occur.[71] In addition, the nature of civil war has changed dramatically over the last 50 years. Initially the post-World War II literature dealing with rebels focused on armed forces that continued to fight once the state had admitted defeat (there was much discussion of German forces acting as rebels and of groups fighting outside invading forces amounting to rebels).[72] By the 1950s and 1960s, however, the dominant type of civil war was the post-colonial war of liberation, which raised issues of self-determination and anti-colonialism.[73] The contemporary world arena, in contrast, is dominated by civil wars with ethnic cleansing or religious aims—such as in Rwanda or the former Yugoslavia—or wars with clear financial incentives for the rebels, such as those in Sierra Leone, Democratic Republic of the Congo, Sudan, or Colombia.

Finaly, for the purposes of this book, "coup d"état" is taken to mean any attempt to overthrow a government by force. This definition does not turn on whether injury or death results, since it is implicit that violence would have been used if necessary.

---

69 ADAM ROBERTS AND RICHARD GUELFF, DOCUMENTS ON THE LAWS OF WAR (3d ed., 2000).

70 *See, e.g.*, Prosecutor v. Tadic, Case No. IT-94-1-A, Judgment of the Appeals Chamber (July 15, 1999) [hereinafter *Tadic*, Judgment of the Appeals Chamber]: an internal conflict may become international "if (i) another State intervenes in that conflict through its troops, or alternatively (ii) some of the participants in the internal armed conflict act on behalf of that State."

71 *See* a review of different contexts and different types of conflicts in FALK, *supra* note 2, at 17–22. See the categorization of conflicts in 1969, Higgins, *supra* note 12, at 82–83.

72 *See, e.g.*, Iosee Trainin, *Questions of Guerrilla Warfare in the Law of War*, 40 AM. J. INT'L L. 534 (1946); Lester Nurick and Roger W. Barrett, *Legality of Guerrilla Forces Under the Laws of War*, 40 AM. J. INT'L L. 563 (1946).

73 *E.g.*, WILSON, *supra* note 2.

2. Intervention Prohibited

As the one exception to the otherwise substantially under-developed legal and policy discourse surrounding civil conflict, the law governing intervention in civil conflict has received sustained attention. However, the issue is far from settled. In theory, intervention by outside states into civil conflicts is largely prohibited. This derives from the well-established duty of states not to intervene or interfere[74] in the internal affairs of other states.[75]

In the words of *Oppenheim's International Law*, "when there exists a civil war and control of a State is divided between warring factions, any form of interference or assistance (except probably of a humanitarian character) to any party amounts to intervention contrary to international law."[76] Assistance to rebels is also prohibited irrespective of the level of conflict or the purpose of the war.[77] The International Court of Justice in *Nicaragua* rejected any exceptions to this rule based on the rebel's aims or political or moral values, although it did not address the case of assistance to liberation movements.[78]

The one area of contention is the degree to which consensual intervention is restricted. Though states may invite intervention while a civil disturbance falls below the level of intensity of a civil conflict, some have argued that when the conflict reaches the level of a civil conflict, third-party states may no longer intervene to assist the government, irrespective of consent.[79]

---

[74] Both terms are used in the relevant General Assembly declarations.

[75] *See, e.g.*, Committee of Enquiry into Breaches of International Law, *Report and Findings of Committee of Enquiry into Breaches of International Law Relating to Intervention in Spain*, S/32 and S/34 SCOR (1936), 1.1 Supp 2 at 54–55, Security Council, Apr. 17, 1946, SCOR 1.1 N2, 167; Titus Komarnicki, *L'Intervention en Droit International Moderne*, *in* REVUE GENERALE DE DROIT INTERNATIONAL PUBLIC 521 (1956) (Fr.); Tom J. Farer, *Harnessing Rogue Elephants: A Short Discussion on Foreign Intervention in Civil Strife*, 82. HARV. L. REV. 511 (1969); Moore, *supra* note 9, at 1.

[76] JENNINGS AND WATTS, *supra* note 56, at 438.

[77] Higgins, *supra* note 12; CASSESE, *supra* note 61, at 66–69; Mary Ellen O'Connell, *Regulating the Use of Force in the 21st Century: The Continuing Importance of State Autonomy*, *in* POLITICS, VALUES AND FUNCTIONS: INTERNATIONAL LAW IN THE 21ST CENTURY 443, 448 (Jonathan I. Charney et al. eds., 1998).

[78] *Nicaragua*, Merits, *supra* note 47, ¶ 209.

[79] *See, e.g.*, GRAY, *supra* note 2, at 51–52; WILSON, *supra* note 2, at 30–32; Bowett, *supra* note 8, at 42; Institut De Droit International, *Resolution*, 56 ANNUAIRE DE L'INSTITUT DE DROIT INTERNATIONAL 544, 546 (1975).

However, the practice has diverged starkly from all of the theoretical prohibitions on intervention. Intervention in civil conflicts is widespread and consistent. Falk goes so far as to consider the restatement of the general rule in General Assembly resolutions as a "hypocritical normative assertion since it contradicts the attitudes and policies of many governments."[80] Higgins argues: "If one would look behind the legal rhetoric to the reality . . . , it is clear that the law has to be restated."[81] Franck and Rodley also call for such reformulation: "One advantage of legitimating what is in any event happening—the general intervention of third States in civil wars—is that it permits international law to regulate the nature and scope of these interventions on the basis of reciprocal principles."[82] There has been much debate whether this extensive practice of intervention into civil conflict, which contradicts the traditional legal position that such intervention is prohibited, supports the emergence of new norms permitting intervention into such conflicts. However, the question of whether this practice reflects a change in international policy with respect to civil conflict, or in perception about the legality of civil conflict itself, has been largely overlooked.

3. Self-Determination and Secession

As wars of self-determination have been accorded special status with respect to the norms of *jus in bello*, there has been some suggestion that such wars may constitute an exception to the prohibition on intervention to assist rebel forces and even that international law may in fact develop to authorize the use of force by national liberation movements.[83]

National liberation wars are "upgraded" to the equivalent of international wars through the 1977 Geneva Additional Protocol I, and the International Court of Justice in *Nicaragua* deliberately kept open the option of an exception to the prohibition on intervention when it excluded such wars from its judgment prohibiting assistance to rebel forces.[84] Nonetheless, so far, no such exceptions have crystallized. As

---

80 FALK, *supra* note 2, at 7. *See also* Farer, *supra* note 9, at 516.

81 Higgins, *supra* note 44, at 183.

82 Franck and Rodley, *supra* note 39, at 732.

83 *Id.* at 136.

84 *Nicaragua*, Merits, *supra* note 47, ¶ 206. Note that Judge Schwebel rejected this aspect of the majority judgment. *Id.*, ¶¶ 179–80. *But see* Antonio Cassese, *Le Droit International Et La Question De L'assistance Aux Mouvements De Libération Nationale,* 19

Wilson explained, even in such cases, the use of force "remained a matter of self-help beyond the purview of international law."[85]

Even a civil conflict that seeks to achieve secession is not supported under international law. The generally accepted position is that international law does not recognize a unilateral right to secession.[86] The doctrine of *uti possidetis*, which provides that colonial boundaries will become international boundaries at independence,[87] seems to have played a role in preventing the emergence of a right to secession via self-determination.[88] However, once the new state is established, the principle of *uti possidetis* should give way to the principle of territorial integrity.[89]

It would appear that, as the Canadian Supreme Court held in the *Quebec Secession Case*, international law leaves the question of secession to be determined by the state.[90] The Court did suggest that the right to self-determination may ground a right to unilateral secession "when a people is blocked from the meaningful exercise of its right to self-determination internally, it is entitled, as a last resort, to exercise it by secession."[91] However, the matter did not ultimately arise for resolution in that case.[92]

REVUE BELGE DE DROIT INTERNATIONAL 307, 325 (1986); Bowett, *supra* note 8, at 43. *See also* JENNINGS AND WATTS, *supra* note 56, at 445–46, who limit the permissible assistance to humanitarian or economic.

[85] WILSON, *supra* note 2, at 28.

[86] Reference Re Secession of Quebec [1998] 2 S.C.R. 217, para. 112 (Can.). James Crawford, *State Practice and International Law in Relation to Secession*, 69 BRIT. Y.B. INT'L L. 85 (1999).

[87] See OAU Res. 16, para. 1 (1964) (Cairo), in which member states pledged to respect each others' colonial frontiers at the moment of decolonialization.

[88] For instance, the Yugoslav Arbitration Commission maintained: "[I]t is well established that, whatever the circumstances, the right to self-determination must not involve changes to existing frontiers at the time of independence (*uti possidetis juris*) except where the states concerned agree otherwise." *Yugoslavia Arbitration Commission Opinion 2*, 31 I.L.M. 1497 (1992).

[89] Frontier Dispute (Burk. Faso/Mali), 1986 I.C.J. 554, 565 (Dec. 22). For a discussion of this doctrine, *see* PAUL R. HENSEL ET AL., THE COLONIAL LEGACY AND BORDER STABILITY: UTI POSSIDETIS AND TERRITORIAL CLAIMS IN THE AMERICA (2004).

[90] Reference Re Secession of Quebec [1998] 2 S.C.R. 217.

[91] *Id.*, paras. 135, 138.

[92] *Id.*, para. 135. *See also* Crawford, *supra* note 86, paras. 10, 26, which maintains

One point to note is that the violent *repression* of self-determination is likely to be governed by international law. Although this has not yet been applied in practice, Bowett maintains that denial of self-determination is an international wrong,[93] and, accordingly, forceful intervention is permissible, at least where the Security Council or General Assembly has confirmed the denial of the right to self-determination and has authorized the intervention.[94]

4. Humanitarian Laws in Armed Conflict

Jus in bello norms, also known as humanitarian laws in armed conflict, seek to regulate the actual use of force in conflicts without judging whether the cause of war was legitimate. The protection, so far as possible, of civilians from violence is a cardinal aspect of humanitarian law.[95] Humanitarian principles increasingly apply to civil conflicts. Initially only Common Article 3 of the 1949 Geneva Conventions applied to non-international conflicts and, even then, only to situations recognized as "armed conflicts." The article prohibits "[v]iolence to life and person, in particular murder of all kinds, mutilation, cruel treatment and torture," against "[p]ersons taking no active part in the hostilities, including members of armed forces who have laid down their arms and those placed hors de combat by sickness, wounds, detention, or any other cause."

The Additional Protocol I to the Geneva Conventions extends a series of protections to conflicts involving self-determination against colonial or racist regimes,[96] and the Additional Protocol II aims to apply to

---

that "international law does not confer any right to unilateral secession outside the colonial context," and points out that "[s]ince 1945 the international community has been extremely reluctant to accept unilateral secession of parts of independent states, in situations where the secession is opposed by the government of that state," that, in fact, since 1945, no such state has been admitted to the United Nations against the wishes of the predecessor state, and there are many examples of attempted secession that have failed. *See also* Commission of Jurists, *Aaland Islands Situation*, LEAGUE OF NATIONS O. J., Spec. Supp. No. 3 (1920): "Positive International law does not recognise the right of national groups, as such, to separate themselves from the State of which they form a part by the simple expression of a wish."

93 Bowett, *supra* note 8, at 43.

94 *Id.* at 44.

95 *See* ROBERTS AND GUELFF, *supra* note 69, at 615–17; and Rome Statute of the International Criminal Court art. 8, U.N. Doc. No. A/CONF.183/9 (July 17, 1998).

96 *See* Additional Protocol II, *supra* note 64, art. 1, para. 4.

all other armed conflicts involving armed forces of organized groups under responsible command and exercising control over a part of the territory.[97] According to Additional Protocol II, "The civilian population as such, as well as individual civilians, shall not be the object of attack. Acts or threats of violence the primary purpose of which is to spread terror among the civilian population are prohibited."[98]

Jus in bello norms are increasingly being applied to all civil conflicts, both through the creation of the International Criminal Tribunals for the former Yugoslavia (ICTFY) and for Rwanda (ICTR),[99] and following the decision of the ICTFY in *Tadic*, which held that Article 3 of the Geneva Conventions was part of customary law and thus applicable to all conflicts. In *Tadic*, the Court of Appeal also found that the grave breaches provisions of the Geneva Conventions could apply in the conflict in the former Yugoslavia, as a conflict could be internationalized if another state intervenes through its troops or if participants in the conflict act on behalf of another state.[100]

5. Coup d'État

Traditionally, the question of regime change through coup d'état was considered a matter for the state in question, not for the international community. While democratic states have expressed a policy preference for democratic states, there was little in international law to suggest that regime change through coup d'état was a matter for international concern. However, a series of regional agreements in Africa and Latin America have begun addressing the legitimacy of forceful regime change, at least when the targeted government was "democratically elected." The African Union, for instance, adopted the Lomé Declaration on Unconstitutional Changes of Government (2000), which rejected and condemned such unconstitutional change of government, defined as military coup d'état against a democratically elected government; intervention by mercenar-

---

97 *See id.*, art. 1, para. 1.

98 *See id.*, art. 13.

99 Note that while ICTFY provides for prosecution of the laws or customs of war, in the case of ICTR, the statute appears to provide only for prosecution of violations of Common Article 3 or of Additional Protocol II. *See* Statute of the International Criminal Tribunal for Rwanda art. 4, *available at* http://www.ohchr.org/english/law/itr.htm. It does, however, extend international criminality to such violations.

100 Prosecutor v. Tadic, Case No. IT-94-1-AR72, Appeal on Jurisdiction, para. 127 (Oct. 2, 1995); *Tadic*, Judgment of the Appeals Chamber, Case No. IT-94-1-A.

ies to replace a democratically elected government; replacement of democratically elected governments by armed dissident groups and rebel movements; or the refusal by an incumbent government to relinquish power to the winning party after free, fair, and regular elections.[101]

The Economic Community of West African States, has also listed the "overthrow or attempted overthrow of a democratically elected government" as enlivening the jurisdiction of its Mechanism for Conflict Prevention, Management, Resolution, Peacekeeping and Security, which permits intervention to "prevent, manage and resolve internal and inter-State conflicts," and "maintain and consolidate peace, security and stability within the Community."[102] Such a principle is also supported by the treaty regime of the Organization of American States, which specifically supports the use of collective measures to restore democracy where it has been overthrown unconstitutionally.[103]

The impact of these treaties on international policy and law with respect to violent regime change is explored further in Chapter 4, Section D.

D. OUTLINE

In this context, this book considers how the practice of the international community responding to certain forms of extreme political violence has influenced the international law and international policy perspective. It reviews the accumulating practice of the international community rejecting and condemning civil conflict and coups d'état, which

---

101 Lomé Declaration on the Framework for an OAU Response to Unconstitutional Changes of Government (2000) AHG/Decl.5 (XXXVI), *available at* http://www.africanreview.org/docs/govern/govchange.pdf.

102 ECOWAS Protocol on Democracy and Good Governance, art. 25, Dec. 2001, A/SP1/12/01, *available at* http://www.issafrica.org/AF/RegOrg/unity_to_union/pdfs/ecowas/12ProtDemocGood.pdf.

103 Inter-American Democratic Charter, Sept. 11, 2001, OEA/Ser.G CP-1, *available at* http://www.oas.org/OASpage/esp/Publicaciones/CartaDemocratica_spa.pdf; Organization of American States (OAS), The Santiago Commitment to Democracy and the Renewal of the Inter-American System, G.A. 3d plen. sess. (June 4, 1991) OEA/SerP/XXIO2; OAS, Representative Democracy, G.A. Res. 1080, 5th plen. sess., OAS Doc. AG/RES. 1080 (XXI-O/91) (June 5, 1991); OAS, Inter-American Democratic Charter, Resolution of San Jose Costa Rica, G.A. Res. 1838, 4th plen. sess., OAS Doc. G/RES. 1838 (XXXI-O/01) (June 5, 2001). *See, e.g.*, OAS Permanent Council Emergency Meeting (Apr. 13, 2003), for the condemnation of the attempted coup in Venezuela in April 2003.

up to now has not been systematically analyzed, and seeks to explore what changes it evidences in international policy, and/or in the relationship between political violence and international law. In this regard, it considers the emergence of possible norms of *jus ad bellum internum*[104] under traditional customary law or international law more broadly.

The book begins with a discussion of methodology to set out the way in which the practice will be approached. It then reviews and analyzes the practice of the Security Council in the 32 civil conflict/coups d'état situations in which it had been involved through September 30, 2003, followed by three recent case studies providing an in-depth overview of the response of the international community to such examples of extreme political violence. The final chapter seeks to pull the practice together through an analysis of how this practice reflects changing international policy norms and emerging international law perspective.

---

[104] This question is distinct from the question of whether a *response* by a state or regional body *is* legal, which is concerned with whether new rules governing intervention into civil conflicts are emerging. That question has been extensively, albeit inconclusively, debated, and there is no intention to reopen it here. *See, e.g.*, Friedmann, *supra* note 9; Farer, *supra* note 9; Moore, *supra* note 9; DAMROSCH, *supra* note 9; Ofodile, *supra* note 9; MAYALL, *supra* note 9; MERON, *supra* note 9; Fielding, *supra* note 9; TESÓN, *supra* note 9; CHESTERMAN *supra* note 9.

CHAPTER 2
METHODOLOGICAL ISSUES

A discussion of emerging international policy on civil conflict and coup d'état can be based on a descriptive analysis of the practice, to determine whether certain policy positions are gaining widespread support and becoming established. However, the discussion of customary law requires a more extensive methodological framework, both with respect to what broad approach is appropriate in the context of civil conflict and coup d'état, and also with respect to the role the Security Council plays in shaping new international law. This role is markedly under-theorized—in contrast to the widely debated General Assembly practice in customary law formation—but is central because of the remarkable scope of Council practice that has been accumulating in response to civil conflicts and coups d'état.

A. AN APPROPRIATE CUSTOMARY LAW METHODOLOGY

In formal terms, the formation of customary law requires evidence of both *opinio juris* and material practice. However, the question of how customary norms emerge and what is required to establish their existence is a long-standing controversial issue in international law. A search for a methodological framework must take account of a number of related issues, notably what and whose practice is relevant to customary norm formation, the proper balance between *opinio juris* and practice, the assessment of the practice, and the relative weight to be ascribed to oral and physical conduct. In order to determine an appropriate methodological framework for this book, it is useful to consider the debate surrounding the emergence of human rights customary law norms, which raises similar issues to the field under consideration.

1. Legal Methodology and the Emergence of Human Rights Customary Law Norms

The International Court of Justice (I.C.J.) and the international tribunals have repeatedly stated basic principles in relation to customary law formation: there must be practice[1] and *opinio*

[1] Military and Paramilitary Activities in and Against Nicaragua (Nicar. v. U.S.), Merits, 1986 I.C.J. 14 (June 27) [hereinafter *Nicaragua*, Merits]: "[T]he shared view of

juris.[2] However, the extent to which practice must be established and systematically reviewed, and the extent to which both *opinio juris* and practice must be separately established rather than implied, remain open to debate. In the human rights context, the emphasis has been on the dominance of *opinio juris* over inconsistent practice.[3] However, the reverse proposition, that where appropriate practice exists "it is not necessary to prove the existence of an *opinio juris*," has also recently been adopted by the Committee on the Formation of Customary Law.[4]

In the human rights context, the nature of the available practice raised methodological questions regarding how to assess a proliferation of conventions, General Assembly resolutions, and governmental statements subscribing to the norms, but little practical compliance or enforcement. The value-laden nature of such norms squarely raised the positivist-natural lawyer divide. The mainstream position in support of the existence of such norms argues that the nature of human rights is such that a broad category of practice must be considered, and that practice in favor and against each human right must be considered individually to determine whether that particular norm has crystallized into custom.[5] Schachter illustrates this approach. He rejects the "usual process of customary law formation," as "States do not usually make claims on other States or protest violations that do not affect their nationals,"[6] and

---

the Parties as to the content of what they regard as the rule is not enough. The Court must satisfy itself that the existence of the rule in the *opinio juris* of States is confirmed by practice."

[2] North Sea Continental Shelf Cases, 1969 I.C.J. 3, 44 (Feb. 20): acts must "be such, or be carried out in such a way, as to be evidence of a belief that this practice be rendered obligatory by the existence of a rule requiring it."

[3] *See* THEODOR MERON, HUMAN RIGHTS AND HUMANITARIAN NORMS AS CUSTOMARY LAW 99 (1989). *But see* Bruno Simma and Philip Alston, *The Sources of Human Rights Law: Custom, Jus Cogens, and General Principles*, 12 AUSTL. Y.B. INT'L L. 82, 96 (1989), who favor a strict approach to customary norm formation and reject undue reliance on *opinio juris*.

[4] International Law Association, *Final Report of the Committee on Formation of Customary General International Law* 742 (2000).

[5] *See, e.g.*, MERON, *supra* note 3; RESTATEMENT (THIRD) OF FOREIGN RELATIONS LAW OF THE UNITED STATES 161 (1987); Oscar Schachter, *International Law in Theory and Practice*, 178 RECUEIL DES COURS 13, 333 (1982), in favor of human rights customary law norms.

[6] Schachter, *supra* note 5. *See* Isabelle Gunning, *Modernizing Customary International Law: The Challenge of Human Rights*, 31 VA. J. INT'L L. 212 (1991).

instead argues that in the human rights context greater emphasis can validly be placed on General Assembly resolutions and multilateral treaties. According to this approach, he concludes that a review of available practice—conventions, declarations, U.N. resolutions, the incorporation of human rights provisions into domestic laws and condemnation by states of human rights violations by other states, as well as repeated breaches of human rights norms—suggests that some, but not all, of the norms in the Universal Declaration of Human Rights have crystallized into custom.[7] Charlesworth's methodology is similar, in that she points out that that modern custom does not accord with the traditional rhetoric of custom.[8]

A variation on this approach emphasizes reliance on the role of the moral value of human rights in assessing whether such norms exist. Cassese considers that when it comes to proof of the emergence of norms based on the dictates of public conscience, the requirement of practice may be less stringent than in other cases, and the *opinio juris* may take on a special prominence.[9] Kirgis similarly suggests: "When issues of armed force are involved, it may well be that the need for stability explains an international decision maker's primary reliance on normative words rather than on a combination of words and consistent deeds."[10]

Meron, interestingly, acknowledges that it is "to be expected that those rights which are most crucial to the protection of human dignity and of universally accepted values of humanity, and whose violation triggers broad condemnation by the international community, will require a lesser amount of confirmatory evidence."[11] However, he then goes on to assess the question on the basis of a largely positivist approach.[12] Nevertheless, he

---

7 Schachter, *supra* note 5, at 336. Richard B. Lillich, *The Growing Importance of Customary International Human Rights Law,* 25 GA. J. INT'L & COMP. L. 1, 9–10 (1996), adopts a similar approach.

8 Hilary C.M. Charlesworth, *Customary International Law and the Nicaragua Case,* 11 AUSTL. Y.B. INT'L L. 1 (1984–87).

9 ANTONIO CASSESE, INTERNATIONAL LAW 122 (2001).

10 Frederic L. Kirgis, Jr., *Custom on a Sliding Scale,* 81 AM. J. INT'L L. 146, 147 (1987).

11 MERON, *supra* note 3, at 92.

12 For a criticism of Meron's lack of radical revision, *see* Martti Koskenniemi, Book Review, 88 MICH. L. REV. 1946 (1990) (reviewing THEODOR MERON, HUMAN RIGHTS AND HUMANITARIAN NORMS AS CUSTOMARY LAW (1989)).

recognizes the relevance of statements and resolutions, pointing out that "the repetition of the articulation and the assertion of certain norms in various resolutions and declarations and treaties play an important role" in the formation of new customary norms of human rights.[13]

A more extreme position can be seen in the reasoning of scholars who rely more directly on a Dworkinian approach. The influence of the natural law school is particularly evident in Tesón's recent analysis of humanitarian intervention, where he argues that "moral philosophy is necessarily part of the articulation of legal propositions."[14] Tesón points out that any approach to customary law is permeated by values and is inevitably purposive[15] and therefore uses moral theory to assist the selection of relevant precedents.[16] He rejects the traditional inductive approach[17] in favor of a claim-oriented approach,[18] which, he argues, takes better account of the exceptional and in extremis nature of humanitarian intervention.[19]

Koskenniemi similarly emphasizes that the nature of the rules is fundamental to their assessment. He writes:

> [I]t is really our certainty that genocide or torture is illegal that allows us to understand state behavior and to accept or reject its legal message, not state behavior itself that allows us to understand that these practices are prohibited by law. It seems to me that if we are uncertain of the latter fact, then there is really little in this world we can feel confident about.[20]

Higgins, on the other hand, rejects the natural law-influenced perspective of hierarchical normativity where certain rules, as those against

---

13 MERON, *supra* note 3, at 99.

14 FERNANDO R. TESÓN, HUMANITARIAN INTERVENTION: AN INQUIRY INTO LAW AND MORALITY 6 (2d ed. 1997).

15 *Id.* at 176–77.

16 *Id.* at 11.

17 GEORG SCHWARZENBERGER, THE INDUCTIVE APPROACH TO INTERNATIONAL LAW (1965).

18 Also favored by ANTHONY D'AMATO, THE CONCEPT OF CUSTOM IN INTERNATIONAL LAW 18–20 (1971).

19 TESÓN, *supra* note 14, at 176.

20 Koskenniemi, *supra* note 12, at 1952.

aggression and self-defense, have "higher normativity"[21] than other international rules and require different compliance.[22] She also rejects an unduly positivistic, "law-as-rules" approach and instead argues for a "law-as-process" approach that "encourages interpretation and choice that is more compatible with values we seek to promote and objectives we seek to achieve."[23] Ultimately, she maintains that the reason certain norms, such as the prohibition on torture, retain their status despite breaches is that there remains strong *opinio juris* in their favor.[24]

Among those that deny the existence of customary human rights norms, there are those who reject the assessment of the practice, while agreeing that an inclusive approach is appropriate,[25] and those who reject all aspects of the methodology. Simma and Alston represent the latter view, rejecting the entire approach, which they see as a way of bending the formal criteria of customary law "in order to reach a certain policy result."[26] Instead, they favor a strict approach to customary norm formation, rejecting the reliance on *opinio juris* over state practice and even reliance on practice, such as General Assembly resolutions and conventions.[27] They suggest that human rights norms should be acknowledged as legally binding as "general principles of law recognized by civilized nations" under Article 38 of the I.C.J. statute.[28] However, their

---

[21] Oscar Schachter, *Entangled Treaty and Custom, in* INTERNATIONAL LAW AT A TIME OF PERPLEXITY: ESSAYS IN HONOUR OF SHABTAI ROSENNE 717, 734 (Yoram Dinstein ed., 1989).

[22] ROSALYN HIGGINS, PROBLEMS AND PROCESS: INTERNATIONAL LAW AND HOW WE USE IT 20 (1994).

[23] *Id.* at 10.

[24] *Id.* at 22.

[25] *See, e.g.*, Arthur M. Weisburd, *The Significance and Determination of Customary International Human Rights Law*, 25 GA. J. INT'L & COMP. L. 99, 135–36 (1996), which questions the point of relying on evidence which parties flout and fail to enforce.

[26] Simma and Alston, *supra* note 3, at 96.

[27] *Id.* at 96. For examples of other authors that reject the emergence of human rights customary law norms, *see* G.J.H. VAN HOOF, RETHINKING THE SOURCES OF INTERNATIONAL LAW 107 (1983).

[28] In their view, this would accommodate a process of "express articulation of principles in the first instance, *ab initio* or progressively being 'accepted and recognised' as binding and peremptory by the "international community of States as a whole." Simma and Alston, *supra* note 3, at 104. This approach also requires bending of the formal requirements, as the original debates surrounding U.N. Charter Article 38, paragraph 1(c) favor the view that this source of law was intended to refer to general

approach is out of step with that of the mainstream[29] and the view of the I.C.J.[30]

These divergent approaches present a spectrum of attitudes responding to the type of practice and *opinio juris* available in the human rights context. The mainstream approach considers that a broad range of practice should be treated as relevant and that the emphasis on the type of practice and the relevance of material practice and *opinio juris* must take into account how states act in that particular context. It suggests that customary law methodology must be tailored to the context of the norms investigated. To develop a methodology in this case, it is therefore essential to investigate how the civil conflict and coup d'état context will affect the practice and *opinio juris* required to establish customary law.

2. Elements of the Customary Law Context

a. *Whose Practice Is Relevant?*

Generally, new customary law norms are manifested in the conduct of states. In the case of permissive norms, the focus is on practice consistent with, and statements upholding, the positive obligation that underlies them.[31] In contrast, norms of prohibition are more difficult to examine, as the primary practice is absence of action, in effect refraining from practice.

---

principles within the domestic rather than the international sphere. For instance, Lord Phillimore specified that what was intended was laws accepted by "all civilized nations in foro domestico." Proces-Verbaux Du Comité Consultatif Des Juristes, 16 Juin/24 Juillet, 306, 335 (1920). *See* Lillich, *supra* note 7. For the alternative view, *see, e.g.*, Simma and Alston, *supra* note 3, at 104. In the environmental rights context, *see* Daniel Bodansky, *Customary (and Not So Customary) International Environmental Law*, 3 IND. J. GLOBAL LEGAL STUD. 105, 116–19 (1995), which also seeks to justify customary law as a new form of universal declaratory law.

29 *See* Lillich, *supra* note 7, at 12–13.

30 *See* esp. *Nicaragua*, Merits, *supra* note 1; and Advisory Opinion on the Legality of the Threat or Use of Nuclear Weapons, 1996 I.C.J. 226 (July 8) [hereinafter *Legality of the Threat or Use of Nuclear Weapons*].

31 For instance, in Fisheries (U.K. v. Nor.), 1951 I.C.J. 116 (Dec. 18), the Court considered the practice of states, which had asserted an extension of the fisheries limits, and preparatory documents to the third Conference on the Law of the Sea, which included the principle of preferential rights for coastal states (para. 53). It also considered resolutions at conferences as showing "overwhelming support for the idea" (para. 58) and noted that the practice of the North East Atlantic fisheries commissions (of which the parties were members) had adopted the principle in question.

The *Nuclear Weapons Advisory Opinion* shows that an absence of action is difficult to interpret. In that case, certain states argued that the consistent practice of non-utilization of nuclear weapons since 1945 supported the existence of a customary international law prohibiting their use.[32] However, other states argued that the non-use was referable not to emerging customary prohibition, but to the fact that circumstances that might justify their use had not arisen.[33] Ultimately this division of opinion led the Court to discount the importance of the practice.[34]

In the case of civil conflicts and coups d'état, cases of disagreements that could have led to conflicts but were peacefully resolved are not easy to locate and are unlikely to have attracted international community interest. However, the response of the international community to the cases in which recourse to force occurs can be identified. The question that arises is whether the regular disapproval of certain types of conduct expressed through condemnation or intervention amounts to a response to the breach of a legal norm. While such an approach would not be strictly orthodox, it is consistent with an aspect of the opinion of the Court in *Nicaragua*, which emphasized that " instances of State conduct inconsistent with a given rule *should generally have been treated as breaches of that rule*, not as indications of the recognition of a new rule."[35]

Morgenthau points out that "a rule, be it legal, moral, or conventional, is valid when its violation is likely to be followed by an unfavorable reaction, that is, a sanction against its violator."[36] Weisburd similarly emphasizes: "What is crucial, however, to permit the characterization of a norm as a rule of customary law, is that States refuse to acquiesce in a breach of the norm, but on the contrary actively seek to reverse the effects of the breach."[37] Schachter also highlights the importance of assessing the intensity and depth of third-party condemnation of viola-

---

32 *Legality of the Threat or Use of Nuclear Weapons*, *supra* note 30, paras. 65–66.

33 *Id.*, paras. 65–66.

34 *Id.*, para. 67. It also considered the impact of General Assembly resolutions affirming the illegality of nuclear weapons but held that as these were not binding, and were not supported by all nuclear states, these were insufficient to establish the requisite *opinio juris*. *See* paras. 68–69.

35 *Nicaragua*, Merits, *supra* note 1, para. 186 (emphasis added).

36 Hans Morgenthau, *Positivism, Functionalism, and International Law*, *in* THE NATURE OF INTERNATIONAL LAW 159, 175 (Gerry Simpson ed., 2001).

37 Weisburd, *supra* note 25, at 103.

tion in determining the emergence of a norm.[38] In practical terms, therefore, the customary law norm would be founded on the practice of the international community in response to the recourse to force in civil conflicts and coups d'état, rather than on an assessment of the extent to which states resolve their internal differences through political means, as opposed to violence.

The question remains whether the disapproval is based on a policy decision or is hardening into a legal prohibition. This turns on the issue of intention. Was the statement intended to protest against the violation of a legal obligation? To some extent, this can be determined through consideration of how the statement is formulated: whether it implies a legal obligation and uses legal terminology, whether it is perceived as binding by different actors, and how the international community responds to its breach. A focus on intention is consistent with the emphasis on *opinio juris* in customary law but also inherits similar difficulties, particularly, how to balance what states actually believe with what they claim.[39]

b. *Condemnation Followed by Sanctions*

This book takes the view that instances in which non-injured parties respond to a situation, by explicitly condemning the conduct and then seeking to impose sanctions, constitute crucial practice. Such responses, which appear to represent attempts at enforcement of a prohibition by non-injured states, are unusual in the realm of international law.[40] In fact,

---

[38] He was discussing human rights norms. Schachter, *supra* note 5, at 335–36.

[39] For a helpful discussion of the problems raised by *opinio juris, see* MICHAEL BYERS, CUSTOM, POWER AND THE POWER OF RULES: INTERNATIONAL RELATIONS AND CUSTOMARY INTERNATIONAL LAW 130–42 (1999). *See also* Michael Akehurst, *Custom as a Source of International Law,* 47 BRIT. Y.B. INT'L L. 1, 32 (1974–75). *See* GENNADY M. DANILENKO, LAW-MAKING IN THE INTERNATIONAL COMMUNITY 98–129 (1993), for a further discussion of the traditional role of *opinio juris* and its current role. For a striking criticism of Danilenko's strongly Positivist approach, *see* Jose E. Alvarez, *Positivism Regained, Nihilism Postponed,* 15 MICH. J. INT'L L. 747 (1994) (reviewing GENNADY M. DANILENKO, LAW-MAKING IN THE INTERNATIONAL COMMUNITY (1993). Note that in the case of *opinio juris,* Byers, for instance, maintains that rather than searching for beliefs, the Court is essentially searching for "convergent expectations," and it is doing so by examining "what States have openly done or admitted to doing, what in some cases they have not done, what State representatives have or in some cases have not said, and the contexts in which these various kinds of State practice have taken place." BYERS, *supra* at 151.

[40] Few international law norms are consistently enforced, and the absence of enforcement is one of the structural weaknesses of international law. Thus, while

according to orthodox international law, they are of uncertain legality, at least when they involve the use of force. Regardless, they must be acknowledged to represent a particularly strong rejection of the conduct taking place. Rejection and disapproval of conduct does not necessarily imply that such conduct is illegal. However, sanctions are a manifestation of the belief of a state that the conduct should be rejected. While the practice of rejecting aspects of civil conflicts has generally been analyzed from the perspective of whether these imply new norms permitting recourse to force (focusing on *legality of intervention*), such an approach obscures the question of whether the practice can impact on the legality of the conduct. A series of interventions by states condemning the overthrow of democratic governments by force, for instance, must be relevant to the question of whether there is an emerging principle that prohibits the overthrow of democracies by force.

It is uncontroversial that states may take actions in support of the international legal order, especially by applying economic and political sanctions. As Kelsen maintains, "there is nothing to prevent us from calling reprisals sanctions of international law. For reprisals are reactions against violations of international law."[41] Nonetheless counter-measures are typically only open to the state victim of the breach, although if such an obligation were owed *erga omnes*, it would, in theory, be open to enforcement by all states. In such limited fashion, non-forceful sanctions that aim at stopping or preventing conduct that has been condemned imply that the principles sought to be enforced are binding principles, not merely guidelines or policies.

Forceful responses to civil conflicts raise more complex issues, however, as these forceful counter-measures are *prima facie* illegal under the Charter.[42] While the legality of the actions themselves is not the focus of this discussion, the question of how to interpret this practice, in the light of its *prima facie* inconsistency with the prohibition on recourse to force under the Charter and the rejection of the legality of forceful counter-measures, does arise.

---

attempts at enforcement are striking and suggest that the norm is considered of particular importance by the international community, the reverse is not necessarily true. A failure to act to enforce a particular rule does not strongly contradict the existence of that norm.

41 HANS KELSEN, PRINCIPLES OF INTERNATIONAL LAW 21–22 (Robert W. Tucker rev. ed., 2d ed. 1966).

42 IAN BROWNLIE, INTERNATIONAL LAW AND THE USE OF FORCE BY STATES 281 (1963); *Nicaragua*, Merits, *supra* note 1, at 110–11.

According to Oppenheim, while states formerly had the right to intervene to secure "the observance by other states of universally accepted rules of international law, or of their treaty obligations," in the form of a quasi "police action," such intervention can no longer be justified, since the responsibility for policing now rests with the United Nations.[43] As the Court stated in *Nicaragua*, even if Nicaragua had made, and then breached, a commitment to hold elections, the United States could not use force as a remedy.[44]

Nevertheless, in practice, states have resorted to forceful reprisals on many occasions. Arend and Beck acknowledge that, despite the apparent prohibition, states have frequently maintained that force was used for purposes of deterrence or punishment and have claimed the right to resort to reprisals.[45] Bierzanek considers that "as long as the traditional structure of international relations exists, such imperfect methods of maintaining the international legal order are justified and are hardly to be avoided."[46] And, as Bowett has stated:

> As states have grown increasingly disillusioned about the capacity of the Council to afford them protection against what they would regard as illegal and highly injurious conduct directed against them, they have resorted to self-help in the form of reprisals and have acquired the confidence that, in so doing, they will not incur anything more than a formal censure from the Council. The law on reprisals is, because of its divorce from actual practice, rapidly degenerating to a stage where its normative character is in question.[47]

---

[43] ROBERT JENNINGS AND ARTHUR WATTS, OPPENHEIM'S INTERNATIONAL LAW 439–40, n.4 (9th ed. 1992). *See also* BROWNLIE, *supra* note 42, at 281.

[44] *Nicaragua*, Merits, *supra* note 1, at 131–33.

[45] ANTHONY C. AREND AND ROBERT J. BECK, INTERNATIONAL LAW AND THE USE OF FORCE: BEYOND THE UN CHARTER PARADIGM 42–43 (1993). *See also* William V. O'Brien, *Reprisals, Deterrence and Self-Defense in Counterterror Operations*, 30 VA. J. INT'L L. 421 (1990). Moreover, MYRES S. MCDOUGAL AND FLORENTINO P. FELICIANO, LAW AND MINIMUM WORLD PUBLIC ORDER: THE LEGAL REGULATION OF INTERNATIONAL COERCION (1961) point out that, frequently, reprisals are the only protection to ensure that other states will do their duty under international law.

[46] Remigiusz Bierzanek, *Reprisals as a Means of Enforcing the Laws of Warfare: The Old and the New Law, in* THE NEW HUMANITARIAN LAW OF ARMED CONFLICT 232, 233 (Antonio Cassese ed., 1979).

[47] Derek Bowett, *Reprisals Involving Recourse to Armed Force*, 66 AM. J. INT'L L. 1, 2 (1972).

This controversy prevents a straightforward correlation between the use of force by states and regional bodies and the legality of the principles they seek to enforce. Nevertheless, these enforcement actions should not be discounted. The decision to use force is not taken lightly by a state, and it must indicate that the principle it seeks to enforce is of considerable importance. This is reinforced by the fact that such use of force remains illegal according to traditional theory—even though, in this latest incarnation, it has generally not been condemned by the international community.[48] Therefore, irrespective of the formal legality of these actions, they support the emergence of a legal prohibition that they seek to enforce. Recourse to forceful measures indicates a high level of commitment by a state to the principle it is seeking to enforce. Moreover, while in the short term it is not unthinkable that a pattern of enforcement could emerge without the conduct becoming illegal, it would be contrary to logic and fairness for such a situation to persist in the longer term.

c. *Verbal Acts and Physical Actions*

Concurrent with the human rights debate and the debate surrounding the weight to be given to *opinio juris*, a question arises of how much weight is to be accorded to verbal acts of states, in contrast with physical actions, in the civil conflict and coup d'état context. At one level, this involves the issue of the extent to which verbal acts can contribute to practice, as well as *opinio juris*;[49] at another, it raises the question of how much weight to accord to a range of different types of practice during the process of making an assessment of whether a customary rule has emerged.

Many commentators have maintained that physical acts are the most important element of practice. This view is supported by D'Amato, for instance, who argues that a statement by a state can only be considered as evidence of *opinio juris* but not as evidence of the material component of custom.[50] Simma and Alston similarly emphasize that actions, not

---

48 Consider, for instance, the Nigerian and U.K. intervention in Sierra Leone and French interventions in Côte d'Ivoire.

49 *See* Theodor Meron, *Editorial Comment: The Continuing Role of Custom in the Formation of International Humanitarian Law*, 90 AM. J. INT'L L. 238, 239 (1996).

50 D'AMATO, *supra* note 18, at 88. *See also* Gerald Fitzmaurice, *Law and Procedure of the International Court of Justice: General Principles and Sources of Law*, 30 BRIT. Y.B. INT'L L. 1, 68 (1953); KAROL WOLFKE, CUSTOM IN PRESENT INTERNATIONAL LAW (2d ed. 1993).

words, should have precedence, as deeds "are hard and solid; they have been carefully hammered out on the anvil of actual, tangible interaction among States; and they allow reasonably reliable predictions as to future State behavior."[51]

In essence, however, the issue is not whether verbal acts can amount to practice, which in the view of the Committee on Formation of Customary Law they do, but rather that, in some instances, more weight should be attributed to conduct than to verbal acts.[52] Moreover, as Mendelson points out, different verbal acts carry different weights as well: "a formal statement of position by a head of State or Government, or a formal diplomatic communication at the highest level, plainly must be taken seriously."[53]

Ultimately, a process of weighing different types of practice and supporting and opposing behavior is essential to the search for a customary law rule. Commentators have adopted differing approaches to this process. O'Connell, for instance, favors taking into account "the number of protests, the vehemence of the protests, the subsequent actions of all parties, the importance of the interests affected and the effluxion of time."[54] Schachter focuses on the intensity and depth of condemnation of violations.[55] These approaches have in common an assessment of practice that seeks to take into account and weigh up the vehemence, importance, and nature of actions.

In applying a similar approach to the norms considered in this work, it is useful to undertake a rough categorization of conduct. A commonsense approach suggests that certain actions will carry greater weight, because they indicate greater or clearer commitment to a particular position. The strongest reaction would be an insistence through military force that other states follow the rule, and the weakest would be a verbal expression of concern. Therefore, the following scale—ranging from

---

[51] Simma and Alston, *supra* note 3, at 89.

[52] International Law Association, *supra* note 4, at 724–25.

[53] Mendelson "*The Formation of Customary International Law*," 272 HAGUE ACADEMY OF INTERNATIONAL LAW, RECUEIL DES COURS 155, at 205 (1998).

[54] D.P. O'Connell, *Mid-Ocean Archipelagos in International Law*, 45 BRIT. Y.B. INT'L L. 1, 63 (1971).

[55] Schachter, *supra* note 5, at 338. MERON, *supra* note 3, at 92, also supports this approach.

weakest to most significant categories of practice—is adopted to assist in the balancing process: expressions of concern and condemnation of civil conflicts or particular actions in them; explicit calls for specific outcomes or actions; the imposition of sanctions against, or the provision of non-military assistance to, either side in a civil conflict; and indirect and direct forceful intervention. In addition, the reactions by other states either supporting or challenging the legality of the above actions are also considered practice of great import.

d. A Question of Consent?

The impact of consent by a state to third-party intervention can be perplexing, and it may seem counter-intuitive.[56] Consent by a state has, in general, been considered a dominant rationale for intervention, and therefore where consent can be identified, no other justifications for the intervention are given any weight. Nonetheless, consent can support the emergence of new legal norms prohibiting conduct.

Traditionally, the emergence of international law is based on the consent of states. An example is the emergence of the norm favoring a right to send satellites into orbit without the agreement of the underlying territorial states based on the accumulation of examples of states willingly consenting to it. By analogy, the consent by party states to the actions of the international community rejecting recourse to force in initiating civil conflict could support the emergence of a consensus prohibiting the recourse to force. This is in accord with the *Nicaragua* decision where the Court highlighted (in the context of General Assembly resolutions):

> The effect of *consent* to the text of such resolutions cannot be understood as merely that of "reiteration or elucidation" of the treaty commitment undertaken in the Charter. On the contrary, it may be understood as an *acceptance of the validity of the rule* or set of rules declared by the resolution by themselves.[57]

Consent is fundamental to the emergence of a new norm. A state's vehement rejection of the rules formulated by the Security Council (and its attempts to enforce them) must count against the emergence of new norms. On the other hand, a state's consent to the rules—whether it

---

[56] Further discussion of the issue of consent in the practice is undertaken in Chapter 5.

[57] *Nicaragua*, Merits, *supra* note 1, para. 188 (emphasis added).

does so willingly, feels bound to, or has no realistic alternative—supports the view that a new norm is crystallizing.

Moreover, the existence of consent does not *prevent* the emergence of norms based on other principles, unless the practice suggests that condemnation may *only* take place where there is consent. In the practice reviewed, the condemnation and intervention seem not to have been formulated as pre-determined by the consent (although consent was acknowledged), particularly where the international community's response was based on a Chapter VII resolution.[58]

e. *Inconsistent Practice*

The extent to which inconsistent practice undermines the emergence of a legal norm depends on the reasons for such inconsistency. If the conduct is caused by a belief that such matters are domestic, or acceptable conduct, then the lack of response undermines the emergence of a relevant consensus. Alternatively, inconsistency may indicate that the law and practice is still in flux. The case of inconsistent enforcement must also be considered separately, as enforcement in international law is an exception and can be highly influenced by geopolitical considerations.[59]

It is often difficult to determine the true rationale for the lack of response. A lack of response by the Security Council, for instance, could be an exception to a rule or a failure to intervene based on political

---

[58] In East Timor, for instance, the Council only intervened once the consent of Indonesia was secured. S.C. Res. 1236, U.N. Doc. S/RES/1236 (May 7, 1999). However, it authorized the force on the basis of a finding of a threat to international peace and security. S.C. Res. 1264, U.N. Doc. S/RES/1264 (Sept. 15, 1999). Similarly, in Liberia the cease-fire agreement was mentioned, but the intervention was in fact authorized on the basis of the deterioration of the situation, which constituted a threat to international peace and security. S.C. Res. 866, U.N. Doc. S/RES/866 (Sept. 22, 1993). In addition, a number of the peace-keeping forces have been authorized under Chapter VII without reference to the consent of the parties. UNPROFOR in Croatia was authorized to use force in self-defense under Chapter VII, S.C. Res. 871, U.N. Doc. S/RES/871 (Oct. 4, 1993), and in Bosnia, the mandate was extended to the protection of the safe areas under Chapter VII, S.C. Res. 836, U.N. Doc. S/RES/836 (June 4, 1993).

[59] For instance, the Secretary-General has indicated that in the case of Rwanda, the political will and the troops were lacking, and hence no enforcement measures were taken, but this does not undermine the existence of the norm prohibiting genocide. Press Release, Secretary-General, Statement at Memorial Ceremony in New York, U.N. Doc. SG/SM/9223 (Mar. 26, 2004).

grounds; it could indicate the non-existence of a rule or it could reflect the belief that the Council is precluded from responding because of the domestic nature of the matter.[60]

3. International Law and Non-State Actors

Additional complexities arise from the fact that any norms involving the actors in civil conflict or coup d'état would apply to a non-state party. The traditional roles of the state as subject, and of the individual as object, of international law seem to be gradually eroding in international law, but the enforcement of international law against non-state actors remains controversial. There are some areas, however, in which clear norms supporting the enforcement of international law against individuals or non-state actors are emerging.

The first is the field of individual criminal responsibility. Since the Nuremberg Trials, individual responsibility for serious human rights violations has been well established in international law.[61] The Genocide Convention also provides for criminal responsibility of individuals, which it anchors in the criminality of genocide under customary international law.[62] The statutes of the criminal tribunals for the former Yugoslavia and Rwanda both provide for individual responsibility for crimes against humanity. The new International Criminal Court also adopts individual responsibility for a range of crimes in its Rome Statute. Simma and Paulus consider that "the law increasingly renders individuals accountable for violations of the most basic humanitarian rules" and that "[t]his development is being brought about by the traditional means of international lawmaking through state consent."[63] The International Law Commission has long accepted some form of individual responsibility. In the 1951 Draft Code of Offences Against the Peace and Security of Mankind, Article 1 provided that "offences against the peace and secu-

---

60 For a discussion of the interplay between Security Council intervention and Article 2(7), *see* Fernando R. Tesón, *A Symposium on Re-Envisioning the Security Council: Collective Humanitarian Intervention*, 17 MICH. J. INT'L L. 323, 353–54 (1996). *See also* ROSALYN HIGGINS, THE DEVELOPMENT OF INTERNATIONAL LAW THROUGH THE POLITICAL ORGANS OF THE UNITED NATIONS 58–130 (1969).

61 *See* LYAL S. SUNGA, INDIVIDUAL RESPONSIBILITY IN INTERNATIONAL LAW FOR SERIOUS HUMAN RIGHTS VIOLATIONS (1992).

62 Bruno Simma and Andreas Paulus, *Symposium on Method in International Law: The Responsibility of Individuals for Human Rights Abuses in Internal Conflicts: A Positivist View*, 93 AM. J. INT'L L. 302, 308 (1999).

63 *Id.* at 316.

rity of mankind are crimes under international law, for which the responsible individual shall be punished." The 1996 text now provides in Article 2, "A crime against the peace and security of mankind entails individual responsibility."[64]

The second area is the field of humanitarian laws of war. Additional Protocol II to the Geneva Conventions applies to non-state entities and renders certain conduct illegal. It clearly binds "dissident armed forces or other organized armed groups which, under responsible command, exercise such control over a part of its territory as to enable them to carry out sustained and concerted military operations and to implement this Protocol,"[65] and breaches of that Protocol by a non-state actor would be considered a breach of international law.[66]

A number of domestic courts have made rulings against individuals on the basis of individual responsibility for international crimes. In *Kadic v. Karadzic*,[67] the court maintained that since the time of piracy, non-state actors had been held liable for certain violations of international law. It confirmed that individual non-state actors are capable of violating international laws prohibiting genocide and war crimes and held therefore that a U.S. court could have jurisdiction over a non-state actor, under the Alien Tort Claims Act,[68] accused of committing genocide or war crimes in violation of international law. The Special Court for Sierra Leone and the International Commission of Inquiry on Darfur similarly held that the Revolutionary United Front of Sierra Leone and the Sudan Liberation Movement/Army were bound by customary humanitarian law principles.[69] According to Sandesh Sivakumar, it is uncontroversial that

---

64 Draft Code of Crimes Against the Peace and Security of Mankind (1996), *at* untreaty.un.org/ilc/texts/instruments/english/draft%20articles/7_4_1996.pdf.

65 Protocol Additional to the Geneva Conventions of 12 August 1949, Relating to the Protection of Victims of Non-International Armed Conflicts, art. 1, 16 I.L.M. 1442 (1977).

66 Individuals, in grouping themselves such that they become a party to an internal armed conflict, are granted a sufficient degree of personality so as to be able to hold rights and be subject to obligations imposed on them by the rules governing internal armed conflict. GERALD I.A.D. DRAPER, THE RED CROSS CONVENTIONS 17 (1958).

67 Kadic v. Karadzic, 70 F.3d 232 (2d Cir. 1995); see the review by Theodore R. Posner, "Kadic v Karadzic", 90 AM. J. INT'L L. 658 (1996).

68 28 U.S.C. § 1350 (1988).

69 *See* Prosecutor v. Morris Kallon, Brima Bazzy Kamara, SCSL 2004-15-AR72(E),

armed opposition groups can be bound under customary international law.[70] The I.C.J. already held in 1949 that the United Nations could bring an action against a state, thus recognizing the possibility of entities other than states having legal personality.[71]

Sivakumar questions whether the practice of armed groups is relevant to the formation of customary international law, which, he maintains, remains uncertain and controversial. The ICRC study on customary international humanitarian law found that legal significance for the practice of armed opposition groups was unclear and that is constituted "other practice."[72] However, Higgins, for instance, is prepared to grant to individuals a much greater status in international law, rejecting the traditional subject/object dichotomy.[73] Nonetheless, the weight to be accorded to practice of armed groups remains somewhat uncertain, and hence such practice should be evaluated with care.

B. THE NORMATIVE IMPACT OF SECURITY COUNCIL PRACTICE

One of the key elements of the methodological framework is the relevance of Security Council decisions to the emergence of policy and legal norms. The nature and impact of Council practice has been addressed as an aside to the question of the I.C.J. review of Council decisions.[74]

SCSL-2004-16-AR72(E), Decision on Challenge to Jurisdiction: Lomé Accord Amnesty, para. 47, Mar. 13, 2004; International Commission of Inquiry on Darfur, *Report of the International Commission of Inquiry on Darfur to the United Nations Secretary-General*, para. 172 (Jan. 25, 2005), *available at* http://www.un.org/News/dh/sudan/com_inq_darfur.pdf.

70 Sandesh Sivakumar, *Binding Armed Opposition Groups*, 55 INT'L & COMP. L.Q. 369, 373 (2006).

71 Reference to Reparations for Injuries Suffered in the Service of the United Nations, 1949 I.C.J. 174, 178, Advisory Opinion (Apr. 11).

72 Jean-Marie Henckaerts and Louise Doswald-Beck eds., *Study on Customary International Humanitarian Law: A Contribution to the Understanding and Respect for the Rule of Law in Armed Conflict*, 87 INT'L REV. RED CROSS 175, 179–80 (2005).

73 HIGGINS, *supra* note 22, at 50.

74 For an overview of that debate, *see* Questions of Interpretation and Application of the 1971 Montreal Convention Arising from the Aerial Incident at Lockerbie, (Libya v. U.K.), Provisional Measures, 1992 I.C.J. 114 (Apr. 14) [hereinafter *Lockerbie Case*]. *See* Thomas F. Franck, *The 'Powers of Appreciation': Who Is the Ultimate Guardian of UN Legality?*, 86 AM. J. INT'L L. 519 (1992); Derek Bowett, *The Impact of Security Council Decisions on Dispute Settlement Procedures*, 5 EUR. J. INT'L L. 89 (1994);

Nonetheless, the Council provides an abundant source of accessible, published, and organized practice. Moreover, the Council's nature as a powerful and influential decision-making body, which can pass binding resolutions and impose serious consequences and sanctions, suggests that any principles that are emerging within its practice will be of great importance.

This section reviews the ways in which Council practice influences international law. It focuses on the impact of resolutions that condemn conduct (without declaring it to be illegal) and goes on to impose sanctions. There are many such resolutions, and hence their impact is of key importance to the discussion of norms in the civil conflict context.

1. The Relevance of Resolutions

a. *Textual Interpretation*

Before turning to a normative discussion of the impact of Security Council practice, the question of how to investigate the practice of the Council, given its highly political nature, on the basis of its resolutions must be addressed. Is the text of a resolution a good indication of the intentions of the Council, or should it be discounted as merely the result of a series of compromises and deals?

The literature has touched on rules of interpretation of Council resolutions, relying primarily on the I.C.J.'s decision in *Namibia*.[75] It supports the view that the intended meaning of a resolution must be determined in each case, taking into account the language of the resolution, the discussions leading to it, the U.N. Charter provisions invoked, and all surrounding circumstances.[76]

MOHAMMED BEDJAOUI, THE NEW WORLD ORDER AND THE SECURITY COUNCIL: TESTING THE LEGALITY OF ITS ACTS (1994); Jose E. Alvarez, *Judging the Security Council*, 90 AM. J. INT'L L. 1 (1996). In other instances, it has only been touched upon. *See, e.g.*, HIGGINS, *supra* note 60. For a more focused investigation, although with little theoretical discussion, *see* Steven R. Ratner, *The Security Council and International Law: Deciphering the Normative Messages of a Political Organ, in* THE UNITED NATIONS SECURITY COUNCIL AFTER THE COLD WAR (David Malone ed., 2004).

[75] For a thorough discussion of the general principles to be applied to the interpretation of Security Council resolutions, *see* Michael C. Wood, *The Interpretation of Security Council Resolutions*, 2 MAX PLANK Y.B. U.N. L. 73 (1998).

[76] In that case, the issue was the binding nature of a resolution. Legal Consequences for States of the Continued Presence of South Africa in Namibia (South

Despite the fact that many resolutions result from a combination of geopolitical factors, it is largely not possible to go behind the public statements and justifications in the resolution and the published debates, as these form the official justification for the actions. Clearly the realpolitik rationale for any resolution will vary depending on which actors are interviewed. This is even more difficult in the case of the use of the veto blocking a resolution. In some cases, the realpolitik rationale is known, because it is the intention of the vetoing state that it be known—such as China's veto of the continuation of the Macedonian peace-keeping mission in response to Macedonia's recognition of Taiwan—but, frequently, the true rationale for the veto is not directly expressed. In such circumstances, the conclusion that the principle under consideration was rejected would be entirely artificial, if in fact it was evident that the reasons for the veto were geopolitical.

b. When Are Resolutions Binding?

Although the I.C.J. expressly considered the binding nature of Security Council resolutions in the *Advisory Opinion on Namibia,*[77] this remains a difficult and controversial topic.[78] Two issues in particular arise in this text: whether Council resolutions can bind non-state actors; and the extent to which resolutions authorized under Chapter VI of the U.N. Charter can impose binding obligations.

While the Council appears to consider itself to have power to bind all parties to all conflicts (including civil conflicts) with or without relying on Chapter VII, an interesting distinction appears to be emerging in the practice between resolutions addressing parties and those addressing the greater U.N. membership. In fact, despite the reasoning in *Namibia,* the Council has rarely imposed demands on the greater membership outside of Chapter VII, whereas it has done so frequently in the case of parties to a dispute. This differential approach to parties to a dispute seems to reflect the wording of the Charter, and it is consistent with its scheme that places the responsibility to maintain peace and security on the Council.

West Africa) Notwithstanding Security Council Resolution 276 (1970), Advisory Opinion, 1971 I.C.J. 16 (June 21) [hereinafter *Advisory Opinion on Namibia*].

[77] *Id.*

[78] The discussion of Article 25 in BRUNO SIMMA AND HERMANN MOSLER, THE CHARTER OF THE UNITED NATIONS: A COMMENTARY (2d ed. 2002), for instance, is testimony to the ongoing confusion and difficulty.

i. Non-Chapter VII Resolutions

In the *Advisory Opinion on Namibia*[79] the I.C.J. considered the legal consequences of a Security Council resolution that declared South Africa's presence in Namibia illegal and invalid. This resolution was not passed under Chapter VII of the U.N. Charter, according to which the Council "may call upon the Members of the United Nations to apply such measures,"[80] which would have rendered it binding, nor did it refer to the situation as amounting to a threat to international peace and security. Nevertheless, the majority held that member states were under an obligation to accept and carry it out:

> A binding determination made by a competent organ of the United Nations to the effect that a situation is illegal cannot remain without consequence. Once the Court is faced with such a situation, it would be failing in the discharge of its judicial functions if it did not declare that there is an obligation, especially upon Members of the United Nations, to bring that situation to an end.[81]

The Court rejected the view that only resolutions under Chapter VII could be binding on the basis that to limit Article 25[82] to enforcement actions under Chapter VII would render it "superfluous," as Articles 48 and 49 already assure the same effect.[83] This approach was strongly opposed by the minority, who argued that Article 25 could not have the effect of evading the conditions in Chapter VII.[84]

The *Namibia* decision provides that binding resolutions may be passed without reliance on Chapter VII and that the question of whether

---

79 *Advisory Opinion on Namibia, supra* note 76. For a discussion of this case, see Tadashi Mori, *Namibia Opinion Revisited: A Gap in the Current Arguments on the Power of the Security Council,* 4 ILSA J. INT'L & COMP. L. 121 (1997); Rosalyn Higgins, *The Advisory Opinion on Namibia: Which UN Resolutions Are Binding under Article 25 of the Charter?,* 21 INT'L & COMP. L.Q. 270, 286 (1972).

80 U.N. CHARTER art. 41; *see also* U.N. CHARTER arts. 48, 49.

81 *Advisory Opinion on Namibia, supra* note 76, at 54.

82 U.N. Charter Article 25, provides that the members "agree to accept and carry out the decisions of the Security Council in accordance with the present Charter."

83 *Advisory Opinion on Namibia, supra* note 76, at 53.

84 *Id.* (separate opinion of Judge Petren), at 136; (dissenting opinion of Judge Fitzmaurice), at 293; (dissenting opinion of Judge Gros), at 341.

a resolution is binding is to be determined in each case, taking into account the language of the resolution, the discussions leading to it, the Charter provisions invoked, and all surrounding circumstances. Despite this decision, however, the debate regarding the binding nature of resolutions continued unresolved in the literature.[85] Even the latest Simma and Mosler commentary on the Charter is inconclusive on the issue. While that commentary leans toward the view that some resolutions outside of Chapter VII may be binding, they suggest that the scope for such resolutions is extremely limited, because resolutions under Chapter VI cannot impose binding obligations but merely repeat the duty of states to settle peacefully.[86]

ii. Resolutions Addressed at Parties vs. U.N. Members

It is useful to distinguish between resolutions addressed to parties to a dispute and those addressed to the general U.N. membership. Even a brief overview of the practice of the Security Council makes clear that a strikingly large number of resolutions addressed at parties to a dispute are formulated as binding, irrespective of whether they rely on Chapter VII or the finding of a threat to international peace and security.[87]

In contrast, Council practice directed at the general U.N. membership rarely uses compulsory language unless the resolution is passed under Chapter VII. Most non-Chapter VII requests addressed to the U.N. membership are general or ambiguous and do not seek to impose binding enforcement action or sanctions.[88]

---

85 *See, e.g.*, Mori, *supra* note 79, at 131 n.78, who also points out that the *travaux preparatoires* appear not to resolve the issue, although in her view the better approach is that only Chapter VII resolutions are binding. Willem Riphagen, *The Legal Consequence of Illegal Acts Under Public International Law*, 20 NETH. INT'L L. REV. 27, 31 (1973); Lawrence L. Herman, *The Legal Status of Namibia and of the United Nations Council for Namibia*, 13 CAN. Y.B. INT'L L. 306, 316 (1975); RENATA SONNENFELD, RESOLUTIONS OF THE UNITED NATIONS SECURITY COUNCIL 127–28 (1988). *See* James A.R. Nafziger and Edward M. Wise, *The Status in United States Law of Security Council Resolutions Under Chapter VII of the United Nations Charter*, 46 AM. J. COMP. L. SUPP. 421, 428–29 (1998); and SYDNEY BAILEY AND SAM DAWS, THE PROCEDURE OF THE UN SECURITY COUNCIL 263–73 (3d ed. 1998). On the interpretation of Article 25, *see* HANS KELSEN, THE LAW OF THE UNITED NATIONS: A CRITICAL ANALYSIS OF ITS FUNDAMENTAL PROBLEMS 444–50 (1st ed. 1950).

86 *See* the discussion of Article 25 by SIMMA AND MOSLER, *supra* note 78, at 452.

87 *See* the discussion of the practice of the Security Council, in Chapter 3.

88 Other than the resolutions in Namibia, there have been few examples of reso-

The emphasis on the responsibility of parties to a dispute to abide by the resolutions of the Council seems consistent with one interpretation of the U.N. Charter. Article 40 explicitly permits the Council to act with respect to parties before determining a threat to international peace and security under Article 39. The Council may "call upon the parties concerned to comply with such provisional measures as it deems necessary" and "shall duly take account of failure to comply [with such measures],"[89] suggesting that it may act to enforce a failure to comply.

Moreover, a terminological distinction between Article 40 and Articles 41, 42, and 43 further supports the view that the Council is able to make binding demands on parties to a conflict without relying on Article 39. Under Article 40, it may call upon "the parties concerned" to comply with provisional measures. However, in Articles 41, 42, and 43, the Council may call upon the "Members of the United Nations" to enforce its measures. The text implies, therefore, that under Article 40, the Council may make binding decisions against any party to a conflict threatening international peace and security.

Furthermore, it seems logical that a party to a dispute that is likely to endanger peace and security[90] would be expected to comply with resolutions of the Council that aim to prevent an aggravation of the situation. Their conduct jeopardizes the peace and security of the other states, and hence they have a serious responsibility to comply with decisions of the Council seeking to maintain international peace and security.[91]

In this light, the text adopts the position that, at least in relation to resolutions addressed to parties to a dispute, the *Namibia* decision—which provides that a resolution, even if not passed under Chapter VII, will be held to be binding, if its formulation evidences that the Council

---

lutions seeking to impose direct obligations without referring to Chapter VII. One possible example occurred in the conflict in Afghanistan, S.C. Res. 1076, U.N. Doc. S/RES/1076 (Oct. 22, 1996) (end the supply of arms and ammunition to both parties), and South Africa, where many explicit demands were made on the parties, without reference to Chapter VII, and a number of calls on other states to impose an arms embargo, *Id.*, ¶ 9. *See also* during the Yugoslav conflict, S.C. Res. 713, U.N. Doc. S/RES/713, 7 (Sept. 25, 1991).

89 U.N. CHARTER art. 40.

90 These are the parties subject to U.N. Charter, Chapters VI and VII; *see* U.N. CHARTER art. 33.

91 *Id.*, art. 24.

intends it to be binding—should be applied. Thus, while a Chapter VII resolution is clearly binding, a non-Chapter VII resolution aimed at the parties to a dispute may also be binding if it is formulated in a binding fashion.

iii. Non-State Actors?

To what extent do Security Council resolutions bind non-state actors? Arguably, Chapter VI places obligations on all parties to a dispute, including non-state parties, and gives the Council power to call on all such parties to settle their disputes by peaceful means.[92] A literal reading of Article 33 supports this position as the article uses the term "parties" rather than "States" or "Members" (which are used to indicate state parties to the U.N. Charter in other provisions of the Charter). Nonetheless, in their commentary on the Charter, Goodrich et al. use the terminology of "members" or "states" interchangeably with "parties," suggesting that the Charter only anticipates state actor parties.[93] The later commentary on the Charter by Simma and Mosler does note that the literal meaning of Article 2(3) includes disputes with non-state actors, such as international organizations, *de facto* regimes, ethnic communities, or national liberation movements. However, it goes on to argue that "since the Charter is a multilateral treaty between the member States of the UN, and since Art 33(1) must be viewed as covering a sector from the larger scope of Art 2(3), it must be concluded that the members of the UN are the primary addressees here as well."[94]

On the other hand, it could be argued that under Chapter VII (and particularly Article 40) the Council does have power to bind parties, including non-state actors. This position would reflect the broad powers that the Council has under Chapter VII to "make recommendations, or decide what measures shall be taken"[95] to maintain and restore international peace and security. There is no explicit limit on the potential measures the Council may impose once Article 39 is activated; why would these be restricted to measures directed at state parties or even at the parties to the conflict?

---

[92] *Id.*, art. 33.

[93] *See* LELAND M. GOODRICH ET AL., CHARTER OF THE UNITED NATIONS: COMMENTARY AND DOCUMENTS 260 (3d ed. 1969).

[94] SIMMA AND MOSLER, *supra* note 78, at 585.

[95] U.N. CHARTER art. 39.

The practice of the Council supports the view that non-state parties can be bound by resolutions. The Council habitually calls upon rebel groups, or sub-state groups involved in conflicts, to act in specific ways. The trend can be traced to the practice of the Council in Angola demanding that the United Front for the Total Liberation of Angola (UNITA) and Jonas Savimbi stop hostilities and respect the result of the elections. The Council also imposed a military and petrol embargo on UNITA,[96] demanding that it withdraw its troops from certain areas and condemning its breach of the peace accords.[97] The discussions in the Council, which led to these resolutions, support the view that the Council is entitled to bind UNITA despite it being a non-state party.[98] Other striking practice includes a resolution under Chapter VII, which insisted that the Taliban "cease the provision of sanctuary and training for international terrorists and their organisations"[99] and a resolution demanding

---

[96] S.C. Res. 864, U.N. Doc. S/RES/864, ¶¶ 17–19 (Sept. 15, 1993).

[97] *Id.*, ¶¶ 8–9. *See also* S.C. Res. 1127, U.N. Doc. S/RES/1127 (Aug. 28, 1997): S.C. Res. 1173, U.N. Doc. S/RES/1173 (June 12, 1998).

[98] For instance, the representative for Angola noted: "In all civilized democratic nations, those who break the law and who commit crimes are penalized. In the modern world there are countries or individuals who are penalised for not fulfilling their international commitments." S.C. 3168th mtg., U.N. Doc. S/PV.3168, at 11–12 (Jan. 29, 1993). Brazil emphasized that it was important to take action against UNITA, as it would be interpreted as a measure of the willingness of the United Nations "in promoting the principle that conflicts must be settled peacefully and that the use of force must never be rewarded." *Id.* at 26–30. The Russian Federation emphasized that "the time has come when the international community must immediately demonstrate responsibility and firmness in dealing with those forces which are ignoring the resolutions of the Security Council, and to that end, use must be made of every means available to individual States for exerting influence on UNITA." S.C. 3182d mtg., U.N. Doc. S/PV.3182 (Mar. 12, 1993), at 12. In meeting 3277, which led to the imposition of sanctions, the discussion similarly assumed that the Security Council was entitled to bind UNITA. The Russian Federation stated that it is only through "determined and forceful measures on the part of the international community that we can force UNITA to fulfil its obligations under existing agreements and to embark unreservedly on the process of seeking a peaceful settlement in the country." S.C. 3277th mtg., U.N. Doc. S/PV.3277 (Sept. 15, 1993), at 46. Nigeria agreed that the United Nations must "send out the strongest possible signals to the rebel party in Angola, UNITA, that enough is enough and that its patience is running out." S.C. 3277th mtg., *supra* at 3. Brazil specified that UNITA must "understand that the United Nations will not turn a blind eye to violations of Security Council resolutions and that this Organisation would be betraying its most basic principles if it were to allow force to prevail over the rule of law." S.C. 3277th mtg., *supra.* It also emphasized that the international community will hold UNITA responsible and "will not tolerate its continued attempts to wage war on its own people in an effort to conquer militarily what it could not win in a democratic election." S.C. 3277th mtg., *supra* at 31.

[99] S.C. Res. 1267, U.N. Doc. S/RES/1267 (Oct. 15, 1999).

that "all parties and others concerned in the former Yugoslavia, and all military forces in Bosnia and Herzegovina, immediately cease and desist from all breaches of international humanitarian law."[100]

2. The Security Council and Customary Law

Determining the extent to which customary law is modified and developed by the practice of the Security Council is of increasing importance given the range and volume of its practice in the civil war context. Although Council resolutions have been referred to by both courts and commentators, there has been little discussion of how best to characterize the impact of the practice.

a. *The Approach of the Court and Commentators*

i. The International Court of Justice

Though the way in which the I.C.J. has approached the question would be a useful starting point, in practice, the Court has not undertaken a systematic review of the role of Security Council practice. In passing, it has relied on Council resolutions in a rather ambiguous fashion, without clear justification as to their relevance to customary law.

For instance, in the *Hostages Case*, the Court maintained that a statement by the Secretary-General and a Council resolution supporting particular principles could be seen as "evidencing the importance attached by the international community as a whole to the observance of those principles."[101] In the *Threat or Use of Nuclear Weapons Case*, the Court also relied upon a statement by the Secretary-General, approved by the Council, that the Geneva Conventions had become part of customary law.[102] However, it did not undertake a discussion of the relevance of the resolutions or justify reliance on them, in contrast to its extensive discussion of the relevance of General Assembly resolutions.[103] Similarly, the

---

100 S.C. Res. 771, U.N. Doc. S/RES/771, ¶ 3 (Aug. 12, 1992). *See also* with respect to Sierra Leone rebels, S.C. Res. 1132, U.N. Doc. S/RES/1132, ¶ 1 (Oct. 8, 1997); S.C. Res. 1260, U.N. Doc. S/RES/1260 (Aug. 20, 1999); and the Rwandan civil war, S.C. Res. 812, U.N. Doc. S/RES/812 (Mar. 12, 1993); S.C. Res. 925, U.N. Doc. S/RES/925 (June 8, 1994).

101 United States Diplomatic and Consular Staff in Teheran, Judgment, 1980 I.C.J. 3, para. 36 (May 24), adopting the statement made in the Provisional Measures decision, United States Diplomatic and Consular Staff in Teheran, Provisional Measures, 1979 I.C.J. 7 (Dec. 15).

102 *Legality of the Threat or Use of Nuclear Weapons, supra* note 30, at 258.

103 *Id.* at 254–55.

International Tribunal for the former Yugoslavia relied on Council resolutions in support of the proposition that persons committing serious violations of international humanitarian law in the former Yugoslavia would be held individually responsible for such violations, again without justifying the reliance.[104] Nevertheless, it seems implicit in these decisions that such resolutions are relevant evidence of customary law.

ii. The View of Commentators

The approach by commentators to the practice of the Security Council also seems cursory and provides little insight into how best to analyze its impact on customary law. Higgins's early influential treatise on the development of international law through the United Nations only briefly discusses the question of Council practice.[105] In later writings, Higgins largely rejects the view that Council resolutions could be a source of international law other than as *ad hoc* binding obligations, although she does admit that there is some indistinct way in which they may have an effect on customary law.[106] Tunkin, the Russian socialist international law theorist, suggests that Council resolutions have a norm-forming role, although it is also uncertain whether this arises from an amorphous impact on state practice or some more direct impact. He argues:

> Resolutions of the Council adopted in conformity with the Charter may in a number of instances create a specific practice or contribute to the formation of an international practice that can crystallize into a rule of conduct and therefore be a definite stage in the process of forming a customary norm of international law.[107]

He also states that resolutions—and in this respect he did not differentiate between the General Assembly and Council—"may enter into the process of norm-formation and play a definite role in forming new principles and norms of international law and in affirming, strengthening, developing and interpreting existing principles and norms."[108]

---

104 Prosecutor v. Tadic, Case No. IT-94-1–A, Judgment of the Appeals Chamber, para. 186 (July 15, 1999) [hereinafter *Tadic*, Judgment of the Appeals Chamber].

105 HIGGINS, *supra* note 60, at 2–5.

106 HIGGINS, *supra* note 22, at 28.

107 GRIGORII I. TUNKIN, THEORY OF INTERNATIONAL LAW 187 (2d ed. 2003).

108 *Id.* at 187.

Ratner also comments that the law-making function of the Council is most significant in the formation of customary law.[109] However, he then considers the role of the Council in formulating legal principles and findings, interpreting the U.N. Charter, encouraging states to abide by international law, and enforcing such laws. He does comment that the resolutions are "critical evidence" of "how expectations of states change over time,"[110] but he does not go on to consider in what ways these are evidence or how such resolutions affect customary law.

Other commentators have dealt with Council resolutions in a way reminiscent of the approach of the courts, simply referring to them without explanation. Meron, for instance, states that in relation to the customary norm value of the Geneva Conventions, relevant practice includes "Council's appeals to parties to conflicts to apply the Geneva Conventions, and Council resolutions providing that Geneva Convention No IV applies to the territories occupied by Israel and requesting Israel to abide by its obligations under that Convention."[111] This approach seems unsatisfactory in that it does not attempt to analyze the relevance of the practice.

Similarly, the publication of the practice of the Council in the *Repertoire of the Practice of the Council* implies that it is widely accepted that such practice is relevant to international customary law. The practice is accompanied by a note explaining that it is published at the request of the General Assembly as part of the "[w]ays and means for making the evidence of customary international law readily available."[112] The *Repertoire* does not, however, elucidate in what way this practice is relevant.

Finally, a number of commentators consider Council resolutions to be analogous to General Assembly resolutions and relevant in similar ways. For instance, Secretary-General Javier Perez de Cuellar maintained that resolutions could represent *opinio juris.* He relied on Council resolutions and General Assembly resolutions in establishing the *opinio juris* of the international community regarding the Israeli deportation of civilians.[113] Kirgis

---

109 Ratner, *supra* note 74, at 593–95.

110 *Id.* at 602.

111 MERON, *supra* note 3, at 55–56.

112 G.A. Res. 686(VII), para. 1(b) (Dec. 5, 1952), *available at* http://www.un.org/documents/ga/res/7/ares7.htm.

113 The Secretary-General, *Report Submitted to the Security Council in Accordance with Resolution 605(1987)*, at 9, U.N. Doc. S/19443 (Jan. 21, 1988).

similarly acknowledges this possibility but points out that in comparison to General Assembly resolutions, the Council suffers from being a "fifteen-member UN body dominated by one or a few states."[114] Gray, on the other hand, argues that at least in relation to the interpretation of the Charter and the development of the law on the use of force, Council and General Assembly resolutions are of equal importance: they are both "fora in which states can set out their legal justifications for the use of force and appeal to other states for support," and the fact that the General Assembly is more representative is balanced by the Council's having primary responsibility for the maintenance of international peace and security.[115]

b. *Evidence of Practice and* Opinio Juris *of States*

Thus, commentators and courts have tended to acknowledge the impact Security Council practice has on customary law in passing but largely without explicit investigation of what form this influence takes. What then can be said about the role of this practice in the formation of customary law?

In undertaking such an analysis, the theoretical perspective adopted will affect the way in which the practice is analyzed. Positivists, for instance, tend to rely on a clear distinction between actions relevant to *opinio juris* and those forming customary law practice. It also emphasizes the traditional view of customary law as defined in Article 38 of the I.C.J. Statute, particularly the importance of the actions of states over those of other international bodies. The Law as Process school, on the other hand, tends to take a more flexible approach, looking for real impact rather than seeking to fit the practice into a particular category. Overall, however, the current trend in customary law norm analysis in all schools is to lean toward an inclusive approach to relevant practice, which is also the approach adopted here.[116]

---

114 Frederic L. Kirgis, Jr., *The United Nations at Fifty: The Security Council's First Fifty Years*, 89 AM. J. INT'L L. 506, 529 (1995).

115 CHRISTINE GRAY, INTERNATIONAL LAW AND THE USE OF FORCE 13 (2000).

116 Both the Positivist and Law as Process schools have tended to support an inclusive approach, as has the Natural Law school. *See* HIGGINS, *supra* note 22, at 10. *See also* MERON, *supra* note 3; Lillich, *supra* note 7; Schachter, *supra* note 5, at 333–38; and IAN BROWNLIE, PRINCIPLES OF PUBLIC INTERNATIONAL LAW 5 (5th ed. 1998).

i. The Practice of an International Organization

How can the practice of the Security Council, as an international organization, be relevant to customary law formation? The practice of international organizations can, in theory, be relevant in three ways. Traditionally, customary law has been formed from the practice of states rather than any other bodies or international organizations.[117] Thus, the majority of commentators have taken the view that the predominant relevance of international organization practice is that it constitutes practice of individual member states. Higgins, for instance, argues that the United Nations is relevant to customary law, because "international custom is to be deduced from the practice of States, which includes their international dealings as manifested by their diplomatic actions and public pronouncements."[118]

A more controversial prospect is that the actions of the organization could amount to practice in their own right. Mendelson argues: "To a varying extent, intergovernmental organisations participate in international relations in their own name, and not that of the members who constitute them. As such, they are subjects of international law who play their own part in the law-making process."[119] Similarly, the International Law Association Committee on Customary Law Formation maintains that international organizations could be "international persons in their own right, and are capable of performing acts which contribute to the formation of international law."[120] However, it is not clear how such practice can be taken into account according to the general theory of customary law,[121] and it is still principally through the notion of resolutions, as actions by the constituent states, that its relevance is understood.[122]

Finally, it is widely accepted that the practice of international organizations will also have an indirect influence on customary law, as a cat-

---

117 Mendelson, *supra* note 53, at 198.

118 HIGGINS, *supra* note 60, at 2.

119 Mendelson, *supra* note 53, at 201.

120 International Law Association, *supra* note 4, at 730.

121 VAN HOOF, *supra* note 27, at 63.

122 Mendelson, *supra* note 53, at 201. *See also* International Law Association, *supra* note 4, at 730.

alyst for the emergence of international customs[123] or by encouraging states to adopt certain behaviors.[124]

ii. Analogy with the General Assembly?

To what extent can Security Council resolutions be treated analogously to General Assembly resolutions? While there are clear similarities, particularly the fact that both originate in international fora formed of individual member states, substantial differences exist. Some of these would undermine the Council's role in customary law formation, and others would strengthen it.

Before considering the impact of these differences, however, it is useful to recapitulate briefly the way in which General Assembly resolutions are considered relevant to customary international law. This has been a controversial matter.[125] Some have argued that General Assembly resolutions have little, if any, impact, as they are non-binding, formalistic, and often not intended to be followed by the states adopting them.[126] Nonetheless, it is generally accepted that General Assembly resolutions evidence *opinio juris* of the member states involved, at least to the extent that the principles are of a normative character and are formulated as a matter of law.[127] Even Simma and Alston, who take a restrictive view,

---

[123] *See* DEREK BOWETT ET AL., BOWETT'S LAW OF INTERNATIONAL INSTITUTIONS 290 (5th ed. 2001); *see also* BEN CHIGARA, LEGITIMACY DEFICIT IN CUSTOM: A DECONSTRUCTIONIST CRITIQUE 205 (2001).

[124] International Law Association, *supra* note 4, at 272.

[125] *See* HIGGINS, *supra* note 60; Stephen M. Schwebel, *United Nations Resolutions, Recent Arbitral Awards and Customary International Law, in* REALISM IN LAW-MAKING: ESSAYS ON INTERNATIONAL LAW IN HONOUR OF WILLEM RIPHAGEN 203 (Adriaan Bos and Hugo Siblesz eds., 1986); MARK E. VILLIGER, CUSTOMARY INTERNATIONAL LAW AND TREATIES: A MANUAL ON THE THEORY AND PRACTICE OF THE INTERRELATION OF SOURCES (2d ed. 1997).

[126] *See, e.g.*, Gaetano Arangio-Ruiz, *The Normative Role of the General Assembly of the United Nations and the Development of Principles of Friendly Relations*, 137 RECUEIL DES COURS 431 (1972); DANILENKO, *supra* note 39, at 121; Stephen M. Schwebel, *The Effect of Resolutions of the United Nations General Assembly on Customary International Law*, 73 PROC. ANN. MEETING OF ASIL 301 (1979); James L. Taulbee, *Governing the Use of Force: Does the UN Charter Matter Anymore?*, 4 CIVIL WARS 1 (2001).

[127] *See Nicaragua*, Merits, *supra* note 1; DANILENKO, *supra* note 39, at 120–22; International Law Association, *supra* note 4, at 771, art. 31. For a review of the controversy surrounding the relationship between *usus* and *opinio juris* and what is required to establish customary law, *see* VAN HOOF, *supra* note 27, ch. 6. This view seems consistent with the I.C.J. position in *Nicaragua*, Merits, *supra* note 1, at 99–100.

accept that General Assembly resolutions may be relevant "as starting points for the possible development of customary law in the event that State practice eventually happens to lock on to these proclamations."[128]

In the *Threat or Use of Nuclear Weapons Case*, the Court held that "General Assembly resolutions, even if they are not binding, may sometimes have normative value. They can, in certain circumstances, provide evidence of a rule or the emergence of an *opinio juris*."[129] In order to determine the impact of a particular resolution, the Court held that it is "necessary to look at its content and the conditions of its adoption; it is also necessary to see whether an *opinio juris* exists as to its normative character."[130] In that particular instance, however, the Court held that the resolutions had been adopted with a substantial number of negative votes and abstentions and thus that "although these resolutions are a clear sign of deep concern regarding the problem of nuclear weapons, they still fall short of establishing the existence of an *opinio juris* on the illegality of the use of such weapons."[131]

According to the Committee on the Formation of Customary Law, General Assembly resolutions may also constitute a form of state practice as verbal acts.[132] Certain General Assembly resolutions have also been viewed as providing more general evidence of the existence of a customary law rule.[133] In Schwebel's words, certain resolutions "viewed as expressions of the assembled States of the world community rather than as acts within the constitutional or acquired authority of a quasi-legislative body" may be declaratory, though not creative, of international law.[134]

iii. Authority of the Council

The Security Council derives authority and legitimacy from its position in the institutional hierarchy in the United Nations, as the sole body that is entitled to authorize the use of force, and also through its mem-

---

128 Simma and Alston, *supra* note 3, at 89–90.

129 *Legality of the Threat or Use of Nuclear Weapons*, *supra* note 30, at 254.

130 *Id.* at 254.

131 *Id.*

132 International Law Association, *supra* note 4, at 772.

133 *See also id.*, art. 29; Akehurst, *supra* note 39, at 6.

134 Schwebel, *supra* note 125, at 209.

bership, which includes the powerful Permanent Five members. It is empowered to act on behalf of all the member states when passing a resolution, and thus its practice represents substantially more than the view of its small membership. Article 24(1) specifies that the Council acts on the behalf of the members when carrying out its duties related to the maintenance of peace and security. Although the meaning of this provision has been the subject of debate,[135] and there is little legislative history to shed light on it,[136] it must at least mean that actions of the Council are attributable to the "UN organisation as a whole and not to individual members, such as, for instance, the members of the SC."[137] Ecuador explained during the debates that this meant that the Council "must act in the name and on behalf of all members of the Organisation."[138] Moreover, under Article 25 of the U.N. Charter, members agree to accept and carry out Council decisions, thus reinforcing the view that the numeric size of the Council is not representative of the weight that ought to be accorded to its resolutions.

The numerical weight of the Council must be addressed in considering the impact of its practice on customary international law. Bedjaoui, for instance, has argued:

> Nothing would in principle prevent States from . . . creating new custom within an international organisation in the framework of its activity, provided the organisation is genuinely universal and the custom is created by States within the most representative organ. The Council could scarcely be the organ for such a role, given its very narrow composition.[139]

However, the decisions of the Council represent more than the view of a small number of member states. Political reality dictates that the Council cannot make decisions that do not have the support of a vast majority of the U.N. membership, because, as Fox points out, "members

---

135 *See* SIMMA AND MOSLER, *supra* note 78, at 442. *See also* KELSEN, *supra* note 85, at 280.

136 *See* the discussions regarding Article 24(1) at the United Nations Conference on International Organization, San Francisco, April 25–June 26, 1945.

137 SIMMA AND MOSLER, *supra* note 78, at 449.

138 Comments of Ecuador on the Dumbarton Oaks Proposals at 407. *See also* BAILEY AND DAWS, *supra* note 85, at 22.

139 BEDJAOUI, *supra* note 74, at 32.

are acutely aware that undertaking large or risky operations without a broad base of support among the membership is simply pointless."[140]

Moreover, while only the Council members may formally vote, many more states attend and participate in Council debates.[141] This is provided for in Article 31 according to which any member may participate in the discussion of any question brought before the Council whenever its interests are especially affected. Also, the number of states involved in a particular ongoing issue will grow, since the non-permanent membership of the Council rotates every two years.[142]

iv. Seriousness and Binding Nature of Resolutions

The principal argument against the customary law relevance of General Assembly resolutions is that these are non-binding resolutions, and the states do not mean them to be followed when they are passed.[143] The Security Council is also a political decision-making body. Its function is a practical one—to address and resolve situations that are a threat to international peace and security. Hence, it could be argued that the states participating in the decisions have no intention of creating customary law through their actions.

---

[140] Gregory H. Fox, *International Law and Civil Wars*, 26 N.Y.U. J. INT'L L. & POL. 633, 643 (1994), referring to and agreeing with Paul Szasz, *Centralized and Decentralized Law Enforcement: The Security Council and the General Assembly Acting Under Chapters VII and VIII*, paper presented to the International Symposium on Allocation of Law Enforcement Authority (Kiel, Germany, Mar. 23–25, 1994).

[141] States may participate in accordance with Rule 37 of the Council's Provisional Rules of Procedure. Numbers of participants vary. For example, Norway and Nepal participated in S.C. 4824th mtg., U.N. Doc. S/PV.4824 (Sept. 15, 2003); Albania, Italy, and Serbia and Montenegro participated in S.C. 4828th mtg., U.N. Doc. S/PV.4828 (Sept. 16, 2003); the Democratic Republic of the Congo, Rwanda, and Tanzania, in S.C. 4775th mtg., U.N. Doc. S/PV.4775 (June 18, 2003), Greece (speaking on behalf of the European Union, the acceding states of Cyprus, the Czech Republic, Estonia, Hungary, Latvia, Lithuania, Malta, Poland, Slovakia, Slovenia, Bulgaria, Romania, and the European Free Trade Association of the Economic Area of Iceland), Bahrain, Switzerland, Canada, Philippines, Monaco, Rwanda, Ukraine, Egypt, Austria, Nepal, Israel, Ethiopia, Costa Rica, Indonesia, Sierra Leone, Slovenia, Myanmar, Colombia, Malawi, Liechtenstein, DRC, Burundi, Japan, Namibia, Ecuador, Palestine, and Rwanda, in S.C. 4684th mtg., U.N. Doc. S/PV.4684 (Jan. 14, 2003).

[142] U.N. CHARTER art. 23.

[143] *See, e.g.*, Arangio-Ruiz, *supra* note 126, at 431; DANILENKO, *supra* note 39, at 121–22; Schwebel, *supra* note 126.

However, Council resolutions are markedly different from General Assembly resolutions. The Council is the primary body responsible for the grave matters of international peace and security. It is empowered to make binding decisions and impose economic sanctions or military enforcement. As Simma and Mosler point out, the Council is "the politically more important organ which, according to the intentions of the authors of the Charter, is supposed to take the necessary prompt and effective measures for the maintenance of peace, and which possesses the corresponding powers to do so."[144] The power of the Council to pass binding resolutions is a further distinction. A binding resolution has particular force, it has an immediate quasi-judicial impact, and as the Court in *Namibia* pointed out, it means that all members must comply with the decision, "including those members of the Council which voted against it and those Members of the United Nations who are not members of the Council."[145]

v. Decision-Making Body

Another relevant distinction with the General Assembly is that the Security Council is a decision-making body. The General Assembly is only empowered to "discuss" and "make recommendations" and in some circumstances "initiate studies."[146] It is a forum for debate, and its actions are verbal. The Council, on the other hand, may establish subsidiary organs,[147] "call upon parties to settle their dispute,"[148] "investigate,"[149] and "recommend procedures."[150]

Importantly it can also "determine the existence of any threat to the peace" and "make recommendations" or "decide what measure shall be taken."[151] Its resolutions range from expressions of concern to decisions to use force. These resolutions are verbal conduct in one sense, but lead

---

144 SIMMA AND MOSLER, *supra* note 78, at 447.

145 *Advisory Opinion on Namibia, supra* note 76, at 54.

146 U.N. CHARTER arts. 10, 13. Note that it has other powers under the trusteeship arrangements.

147 U.N. CHARTER art. 29.

148 *Id.*, art. 33, para. 2.

149 *Id.*, art. 34.

150 *Id.*, art. 36.

151 *Id.*, art. 39.

to physical actions, which may have dramatic impacts. Thus, they can be considered to have a greater weight than General Assembly resolutions and be relevant not only as *opinio juris* but also as a form of practice.

vi. Consequential Practice of States Under Resolutions

The fact of a preexisting obligation complicates the question of whether the consequential practice of states (enforcing Security Council resolutions) is relevant to customary law. The case of practice undertaken pursuant to a treaty may provide a useful analogy. Such practice is usually considered not to contribute to customary norms, as it is not referable to a "general practice accepted as law,"[152] but rather a treaty obligation. The Committee on the Formation of Customary Law maintains that "what states do in pursuance of their treaty obligations is *prima facie* referable only to the treaty, and therefore does not count towards the formation of a customary rule."[153] This is nonetheless a matter to be determined in each case, and some practice will be relevant to customary law formation.[154]

In the case of the Council, the question is a little more complex. As mentioned above, the implication, in much of Council practice, is that the legal rule underlying a binding obligation is not created in the resolution, but rather is enforced through that resolution. If this were the correct analysis of such obligations, then the actions undertaken in pursuance of the resolution would be relevant evidence of practice supporting the underlying obligation. In that case, the practice upholds that norm despite being most proximately referable to the Council resolution.

In those instances where the resolution is neither restating nor referring to an obligation already existing under international law, the conduct consequential to Council resolutions is likely to amount to relevant practice only where it is not only referable to a binding resolution, such as when it takes place according to a recommendatory resolution, or is undertaken independently from the obligation. Finally, the consequen-

---

152 Statute of the International Court of Justice, June 26, 1945, art. 38, para. b, *available at* http://www.icj-cij.org/icjwww/ibasicdocuments/ibasictext/ibasicstatute.htm.

153 International Law Association, *supra* note 4, art. 24, at 757. This is consistent with the position of the I.C.J. in North Sea Continental Shelf Cases, 1969 I.C.J. 3, at 43–44.

154 MERON, *supra* note 3, at 50.

tial practice under binding resolutions will play a part in shaping the opinion of the international community and act as a crystallizing force in relation to the acceptance of a particular norm.

c. Conclusion

Security Council resolutions, at the very least, provide evidence of *opinio juris* and verbal acts of the states members of the Council, and arguably also reflect a broader consensus. Moreover, the Council's special status in the international community causes it to shape the views of the broader international community on matters on which it passes resolutions, thus creating consensus views aligned with its resolutions, and hence its practice can be considered to indicate the future direction of evolution of customary law on those matters.

By analogy with General Assembly resolutions, its resolutions may contribute to customary law as *opinio juris* of individual states and as verbal practice. In addition, certain resolutions lead to physical actions, which may be a form of state practice so long as they are not merely the implementation of an obligation created by the resolution.

The weight of Council resolutions is greater than that of General Assembly resolutions. Despite the Council's more limited membership, these resolutions represent more than merely the view of the members of the Council, and they are serious and considered statements. Moreover, they are binding, and the Council can pass sanctions to reinforce their weight. The impact of the resolutions will still depend on their particular wording and the surrounding circumstances. They are most likely to be direct evidence of *opinio juris* when they formulate legal principles in a deliberate way or specify that a particular action is contrary to international law. Nevertheless, it is difficult to see why repeated calls for states to abide by particular behavior or principles, even when not formulated as illegal, will not, in time, serve as the foundation for new customary law norms. This is particularly true where the Council imposes conduct or standards through sanctions or forceful intervention. A migration of the principles it seeks to impose as Council-prohibited conduct to customary law could be anticipated in such situations, given the hierarchical authority of the Council, and the fact that it represents the most prominent members of the international community. Naturally, however, the emergence of a customary law norm would require reinforcing practice outside the Council.

3. Quasi-Legislative Impact

The notion that the Security Council can have a quasi-judicial impact where it makes explicit findings of illegality or interprets provisions of the U.N. Charter or legal principles is broadly accepted.[155] However, the question of how the Council can have a quasi-legislative impact—defined as one involving the creation or modification of some element of a legal norm that is "directed to indeterminate addressees and capable of repeated application in time"[156]—has received less attention and has also been somewhat more contentious. This section considers two forms of quasi-legislative impact, the first derived from resolutions explicitly maintaining that certain conduct is illegal, and the second considering whether, even when the Council does not explicitly make a finding of illegality, it can, through frequent repetition of prohibitions in different instances, and the adoption of enforcement measures under Chapter VII, create a quasi-legislative prohibition on certain conduct.

a. *Quasi-Judicial*

The I.C.J. in the *Advisory Opinion on Namibia*[157] implicitly accepted that the Security Council could make a quasi-judicial finding of illegality. It held:

> A binding determination made by a competent organ of the United Nations to the effect that a situation is illegal cannot remain without consequence. Once the Court is faced with such a situation, it would be failing in the discharge of its judicial functions if it did not declare that there is an obligation, especially upon Members of the United Nations, to bring that situation to an end.[158]

---

[155] Vera Gowlland-Debbas, *The Relationship Between the International Court of Justice and the Security Council in the Light of the Lockerbie Case*, 88 AM. J. INT'L L. 643 (1994); *see also* Keith Harper, *Does the United Nations Security Council Have the Competence to Act as Court and Legislature?*, 27 N.Y.U. J. INT'L L. & POL. 103 (1994); Kirgis, *supra* note 114; Alvarez, *supra* note 74, esp. n.115, at 21; and PHILIP C. JESSUP, TRANSNATIONAL LAW 103–04 (1956).

[156] Kirgis, *supra* note 114, at 520, adopts EDWARD YEMIN, LEGISLATIVE POWERS IN THE UNITED NATIONS AND SPECIALIZED AGENCIES 6 (1969).

[157] *Advisory Opinion on Namibia*, *supra* note 76.

[158] *Id.* at 54.

It went on to find: "The decisions are consequently binding on all States Members of the United Nations, which are thus under obligation to accept and carry them out."[159] Thus, members were prohibited from disregarding such illegality or recognizing violations of law resulting from it. Judge Onyeama described the nature of the Council resolution as "in effect, a judicial determination."[160]

The reasoning of the Court in the *Lockerbie Case* also supports the view that the Council resolutions have a legal impact and can even prevail over other legal obligations.[161] The Court held that the Council resolutions were binding under Article 25. It stated that "prima facie this obligation extends to the decision contained in resolution 748 (1992); and whereas, in accordance with Article 103 of the Charter, the obligations of the Parties in that respect prevail over their obligations under any other international agreement."[162]

The resolutions that most clearly purport to have a quasi-judicial application are those in which the Council finds that certain conduct by a state or non-state actor is illegal.[163] The impact of such resolutions is particularly clear when the Council then goes on to request actions or impose enforcement measures.[164] Illegality can also be implied. For instance, in the case of Libya, the Council stated that "every State has the

---

159 *Id.* at 53.

160 *Id.* at 147.

161 *See* Bowett, *supra* note 74, for criticism of this position.

162 *Lockerbie Case, supra* note 74, para. 42.

163 For example, the Security Council maintained that the secessionist activities by the province of Katanga during the war in the Republic of Congo were illegal, S.C. Res. 169, U.N. Doc. S/5002 (Nov. 24, 1961). It declared that the continued presence of South Africa in Namibia was illegal and that all acts by the South African government concerning Namibia were invalid, S.C. Res. 276, U.N. Doc. S/INF/25 (Jan. 30, 1970). It declared that the capture and murder of diplomats by the Taliban were flagrant violations of international law, S.C. Res. 1193, U.N. Doc. S/RES/1193 (Aug. 28, 1998) and S.C. Res. 1267, *supra* note 99, as were acts of genocide in Rwanda, S.C. Res. 925, *supra* note 100, and attacks against U.N. personnel, *see, e.g.*, S.C. Res. 912, U.N. Doc. S/RES/912 (Apr. 21, 1994) (also in the case of Rwanda).

164 Examples include Southern Rhodesia, South Africa, Iraq, the former Yugoslavia, Libya, and Somalia. *See* Alvarez, *supra* note 74, at 20–21. For instance, it called on Israel "to rescind these illegal measures and to facilitate the immediate return of the expelled Palestinian leaders so that they can resume the functions for which they were elected and appointed." S.C. Res. 468, U.N. Doc. S/RES/468 ¶ 1, (May 8, 1980). In relation to Iraq's invasion of Kuwait, the Council called on the international community not to recognize the annexation, S.C. Res. 662, U.N. Doc. S/RES/662 (Aug. 9,

duty to refrain from organizing, instigating, assisting or participating in terrorist acts in another State" and found that Libya's failure to demonstrate, by concrete actions, its renunciation of terrorism constituted a threat to international peace and security. It then requested that Libya discharge its responsibility by surrendering two of its nationals.[165] Similarly, after the coup in Haiti, the Council referred to the new regime as the "illegal *de facto* regime" and authorized the use of force "to facilitate the departure from Haiti of the military leadership."[166]

Despite the expressed concern some commentators have expressed regarding the extent to which the Council may validly develop its influence and authority unchecked,[167] most scholars have acknowledged that these resolutions have important consequences and have conceived of them as quasi-judicial.[168]

b. *Explicit Quasi-Legislative Determinations*

The role of the Security Council in shaping general international law principles is less well recognized, although commentators acknowledge that the Council has, in some instances, affected the meaning of legal terms or modified or created legal rules of general application. Szasz points out a particularly striking example of such conduct in the case of the recent resolution on terrorism, in which the Council relied on Chapter VII to order states to take and refrain from certain actions in an outright legislative manner.[169] Kirgis recognizes this form of "legislative

---

1990), imposed a binding settlement with regard to the boundary dispute, S.C. Res. 687, U.N. Doc. S/RES/687 (Apr. 8, 1991), and made findings with respect to responsibility for damages, S.C. Res. 686 (1991); S.C. Res. 687, *supra*; S.C. Res. 705, U.N. Doc. S/RES/705 (Aug. 15, 1991).

165 S.C. Res. 748, U.N. Doc. S/RES/748 (Mar. 31, 1992). *See* Gowlland-Debbas, *supra* note 155, at 660.

166 S.C. Res. 940, U.N. Doc. S/RES/940, ¶¶ 3–4 (July 31, 1994).

167 *See* Franck, *supra* note 74; Bowett, *supra* note 74; BEDJAOUI, *supra* note 74; Alvarez, *supra* note 74. NIGEL D. WHITE, KEEPING THE PEACE: THE UNITED NATIONS AND THE MAINTENANCE OF INTERNATIONAL PEACE AND SECURITY 98 (2d ed. 1997), questioned the authority of the Council to undertake the quasi-judicial determination of the Kuwait border and the punishment of Iraq.

168 Gowlland-Debbas, *supra* note 155; *see also* Harper, *supra* note 155; Kirgis, *supra* note 114; Alvarez, *supra* note 74, esp. n.115, at 21; and, JESSUP, *supra* note 155, at 103–04.

169 Paul Szasz, *The Security Council Starts Legislating*, 96 AM. J. INT'L L. 901 (2002), referring to S.C. Res. 1373, U.N. Doc. S/RES/1373 (Sept. 28, 2001).

authority" when there is a threat to, or breach of, the peace.[170] He points to the Council Chapter VII tax on Iraq's oil exports and the subsequent transfer of frozen proceeds,[171] which gave the commission set up to administer the compensation fund for damage to be paid by Iraq a way to execute its decisions.[172]

Alvarez points out that Resolution 688, which deals with the entry of humanitarian organizations into Iraq to protect the Kurds, is a decision that, "like many others the Council has recently made, bears on the meaning of Article 2(7) and the present status of human rights law."[173] Moreover, once the Council has found, for instance, that mass rape constitutes a breach of humanitarian law, this position is effectively crystallized in the law, even if the rule was originally of conventional or customary law origin.[174]

Tesón has also argued that the Council has, through its practice, established its power to authorize the use of force to remedy serious human rights violations, thus developing the substantive law of the U.N. Charter.[175] Moreover, the accumulation of individual resolutions can cause a gradual evolution of meaning.[176]

Some commentators, however, have questioned whether the Council has the authority to make such legal determinations. Higgins, for one,

---

170 Kirgis, *supra* note 114, at 522. *See also* Harper, *supra* note 155; Vera Gowlland-Debbas, *Security Council Enforcement Action and Issues of State Responsibility*, 43 INT'L & COMP. L.Q. 55 (1994); JOHN FOSTER DULLES, WAR OR PEACE 194 (1950); TAE JIN KAHNG, LAW, POLITICS, AND THE SECURITY COUNCIL: AN INQUIRY INTO THE HANDLING OF LEGAL QUESTIONS INVOLVED IN INTERNATIONAL DISPUTES AND SITUATIONS 13 (1964).

171 S.C. Res. 705, *supra* note 164 and S.C. Res. 706, U.N. Doc. S/RES/706 (Aug. 15, 1991); S.C. Res. 778, U.N. Doc. S/RES/778 (Oct. 2, 1992). *See* Kirgis, *supra* note 114, at 525–26.

172 Kirgis, *supra* note 114, at 525–26.

173 Alvarez, *supra* note 74, at 22. *See also* Gowlland-Debbas, *supra* note 170, at 63–68.

174 *See* Theodor Meron, *War Crimes in Yugoslavia and the Development of International Law*, 88 AM. J. INT'L L. 78 (1994); Jordan J. Paust, *Applicability of International Criminal Law to Events in the Former Yugoslavia*, 9 AM. U. J. INT'L L. & POL'Y 499 (1994); ANNE T. GOLDSTEIN, RECOGNIZING FORCED IMPREGNATION AS A WAR CRIME UNDER INTERNATIONAL LAW (1993).

175 Tesón, *supra* note 60, at 353–54.

176 Kirgis, *supra* note 114, at 526–27, and generally Ratner, *supra* note 74.

argues that the Council is not authorized under the Charter to make legal findings and hence questions the authoritativeness of such resolutions.[177] Nonetheless, until resolutions explicitly declaring illegality or defining legal meaning are delegitimized, perhaps by an I.C.J. ruling, they remain authoritative and binding.

c. *Implicit Quasi-Legislative Prohibitions?*

One particularly interesting issue is whether, even when the Security Council does not explicitly make a finding of illegality, it can, through the formulation, seriousness, frequent repetition in different instances, and enforcement measures under Chapter VII, create a quasi-legislative prohibition on certain conduct. The great majority of Council practice considered in this book does not specify that conduct is illegal but consists of statements condemning particular conduct and calling on parties to cease the conduct.

This section argues that, indeed, although this effect has as yet been largely overlooked, in fact, the Council can create a quasi-legislative prohibition on certain conduct by force of repetition, accumulated condemnation, and enforcement, where the practice is shown to amount to more than *ad hoc* policy decisions. This derives from the Council's ability to enforce its decisions and an informal precedent system within the Council. While such prohibitions are difficult to characterize under international law, they have substantial de facto impact.

i. *Ad Hoc* Policy or Binding Prohibitions?

The Security Council, like most decision-making bodies of an executive nature, has broad discretion in its practice. The extent of this discretion, and whether it must be guided by standards or law, remains somewhat uncertain.[178] However, the key question, for the purposes of

---

177 Rosalyn Higgins, *The Place of International Law in the Settlement of Disputes by the Security Council*, 64 AM. J. INT'L L. 1, 5 (1970). *See also* Kirgis, *supra* note 114, at 529; Bowett, *supra* note 74.

178 The Appeals Chamber decision in *Tadic* suggested that it would be subject to some restrictions, deciding that even though the determination of a threat to the peace "is more of a political concept . . . the determination that there exists such a threat is not a totally unfettered discretion, as it has to remain, at the very least, within the Purposes and Principles of the Charter." *Tadic*, Judgment of the Appeals Chamber, *supra* note 104. This is consistent with Tesón's reasoning that the notion of discretion, which "conceives of the official as deciding the case anew, as creating fresh law," does

this book, is whether the Council can voluntarily establish a general norm through its practice. This question will turn on whether the Council intends to simply resolve a particular threat to international peace and security or to formulate a prohibition of more general application, as evidenced in the wording of the resolution and extent to which it is restated in analogous cases.

An important factor will be whether the Council formulates similar principles across a wide variety of analogous situations. Even if they are initially formulated as mere policy, over time, the repetition of these principles by states in Council debates (and outside of the Council) and in later resolutions may suggest that a consensus is forming around a particular proposition. A large volume of similar practice is difficult to account for unless the policy of the Council is informed by a common understanding of the way in which the parties should behave. This is in accord with the view that political restrictions on the Council require it to act in a coherent and fair manner, inasmuch as this is possible, to maintain its legitimacy.[179] The Council, as a predominantly executive body with broad discretion to enforce international peace and security, is not bound by its prior decisions. However, the repeated condemnation of certain conduct, and maintenance of the importance of particular principles, must create within the body of the Council a set of principles that influence future Council practice, even if not binding. Higgins acknowledged, for instance, that "sometimes the substance of the Council work, and the fact that it is legal work repeated year in and year out, makes it engage in the processes of customary development as well as the mere imposing of obligation."[180]

A resolution by the Council condemning conduct must be taken seriously. The Council is the primary decision-making body responsible for international peace and security, and a failure to comply with its decisions may cause a state to become an international pariah and face sanctions or forceful intervention.[181] Moreover, the Council's power is reinforced by the fact that its permanent members are the most powerful economic and

---

not apply to the Council, which is subject to international law and standards, even if its decisions may not be subject to review by the I.C.J. *See* Tesón, *supra* note 60, at 339.

[179] *See* THOMAS M. FRANCK, FAIRNESS IN INTERNATIONAL LAW AND INSTITUTIONS (1995).

[180] HIGGINS, *supra* note 22, at 28.

[181] See, for instance, Iraq, but consider the extent to which the same could be said of Israel, which has also failed to abide by Security Council resolutions.

military states. Political reality dictates that decisions are usually only taken when the majority of states in the General Assembly support them—despite the limited number that officially makes the decision—and thus they are actually representative of a widely accepted position.

Therefore, in the international context where no other mechanism of regulation is associated with any enforcement power, the role of the Council in shaping the conduct of states through its power to reject certain conduct and effectively prohibit it, takes on particular prominence.

ii. Council Sanctions and Illegality

The relationship between conduct that is *de facto* prohibited through force of repeated Security Council action condemning conduct and then imposing sanctions and illegality under traditional international law is somewhat uncertain. The Council does not formally require a breach of international law or of the U.N. Charter before it can act.[182] In Kelsen's words, "The purpose of the enforcement action under Article 39 is not to maintain or restore the law, but to maintain, or restore peace, which is not necessarily identical with the law."[183] Therefore, the mere fact that the Council imposes sanctions does not render the conduct illegal.

Nonetheless, there is a complex if intuitive link between Council sanctions and illegality under international law. Many factors reinforce the perception that actions subject to Council censure are illegal, including the binding nature of resolutions, the gravitas of the Council, and the use of sanctions to enforce decisions. Despite being difficult to quantify, an assumption exists that when the Council imposes sanctions, the party being sanctioned was acting contrary to international law. The Council has sought to impose sanctions following a breach of international law by a state.[184] Moreover, states frequently assert non-compliance with the Charter or international law as a basis for Council intervention. This practice, which Higgins considers to arise from "the psychological need for legal justification,"[185] is generally acknowledged.[186] In addition, it

---

182 *See* Higgins, *supra* note 177, at 16; Oscar Schachter, *United Nations Law*, 88 AM. J. INT'L L. 1, 12 (1994).

183 KELSEN, *supra* note 85, at 294.

184 *See* Alvarez, *supra* note 74, at 21; Schachter, *supra* note 182, at 12; Gowlland-Debbas, *supra* note 155, at 660.

185 Higgins, *supra* note 177, at 11.

186 *Id.* at 17. *See also* Oscar Schachter, *The Quasi-Judicial Role of the Security Council and the General Assembly*, 58 AM. J. INT'L L. 960, 960–61 (1964).

reinforces the perception that states look to the Council to enforce international law.[187]

Moreover, a theoretical link between condemnation and sanctions and a violation of law is implicit in most legal theory. Dicey, in his exposition of the rule of law, emphasized that "a man may with us be punished for a breach of law, but he can be punished for nothing else."[188]

Consider also Kelsen's explanation, that "sanctions are forcible interference in the sphere of interests normally protected by the law. They apply only on the condition that a delict has been committed or, what amounts to the same, that an obligation established by the law has been disregarded, and only against the delinquent."[189] Some commentators have acknowledged a more specific link between Council sanctions and perceived illegality. Alvarez, for instance, asked—without venturing to provide an answer—"whether the activities that prompted Council actions should generally be regarded as violations of international law."[190] Gowlland-Debbas took the matter further:

> [W]e can no longer speak of two alternative methods of dispute settlement, the one political and the other legal, but of two alternative processes available to states within the legal framework of state responsibility: the distinction between the function of the Court and that of the Council becomes the distinction between judicial settlement procedures in disputes concerning responsibility and institutionalized countermeasures or sanctions.[191]

Gowlland-Debbas seems to consider Council sanctions to be a form of enforcement of international law, while acknowledging that the condition for the application of the sanctions is strictly not an international wrongful act. This position is an extension of the reasoning of the International Law Commission, which defined sanctions, including Council sanctions as "reactive measures applied by virtue of a decision

---

187 *See* Ratner, *supra* note 74, at 601.

188 ALBERT V. DICEY, INTRODUCTION TO THE STUDY OF THE LAW OF THE CONSTITUTION 202–03 (10th ed. 1959).

189 KELSEN, *supra* note 85, at 706.

190 Alvarez, *supra* note 74, at 21; *see also* Gowlland-Debbas, *supra* note 155.

191 Gowlland-Debbas, *supra* note 155, at 661.

taken by an international organisation following a breach of an international obligation."[192]

Higgins also points out the implicit creation of legal norm through the mere fact of support of one side in a dispute. For instance, when the Council and the General Assembly called on Israel, after the 1967 war, not to alter the status of Jerusalem, an assumption grew out of that resolution that "Jordan has a legal title in Old Jerusalem which is preferable to that of Israel's."[193] The converse is also true, that "in practice an authorization by the Council has almost invariably been universally accepted as conferring international legality on an action."[194]

The link between sanctions and illegality is further reinforced by the fact that once a binding resolution has been passed, actions in breach of that resolution become illegal from that point on. A failure to abide by a binding Council resolution has been considered grounds for enforcement measures.[195] In Resolution 1193, for instance, the Council reminded "all parties of the obligation to abide strictly by the decisions of the Council and expresse[d] its firm intention, in accordance with its responsibility under the Charter, to consider such further steps as may be required for the implementation of this resolution."[196]

Moreover, the fact that under Article 1(1), the Council, as an organ of the United Nations, must act "in conformity with the principles of justice and international law" could be seen to reinforce the relationship between Council sanctions and the illegality of the underlying conduct. However, the interpretation of this article has been controversial. According to Kelsen, the restoration of peace is different from the restoration of law, allowing the Council "to enforce a decision which it considered to be just though not in conformity with existing law."[197]

---

192 International Law Commission, *Draft Articles on State Responsibility*, [1980] 2 Y.B. Int'l L. Comm'n, pt. 2, at 30, U.N. Doc. A/CN.4/SER.A/1980/Add.1 (81.V.4).

193 Higgins, *supra* note 177, at 7.

194 INTERNATIONAL COMMISSION ON INTERVENTION AND STATE SOVEREIGNTY, RESPONSIBILITY TO PROTECT, para. 6.16 (2001).

195 Michael L. Cornell, *A Decade of Failure: The Legality and Efficacy of United Nations Actions in the Elimination of Iraqi Weapons of Mass Destruction*, 16 CONN. J. INT'L L. 325, 352 (2001). *See* GOODRICH ET AL., *supra* note 93, at 276–81.

196 S.C. Res. 1193, *supra* note 163, ¶ 16.

197 KELSEN, *supra* note 85, at 295, 366.

Other commentators, however, have taken the view that the Council is restricted by international law.[198]

d. Conclusion

Thus, the view adopted in this book is that the Council can create a quasi-legislative prohibition on certain conduct by force of repetition, accumulated condemnation, and enforcement, when the practice is shown to amount to more than *ad hoc* policy decisions. This view is also supported by the basic notions underpinning the rule of law requiring that punishment and sanctions only be imposed in the case of a breach of law. While the conduct censured need not be illegal under international law, it does, in practice, become prohibited by the Council, which will, in turn, affect international opinion of the legality of the conduct.

4. Shaping International Policy

Finally, it is clear that the Security Council leads and shapes general international policy. Council practice affects what is being condemned, rejected, and prohibited in the international community. The imposition of sanctions and binding resolutions forces individual states to change their behavior, as well as changes their long-term expectations.

a. Crystallizing the Opinion of the International Community

Security Council resolutions drive and shape the opinion of the international community. This undeniable influence has been recognized since the Council's inception. As the Netherlands representative commented during the San Francisco debates, even a non-binding censure "would have a considerable moral effect on world opinion and might therefore be an effective deterrent to potential aggressors."[199]

Every day the Council assesses situations and applauds or condemns actions, it determines what conduct is acceptable, calls on parties to behave in certain ways, and ultimately can take steps to enforce its view through sanctions or enforcement action. In this fashion the Council

---

[198] BEDJAOUI, *supra* note 74, at 29–36. Note the justice/international law distinction and the extent to which this implies that the Security Council need not act consistently with international law. Higgins, *supra* note 177, at 8–9. *See, e.g.*, the Statement of the United States to Committee III/1 (S1945) 11 UNCIO 379, at 379.

[199] Statement of the Netherlands to Committee III/1 (1945) 11 UNCIO 329, at 329.

plays a key role in crystallizing the opinion of the international community. This is particularly true in relation to the perception of what is legal.

b. *Shaping the Practice of States*

The role of the Security Council in shaping and changing the practice of states is perhaps the most striking aspect of Council practice. The Council affects how states behave, not only through the implementation of a resolution, but also by modifying long-term conduct and expectations. The Council can bind parties to a dispute in a quasi-judicial fashion, as well as require that all member states comply with a particular resolution. It has made explicit findings of illegality and insisted that the rest of the international community act as if those actions were illegal. It has also repeatedly and explicitly condemned certain conduct, demanded that parties modify their behavior, and backed up these demands with stated determination to enforce its resolutions.[200] Moreover, the precedent nature of Council practice, which is reinforced by requirements of fairness and legitimacy,[201] has a norm-forming impact, causing states to expect that certain conduct will be rejected. The Council's practice shapes the practice of states, but it is also formed by such practice. A review of the practice in the Balkans and Western Africa suggests that, at times, the opinion of states was leading the practice of the Council. This is most clear in the case of Yugoslavia where the Council seemed to be adopting the decisions of the EU and Conference for the former Yugoslavia. However, as the practice evolved in the cases of Kosovo and the Former Yugoslav Republic of Macedonia, it appears that the Council was no longer merely adopting principles agreed to in the region or by the parties (for instance, in peace agreements) but was instead insisting on particular principles as intrinsic to the situation. Similarly, in the case of Sierra Leone, the Council adopted the principles already formulated by the regional organization and individual states. However, the later decisions in Côte d'Ivoire and Liberia also seem to derive more from intrinsic Council authority.

The recent amendments to the regional conventions of the Economic Community of West African States (ECOWAS) and African Union (A.U.) to mirror the principles that have received extensive and consistent support in the Council are evidence that these principles are gain-

---

200 *See, e.g.*, S.C. Res. 1267, *supra* note 99; S.C. Res. 771, *supra* note 100, ¶ 7. *See also* S.C. Res. 757, U.N. Doc. S/RES/757 (May 30, 1992).

201 FRANCK, *supra* note 179.

ing widespread acceptance. Clearly, these treaties are not negotiated out of historical or chronological context. The practice of the Council and that of individual states repeating the principles legitimized them for many years before the amendments to the ECOWAS Convention in 2001 and the creation of the A.U. Constitution in 2002. These conventions are a form of codification of the practice. Given that they reflect the same evolution on the nature of civil conflict as that of the Council, this must at least *prima facie* imply that the decisions taken by the Council have impacted on the practice of the region.

5. Conclusion

The general practice of the Security Council, which includes the reasons it puts forward to justify its positions and the principles it cites and relies upon in the preambles to resolutions, provides a strong indication of the direction in which international law is evolving. The practice of the Council is both evidence of *opinio juris* and verbal action, and shapes what is considered prohibited and illegal in the international community. Many factors reinforce the perception that actions subject to Council censure are illegal, including the binding nature of resolutions, the gravitas of the Council, and the use of sanctions to enforce decisions. The imposition of sanctions and binding resolutions forces individual states to change their behavior, as well as changes their long-term expectations.

Even if the statements in the Council are initially policy decisions, if they are binding and repeated sufficiently, they can become a form of quasi-legislative Council prohibited conduct. While this is not the same as saying that the practice renders the conduct illegal under international law, it does however, create a *de facto* prohibition on such conduct. Such practice may provide instigation for the emergence of customary international law. This will depend on the extent to which the principles are incorporated into state and regional organization practice and treaties independently of Council practice.

CHAPTER 3

THE SECURITY COUNCIL RESPONSE TO EXTREME POLITICAL VIOLENCE

The Security Council has been involved in civil conflicts and coups d'état virtually since its inception and has accumulated a considerable amount of practice. This chapter undertakes a review of the resolutions of the Council in the 32 civil conflicts it had been involved through September 30, 2003. It looks at whether certain forms of political violence are consistently being rejected. Do Council interventions aim to stop or prevent a certain sort of violent political conduct? And does the Council reject this conduct on behalf of the international community? At the core of this investigation is the question of whether the Council is merely making *ad hoc* pragmatic decisions or creating and enforcing particular policy or legal principles.

To assist this determination, the practice is divided into three tiers of significance: demands and statements, economic or military embargoes, and forceful intervention. A gradient from condemnations and demands to sanctions and enforcement actions is taken to indicate increasing seriousness, with a stronger response implying a more strongly held view. Nonetheless, explicit condemnation of particular conduct has special weight, as it provides clear indication of the response of the Council to that conduct.[1] A distinction is drawn between what is *disapproved of*, in the sense of being condemned and rejected through the practice, and what is *illegal* under international law. The first is descriptive of emerging international policy, which is based in practice and recognizes that such policy norms can be expected both to predict and shape future conduct of international actors, without creating binding obligations. The second refers to a norm that satisfies the criteria for recognition in international law and hence creates a binding obligation.

A. THE LEGAL FRAMEWORK

The Security Council has the primary responsibility to maintain international peace and security pursuant to the powers granted in

1 For a more detailed discussion of methodological issues, see Chapter 4.

Chapters VI, VII, and VIII of the U.N. Charter.[2] However, its authority is limited when dealing with matters falling within the domestic jurisdiction of states.

The Charter provides little guidance to the Council on how to address civil conflicts: the original debates suggest that the Charter did not anticipate the Council addressing civil conflicts. This understanding is reinforced by the restrictions on the Council authority over matters considered domestic.[3] Although there is little legal guidance in the Charter on the role of the Council in civil conflict, there is extensive Council practice responding to civil conflicts.

1. Pacific Settlement of Disputes

Prima facie the powers granted to the Council under Chapter VI, which address the "pacific settlement of disputes," were not intended to apply to the civil conflict context.[4]

Article 33 provides:

> 1. The parties to any dispute, the continuance of which is likely to endanger the maintenance of international peace and security, shall, first of all, seek a solution by negotiation, enquiry, mediation, conciliation, arbitration, judicial settlement, resort to regional agencies or arrangements, or other peaceful means of their own choice.
>
> 2. The Security Council shall, when it deems necessary, call upon the parties to settle their dispute by such means.

The word "international" was deliberately inserted into Article 2(3), and thus implicitly into Article 33, at the San Francisco Conference, "for the specific purpose of underlining the necessity of a transborder dimension."[5] This intent is reinforced by Article 2(7), which prohibits inter-

---

[2] U.N. CHARTER art. 24, para. 2.

[3] *Id.*, para. 7.

[4] For a general discussion of the power of the Security Council under Chapter VI, *see* NIGEL D. WHITE, KEEPING THE PEACE: THE UNITED NATIONS AND THE MAINTENANCE OF INTERNATIONAL PEACE AND SECURITY 81 (2d ed. 1997).

[5] BRUNO SIMMA AND HERMANN MOSLER, THE CHARTER OF THE UNITED NATIONS: A COMMENTARY 108 (2d ed. 2002); (1945) UNCIO III, at 623.

vention into matters within the domestic jurisdiction of states.[6] Article 2(7) has been interpreted to prohibit any "recommendatory resolution addressed to a particular state . . . urging that state to change its policy in a matter regarded as domestic"[7] but not mere discussion or placement on the agenda.[8] It only prohibits intervention into matters "essentially" within the domestic jurisdiction. This has been taken to narrow the domestic jurisdiction of states,[9] although, on its face, the clause was "designed to reinforce and widen the scope of the domestic jurisdiction clause."[10]

2. Intervention Under Chapter VII

Under Chapter VII, the Security Council can impose enforcement measures in relation to a "threat to the peace, breach of the peace, or act of aggression."[11] The drafters of the U.N. Charter "clearly did not intend this phrase to encompass internal conflicts."[12]

There has been an extensive debate over whether the Council has complete discretion in determining a threat to international peace and security.[13] Various arguments seeking to limit the Council's authority

---

6 U.N. CHARTER art. 2, para. 7:

> Nothing contained in the present Charter shall authorize the United Nations to intervene in matters which are essentially within the domestic jurisdiction of any State or shall require the Members to submit such matters to settlement under the present Charter; but this principle shall not prejudice the application of enforcement measures under Chapter VII.

7 Oscar Schachter, *The United Nations and Internal Conflict, in* LAW AND CIVIL WAR IN THE MODERN WORLD 401, 421 (John Norton Moore ed., 1974).

8 *Id.* at 421; *Resolution of the Institut de Droit International* (Apr. 29, 1954). *See also* LELAND M. GOODRICH ET AL., CHARTER OF THE UNITED NATIONS: COMMENTARY AND DOCUMENTS (3d ed. 1969); Ruth Gordon, *United Nations Intervention in Internal Conflicts: Iraq, Somalia, and Beyond*, 15 MICH. J. INT'L L. 519, 536 (1994).

9 SIMMA AND MOSLER, *supra* note 5, at 158.

10 *Id.* According to GOODRICH ET AL., *supra* note 8, at 63, the term "essentially" was substituted for the term "solely," because in the modern world it was not easy to find a matter that was "solely domestic."

11 U.N. CHARTER art. 39.

12 Gregory H. Fox, *International Law and Civil Wars*, 26 N.Y.U. J. INT'L L. & POL. 633, 638 (1994).

13 It is likely to be limited by some "substantive notion" of what would amount to such a threat. Mary Ellen O'Connell, *Continuing Limits on UN Intervention in Civil War*,

have been made. For example, Fielding argues that "the Charter does not contemplate that U.N. armed force should be used in order to put down internal rebellion."[14] Schachter similarly maintains that international peace and security "does not include the elimination of internal conflicts *per se*"[15] and that the United Nations is not entitled to use force "to bring about the victory of one faction or another in an internal conflict."[16]

In practice, however, the Council has intervened repeatedly in situations that could be considered purely domestic on one or the other side of the conflict.[17] This has generally been justified in the literature on the basis of some internationalizing factor—such as significant refugee flows, regional disruption, or the likelihood of intervention by outside states,[18] and self-determination[19]—or the impact on the broader international

---

67 IND. L.J. 903, 911 (1992). *See also* Lois E. Fielding, *Taking a Closer Look at Threats to Peace: The Power of the Security Council to Address Humanitarian Crises*, 73 U. DET. MERCY L. REV. 551, 558 (1996). For a discussion of the legitimacy of Security Council decisions from a procedural standpoint, *see* David D. Caron, *The Legitimacy of the Collective Authority of the Security Council*, 87 AM. J. INT'L L. 552 (1993); IAN BROWNLIE, THE RULE OF LAW IN INTERNATIONAL AFFAIRS (1998); Frederic L. Kirgis, Jr., *The United Nations at Fifty: The Security Council's First Fifty Years*, 89 AM. J. INT'L L. 506, 516 (1995). For a view of it having wide discretion, *see* Peter H. Kooijmans, *The Enlargement of the Concept 'Threat to the Peace,' in* PEACE-KEEPING AND PEACE-BUILDING, THE DEVELOPMENT OF THE ROLE OF THE SECURITY COUNCIL 111 (René-Jean Dupuy ed., 1992); Michael Reisman, *Comment, Summing Up, in* THE DEVELOPMENT OF THE ROLE OF THE SECURITY COUNCIL: PEACE-KEEPING AND PEACE-BUILDING, *supra*, at 140; James L. Taulbee, *Governing the Use of Force: Does the UN Charter Matter Anymore?*, 4 CIVIL WARS 1, 7 (2001).

14 Fielding, *supra* note 13, at 563. *See also* Oscar Schachter, *Authorized Uses of Force by the United Nations and Regional Organisations, in* LAW AND FORCE IN THE NEW INTERNATIONAL ORDER 86 (Lori F. Damrosch and David J. Scheffer eds., 1991).

15 Schachter, *supra* note 7, at 404.

16 *Id.* at 423.

17 Lori F. Damrosch, *Changing Conceptions of Intervention in International Law, in* EMERGING NORMS OF JUSTIFIED INTERVENTION: A COLLECTION OF ESSAYS FROM A PROJECT OF THE AMERICAN ACADEMY OF ARTS AND SCIENCES 105 (Laura W. Reed et al. eds., 1993).

18 *See* William Chip, *A United Nations Role in Ending Civil War*, 19 COLUM. J. TRANSNAT'L L. 15 (1981); Thomas F. Franck, *United Nations Law in Africa: The Congo Operation as a Case Study*, 27 LAW & CONTEMP. PROBS. 632 (1962).

19 Paul Szasz, *Role of the United Nations in Internal Conflicts*, 13 GA. J. INT'L & COMP. L. 345, 347–51 (1983). *See* Gordon, *supra* note 8, at 537–38.

community.[20] Goodrich et al. maintain: "There has been a reluctance to dismiss any dispute or situation even when the danger to peace, or indeed the international character of the question, has seemed highly doubtful."[21] However, this approach does not really limit the scope for intervention, as it is always possible to find some consequential impact on the region, if not on the world, arising from a civil conflict.[22]

3. Peace-Keeping Forces

Finally, the authority to send peace-keeping forces (to any conflict, not only civil) is not explicitly provided for in the U.N. Charter. Dag Hammarskjold, the second U.N. Secretary-General, referred to it as belonging to "Chapter Six and a Half" of the Charter, thus placing it between Chapter VI methods of resolving disputes peacefully, such as mediation and fact-finding, and Chapter VII, more forceful action, such as embargos and military intervention. Such operations have been acknowledged as legal by the International Court of Justice (I.C.J.) in the *Certain Expenses Advisory Opinion.*[23] However, they are considered to rely on the consent of the parties,[24] which does raise additional ques-

---

20 O'Connell comments that "the Charter meant to restrict the Council's authority to intervene in civil war despite such wars being breaches of 'peace.'" Mary Ellen O'Connell, *Regulating the Use of Force in the 21st Century: The Continuing Importance of State Autonomy, in* POLITICS, VALUES AND FUNCTIONS: INTERNATIONAL LAW IN THE 21ST CENTURY 443, 450–451 (Jonathan I. Charney et al. eds., 1998).

21 GOODRICH ET AL., *supra* note 8, at 268. *See also* JEAN-PIERRE COT ET AL., LA CHARTE DES NATIONS UNIES: COMMENTAIRE ARTICLE PAR ARTICLE 572 (1985), which takes a similar view.

22 Serious human rights violations, for instance, have been used to justify intervention, despite their not being a threat to international peace and security in a traditional sense. Schachter, *supra* note 7. Kirgis reviews the discussions surrounding the resolutions finding a threat to international peace and security in Somalia, Haiti, and Angola, and concludes that these "lead unavoidably and quite properly to a much expanded definition of 'threat to international peace' than could have been intended fifty years ago." Kirgis, *supra* note 13, at 517.

23 The Court held that the power to send peace-keeping forces was implied even when the Security Council did not resort to enforcement action against a state. Certain Expenses of the United Nations (U.N. Charter, art. 17, para. 2), 1962 I.C.J. 151 (July 20); WHITE, *supra* note 4, at 224.

24 Former U.N. Secretary-General Boutros Boutros-Ghali defined peacekeeping as "The deployment of a United Nations presence in the field, hitherto with the consent of all the parties concerned, normally involving United Nations military and/or police personnel and frequently civilians as well." The Secretary-General, *An Agenda for Peace: Preventive Diplomacy, Peacemaking and Peacekeeping, Report of the Secretary-General,* U.N.

tions about their legitimacy in civil conflicts. As White points out, consent is usually obtained from the governments concerned.[25] However, the authority of the government is put into question in a civil conflict, which may result in it no longer being a meaningful gauge of the will of the state.[26] Thus, it may be that only peace-keeping operations, with the consent of all factions in a civil war, can be justified according to traditional theory.

B. THE PRACTICE OF THE COUNCIL

In order to undertake an analysis of Security Council practice, a multi-step analysis was adopted. First, Council practice in the relevant 32 civil conflicts was identified. An overview of that practice revealed that certain responses were typical and repeated and provided the basis for categorization according to possible emerging principles. The practice was thus tabulated according to conflict and type of response.[27] Second, the table was analyzed to identify the principles that received repeated support across different conflicts.

This section is the result of that analysis and considers the practice in five categories: (1) rejecting violence to resolve political disputes; (2) rejecting the violent overthrow of a democratically elected government; (3) requiring that conflicts be resolved peacefully; (4) rejecting violence against civilians; and (5) rejecting violent breach of a cease-fire or peace agreement. The significance of this practice must be assessed in the light of whether the resolutions are binding or aspirational and whether they are restricted to the particular conflict or are of a more general application.

Doc. A/47/277, S/24111, at 207 (June 17, 1992). *See* UNITED NATIONS, THE BLUE HELMETS: A REVIEW OF UNITED NATIONS PEACE-KEEPING (3d ed. 1996); O'Connell, *supra* note 20, at 451. For a comprehensive discussion of peacekeeping, *see* WHITE, *supra* note 4, at 172–76.

[25] WHITE, *supra* note 4, at 232.

[26] *See* David Wippman, *Treaty-Based Intervention: Who Can Say No?*, 62 U. CHI. L. REV. 607 (1995); WHITE, *supra* note 4, at 232, 610.

[27] The categories adopted were resolutions expressing: "concern, comments and acknowledgements"; "condemnation"; "resolutions calling for, or demanding, particular actions or outcomes"; "sanctions"; the sending of "bserver or peacekeeping forces"; "authorizations of use of force"; "encouragement or authorisation of third party actions"; the "applicability of humanitarian laws of war"; issues of "sovereignty and territorial integrity"; and findings of "threats to international peace and security."

In order to determine what principles are emerging from Council practice, a number of questions must be addressed: Whose resort to political violence is being rejected—rebels (which would suggest a state-centric status quo approach) or both parties? Are only specific types of political violence rejected (e.g., recourse to force to gain political power, force following the signing of a peace agreement, violence against civilians)? Has the Council tended to condemn the political violence as soon as it becomes involved in the conflict? Are these demands and calls to renounce force binding? Does the Council expect them to be followed? Have the condemnations and calls to stop using force been formulated in a broad fashion—i.e., rejecting all political violence—or are they a response to the particular situation considered by the Council? Can trends be identified?

1. Rejecting Violence to Resolve Political Disputes

The Council has repeatedly condemned violence in civil conflicts and coups d'état and demanded that parties stop using such force. During the 1990s, it became increasingly usual for the Council to condemn the recourse to force and then call on parties to stop fighting. The explicit rejection of the use of violence to resolve political disputes has been a central aspect of Council practice in relation to many conflicts.[28] The Council has also repeatedly rejected the use of "force," which seems to be used as a synonym for "violence."[29]

---

[28] In Georgia, it demanded that all parties "refrain from the use of force," S.C. Res. 876, U.N. Doc. S/RES/876 (Oct. 19, 1993). *See also* S.C. Res. 881, U.N. Doc. S/RES/881, ¶ 3 (Nov. 4, 1993), and also explicitly welcomed the "commitment of the parties not to use force for the resolution of any disputed questions" and to refrain from "propaganda aimed at the solution of the conflict by force," S.C. Res. 1311, U.N. Doc. S/RES/1311, ¶ 5 (July 28, 2000). In Afghanistan, it called on all parties to "renounce the use of force." S.C. Res. 1076, U.N. Doc. S/RES/1076, ¶ 1 (Oct. 22, 1996). *See also* S.C. Res. 1193, U.N. Doc. S/RES/1193, ¶ 2 (Aug. 28, 1998); S.C. Res. 1214, U.N. Doc. S/RES/1214, ¶ 1 (Dec. 8, 1998). In Burundi, it also specifically demanded that all parties refrain from "seeking to destabilize the security situation or depose the Government by force or by other unconstitutional means." S.C. Res. 1049, U.N. Doc. S/RES/1049, ¶ 3 (Mar. 5, 1996).

[29] Similar demands, with varying formulations, were made in Lebanon: the Security Council condemned the violence and called on "all those involved in hostilities in Lebanon to put an end to acts of violence." S.C. Res. 436, U.N. Doc. S/RES/436, ¶ 1 (Oct. 6, 1978); S.C. Res. 490, U.N. Doc. S/RES/490, ¶ 1 (July 21, 1981); S.C. Res. 512, U.N. Doc. S/RES/512, ¶ 1 (June 19, 1982). *See also* S.C. Res. 513, U.N. Doc. S/RES/513, ¶ 1 (July 4, 1982), with respect to violence against civilians. In Rwanda, the Security Council did ultimately demand "an end to the mindless violence and carnage which are engulfing Rwanda." S.C. Res. 912, U.N. Doc. S/RES/912, ¶ 6

a. Overview of the Practice

The most illuminating practice has, on the whole, taken place in the last 15 years. However, one instance of early practice is worth highlighting, because it did foreshadow the principles emerging in the 1990s—the practice of the Council in Congo Brazzaville in 1961,[30] which explicitly aimed to prevent civil conflict. The Council sent a peace-keeping force to "prevent the occurrence of civil war."[31] It highlighted the threat to international peace and security and went on to urge the forces to "take immediately all appropriate measures to prevent the occurrence of civil war in the Congo, including arrangements for cease-fires, the halting of all military operations, the prevention of clashes and the use of force if necessary in the last resort."[32] For many years after this intervention, the

(Apr. 21, 1994); S.C. Res. 918, U.N. Doc. S/RES/918 (May 17, 1994); S.C. Res. 925, U.N. Doc. S/RES/925 (June 8, 1994). Similarly in Cambodia: S.C. Res. 880, U.N. Doc. S/RES/880, ¶ 5 (Nov. 4, 1993). In Burundi: S.C. Res. 1049, *supra* note 28, ¶¶ 3, 4; S.C. Res. 1072, U.N. Doc. S/RES/1072 (Aug. 30, 1996) (including demands that parties refrain from incitement to violence); S.C. Res. 1049, *supra* note 28, ¶¶ 3, 4. *See also* in the Democratic Republic of the Congo (DRC), expressing concern at "acts of and incitement to ethnic hatred and violence by all parties to the conflict," S.C. Res. 1234, U.N. Doc. S/RES/1234 (Apr. 9, 1999). In Sierra Leone, the resolutions were passed pursuant to Chapter VII and were thus explicitly binding. S.C. Res. 1132, U.N. Doc. S/RES/1132, ¶¶ 1, 2 (Oct. 8, 1997). In Albania, the explicit calls to end violence were made after determining that the situation amounted to a threat to international peace and security. S.C. Res. 1101, U.N. Doc. S/RES/1101 ¶ 1, (Mar. 28, 1997). This formulation was repeated in S.C. Res. 1114, U.N. Doc. S/RES/1114 ¶ 1, (June 19, 1997). *See* Albania: S.C. Res. 1101, *supra*, pmbl. East Timor: S.C. Res. 1264, U.N. Doc. S/RES/1264, ¶ 1 (Sept. 15, 1999) (acting under Chapter VII, repeatedly condemned "all acts of violence in East Timor" and called for their immediate end). *See also* S.C. Res. 1246, U.N. Doc. S/RES/1246, ¶ 11 (June 11, 1999); S.C. Res. 1272, U.N. Doc. S/RES/1272, ¶¶ 12, 16 (Oct. 25,1999). Central African Republic (CAR): the Council called on the Government "to take urgent steps to bring an end to all acts of violence." President of the Security Council, *The Situation in the Central African Republic*, Statement, U.N. Doc. S/PRST/2001/18 (July 17, 2001).

[30] Note that the practice of the Security Council in relation to the more recent civil uprising in 1997 has been very limited. It did not send peacekeepers despite requests by the OAU and the Congolese government. It did find that the factional fighting, the plight of civilians, and the severe humanitarian conditions were "likely to endanger peace, stability and security in the region." However, it maintained that a force would only be sent if there was "complete adherence to an agreed and viable ceasefire, agreement to the international control of Brazzaville airport and a clear commitment to a negotiated settlement covering all political and military aspects of the crisis." President of the Security Council, Statement, U.N. Doc. S/PRST/1997/43 (Aug. 13, 1997).

[31] S.C. Res. 161, U.N. Doc. S/4741, ¶ 1 (Feb. 21, 1961).

[32] *Id.*

Council seemed to have retreated from this stance and failed to intervene in further civil conflicts. However, the practice of the last decade and a half seems to be reinstating the principles underlying that early intervention.

Two sets of conflicts are worth investigating in more detail in relation to the emergence of new trends, those in the Balkans and those in Western Africa. These conflicts have elicited the entire range of Council responses—from condemnation to intervention—and provide useful insight into the formulation and justification of the emerging principles. In the Balkans, a progression is visible from the practice in the early 1990s (the former Yugoslavia, Bosnia and Herzegovina, and Croatia) to the practice in the late 1990s (Kosovo and the Former Yugoslav Republic of Macedonia). The practice in Western Africa similarly can be traced from the mid-1990s intervention in Sierra Leone to the most recent interventions in Côte d'Ivoire and Liberia in the early 2000s. The practice in the Balkans is reviewed here, whereas the practice in Western Africa is reviewed as part of the more comprehensive case studies in the next chapter.

i. The Balkans

Security Council practice in the Balkans involved condemnations and calls to cease the violence. Much of that practice was interlinked, arising from the break-up of the former Yugoslavia,[33] and taking place against the backdrop of intense European involvement. Early in the conflict, in June 1991 the European Community, the Organization for Security and Cooperation in Europe (OSCE), and the United States

[33] The break-up of the former Yugoslavia in the early 1990s evolved as a series of civil conflicts and led to the creation of a number of new states. At least the early stages of the complex series of disintegrations resulting from the break-up of the former Yugoslavia can be viewed as a civil war within the former Yugoslavia. This was later internationalized when the breakaway entities were accorded international recognition. Slovenia (July 1990 declaration of Sovereignty, referendum December 1990), and Croatia were the first to seek to secede. They were followed by Bosnia and Herzegovina and Macedonia. The European Community nations extended recognition to these Yugoslav republics seeking independence subject to certain conditions. Kosovo, however, was not included in these arrangements. Bosnia and Herzegovina claimed independence from Yugoslavia in October 1991 and voted by a referendum for independence in 1992. The Bosnian Serbs responded with armed resistance aimed at partitioning the republic along ethnic lines and joining Serb-held areas to form a "greater Serbia." By 1992, the Security Council considered that the Socialist Federal Republic of Yugoslavia had ceased to exist, and the remaining republics of Serbia and Montenegro declared a new Federal Republic of Yugoslavia (FRY) under President Slobodan Milosevic.

maintained that they would not recognize Slovenia or Croatia as international subjects.[34] The European Community sought a mediated solution to the crisis in June 1991, leading to a form of interim peace agreement, under which independence would be suspended for three months. However, this broke down immediately, and it became clear that Serbia aimed to exploit the situation to create a "greater Serbia." The International Crisis Group points to this as the time when the "United States and Germany switched positions from insisting on the maintenance of territorial integrity to an opposition to the use of force to maintain such integrity."[35] On August 27, 1991, the European Community established the Yugoslav Peace Conference to attempt a peaceful resolution of the conflict. It also created the Arbitration Commission to resolve disputes arising during the negotiations.[36]

Against this backdrop, the Council intervened on September 25, 1991, through Resolution 713. It noted the principle from the declaration coming out of the OSCE conference of September 3, 1991, that "no territorial gains or changes within Yugoslavia brought about by violence are acceptable." It also emphasized its alarm at the violations of the ceasefire and the continuation of the fighting.

The Council held that the situation amounted to a threat to international peace and security, and "[a]ppeal[ed] urgently to and encourage[d]" all parties to settle their disputes peacefully and through negotiation at the Yugoslav Peace Conference, mentioned above.[37] Nonetheless, it decided under Chapter VII to impose a complete embargo on arms "for the purposes of establishing peace and stability in Yugoslavia."[38] Thus, while the Council adopted the principle of peaceful settlement of disputes as a policy objective, it sought to ensure "peace and stability" in Yugoslavia through enforcement measures. This required the Council to reject the recourse to civil conflict as an option for the parties. Nonetheless, these early resolutions are quite different from the

---

[34] U.S. Department of State, Press Release, "Yugoslavia: Croatian and Slovenian Unilateral Assertions of Independence," June 26, 1991. *See* International Crisis Group (ICG), *Current Legal Status of the Federal Republic of Yugoslavia and of Serbia and Montenegro, ICG Balkans Report No. 101* (2000).

[35] ICG, *supra* note 34.

[36] Conference on Yugoslavia Arbitration Commission Opinions, 31 I.L.M. 1488 (1992).

[37] S.C. Res. 713, U.N. Doc. S/RES/713, ¶ 5 (Sept. 25, 1991).

[38] *Id.* ¶ 6.

way the Council later dealt with Kosovo. The focus here was on enforcing and abiding by the peace agreements and the principles put forward by the European Community. The formulation rejecting recourse to force was tentative and seemed more policy driven than a binding principle. Moreover, the Council emphasized that the peacekeepers would not be sent until violence stopped,[39] implying a traditional view of their role in conflicts.

The European Community continued to take the lead in those conflicts and reinforced the importance of peaceful settlement and rejection of recourse to force. In December 1991, the European Guidelines on the Recognition of New States in Eastern Europe and the Soviet Union was adopted. It decided that the European Community would

> recognise, subject to normal standards of international practice and the political realities in each case, those new states which, following the historic changes in the region, have constituted themselves on a democratic basis, have accepted the appropriate international obligations and have committed *themselves in good faith to a peaceful process and to negotiations.*[40]

The criteria set out included a "[c]ommitment to settle by agreement, including where appropriate by recourse to arbitration, all questions concerning State succession and regional disputes."[41] Serbia objected to these principles, asserting that they encouraged secession and civil strife.[42] Nonetheless, the declaration on the Formation of the Federal Republic of Yugoslavia, which set up the Federal Republic of Yugoslavia (FRY), provided that the FRY would not use force to settle questions related to the dissolution of Yugoslavia.[43]

---

39 S.C. Res. 721, U.N. Doc. S/RES/721 (Nov. 27, 1991).

40 *European Guidelines on Recognition of New States in Eastern Europe and the Soviet Union, Adopted by the European Community and Its Member States,* 92 INT'L L. REV. 174 (1991) [hereinafter *European Guidelines*] (emphasis added).

41 European Community Declaration on Yugoslavia (Dec. 16, 1991) (emphasis added). The European Community then announced recognition of Slovenia and Croatia on January 15, 1992, and of Bosnia, on April 6, 1992. However, it denied recognition to Macedonia. European Community Declaration on Yugoslavia (Apr. 6, 1992). The United States then recognized Slovenia, Croatia, and Bosnia as independent states on April 7, 1992.

42 ICG, *supra* note 34.

43 Declaration on the Formation of the Federal Republic of Yugoslavia (Apr. 27, 1992).

The Council did become more determined in its calls for the rejection of recourse to force as time passed, although generally in parallel with calls on parties to enforce peace agreements or the principles that were decided at the Yugoslav Peace Conference.[44] It also called on parties and others "not to resort to violence."[45] Resolution 752 (1992) and the follow-up Resolution 757 (1992) are particularly striking. In the first resolution the Council demanded that

> all parties and others concerned in Bosnia and Herzegovina stop the fighting immediately, respect immediately and fully the cease-fire signed on 12 April 1992 and cooperate with the efforts of the European Community to bring about urgently a negotiated political solution respecting the principle that any change of borders by forces is not acceptable.[46]

In the same resolution, it also explicitly warned that it would consider further steps to achieve a peaceful solution of the conflict in conformity with its relevant resolutions.[47]

In Resolution 757, the Council sought to enforce its demands in Resolution 752, highlighting that they had not been complied with, and "affirming its determination to take measures against any party or parties which fail to fulfil the requirements of resolution 752 (1992) and its other relevant resolutions." It specified that it was "[d]etermined in this context to adopt certain measures with the sole objective of achieving a peaceful solution and encouraging the efforts undertaken by the European Community and its member States"; it went on to apply various Chapter VII sanctions, including a trade embargo on the FRY. In Resolution 770, the Council was making demands under Chapter VII that "all parties and others concerned in Bosnia and Herzegovina stop the fighting immediately."

Resolution 847 spoke of the "overwhelming importance" of seeking "comprehensive political solutions to the conflicts." It also "strongly" con-

---

44 S.C. Res. 740, U.N. Doc. S/RES/740, ¶ 7 (Feb. 7, 1992): "Calls upon the Yugoslav parties to cooperate fully with the Conference on Yugoslavia in its aim of reaching a political settlement consistent with the principles of the Conference on Security and Cooperation in Europe."

45 S.C. Res. 749, U.N. Doc. S/RES/749, ¶ 5 (Apr. 7, 1992).

46 S.C. Res. 752, U.N. Doc. S/RES/752, ¶ 1 (Apr. 7, 1992).

47 *Id.*, ¶ 14.

demned continuing military attacks within the territory of the Republics of Croatia and of Bosnia and Herzegovina.

Thus, between 1991, when the violence began, and November 21, 1995, when the U.S.-mediated General Framework for Peace in Bosnia and Herzegovina (the Dayton Peace Accord) was completed, the Council repeatedly upheld the principle of peaceful resolution of the conflicts and called on all parties "not to resort to violence."[48] This practice did, at times, rely on individual peace agreements rather than a common principle. Nonetheless, the fact that these principles were adopted explicitly and sought to be enforced under Chapter VII suggests that they were considered important and binding on the parties. After the Dayton Peace Accord, the Council was even more determined in its resolutions to reject any "attempt to resolve the conflict . . . by military means."[49]

Moreover, in Croatia,[50] the Council called "*upon* the Government of the Republic of Croatia and the local Serb authorities to refrain from the threat or use of force and to reaffirm their commitment to a peaceful resolution of their differences"[51] and backed up these demands by a statement under Chapter VII that parties were to comply or face coercive enforcement.[52]

In summary, in this early-1990s practice, the Council relied on the existence of peace agreements and European Community decisions and declarations as justifications on which to base its calls for the rejection of recourse to force and demand for peaceful resolution of the disputes.

---

48 The former Yugoslavia, S.C. Res. 749, *supra* note 45, ¶ 5.

49 Bosnia and Herzegovina, S.C. Res. 1004, U.N. Doc. S/RES/1004, pmbl. (July 12, 1995).

50 Croatia was the first of the republics to break away from the former Yugoslavia. After its declaration of independence in 1991, Croatia was admitted to the United Nations in 1992, but armed conflict within Croatia continued. Any characterization of the conflict as strictly civil or international during this period may seem arbitrary given the complexity of the conflict. The continued conflict after independence could be considered partly international, given that local Serb forces were assisted by outside forces from Serbia, but, on the other hand, the fighting involved the very issue of independence and was certainly, in essence, civil.

51 S.C. Res. 981, U.N. Doc. S/RES/981, ¶ 8 (Mar. 31, 1995).

52 *See* S.C. Res. 994, U.N. Doc. S/RES/994, ¶ 10 (May 17, 1995). "Demands that the parties refrain from taking any further military measures or actions that could lead to the escalation of the situation and warns that in the event of failure to comply with this demand it will consider further steps needed to ensure such compliance."

However, there is a sense of increasing determination to the practice of the Council, which demanded that the parties respect its resolutions or face coercive action.

ii. Kosovo

The response to the conflict in Kosovo is particularly instructive and should be considered separately within the Security Council's Balkan practice, as it did not actually result from the initial process of disintegration of the former Yugoslavia.[53] In Kosovo, the Council involvement dates from 1998. In 1992, Kosovo's Albanian majority had voted to secede from Serbia and Yugoslavia and indicated a desire to merge with Albania but were repressed. In 1997, the Kosovo Liberation Army (KLA), then a small militant group, began killing Serb policemen and others who collaborated with the Serbs. In February 1998, Milosevic sent troops into the areas controlled by the KLA. The killing provoked riots in Pristina, the Kosovar capital. It turned the conflict into a guerrilla war and set off ethnic cleansing by the Serbs.

In March 1998, the Council passed Resolution 1160, which called on the FRY under Chapter VII to "take the further necessary steps to achieve a political solution to the issue of Kosovo through dialogue."[54] It also called, under Chapter VII, on "the Kosovar Albanian leadership to condemn all terrorist action" and emphasized that "all elements in the Kosovar Albanian community should pursue their goals by peaceful means only."[55] It is clear from this formulation that the Council's decision was intended to be binding on the parties. This is reinforced by the fact that it was passed under Chapter VII. The resolution appeared to extend the obligation to settle conflicts by peaceful means to the civil conflict in Kosovo.

The resolution followed and welcomed the OSCE decision. The OSCE had found that the crisis in Kosovo "was not solely an internal affair of the Federal Republic of Yugoslavia because of violations of the

---

[53] The conflict in Kosovo took the form of a conflict of secession from the FRY, fought between the Kosovo Liberation Army rebel forces and FRY Serb troops. There are many excellent and detailed accounts of this conflict. *See* INTERNATIONAL CRISIS GROUP, KOSOVO: LETS LEARN FROM BOSNIA: MODELS AND METHODS OF INTERNATIONAL ADMINISTRATION (1999); WILLIAM G. O'NEILL, KOSOVO: AN UNFINISHED PEACE (2002).

[54] S.C. Res. 1160, U.N. Doc. S/RES/1160, ¶ 1 (Mar. 31, 1995).

[55] *Id.*, ¶ 2.

principles and commitments of the [OSCE] on human rights and because it has significant impact on the security of the region."[56] That decision had rejected any terrorist action and had called on "all concerned actively to oppose the use of violence to achieve political aims."[57] It is not evident where the OSCE principles were derived from, as the Helsinki Final Act of 1975 setting out the OSCE principles provides for the peaceful resolution of international, but not internal, conflicts and adopts the usual principle of non-intervention in internal affairs.[58]

In Resolution 1199 (1998) from September, the Council again condemned "all acts of violence by any party." It also emphasized the humanitarian crisis that was being caused by this recourse to force. The resolution stated:

> Acting under Chapter VII of the Charter of the United Nations,
>
> 1. Demands that all parties, groups and individuals immediately cease hostilities and maintain a ceasefire in Kosovo, Federal Republic of Yugoslavia, which would enhance the prospects for a meaningful dialogue between the authorities of the Federal Republic of Yugoslavia and the Kosovo Albanian leadership and reduce the risks of a humanitarian catastrophe.

The Council called on the president of the FRY to implement his commitment of June 16 to resolve the problems by political means, and it also insisted that the KLA "should pursue their goals by peaceful means only." The Council went on to impose an arms embargo "for the purposes of fostering peace and stability in Kosovo."[59] In the later Resolution 1203, adopted after the cease-fire agreement, it demanded compliance by both the KLA and the FRY with Resolutions 1160 and 1199 under Chapter VII.[60]

---

56 Decision 218 on the situation in Kosovo, adopted at the special session of the Permanent Council of the Organisation for Security and Cooperation in Europe, Mar. 11, 1998. Annex of Letter from the Permanent Representative of Poland to the United Nations Addressed to the President of the Security Council (Mar. 17, 1998), U.N. Doc. S/1998/246.

57 *Id.*

58 Final Act of the Conference on Security and Co-operation in Europe (Helsinki Final Act), 14 I.L.M. 1292 (1975).

59 S.C. Res. 1160, *supra* note 54, ¶ 8.

60 S.C. Res. 1203, U.N. Doc. S/RES/1203, ¶¶ 3, 4 (Oct. 24, 1998).

In summary, the principles that the Council sought to enforce in Kosovo did not derive from a peace agreement or a regional agreement, although they were in line with the view of the OSCE member states. While there was a strong underlying concern about the humanitarian impact of the conflict, particularly in reference to ethnic cleansing, these were not explicitly relied on to justify or shape the calls for a political and peaceful resolution. The Council simply condemned the violence in that conflict and demanded an end to recourse to force for political aims.

iii. Former Yugoslav Republic of Macedonia

By the time the Security Council considered the recourse to force in the Former Yugoslav Republic of Macedonia in 2001, on the heels of the Kosovo crisis, a more determined support for a principle rejecting violence to gain political power can be seen. The Council intervened before any peace agreement was negotiated, on March 7, 2001, calling on "all political leaders in the Former Yugoslav Republic of Macedonia and Kosovo, FRY, who are in a position to do so to isolate the forces behind the violent incidents and to shoulder their responsibility for peace and stability in the region."[61] It also highlighted that the government of Macedonia was entitled to address the recourse to force against it, but it should do so with "an appropriate level of restraint and to preserve the political stability of the country."[62] In Resolution 1345, the Council again emphasized that the government should "end the violence in a manner consistent with the rule of law."[63]

Before the peace agreement, the Council condemned recourse to force by armed ethnic extremists and the killing of soldiers.[64] The Council explicitly demanded that those that were engaged in armed action against the state must "immediately cease all such actions, lay down their weapons and return to their homes."[65] Even following the peace agreement, which was entered into on August 13, 2001,[66] the

---

61 President of the Security Council, Statement, U.N. Doc. S/PRST/2001/7 (Mar. 12, 2001).

62 *Id.*

63 S.C. Res. 1345, U.N. Doc. S/RES/1345, ¶ 1 (Mar. 21, 2001).

64 President of the Security Council, Statement, *supra* note 61. *See also* S.C. Res. 1345, *supra* note 63, ¶ 1.

65 S.C. Res. 1345, *supra* note 63, ¶ 8.

66 The agreement was negotiated by the European Community and the United

Council refers to the Framework Agreement, but does not rely on it as the source of its authority to condemn the recourse to force.[67]

In Resolution 1371, the formulation chosen is particularly strong and explicitly rejects recourse to force for political aims. It stated: "[The Council] *rejects the use of violence in pursuit of political aims* and stresses that only peaceful political solutions can assure a stable and democratic future for the Former Yugoslav Republic of Macedonia."[68]

iv. Other Practice

The practice of the Security Council directly condemning the recourse to political violence is striking in its breadth. In some conflicts, the Council has condemned all recourse to force by all sides (Albania, Croatia, Cyprus, Democratic Republic of the Congo (DRC), East Timor, Georgia, Kosovo, and Somalia) and called on all parties to renounce force (Afghanistan, Albania, Bosnia and Herzegovina, Burundi, Cambodia, Congo (Brazzaville), Croatia, DRC, East Timor, FRY, Georgia, Haiti, Kosovo, Lebanon, Liberia, Rwanda, and Somalia). Some resolutions have mainly focused on the rebel groups or elements of the government. For instance, Sierra Leone's Revolutionary United Front (RUF), United Front for the Total Liberation of Angola (UNITA), Albanian extremists, and Serbian police have been singled out and condemned for their recourse to violence.

It is implicit in all these instances that what is being condemned is recourse to violence for political aims. The Council has expressed this explicitly in some conflicts (Burundi, Cambodia, Côte d'Ivoire, Central African Republic, Former Yugoslav Republic of Macedonia, Haiti, and Lebanon). In Haiti,[69] for instance, it called "upon all factions in Haiti explicitly and publicly to renounce, and to direct their supporters to

---

States, and it provided for various constitutional amendments and minority protections, as well as a NATO arms collections force. Signing of the political agreement was the main pre-condition set by NATO, which undertook to send 3,500 troops to Macedonia to collect the weapons of the ethnic Albanian rebels.

[67] *See* S.C. Res. 1371, U.N. Doc. S/RES/1371 (Sept. 26, 2001).

[68] *Id.*, ¶ 3 (emphasis added).

[69] In 1990, decades of dictatorship ended in Haiti with the democratic election of a president. However, President Aristides was overthrown in a military coup in 1991 followed by a wave of violence and instability in the country. The Security Council intervened in 1993, but a new constitutional crisis arose in 2004.

renounce, *violence as a means of political expression.*"[70] Similarly, in Cambodia,[71] it demanded that all parties "put an end to all acts of violence and to all threats and intimidation committed on political or ethnic grounds."[72] Generally, however, it has rejected the political dimensions of the recourse to force implicitly, rejecting the force generically but in the context of civil conflicts that inherently represent a struggle over political power.[73]

In summary, the Council has condemned—a practice stronger than the mere expression of concern—the violence or force in at least eighteen civil conflicts:

- Albania (condemned all acts of violence);
- Angola (condemned UNITA armed attacks);

---

[70] S.C. Res. 867, U.N. Doc. S/RES/867, ¶ 8 (Sept. 23, 1993) (emphasis added).

[71] The Khmer Rouge civil war in Cambodia began in the early 1970s and caused horrific casualties with over 1 million deaths. The Security Council only intervened in 1993 after the parties agreed to U.N.-sponsored elections.

[72] S.C. Res. 810, U.N. Doc. S/RES/810 (Mar. 8, 1993).

[73] In Angola, the Council demanded that UNITA stop armed attacks, S.C. Res. 834, U.N. Doc. S/RES/834, ¶ 4 (June 1, 1993), whereas, in Sierra Leone, it demanded that the RUF "lay down their arms immediately," S.C. Res. 1181, U.N. Doc. S/RES/1181, ¶ 1 (July 13, 1998). *See also* S.C. Res. 1171, U.N. Doc. S/RES/1171 (June 5, 1998), and disband, S.C. Res. 1260, U.N. Doc. S/RES/1260, ¶ 8 (Aug. 20, 1999); S.C. Res. 1270, U. N. Doc. S/RES/1270 (Oct. 22, 1999); and in Kosovo, it demanded that parties "end immediately all offensive actions," S.C. Res. 1244, U.N. Doc. S/RES/1244, ¶ 15 (June 10, 1999). It has also repeatedly called on parties to cease hostilities. In Congo (Brazzaville), this call related to the civil war, which began in 1997 when the military uprising led by former military ruler Dennis Sassou Nguesso, assisted by Angolan troops, overthrew the democratically elected government. President of the Security Council, Statement, U.N. Doc. S/PRST/1997/47 (Oct. 16, 1997). Cyprus, S.C. Res. 360, U.N. Doc. S/RES/360, ¶ 1 (Aug. 16, 1974). Liberia, S.C. Res. 911, U.N. Doc. S/RES/911, ¶ 5 (Apr. 21, 1994). Angola, S.C. Res. 804, U.N. Doc. S/RES/804 (Jan. 29, 1993); S.C. Res. 811, U.N. Doc. S/RES/811 (Mar. 12, 1993). In Rwanda, it repeatedly demanded "an immediate cessation of hostilities," S.C. Res. 912, *supra* note 29; S.C. Res. 918, *supra* note 29; S.C. Res. 925, *supra* note 29. In Somalia the parties were "strongly urged" to cease hostilities immediately, S.C. Res. 733, U.N. Doc. S/RES/733 (Jan. 23, 1992); S.C. Res. 767, U.N. Doc. S/RES/767, ¶ 1 (July 27, 1992); S.C. Res. 751, U.N. Doc. S/RES/751, ¶ 9 (Apr. 24, 1992); S.C. Res. 886, U.N. Doc. S/RES/886, ¶ 6 (Nov. 18, 1994). In the DRC, parties were generally called upon to "cease hostilities," S.C. Res. 1279, U.N. Doc. S/RES/1279, ¶ 1 (Nov. 30, 1999), and the Security Council demanded, pursuant to Chapter VII, that the parties to the conflict in Ituri and Bunia "cease hostilities immediately," S.C. Res. 1484, U.N. Doc. S/RES/1484 (May 30, 2003). In Kosovo, these demands were made pursuant to Chapter VII. S.C. Res. 1199, U.N. Doc. S/RES/1199, ¶ 1 (Sept. 23, 1998).

- Burundi (condemned those responsible for increasing violence and condemned those that resort to violence for political objectives);
- Côte d'Ivoire (condemned those that seize power by force of arms);
- Croatia (condemned attacks leading to loss of civilian and military life);
- Cyprus (condemned the outbreak of violence and the continuing bloodshed);
- Central African Republic (condemned the attempted coup);
- DRC (condemned all acts of violence);
- East Timor (condemned all acts of violence);
- Former Yugoslavia (condemned continuing military attacks within Croatia and Bosnia and Herzegovina);
- Former Yugoslav Republic of Macedonia (condemned the actions of ethnic Albanian extremists and condemned violence for political aims);
- Georgia (condemned the acts of violence by armed groups);
- Haiti (condemned extra-judicial killings, arbitrary arrests, abductions, rapes, and enforced disappearances);
- Kosovo (condemned violence by either party and condemned the use of excessive force by Serbian police forces);
- Lebanon (condemned efforts to disrupt by violence the return of government and condemned the violence);
- Liberia (condemned violence by signatories to the peace agreement and condemned fighting and armed attacks);
- Rwanda (condemned violence against civilians);
- Somalia (condemned fighting and condemned violence against humanitarian efforts); and
- South Africa (condemned massive violence against and killings of the African people).

It has made explicit demands and called on parties—a practice stronger than condemnation—to renounce force or violence in 22 of the conflicts:

- Afghanistan (all parties to renounce the use of force and to stop fighting immediately; decided under Chapter VII that parties were to comply or face coercive enforcement);
- Albania (an end to violence after determining that the situation was a threat to international peace and security);
- Angola (hostilities cease and that UNITA stop armed attacks);

- Bosnia and Herzegovina (rejected any attempt to resolve the conflict by military means; all irregular forces in Bosnia and Herzegovina be disbanded and disarmed, and all parties and others concerned in Bosnia and Herzegovina stop the fighting immediately);
- Burundi (all concerned refrain from acts of violence);
- Cambodia (all parties put an end to all acts of violence and to all threats and intimidation committed on political or ethnic grounds);
- Central African Republic (government to take urgent steps to bring an end to all acts of violence);
- Congo (Brazzaville) (cease hostilities);
- Croatia (parties stop the fighting immediately; decided under Chapter VII that parties were to comply or face coercive enforcement);
- Cyprus (parties cease hostilities and refrain from the threat or use of force or violence as a means to resolve the Cyprus problem);
- DRC (parties cease hostilities and end violence against refugees);
- East Timor (immediate end of all acts of violence);
- Former Republic of Macedonia (all those who are currently engaged in armed action against the authorities of those states immediately cease all such actions, lay down their weapons and return to their homes);
- Former Yugoslavia (parties not resort to violence);
- Georgia (parties refrain from the use of force);
- Haiti (parties renounce violence as a means of political expression, and all factions in Haiti explicitly and publicly to renounce, and to direct their supporters to renounce, violence as a means of political expression);
- Kosovo (parties cease hostilities pursuant to Chapter VII and end all offensive actions, and parties put an immediate and verifiable end to violence and repression);
- Lebanon (all those involved in hostilities in Lebanon to put an end to acts of violence);
- Liberia (parties cease hostilities);
- Rwanda (an end to the "mindless violence" and carnage engulfing Rwanda, and parties cease hostilities);
- Sierra Leone (the RUF lay down arms immediately and disband; resolutions were passed pursuant to Chapter VII and were thus explicitly binding); and

- Somalia ("strongly urged" parties to cease hostilities immediately; maintained that those that resorted to violence would be accountable by the Somali people and the international community; an immediate end to all acts of violence).

And, it has imposed enforcement measures under Chapter VII in 14 of the conflicts. Of these interventions, 13 have taken place since 1991.

- Congo (Brazzaville) (1961) (peace-keeping force to prevent the occurrence of civil war);
- Former Yugoslavia (1991) (complete arms embargo on all parties to establish peace and stability; deplored that its demands in prior resolutions had not been complied with). (1992) (UNPROFOR to create the conditions of peace and security required for the negotiation of an overall settlement of the Yugoslav crisis);
- Somalia (1992) (weapons embargo). (1992) (authorized forceful intervention to restore peace, stability, and law and order with a view to facilitating the process of a political settlement under the auspices of the United Nations);
- Croatia (1993) (UNPROFOR to monitor withdrawal of the Yugoslav Army from Croatia and demilitarization of the Prevlaka peninsula);
- Bosnia and Herzegovina (1993) (UNPROFOR to deter attacks against the safe areas);
- Haiti (1993, 2004) (trade embargo on petrol and arms). (1994) (multi-national force). (2004) (new peace-keeping force);
- DRC (1996, strengthened in 2003) (multi-national intervention to stabilize the security conditions and improve the humanitarian situation in Bunia and contribute to the safety of the civilian population; protect civilians under imminent threat of physical violence);
- Sierra Leone (1997) (arms and petrol embargo). (1998) (arms embargo on RUF). (1999) (peace-keeping force). (2000) (embargo on non-government diamond export);
- Albania (1997) (peace-keeping force to facilitate the safe and prompt delivery of humanitarian assistance, and to help create a secure environment for the missions of international organizations; the call to end all acts of violence, though not stated as an aim of the multi-lateral force, is implicit in the authorization that the civil conflict and acts of violence should cease);

- Kosovo (1998) (arms embargo to foster peace and stability). (1999) (international civil and security presences);
- Afghanistan (1999) (cease all armed hostilities, renounce the use of force, and put aside their differences and engage in a political dialogue; call on states to end immediately the supply of arms and ammunition to the parties of the conflict);
- East Timor (1999) (multi-national force led by Australia to restore peace and security in East Timor);
- Côte d'Ivoire (2003) (peace-keeping troops for the protection of civilians immediately threatened with physical violence); and
- Liberia (1992) (implement the cease-fire, establish conditions for disarmament and demobilization, using all necessary measures; weapons embargo for the purpose of establishing peace and stability in Liberia). (2003) (multinational force).

In addition, in many of the conflicts, separately from the instances of condemnation of violence, the Council has expressed concern over the violence:

- Afghanistan (concern over the continuation and recent intensification of the military confrontation);[74]
- Cambodia (concern over the increasing number of acts of violence perpetrated on political grounds);[75]
- Croatia (concern over the rapid and violent deterioration of the situation);[76]
- El Salvador (urged both parties to exercise maximum and continuing restraint);[77]
- Guinea Bissau (grave concern at the serious humanitarian situation affecting the civilian population);[78]
- Haiti (concern over escalation of politically motivated violence);[79]

---

[74] S.C. Res. 1076, *supra* note 28, pmbl.; S.C. Res. 1193, *supra* note 28, pmbl.

[75] S.C. Res. 810, *supra* note 72.

[76] S.C. Res. 802, U.N. Doc. S/RES/802, pmbl. (Jan. 25, 1993).

[77] S.C. Res. 714, U.N. Doc. S/RES/714, ¶ 6 (Sept. 30, 1991); S.C. Res. 729, U.N. Doc. S/RES/729 (Jan. 14, 1992).

[78] S.C. Res. 1216, U.N. Doc. S/RES/1216 (Dec. 21, 1998).

[79] S.C. Res. 867, *supra* note 70.

- Lebanon (deep grievance at the "loss of life, human suffering and physical destruction");[80]
- Rwanda (deeply disturbed by the magnitude of the human suffering; concern that the parties should cease hostilities and bring to an end the violence and carnage);[81]
- South Africa (concern over the violence destabilizing the peaceful negotiations);[82]
- Former Yugoslavia (concern about the fighting, which is causing a heavy loss of human life and material damage);[83] and
- Western Sahara (appealed to parties to exercise restraint and moderation).[84]

v. Contrary Practice

However, the emergence of any new policy or binding principles in the Security Council must be investigated in light of the conflicts that the Council has not addressed, particularly Algeria, Burma, Chechnya, Colombia, Fiji, Gambia, Northern Ireland, Spain, Sri Lanka, and Sudan.

Nonetheless, the extent to which this practice undermines the emergence of principles is a complex matter. Any contrary practice would put into question the emergence of particular principles. However, explicit statements opposing an action must be distinguished from failures to act. The former would clearly undermine the emergence of principles, whereas the latter would not necessarily do so. Thus, non-intervention could reflect geopolitical realities without denying the emergence of a new principle, or it could reflect a belief that the Council is precluded from intervening because of the domestic nature of the conflict.[85]

---

[80] S.C. Res. 436, *supra* note 29. *See also* S.C. Res. 490, *supra* note 29; S.C. Res. 512, *supra* note 29; S.C. Res. 542, U.N. Doc. S/RES/542 (Jan. 23, 1983).

[81] S.C. Res. 918, *supra* note 29; S.C. Res. 925, *supra* note 29; S.C. Res. 929, U.N. Doc. S/RES/929 (June 22, 1994).

[82] S.C. Res. 765, U.N. Doc. S/RES/765 (July 16, 1992).

[83] S.C. Res. 713, *supra* note 37, pmbl. *See also* S.C. Res. 721, *supra* note 39.

[84] S.C. Res. 377, U.N. Doc. S/RES/377 (Oct. 22, 1975).

[85] *See* Fernando R. Tesón, *A Symposium on Re-Envisioning the Security Council: Collective Humanitarian Intervention,* 17 MICH. J. INT'L L. 323 (1996), for a discussion of the interplay between Security Council intervention and Article 2(7). *See also* ROSALYN HIGGINS, THE DEVELOPMENT OF INTERNATIONAL LAW THROUGH THE POLITICAL ORGANS OF THE UNITED NATIONS 58–130 (1963).

In 1936, the Security Council of the League of Nations considered that it was not entitled to intervene in the civil war in Spain, because it was a domestic matter. The debate in the Security Council in 1946 assumed that Article 2(7) prohibited intervention into civil conflict unless it constituted a threat to international peace and security. No resolution was passed, and no intervention permitted. Poland and Russia suggested that there was a threat to international peace and security, but this was rejected by the United Kingdom and the United States.[86] However, that practice is out of step with the now overwhelming trend to consider such conflicts matters open to Council intervention.

Geopolitics may explain the failure to act in a number of conflicts. In Northern Ireland,[87] despite significant violence and bloodshed and the extension of the conflict to the United Kingdom through terrorism, the Council has not intervened. An attempt to place the question on its agenda in 1969 was strongly rejected by the British Representative on the Security Council; and even if it had made its way on the agenda, it would have undoubtedly faced a U.K. veto. The formal justifications given were that Article 2(7) prevented such intervention and that the conflict in Northern Ireland did not constitute a threat to international peace and security.[88] Since then the Council has clearly intervened in conflicts of similar intensity irrespective of Article 2(7). The conflict in Chechnya,[89] however, is another conflict that is described as a domestic matter by some.[90] This conflict involves many factors that have, in other cases, led

---

86 S/32 and S/34 SCOR, 1.1 Supp 2, at 54–55, Security Council, Apr. 17, 1946, SCOR 1.1 N2, 167.

87 Ireland's struggle for independence from the United Kingdom can be traced back to 1916. By 1921, 26 southern counties obtained independence from the United Kingdom, although the six northern counties remained part of Great Britain. This has sparked decades of civil conflict, both within Northern Ireland with violent clashes between loyalists and republicans, and in London through terrorist actions.

88 U.N. Doc. S/9394 (1969), S.C. Meeting 24, U.N. SCOR 1969.

89 Chechnya's attempt to obtain independence from Russia in 1991 resulted in a vicious civil conflict between Russian troops and Chechen rebels. In 1996, the Khasavyurt Peace Accords were signed in which Russia agreed to withdraw from Chechnya and discuss its independence after five years. In 1997, the Chechens chose a president and a parliament in democratic elections. In May 1997, the new president, Maskhadov, signed a peace treaty with President Yeltsin in Moscow. However, by 1999, Dagestan had become a serious destabilizing force, and Chechen militants, led by warlord Shamil Basayev, were staging violent attacks. This led to Russian forces invading Chechnya for a second time in 1999.

90 *See* comments of U.S. and French Ministers reported in Peter D. DiPaola, *A*

to intervention,[91] and yet—unsurprisingly given Russia's veto power—no action has been taken. The conflicts in Algeria[92] and Tibet also involve veto powers and have not been subject to Council action. Similarly, Cold War politics may explain the failure to act in a number of other conflicts in Africa and Latin America.[93]

There remain a small number of conflicts that have not attracted Council attention seemingly in contradiction to the practice of the 1990s. Algeria, Sri Lanka,[94] and Colombia are the current major ongoing conflicts not on the Council agenda.[95] The civilian massacre in Cambodia, for instance, did not elicit Council intervention for almost 20

Noble Sacrifice? Jus Ad Bellum and the International Community's Gamble in Chechnya, 4 IND. J. GLOBAL LEGAL STUD. 435, 435 (1997).

91 Particularly the overthrow of the democratically elected president and parliament in 1997 and the repeated breaches of the Peace Accords.

92 The most recent conflict in Algeria is a low-grade civil conflict sparked by the success of the fundamentalist Islamic Salvation Front (FIS) party in first-round ballots in December 1991, which caused the army to intervene, crack down on the FIS, and postpone the elections.

93 *See, e.g.*, Guatemala, El Salvador, Nicaragua, Colombia, and Chile. Kenney-Pipe and Jones suggest that Nigeria, Sudan, and Angola were proxy wars influenced by ideology. *See* Caroline Kennedy-Pipe and Clive Jones, *An Introduction to Civil Wars*, 1 CIVIL WARS 1 (1998). For a review of the conflicts in Nigeria and Pakistan, where there was also no action other than humanitarian assistance, *see* BERHANYKUN ANDEMICAEL, PEACEFUL SETTLEMENT AMONG AFRICAN STATES: ROLES OF THE UNITED NATIONS AND THE ORGANISATION OF AFRICAN UNITY, pt. D, ¶ 3 (1972).

94 In Sri Lanka, internal disruption began in 1976 with the emergence of separatist tensions and the formation of Liberation Tigers of Tamil Eelam rebel group. The 1985 Peace Agreement, which provided for an Indian peace-keeping force, failed. Violence between the Sri Lankan Army and separatists continued, and despite substantial international involvement by individual states (Norway had taken forward the latest peace agreement initiative) and pressure to bring the matter to the United Nations (the European parliament adopted a resolution on May 19, 2000, urging this), it has not been the subject of any Security Council resolutions.

95 By January 2007, Sudan seemed to be finally receiving attention. Sudan has been torn by a series of vicious civil wars since at least 1962, aggravated by the discovery of oil in 1978. The latest conflict broke out in 1983, as the government in the North imposed *shari'a* law, and has continued unabated through serious famine. There have been international attempts to find a peaceful solution and many broken peace accords. Moreover, individual states, including the United States, have imposed sanctions against Sudan. However, although the Security Council passed a series of resolutions dealing with the harboring of terrorists, it did not address the civil conflict until 2004. *See* S.C. Res. 1044, U.N. Doc. S/RES/1044 (Jan. 31, 1996); S.C. Res. 1054, U.N. Doc. S/RES/1054 (Apr. 26, 1996); S.C. Res. 1070, U.N. Doc. S/RES/1070 (Aug.

years.[96] The Council only passed a first resolution dealing with Cambodia in 1991, in the run-up to U.N.-sponsored elections. Ironically, this resolution stated that the Council was "[c]onvinced of the need to find an early, just and lasting peaceful solution of the Cambodia conflict."[97]

In addition, in some instances, the Council has suggested that regulation of force is a matter for the government[98] (or sometimes the parties[99]) rather than the international community. It has also made general and seemingly formulaic statements upholding the sovereignty, independence, and territorial integrity of states. These constitute the more important practice, as the Council has recognized state sovereignty in practically all conflicts considered, sometimes repeatedly in successive resolutions in a conflict. The adopted formulation varies little and is generally of the form recognizing or affirming "the sovereignty, independence, territorial integrity and national unity" of the relevant state.[100] This would seem to support the view that these are matters for the state. However, these are frequently contradicted either by direct actions of the Council or other statements within the resolution.

This can be illustrated by the conflicts in Afghanistan and East Timor,[101] for which the Council has particularly emphasized issues of sov-

---

16, 1996); and addressing the conflict, S.C. Res. 1556, U.N. Doc. S/RES/1556 (July 30, 2004); S.C. Res. 1564, U.N. Doc. S/RES/1564 (Sept. 18, 2004).

96 This is striking given the extreme violence against civilians in this conflict, which began in the early 1970s, and is believed to have caused over 1 million deaths from executions and starvation.

97 S.C. Res. 668, U.N. Doc. S/RES/668, pmbl. (Apr. 5, 1991).

98 Cyprus is an example that took place before the principles discussed: the Council did not condemn the violence outright but called on the government to take responsibility to stop it. It emphasized that the government of Cyprus had the "responsibility for the maintenance and restoration of law and order." S.C. Res. 186, U.N. Doc. S/RES/186 (Mar. 4, 1964) is the very first of an ongoing series of resolutions with similar formulations on the war in Cyprus.

99 In Afghanistan, however, it suggested that "the main responsibility for finding a political solution to the conflict lies with the Afghan parties." S.C. Res. 1076, *supra* note 28, ¶ 2. Similar statements were made in Armenia, where the Security Council stressed that "the parties to the conflict themselves bear the main responsibility for reaching a peaceful settlement." S.C. Res. 1236, U.N. Doc. S/RES/1236, ¶ 5 (May 7, 1999).

100 *See, e.g.*, S.C. Res. 1214, *supra* note 28.

101 Indonesia had annexed East Timor by force in 1975, however, the resulting conflict within East Timor seems to have been treated as civil. Following the consultation

ereignty and internal nature. In Afghanistan, the Council made repeated statements "[s]tressing the importance of non-interference in the internal affairs of Afghanistan" and "[r]eaffirming its strong commitment to the sovereignty, independence, territorial integrity and national unity of Afghanistan."[102] However, rather than leaving the matter of the civil conflict for the state to resolve, the Council strongly condemned the use of force in those conflicts and repeatedly demanded that the parties stop fighting, cease armed hostilities, and renounce the use of force.[103] It also imposed a non-Chapter VII arms embargo.[104]

In East Timor, the practice is similarly conflicting. The tone appears deferential to Indonesia. The Council began by stressing that it was Indonesia's responsibility to maintain peace and security in East Timor, "in order to ensure that the consultation is carried out in a fair and peaceful way and in an atmosphere free of intimidation, violence or interference."[105] However, this could be read either as deference to the state's authority or a veiled warning not to encourage recourse to force. Given that the Council went on to insist that the government "take immediate additional steps, in fulfilment of its responsibilities, to disarm and disband the militia,"[106] it seems that it did anticipate that the standard of conduct was to be set by the international community and not the individual state. Despite this, the Council only authorized intervening forces once the consent of Indonesia was secured,[107] although the authorization was on the basis of a finding of a threat to international peace and security.[108]

Overall, however, these cases represent a small number of conflicts in which the Council has not intervened, in comparison to the range and

---

of the East Timorese people, which favored independence, pro-integration militias, and possibly the Indonesian security forces, launched a campaign of violence.

102 S.C. Res. 1076, *supra* note 28, pmbl.; S.C. Res. 1214, *supra* note 28; S.C. Res. 1267, U.N. Doc. S/RES/1267 (Oct. 15, 1999).

103 *Id.*

104 S.C. Res. 1076, *supra* note 28.

105 S.C. Res. 1236, *supra* note 99, ¶ 5. *See also* S.C. Res. 1272, *supra* note 29, stressing the responsibility of Indonesia to ensure safe return of refugees.

106 S.C. Res. 1319, U.N. Doc. S/RES/1319, ¶ 1 (Sept. 20, 2000).

107 S.C. Res. 1236, *supra* note 99, ¶¶ 1–3; S.C. Res. 1264, *supra* note 29, ¶ 3.

108 S.C. Res. 1264, *supra* note 29.

depth of the practice reviewed so far in this chapter. Other than where geopolitics prevents intervention, it seems unlikely in the light of current practice that the Council would not intervene in a civil conflict to demand the end to violence. Moreover, the Council has clearly not recognized civil conflict as a legitimate option. Even the resolutions supporting sovereignty, which could be considered directly in contradiction to a new principle, are undermined by other statements within the same resolutions or the practice of the Council in response to those conflicts.[109] It is the first view that is borne out by the evidence; the majority of the instances of non-response to civil conflict fall into situations where clear geopolitical or veto restrictions came into play.

vi. Rejecting Violent Breach of a Cease-Fire or Peace Agreement

The Security Council has repeatedly rejected and condemned violent breaches of peace or cease-fire agreements[110] and called on parties to abide by their commitments.[111] Technically the legal nature of a peace

---

[109] The impact of sovereignty on the emergence of *jus ad bellum internum* norms is considered in more detail in Chapter 5.

[110] Former Yugoslavia, S.C. Res. 713, *supra* note 37, pmbl. Croatia, S.C. Res. 819, U.N. Doc. S/RES/819 (Apr. 16, 1993); S.C. Res. 820, U.N. Doc. S/RES/820 (Apr. 17, 1993).

[111] Calls under peace agreements: In Georgia, the Security Council emphasized the "importance of implementation by the parties of the obligations to which they have committed themselves." S.C. Res. 896, U.N. Doc. S/RES/896 (Jan. 31, 1994). In Sierra Leone, it called on parties to abide by their agreements. S.C. Res. 1260, *supra* note 73; S.C. Res. 1270, *supra* note 73; S.C. Res. 1289, U.N. Doc. S/RES/1289 (Feb. 7, 2000). In Liberia, it called on all parties "to respect and implement fully and expeditiously all the agreements and commitments they have entered into." S.C. Res. 1020, U.N. Doc. S/RES/1020, ¶ 5 (Nov. 10, 1995). *See also* Croatia, S.C. Res. 762, U.N. Doc. S/RES/762, pmbl., ¶ 2 (June 30, 1992); Lebanon, S.C. Res. 542, *supra* note 80, ¶¶ 3–4; Central African Republic, S.C. Res. 1125, U.N. Doc. S/RES/1125 (Aug. 6, 1997); Mozambique, S.C. Res. 782, U.N. Doc. S/RES/782 (Oct. 13, 1992); Angola, S.C. Res. 696, U.N. Doc. S/RES/696, pmbl. (May 30, 1991); El Salvador, S.C. Res. 729, *supra* note 77, ¶ 5; S.C. Res. 961, U.N. Doc. S/RES/961, ¶ 4 (Nov. 23, 1994).

Calls under cease fire agreements: Georgia, S.C. Res. 1225, U.N. Doc. S/RES/1225 (Jan. 28, 1999). Somalia, S.C. Res. 746, U.N. Doc. S/RES/746 (Mar. 17, 1992); *see also* S.C. Res. 837, U.N. Doc. S/RES/837, ¶ 4 (June 6, 1993), where the Security Council demands under Chapter VII that the parties comply with their commitments; S.C. Res. 886, *supra* note 73, ¶ 6; S.C. Res. 897, U.N. Doc. S/RES/897, ¶ 7 (Feb. 4, 1994). Congo (Brazzaville), President of the Security Council, Statement, *supra* note 30. Former Yugoslavia, S.C. Res. 713, *supra* note 37, ¶ 4. Cambodia, S.C. Res. 766, pmbl., U.N. Doc. S/RES/766 (July 21, 1992). Georgia, S.C. Res. 849, U.N. Doc. S/RES/849 (July 9, 1994). In Mozambique, it called on rebels to "respect scrupulously the cease-

agreement between a government and a rebel group is uncertain under international law. It is not a treaty, since it does not involve sovereign parties. Neither, however, is it a purely domestic matter, as a commercial contract would be.[112] The practice in response to the breach of such agreements could be justified by explicit consent to international enforcement, or it could reflect an expectation that parties that have agreed to particular clauses, and signed a document so doing, abide by their undertakings.

The case studies make clear that parties are expected to abide by their peace agreements.[113] In Angola, for instance, the Council sought to enforce the agreements,[114] sending three UNAVEM missions to do so, imposing punitive sanctions for breaches,[115] and declaring that the par-

---

fire and the commitments entered into under the Agreement." S.C. Res. 797, U.N. Doc. S/RES/797, ¶ 4 (Dec. 16, 1992).

112 The principle of sovereign immunity that exists in most legal systems derived from the common law jurisdictions provides that governments or agents of the government may enjoy immunity for various acts. These are usually limited to acts that emanate from the function of government and do not include those acts that would normally come within the ambit of the activities of private citizens, such as commercial contractual relations or liability for negligence. A similar notion applies under the conflict of laws rules, which preclude the enforcement of claims that constitute an extension of the sovereign power within the territory of another contrary to concepts of independent sovereignties. A foreign state has no international jurisdiction to enforce its law abroad. *See* DICEY AND MORRIS ON THE CONFLICT OF LAWS (Collins et al. eds., 2002).

113 In Sierra Leone, the Council expressly called on the parties "to fulfil all their commitments under the Peace Agreement." S.C. Res. 1270, *supra* note 73, ¶ 2; S.C. Res. 1289, *supra* note 111, ¶ 3. In Liberia, the timing of the international community's response to the conflict correlated with the signing of the ECOWAS negotiated cease-fire agreement on June 17. Violations of the cease-fire repeatedly attracted condemnation. The European Union expressly condemned such breaches and called on the parties to sign a comprehensive peace agreement. Declaration by the Presidency on Behalf of the European Union on the Peace Process in Liberia, 11832/1/03 REV 1, P 92/03 (July 28, 2003). The Council explicitly referred to the positive obligation of the parties to "cease hostilities throughout Liberia and fulfil their obligations under the Comprehensive Peace Agreement and the ceasefire agreement." S.C. Res. 1509, U.N. Doc. S/RES/1509, ¶ 4 (Sept. 19, 2003).

114 The peace accords were accepted as binding by both the government and the rebels and provided for U.N. monitoring. See Peace Accords for Angola, pmbl., Attachment II, Point 4, *available at* http://www.cmi.no/angola/literature/Bicesse_agreement.pdf.

115 S.C. Res. 864, U.N. Doc. S/RES/864 (Sept. 15, 1993); S.C. Res. 1127, U.N. Doc. S/RES/1127 (Aug. 28, 1997).

ties must abide by the agreements, stop military confrontation,[116] and engage in a meaningful dialogue aimed at reconciliation.[117] In Côte d'Ivoire, the Lomé Agreement included an undertaking by both sides that they would refrain from "violations of the accord on cessation of hostilities," and a pledge to urge "their authorities to refrain from any bellicose acts such as abuses and violence."[118] The primary peace agreement, the Linas-Marcoussis Accord,[119] explicitly provided for international enforcement measures: "afin que les mesures de redressement appropriées soient prises."[120] The Council emphasized the binding nature of the agreement and its expectation that it would be implemented, explicitly endorsed the accord, and entrenched the agreement by calling on the parties under Chapter VII to implement it fully and without delay.[121]

In Angola, the Council appeared to act in excess of what had been agreed in the peace accords. While the peace accords did foresee U.N. monitoring of the cease-fire,[122] the Council went much further than anticipated by the accord. It first reaffirmed that "it will hold responsible any party which refuses to take part in such a dialogue" and expressed its readiness to take all appropriate measures "to secure implementation of the 'Acordos de Paz.'"[123] The Council went on to state that the breach of such accords was illegal and "any party which fails to abide by all the commitments entered into under the Acordos de Paz para Angola will be rejected by the international community."[124] In the light of repeated breaches, the Council imposed an embargo on military and petrol sales to UNITA, and threatened further sanctions unless "the Secretary-

---

116 S.C. Res. 793, U.N. Doc. S/RES/793, ¶ 4 (Nov. 30, 1992).

117 *Id.*, ¶ 5.

118 Agence France-Presse, *Ivory Coast Government, Rebels Pledge to End 'Aggressive Acts'* (Oct. 31, 2002).

119 Linas-Marcoussis Accord, Jan. 24, 2003.

120 *Id.*, art. 4 (referring to enforcement by the E.U., A.U., ECOWAS, Secretary-General, Francophonie Organization, the International Monetary Fund and World Bank, G-8, and France).

121 S.C. Res. 1464, U.N. Doc. S/RES/1464 (Feb. 4, 2003).

122 The Peace Accords for Angola (May 15, 1991), art. 4, provided that "The United Nations will be invited to send monitors to support the Angolan parties, at the request of the Government of the People's Republic of Angola."

123 S.C. Res. 785, U.N. Doc. S/RES/785, ¶ 9 (Oct. 30, 1992).

124 *Id.*, pmbl.

General notifies the Council that an effective cease-fire has been established and that agreement has been reached on the implementation of the 'Acordos de Paz.'"[125] Following the signing of the Lusaka Protocol in 1994,[126] the Council again emphasized the urgent need for the government and the rebels to abide by their obligations under the peace agreement. The Council went on to impose travel sanctions on UNITA[127] and freeze UNITA funds.[128]

In Sierra Leone, this principle was supported through condemnation of such breaches and calls on the parties to abide by such agreements. In its preamble, Resolution 1313 maintained that the Abidjan Peace Accord of 1996 continued "to serve as a viable framework for peace, stability and reconciliation,"[129] even as it had been breached and succeeded by two other agreements—the Conakry Peace Plan of 1997 and the Lomé Peace Agreement of 1999, which were also breached.

As the conflict dragged on, the Council increased its attention to the breach of peace agreements and the need to abide by them. The Council welcomed the signing of the Lomé Accord,[130] and called on the RUF and other armed groups "to begin immediately to disband and give up their arms in accordance with the provisions of the Peace Agreement."[131] The Council expressly called on the parties "to fulfil all their commitments under the Peace Agreement to facilitate the restoration of peace, stability, national reconciliation and development in Sierra Leone"[132] and

---

125 S.C. Res. 864, *supra* note 115, ¶ 17.

126 The Lusaka Protocol signed in 1994 provided much more clearly for U.N. intervention. It specifically affirmed the parties' commitment to respect the relevant resolutions of the Security Council. Lusaka Protocol (Nov. 15, 1994), Annex 8, A, I, 1; *see also* Annex I. Moreover, the overall supervision and control of the cease-fire was agreed to be the responsibility of the United Nations. *Id.*, Annex 3 I(3). Thus, the agreed mandate of the United Nations was enlarged, and it was accepted that it "should play an enlarged and reinforced role" in the implementation of the agreements. *Id.*, Annex 8, A, 4. Nevertheless, the Security Council passed the resolution authorizing the intervention under Chapter VII.

127 S.C. Res. 1127, *supra* note 115, ¶ 4.

128 S.C. Res. 1173, U.N. Doc. S/RES/1173, ¶ 11 (June 12, 1998).

129 S.C. Res. 1132, *supra* note 29, pmbl.

130 S.C. Res. 1260, *supra* note 73, ¶¶ 1–2.

131 *Id.*, ¶ 8.

132 S.C. Res. 1270, *supra* note 73, ¶ 2; S.C. Res. 1289, *supra* note 111, ¶ 3.

called on the RUF and AFRC to disband and give up their arms in accordance with the peace agreement.[133] The deployment of the U.N. mission also supported this principle, as part of its mandate was to "cooperate . . . in the implementation of the Agreement."[134]

The demands on the parties to implement the cease-fire and peace accords in Liberia[135] were also supported by a weapons embargo imposed under Chapter VII, aiming to achieve peace and stability.[136] Similarly in the FRY, the Council created conditional sanctions as a form of enforcement mechanism for the peace agreements. The sanctions were to be imposed if the Council was informed "that the Federal Republic of Yugoslavia or the Bosnian Serb authorities are failing significantly to meet their obligations under the Peace Agreement."[137] This practice did not rely on the consent of the parties to Council intervention, as it was in addition to, and prior to, authorization in the Dayton Agreement for a U.N. implementation force to be set up via a Council resolution.[138]

The Council has also sought to "entrench" peace agreements by incorporating them into a resolution under Chapter VII, thus creating the option of enforcement through coercive means. In Resolution 1244, for instance, the Council welcomed the agreement in Belgrade and decided under Chapter VII that "a political solution to the Kosovo crisis shall be based on the general principles in annex 1,"[139] which included the end of violence and repression, withdrawal of military forces from Kosovo, and the deployment of a civil and security presence.

Other examples include the practice in Bosnia and Herzegovina, where the Council called on the parties under Chapter VII to "fulfil in good faith the commitments entered into"[140] and affirmed the need for

---

133 S.C. Res. 1270, *supra* note 73, ¶ 4.

134 *Id.*, ¶ 8(a).

135 S.C. Res. 788, U.N. Doc. S/RES/788 (Nov. 19, 1992).

136 In Liberia, the weapons embargo under Chapter VII had the clear stated aim of achieving peace in the civil conflict. *Id.*, ¶ 8.

137 S.C. Res. 1022, U.N. Doc. S/RES/1022, ¶ 3 (Nov. 22, 1995).

138 The General Framework Agreement for Peace in Bosnia and Herzegovina (Dayton Peace Accords) (Nov. 21, 1995), ANNEX 1A: Agreement on the Military Aspects of the Peace Settlement, Article 1 (1), *available at* http://www.state.gov/www/regions/eur/bosnia/bosagree.html.

139 S.C. Res. 1244, *supra* note 73, ¶ 1.

140 Bosnia and Herzegovina, S.C. Res. 1031, U.N. Doc. S/RES/1031, ¶ 1 (Dec. 15, 1995).

the implementation of the peace agreements in their entirety.[141] In Croatia, it demanded under Chapter VII that "parties and others concerned comply fully with the United Nations peacekeeping plan in Croatia and with other commitments they have undertaken and in particular with their cease-fire obligations."[142] In Côte d'Ivoire, the Council determined that the situation was a threat to international peace and security and then "endorsed" the agreement and called on the parties to implement it.[143]

In addition, the Council has also declared that the international community will not condone the use of force in order to acquire territory during a civil conflict after a peace agreement. In the former Yugoslavia, it took note of the OSCE declaration of September 3, 1991, "that no territorial gains or changes within Yugoslavia brought about by violence are acceptable"[144] and demanded that the parties respect "the principle that any change of borders by force is not acceptable."[145] The Declaration on Yugoslavia[146] both called on parties "to observe their obligations under the cease-fire agreement and the Memorandum of Agreement" and went on to adopt the principle rejecting unilateral changes in frontiers through use of force as the basis of resolution of the dispute.[147]

Such statements are not limited to the break-up of Yugoslavia. Similar statements were made in Angola,[148] in the context of a resolution

---

141 *Id.*, ¶ 30.

142 S.C. Res. 807, U.N. Doc. S/RES/807, ¶ 1 (Feb. 2, 1993).

143 S.C. Res. 1464, *supra* note 121.

144 S.C. Res. 713, *supra* note 38, pmbl.; S.C. Res. 757, U.N. Doc. S/RES/757 (May 30, 1992).

145 S.C. Res. 752, *supra* note 46.

146 Issued at an extraordinary meeting of the European Community, Sept. 3, 1991, The Hague.

147 As discussed under the notion of secession in Chapter 1, Section C.3, this reflected the European Guidelines on Recognition of New States in Eastern Europe and the Soviet Union, adopted by the European Community and its Member States on December 16, 1991, which required "respect for the inviolability of all frontiers which can only be changed by peaceful means and by common agreement." *European Guidelines, supra* note 40.

148 S.C. Res. 864, *supra* note 115, ¶ 8. *See, e.g.*, S.C. Res. 1173, *supra* note 128. The conflict can be characterized as a war of self-determination that evolved into a civil war after independence in 1975. It presented as a complex conflict involving a number of different rebel groups with overt external support. The Security Council became involved in the civil aspect of the conflict in 1991, when most of the external inter-

recognizing the government of Angola following the democratic elections and expressing concern that the peace talks "remain suspended and a cease-fire has not been established." The Council condemned UNITA for continuing military actions and "UNITA's repeated attempts to seize additional territory" contrary to the Acordos de Paz.[149]

One slightly different situation is that of Afghanistan where the Council rejected the use of force to gain territory without there first being an agreement. In 1998, it expressed concern at the Taliban offensive in the northern part of the country, which caused a threat to international peace and security and human suffering. It went on to reiterate:

> [T]he Afghan crisis can be settled only by peaceful means, through direct negotiations between the Afghan factions under United Nations auspices, aimed at achieving a solution accommodating the rights and interests of all Afghans and stresses that territorial gains through military operations will neither lead to a durable peace in Afghanistan, nor contribute to a comprehensive settlement of the conflict in this multi-cultural and multi-ethnic country.[150]

These declarations can be read in a number of ways. They may reflect the notion of territorial integrity or the notion of *uti possidetis*—including the extension of that principle that even a claim for self-determination cannot bring about a change in boundaries other than consensually. Alternatively, they provide support for the view that any breach of a peace agreement is prohibited.

Thus, the practice suggests that the international community may be prepared to intervene to enforce a peace agreement if there is a return to violence, especially if such an agreement provides for international oversight or enforcement. However, there is also striking practice that has not relied on a peace agreement; thus the consent of the parties to such agreements do not govern the practice in this field. For instance, in Kosovo without relying on a peace agreement or a regional agreement, the Council condemned violence by both sides and called on them both

---

vention had subsided, and the government and the UNITA rebel forces had signed the peace accords for Angola.

149 S.C. Res. 864, *supra* note 115, ¶ 8.

150 S.C. Res. 1193, *supra* note 28, ¶ 2.

to cease using violence. Similarly, in the Former Yugoslav Republic of Macedonia in 2001, the Council intervened before any peace agreement was negotiated, on March 7, 2001, calling on all political leaders to isolate the forces behind the violence and shoulder their responsibility for peace and stability.[151] Even before the peace agreement, the Council condemned violence by armed ethnic extremists and the killing of soldiers.[152]

In summary, while the Council has emphasized that parties are expected to abide by the peace agreements they enter into, the Council has not relied in a narrow sense on the terms of these agreements in seeking to enforce them and has also acted before such agreements were signed or where there was no agreement.

b. Ad Hoc *Response to a Threat to International Peace and Security or Binding Principle?*

Can Security Council practice be characterized as merely an *ad hoc* response to a threat to international peace and security—thus being substantially less important to the emergence of new norms—or does it evidence the emergence of new policy or legal norms rejecting the political violence of civil conflict and coups? This issue is relevant to all the norms investigated in this chapter and is considered here in detail.

Much Council practice—especially that which consists of enforcement-style actions, such as sanctions or military intervention—can, at least at some level, be explained as resting solely on its Chapter VII responsibility. The enforcement practice of the Council is necessarily reliant on a formal finding of a threat to international peace and security. Some might say, therefore, that this practice merely reflects the Council's discretionary response to a threat to international peace and security.

However, the consistent rejection by the Council of particular conduct across many conflicts cannot satisfactorily be explained as resulting from *ad hoc* discretionary decisions. Similar principles have been formulated across a wide variety of different conflicts. Even if these principles are initially formulated as mere policy, over time, their repetition by states in Council debates (and outside of the Council), and in later resolutions suggests that agreement is forming around a particular propo-

---

151 President of the Security Council, Statement, *supra* note 61.

152 *Id. See also* S.C. Res. 1345, *supra* note 63, ¶ 1.

sition. The volume of similar practice cannot be accounted for unless the policy of the Council is informed by a common understanding of the way in which the parties should behave.

The mere fact that the Council justifies its intervention as being based on a threat to international peace and security does not prevent it from also developing a rule prohibiting certain conduct in all such conflicts. While one view may be that the description of the practice as a response to a threat against international peace and security under Chapter VII is sufficient, this book adopts a different view. Characterizing this practice as a policy response to a threat to international peace and security may be correct on a formal level. It does not, however, properly explain the dramatic and surprising evolution taking place in this field, and it unduly discounts the principles expressed and supported in the practice. It disregards what the Council and states actually say and do. Overall, the Council and states have not relied on broad statements of threat to international peace and security—although a focus on peace and security is evident in the constitutional documents of a number of regional organizations. Rather, they have formulated general rules condemning certain recourse to force in civil conflict.

Council practice ranges from condemnation to demands that parties renounce violence to measures seeking to enforce these demands. The Council has intervened in 32 civil conflicts since 1945,[153] and there is a trend of increasing interventionism in the last 15 years.[154] The practice shows that the Council has repeatedly rejected the use of "violence," which appears to be used as a synonym for "force." Whether this practice represent an *ad hoc* response to particular circumstances or supports the emergence of a policy principle rejecting recourse to force in civil conflict, or even a binding principle within the Council, must be determined in light of the general trends in the practice, taking into account whether the principles are formulated as binding or recommendatory, and the impact of any contrary practice.

---

[153] In the definition of civil conflict adopted in this text, these are: Afghanistan, Albania, Armenia, former Yugoslavia, FRY and Kosovo, Croatia, Bosnia and Herzegovina, Burundi, Cambodia, Central African Republic, Republic of Congo (Brazzaville), DRC, Colombia, Côte d'Ivoire, Cyprus, East Timor, El Salvador, Georgia, Guatemala, Guinea Bissau, Haiti, Lebanon, Iraq (Kurds), Liberia, the Former Yugoslav Republic of Macedonia, Mozambique, Nicaragua, Rwanda, Sierra Leone, South Africa, Somalia, and Western Sahara.

[154] The exceptions are the Republic of Congo (Brazzaville) (1961), Cyprus (1964), El Salvador (1989), Lebanon (1978), Nicaragua (1983), South Africa (1960), and Western Sahara (1975).

On the one hand, it does not seem from the formulation adopted in the resolutions that the Council intended to enunciate a generic principle; the practice focuses entirely on the particular conflict addressed. On the other hand, the Council has rejected the recourse to political violence in the great majority of the cases it has addressed.

There exists a progression in the Council's approach from its early Balkan practice to that in Kosovo and Macedonia where a principle rejecting recourse to force for political means is put forward more strongly without looking for other justifications (such as peace agreements). A detailed investigation of the practice of the international community, including the Council, in the three recent conflicts in Sierra Leone, Côte d'Ivoire, and Liberia, reviewed in the next chapter, also supports this perspective.

Other than the intervention in Congo Brazzaville in 1961, where the Council explicitly addressed civil conflict, it is the practice since the 1990s that best elucidates the principles guiding Council practice. The explicit rejection of force to resolve conflict has been a central aspect of Council practice in relation to many conflicts. Increasingly, the Council has emphasized that it rejects the use of force to achieve a political outcome.

Council practice in the Balkans in the early 1990s involved condemnations and calls to cease the recourse to force, though it was reliant on the OSCE declarations that "no territorial gains or changes within Yugoslavia brought about by violence are acceptable."[155] The Council also emphasized its alarm at the violations of the cease-fire and the continuation of the fighting. The focus was on enforcing and abiding by the peace agreements and the principles put forward by the European Commission. The formulation rejecting violence was tentative and seems more policy driven than a binding principle. Moreover, the Council emphasized that the peacekeepers would not be sent until violence stopped, implying a traditional view of their role in conflicts.[156]

However, in Georgia, in 1993, the Council demanded that all parties "refrain from the use of force"[157] and also explicitly welcomed the "commitment of the parties not to use force for the resolution of any disputed questions" and to refrain from "propaganda aimed at the solution of the

---

155 OSCE conference of Sept. 3, 1991.

156 S.C. Res. 721, *supra* note 39.

157 S.C. Res. 876, *supra* note 28. *See also* S.C. Res. 881, *supra* note 28, ¶ 3.

conflict by force."[158] In Kosovo, by the late 1990s, the practice was even more striking. The Council condemned violence by both sides, called on them to cease using violence, and demanded under Chapter VII "that all parties, groups and individuals immediately cease hostilities and maintain a ceasefire in Kosovo."[159] Here, the Council did not rely on a peace agreement or a regional agreement, although its demands were in line with the view of the OSCE member states. While there was a strong underlying concern about the humanitarian impact of the conflict, particularly ethnic cleansing, these were not explicitly relied on to justify or shape the calls for a political and peaceful resolution. The Council simply condemned the violence in that conflict and demanded an end to recourse to force for political aims.

By the time the Council considered the violence in the Former Yugoslav Republic of Macedonia in 2001, it reacted with determination rejecting recourse to force in civil conflicts. Even before any peace agreement, the Council called on all political leaders to isolate the forces behind the violence and shoulder their responsibility for peace and stability,[160] and it condemned violence by armed ethnic extremists and the killing of soldiers.[161] The Council explicitly demanded that those who were engaged in armed action against the state must "immediately cease all such actions, lay down their weapons and return to their homes."[162] Moreover, in Resolution 1371, the Council specifically rejected recourse to force for political aims.[163]

Council practice in the recent conflict in Liberia also supports this position. There, the Council urged "the LURD [Liberians United for Democracy and Reconciliation] and MODEL [Movement for Democracy in Liberia] to refrain from any attempt to seize power by force, bearing in mind the position of the African Union on unconstitutional changes of government as stated in the 1999 Algiers Decision and the 2000 Lomé Declaration."[164]

---

158 S.C. Res. 1311, *supra* note 28, ¶ 5.

159 S.C. Res. 1199, *supra* note 73.

160 President of the Security Council, Statement, *supra* note 61.

161 *Id. See also* S.C. Res. 1345, *supra* note 63, ¶ 1.

162 S.C. Res. 1345, *supra* note 63, ¶ 8.

163 S.C. Res. 1371, *supra* note 67, ¶ 3.

164 S.C. Res. 1497, U.N. Doc. S/RES/1497, ¶ 13 (Aug. 1, 2003). Note that this state-

During the mid-to-late 1990s, demands that parties renounce recourse to force were also made, with varying formulations, in a range of other conflicts: Burundi,[165] Central African Republic,[166] East Timor,[167] Rwanda,[168] Lebanon,[169] and Cambodia.[170] In Albania, the calls to end violence were pursuant to a finding of a threat to international peace and security,[171] as they were in Sierra Leone.[172]

It is implicit in much of this practice that what is being condemned is recourse to force for political aims. The Council has expressed this explicitly in some conflicts.[173] For instance, the Council linked its demand in Georgia that all parties "refrain from the use of force"[174] to its support for the "commitment of the parties not to use force for the resolution of any disputed questions," and called on parties to refrain

---

ment took place once President Charles Taylor had stepped down, and it does seem to stretch the intention of the African Union agreement, given the clear doubts surrounding Taylor's democratic legitimacy at that point.

165 S.C. Res. 1049, *supra* note 28, ¶¶ 3–4 and S.C. Res. 1072, *supra* note 29. S.C. Res. 1049, *supra* note 28, ¶¶ 3–4 ("parties refrain from incitement to violence"). *See also* S.C. Res. 1234, *supra* note 29 (expressing concern in the DRC at "acts of and incitement to ethnic hatred and violence by all parties to the conflict)."

166 The Security Council called on the government "to take urgent steps to bring an end to all acts of violence." President of the Security Council, *The Situation in the Central African Republic*, Statement, *supra* note 29.

167 The Security Council repeatedly condemned "all acts of violence in East Timor" and called for their immediate end. S.C. Res. 1264, *supra* note 29, ¶ 1, acting under Chapter VII. *See also* S.C. Res. 1246, *supra* note 29, ¶ 11; S.C. Res. 1272, *supra* note 29, ¶ 12, 16.

168 The Security Council did ultimately demand "an end to the mindless violence and carnage which are engulfing Rwanda." S.C. Res. 912, *supra* note 29, ¶ 6; S.C. Res. 918, *supra* note 29; S.C. Res. 925, *supra* note 29.

169 The Security Council condemned the violence and called on "all those involved in hostilities in Lebanon to put an end to acts of violence." S.C. Res. 436, *supra* note 29; ¶ 1; S.C. Res. 490, *supra* note 29, ¶ 1; S.C. Res. 512, *supra* note 29, ¶ 1. *See also* S.C. Res. 513, *supra* note 29, ¶ 1, with respect to violence against civilians.

170 S.C. Res. 880, *supra* note 29, ¶ 5.

171 S.C. Res. 1101, *supra* note 29, ¶ 1. This formulation was repeated in S.C. Res. 1114, *supra* note 29, ¶ 1. Albania, S.C. Res. 1101, *supra* note 29, pmbl.

172 S.C. Res. 1132, *supra* note 29, ¶ 2.

173 *See* Burundi, Côte d'Ivoire, Central African Republic, Cyprus, Georgia, Haiti, Former Yugoslav Republic of Macedonia, Lebanon, and Liberia.

174 S.C. Res. 876, *supra* note 28. *See also* S.C. Res. 881, *supra* note 28, ¶ 3.

from "propaganda aimed at the solution of the conflict by force."[175] In Cyprus, the Council called on both sides to "refrain from the threat or use of force or violence as a means to resolve the Cyprus problem."[176] In Burundi, it demanded that all parties refrain from "seeking to destabilize the security situation or depose the Government by force or by other unconstitutional means."[177] In Côte d'Ivoire, the Council stated that it "firmly condemns attempts to use force to influence the political situation in Côte d'Ivoire."[178] In Liberia, it similarly rejected "any attempt to seize power by force," acknowledging the Lomé Declaration on unconstitutional changes of government.[179] In Haiti, it called "upon all factions in Haiti explicitly and publicly to renounce, and to direct their supporters to renounce, violence as a means of political expression."[180]

The range and variety of those conflicts, and the different circumstances in which the Council has become involved, suggest that even if the Council is not seeking to formulate a binding principle outside of any individual case, it is effectively applying a general principle rejecting political violence of civil conflicts and demanding that such disputes be resolved by peaceful means only.

The cases clearly establish a principle of general policy and arguably can represent the emergence of a binding Council principle. Given the Council's power of enforcement, certain policy positions are best characterized as binding rules prohibiting certain forms of conflict within the broad category of response to a threat to international peace and security. Given their repetition, these rules no longer constitute unrestricted discretionary responses to a threat but are better characterized as quasi-

---

[175] S.C. Res. 1311, *supra* note 28, ¶ 5.

[176] S.C. Res. 1251, U.N. Doc. S/RES/1251, ¶ 9 (June 29, 1999).

[177] S.C. Res. 1049, *supra* note 28, ¶ 3.

[178] President of Security Council, *Côte d'Ivoire,* Statement, U.N. Doc. S/PRST/2002/42 (Dec. 20, 2002). *See also* Press Release, President of Security Council, Security Council Condemns Attempts at Force to Influence Political Situation, Overthrow Elected Government in Côte d'Ivoire, U.N. Doc. AFR/506, SC/7558 (Oct. 31, 2002) [hereinafter *Security Council Condemns Attempts*].

[179] S.C. Res. 1497, *supra* note 164, ¶ 13.

[180] S.C. Res. 867, *supra* note 70, ¶ 8. In Cambodia, it demanded that all parties "put an end to all acts of violence and to all threats and intimidation committed on political or ethnic grounds." S.C. Res. 810, *supra* note 72. As seen also in the practice in Macedonia, Côte d'Ivoire, and Liberia.

legislative Council prohibitions on certain conduct. The language and formulation of many of the resolutions suggest that these are to be strictly complied with, even when not passed under Chapter VII. A number of factors support this perspective. The Council has passed many resolutions, either making demands of parties or calling on them to cease (or undertake) certain other behavior, without relying on Chapter VII.[181] The use of "calls on" and "demands" appears to imply a binding obligation[182] and can be contrasted with terms such as "urges" or "appeals to" and to "encourage" that do not.[183] Moreover, much of this practice is formulated in a direct and mandatory fashion.[184] Accordingly, the statements are more than merely recommendatory and must be taken to indicate principles that the Council wishes to impose on the parties.

The practice of the Council in Afghanistan[185] and in the former Yugoslavia reinforces this view. The formulation most frequently used is

---

181 The practice in Kosovo is a typical example. The Security Council passed S.C. Res. 1004, *supra* note 49, specifying a list of demands under Chapter VII of the U.N. Charter, including that Serb forces cease their offensive, that the parties respect the safe area of Srebrenica, and that they release unharmed all UNPROFOR personnel. This resolution did not go on to impose any enforcement measures under Chapter VII and only used the verb of "demands," stressing once again the binding nature of the resolution. The demands were reiterated without reference to Chapter VII, however, in S.C. Res. 1034, U.N. Doc. S/RES/1034 (Dec. 21, 1995). The Security Council went on to make further demands under Chapter VII in S.C. Res. 1203, *supra* note 60, and S.C. Res. 1244, *supra* note 73.

182 The Security Council has used the verbs "demands" and "calls on" following an explicit Chapter VII determination, suggesting that such words can convey binding requests. S.C. Res. 1267, *supra* note 102, ¶ 2; S.C. Res. 1160, *supra* note 54, ¶¶ 1–2; S.C. Res. 1199, *supra* note 73; S.C. Res. 871, U.N. Doc. S/RES/871 (Oct. 4, 1993). Note that Article 41 of the U.N. Charter provides that the Council may "decide" what measures are to be applied and may "call upon" the U.N. members to apply them—therefore "call upon" is recognized within the Charter as having a compulsory meaning.

183 *E.g.*, S.C. Res. 713, *supra* note 37.

184 The use of the imperative "to cease all armed hostilities" can be contrasted with resolutions calling upon parties to "reconsider." *E.g.*, S.C. Res. 855, U.N. Doc. S/RES/855 (Aug. 9, 1993).

185 The conflict in Afghanistan became a predominantly civil conflict between the Taliban and the government after the defeat, in 1989, of the invading Russian forces. The Security Council became involved in 1996 when the Taliban took Kabul and declared itself the government of Afghanistan. Following the bombing of the American Embassy in Kenya in 1999, however, and the suspected link between bin Laden and the Taliban, the attention of the Security Council has shifted from matters of civil conflict to those of terrorism. The civil conflict practice is relevant to the discussion here.

of this form: the Council "calls upon all parties immediately to cease all armed hostilities"[186] or "[d]emands that all parties fulfil their obligations and commitments."[187] In Afghanistan, these demands, which were not passed under Chapter VII, were followed by a Chapter VII decision insisting that the parties "comply promptly with its previous resolutions."[188] The explicit reference to Chapter VII leaves no doubt that the Council intended those aspects of its resolution to be binding. The fact that the Council explicitly stated that it expected the parties to comply with its previous resolutions, which had not been passed under Chapter VII, strongly suggests that it considered its previous demands to be binding as well.[189]

The practice in the former Yugoslavia also emphasizes that the Council intends that parties comply with its resolutions. In Resolution 771, it first listed a series of demands in the standard formulation,[190] reaffirmed that the parties were bound to comply with international humanitarian law,[191] and strongly condemned any violation of such law.[192] Explicitly, it decided that, acting under Chapter VII, "all parties and others concerned in the former Yugoslavia, and all military forces in Bosnia and Herzegovina, shall comply with the provisions of the present resolution, failing which the Council will need to take further measures under the Charter."[193]

---

186 *See, e.g.*, S.C. Res. 1076, *supra* note 28, ¶ 1.

187 *See, e.g., id.*, ¶ 10. *See also* S.C. Res. 1193, *supra* note 28; S.C. Res. 1214, *supra* note 28.

188 S.C. Res. 1267, *supra* note 102, ¶ 1.

189 *See also* S.C. Res. 1333, U.N. Doc. S/RES/1333 (Dec. 19, 2000), also under Chapter VII demanding that it comply with S.C. Res. 1267, *supra* note 102.

190 "Demands that all parties and others concerned in the former Yugoslavia, and all military forces in Bosnia and Herzegovina, immediately cease and desist from all breaches of international humanitarian law." S.C. Res. 771, U.N. Doc. S/RES/771, ¶ 3 (Aug. 12, 1992). "Further demands that relevant international humanitarian organisations, and in particular the International Committee of the Red Cross, be granted immediate, unimpeded and continued access to camps, prisons and detention centres." *Id.*, ¶ 4.

191 *Id.*, ¶ 1.

192 *Id.*, ¶ 2.

193 In S.C. Res. 50, U.N. Doc. S/801 (May 29, 1948) (Israel), a similar pattern can be seen, with a series of demands and calls being made on parties followed by explicit statement that if this "present resolution is rejected by either party or by both, or if, having been accepted, it is subsequently repudiated or violated," Chapter VII action would be considered.

The demands made directly pursuant to Chapter VII are unambiguously binding. However, it is difficult to discern a clear pattern or rationale as to when Chapter VII is relied upon. In some cases the Council has relied upon Chapter VII, and in others addressing similar circumstances and seemingly intending its resolutions to be binding, it has not.[194] Nonetheless, it is useful to highlight the principles that the Council has sought to emphasize through its reliance on Chapter VII. One example is the importance of a peaceful resolution of the dispute: the Council demanded under Chapter VII that the FRY "implement immediately the following concrete measures towards achieving a polit-

---

194 *See* Croatia: S.C. Res. 802, *supra* note 76 (no mention of Chapter VII). *But see* S.C. Res. 807, *supra* note 142 (demands made under Chapter VII); S.C. Res. 871, *supra* note 182, and S.C. Res. 1009, U.N. Doc. S/RES/1009 (Aug. 10, 1995) (relied on Chapter VII); S.C. Res. 981, *supra* note 51, and S.C. Res. 994, *supra* note 52 (did not rely on Chapter VII). Bosnia: S.C. Res. 757, *supra* note 144 (the condemnation of the FRY was expressed to be pursuant to Chapter VII, went on to impose trade sanctions). S.C. Res. 752, *supra* note 46, and S.C. Res. 764, U.N. Doc. S/RES/764 (July 13, 1992) (the demands to stop fighting were not related to Chapter VII). S.C. Res. 770, U.N. Doc. S/RES/770 (Aug. 13, 1992) (the same demands were made pursuant to Chapter VII). S.C. Res. 787, U.N. Doc. S/RES/787 (Nov. 10, 1992); S.C. Res. 819, *supra* note 110; S.C. Res. 820, *supra* note 110, relating to cessation of hostilities and the unacceptable practice of taking territory by force (no reference to Chapter VII); *but see* S.C. Res. 824, U.N. Doc. S/RES/824 (May 6, 1993) (the demand that the taking of territory by force stop was made under Chapter VII). East Timor: S.C. Res. 1246, *supra* note 29 (calling for the end of acts of violence); S.C. Res. 1272, *supra* note 29, acting under Chapter VII (calling again for the end of violence and demanding that those responsible be brought to justice). Georgia: similarly, S.C. Res. 858, U.N. Doc. S/RES/858 (Aug. 24, 1993); S.C. Res. 876, *supra* note 28; S.C. Res. 881, *supra* note 28; S.C. Res. 896, *supra* note 111; S.C. Res. 906, U.N. Doc. S/RES/906 (Mar. 25, 1994); S.C. Res. 937, U.N. Doc. S/RES/937 (July 21, 1994); S.C. Res. 1311, *supra* note 28; *cf.* S.C. Res. 858, *supra*, and S.C. Res. 881, *supra* note 28 (contain a finding that the situation amounts to a threat to international peace and security). Iraq (Kurds): S.C. Res. 688, U.N. Doc. S/RES/688 (Apr. 5, 1991) (not passed under Chapter VII but did refer to the demand of Iraq contributing to removing the threat to international peace and security in the region). Rwanda: S.C. Res. 912, *supra* note 29 (demanded cessation of hostilities without Chapter VII). *See also* S.C. Res. 918, *supra* note 29; S.C. Res. 925, *supra* note 29, although in S.C. Res. 918, *supra* note 29, ¶ 13, the Council determined that the situation amounted to a threat to international peace and security and imposed an arms embargo under Chapter VII. Sierra Leone: S.C. Res. 1132, *supra* note 29 (acting under Chapter VII demanded that the junta step down). *See* S.C. Res. 837, *supra* note 111; S.C. Res. 886, *supra* note 73; S.C. Res. 897, *supra* note 111 (the demands and calls were formulated as acting under Chapter VII); *but see* S.C. Res. 1260, *supra* note 73; S.C. Res. 1270, *supra* note 73; S.C. Res. 1289, *supra* note 111 (these remaining calls and demands were not passed under Chapter VII). Somalia: S.C. Res. 751, *supra* note 73; S.C. Res. 767, *supra* note 73; S.C. Res. 794, U.N. Doc. S/RES/794 (Dec. 3, 1992).

ical solution to the situation."[195] In addition, a further statement was made, also under Chapter VII, that all parties are to pursue their goals by peaceful means only.[196]

Demands that parties renounce the recourse to force have also been passed under Chapter VII. For instance, the Council demanded that the FRY "put an immediate and verifiable end to violence and repression in Kosovo,"[197] reaffirmed "its demand that all parties and others concerned in Bosnia and Herzegovina stop the fighting immediately,"[198] and that "any taking of territory by force cease immediately."[199] Similarly, following the military coup in Sierra Leone, it explicitly demanded, under Chapter VII, the reinstatement of the democratically elected government.[200] Overall, it can be seen that a large proportion of the resolutions are formulated as binding on the parties to the conflict, both through mandatory formulation and pursuant to Chapter VII.

c. Conclusion

It is clear that in the last decade and a half it has become routine, once the conflict has been placed on the Security Council agenda, for the Council to condemn the recourse to force and call on the parties to stop fighting and resolve the conflict by peaceful means. The explicit rejection of force to resolve conflict has been a central aspect of the Council practice in relation to many conflicts. Increasingly, the Council has emphasized that it rejects recourse to force to achieve a political outcome. The practice can be seen to evolve from the early Balkan practice to that in Kosovo, Macedonia, Liberia, and Côte d'Ivoire. In the latest of those conflicts, the Council has adopted an explicit principle rejecting recourse to force for political means.

The Council has condemned extreme political violence in the form of civil conflicts or coups d'état in practically all cases since the 1990s, and its formulation indicates that it intends its demands to renounce such force to be binding on the parties involved. The Council has not yet

---

195 S.C. Res. 1199, *supra* note 73, ¶ 4.

196 *Id.*, ¶ 6.

197 S.C. Res. 1244, *supra* note 73, ¶ 3.

198 S.C. Res. 770, *supra* note 194, ¶ 1.

199 S.C. Res. 824, *supra* note 194, ¶ 2.

200 S.C. Res. 1132, *supra* note 29.

formulated a universal principle, however, and the analysis in favor of the emergence of such a principle relies on accumulating practice of condemnation and demands that such conduct stop.

Even if these principles are initially formulated as mere policy, over time, their repetition by states in Council debates (as well as outside of the Council), and in later resolutions, may suggest that a consensus is forming around a particular proposition. A large volume of similar practice is difficult to account for unless the policy of the Council is informed by a common understanding of the way in which the parties should behave.

This practice evidences the emergence, at least, of an international policy principle, and the binding nature of the resolutions and determination of the Council to have them enforced foreshadows the emergence of a binding norm within the practice of the Council of the type discussed in Chapter 2. The fact that the Council has condemned the recourse to force and called for the end of such conduct, irrespective of the type of conflict or what led to it, suggests that a general principle may emerge by force of repetition and precedent. It remains to be seen how this practice impacts on the emergence of a general rule of customary international law.

2. Rejecting Political Violence Against a Democratically Elected Government

One distinct sub-set of the practice consists of the Council's reaction to political violence against democratically elected governments. This practice shows a high level of consistency in the Council's explicit rejection of such political violence.

a. *Overview of the Practice*

The Security Council has supported democratic governments threatened by such violence, although this has not always led to immediate or forceful action.[201] Its practice in Haiti and Sierra Leone is particularly relevant. Following the coup in Haiti that overturned newly elected President Jean-Bertrand Aristide, the Council intervened, in 1993, reaffirming that the international community was committed to resolving the crisis in Haiti and restoring democracy.[202] It underlined the importance

---

201 Note that these conflicts and the practice of the international community, including regional actors and states, are considered in more depth in Chapter 4.

202 S.C. Res. 862, U.N. Doc. S/RES/862 (Aug. 31, 1993).

of democratic issues[203] and deplored that the legitimate government had not been reinstated.[204] It imposed an embargo aimed at resolving the crisis via a "comprehensive and peaceful settlement" and bringing about the reinstatement of the legitimate government.[205] When the Governors Island Agreement, which provided for Aristide's return to power, was breached, the United States led the U.N.-sanctioned "Operation Uphold Democracy," under Chapter VII, to overturn the military coup. The operation aimed to bring to an end the "illegal de facto regime" in Haiti and assure the return of its "legitimately elected President." Its explicit aim was to "facilitate the departure from Haiti of the military leadership."[206]

Even more strikingly, in Sierra Leone the Council condemned the military coup outright[207] and condemned the junta preventing the restoration of the democratically elected government.[208] It repeatedly demanded, under Chapter VII, that "the military junta take immediate steps to relinquish power and make way for the restoration of the democratically-elected Government and a return to constitutional order"[209] and went on to condemn, repeatedly, the resistance of the junta to the authority of the government.[210] These statements were followed by measures seeking to enforce them.[211]

---

203 S.C. Res. 1048, U.N. Doc. S/RES/1048 (Feb. 19, 1996).

204 S.C. Res. 841, U.N. Doc. S/RES/841 (June 16, 1993).

205 *Id.*

206 S.C. Res. 940, U.N. Doc. S/RES/940 (July 31, 1994). "*Determines* that the illegal de facto regime in Haiti has failed to comply with the Governors Island Agreement and is in breach of its obligations under the relevant resolutions of the Security Council." *Id.*, ¶ 3. "*Acting* under Chapter VII of the Charter of the United Nations, *authorizes* Member States to form a multinational force under unified command and control and, in this framework, to use all necessary means to facilitate the departure from Haiti of the military leadership, consistent with the Governors Island Agreement, the prompt return of the legitimately elected President and the restoration of the legitimate authorities of the Government of Haiti, and to establish and maintain a secure and stable environment that will permit implementation of the Governors Island Agreement." *Id.*, ¶ 4

207 S.C. Res. 1132, *supra* note 29.

208 *Id.*

209 *Id.*, ¶ 1, acting under Chapter VII.

210 S.C. Res. 1181, *supra* note 73, ¶ 1.

211 The Council imposed travel embargoes on the junta and prohibited the supply to Sierra Leone of petrol and arms. S.C. Res. 1132, *supra* note 29. Later, it modified

The use of sanctions was aimed at forcing the junta to relinquish power and make way for democratic government.[212] During the Council debate, Kenya asserted: "Africa was saying, and the international community was supporting the clear statement, that military coups overthrowing democratically elected Governments were no longer going to be accepted."[213] The United Kingdom concurred, claiming, "The international community cannot afford to acquiesce in the arbitrary and unconstitutional overthrow of a democratic Government."[214] Egypt referred to a "new, unanimous African position regarding military coups in the countries of the continent."[215] Ultimately, the Council authorized a peace-keeping force under Chapter VII, which can be considered to have intended to assist the democratic government maintain control and prevent a new uprising of the rebel forces.[216]

Other less clear-cut examples also support a trend rejecting the violent overthrow of democracy. In Burundi, the Council strongly condemned the "overthrow of the legitimate government and constitutional order in Burundi"[217] but did not take enforcement action. In Guinea Bissau, it expressed its grave concern when an army uprising and failed coup triggered a civil conflict[218] and welcomed the sending of troops by the Economic Community of West African States (ECOWAS) in response to the coup in 1999.[219] In Congo (Brazzaville) in 1997, the Council did

---

the embargo so that it only applied to the rebels and not to the Sierra Leone government or to ECOMOG. S.C. Res. 1171, *supra* note 73.

212 S.C. Res. 1132, *supra* note 29. *See also* President of the Security Council, Statement, U.N. Doc. S/PRST/1997/42 (Aug. 6, 1997).

213 SC 3822d mtg., U.N. Doc. S/PV.3822 (Oct. 8, 1997).

214 *Id.*

215 Similar statements supporting the protection of democratic regimes were made by all members of the Security Council except China, which supported the resolution but limited its statement to a more ambiguous comment: "Like other Council members, the Chinese delegation is concerned at the changes in the situation in Sierra Leone and feels deep sympathy for the sufferings experienced by the people of that country." *Id.*

216 Particularly in light of the Council's repeated calls on the rebels to step down, disarm and demobilize. S.C. Res. 1270, *supra* note 73, ¶ 8. It further authorized the use force to protect civilians. S.C. Res. 1270, *supra* note 73, ¶ 14; S.C. Res. 1289, *supra* note 111, ¶ 10.

217 S.C. Res. 1072, *supra* note 29, ¶ 1.

218 S.C. Res. 1216, *supra* note 78.

219 S.C. Res. 1233, U.N. Doc. S/RES/1233 (April, 6 1999).

not explicitly condemn the coup but rather expressed concern at the fighting and called on the parties to halt the violence.[220] In the Central African Republic, the Council was explicit in its condemnation when rebel forces within the military again attempted an unsuccessful coup in 2001, although it practically did not respond to the 1996 coup.[221] Similarly in Côte d'Ivoire, the first coup in 1999 elicited little response, but the attempt in 2002 was condemned in clear terms.[222]

In this as well, the Council practice does not point entirely in one direction. It is of course true that the Council has failed to intervene in a number of instances where military forces have overthrown democratic regimes. In Fiji, the Security Council did not intervene following the military coup in May 2000, which overthrew the democratic government elected in 1999. Nor did it intervene in Gambia, despite a coup in 1981, following weeks of violence, and another coup in 1994. In Chad, the Council has barely responded to the conflict, even after the start of the rebellion against the democratic government in 1998, other than with a statement in 1982, "taking note" of the decision of the Organization for African Unity (OAU) to establish a peace-keeping force to maintain peace and security in Chad.[223]

The most recent practice in Haiti is also worth noting, as it could be interpreted as undermining the earlier supporting practice. When a new uprising jeopardized Haiti's stability in March 2004, the international community did not support President Aristide. However, it should be acknowledged that President Aristide's government was by then mired in controversy following the tainted 2002 parliamentary elections, and it had been facing increasingly vocal opposition to the extent that no parliamentary elections had been held, and the parliament's mandate had expired. Accordingly, it may be argued that the president no longer represented a legitimately elected government. Nonetheless, many states in the region criticized the international pressure on Aristide and upheld the general principle that "[t]he unconstitutional removal of any leader

---

[220] President of the Security Council, Statement, *supra* note 30.

[221] President of the Security Council, *The Situation in the Central African Republic*, Statement, *supra* note 29.

[222] The Council condemned the "attempt to seize power by force of arms or to overthrow the democratically elected Government." Press Release, President of Security Council, *Security Council Condemns Attempts*, *supra* note 178.

[223] S.C. Res. 504, U.N. Doc. S/RES/504 (Apr. 30, 1982).

cannot be condoned," as the president of the Caribbean Community and Common Market, Jamaican Prime Minister Patterson, maintained.[224]

Burma is another case that is often cited as contradicting the emergence of a principle rejecting recourse to force against democratically elected governments, as the Council did not intervene to protect the fledging democracy from military suppression following the elections in 1990. Nonetheless, even in that case, there has been vocal denunciation and condemnation of the coup. In particular, the reimprisonment, in May 2003, of the pro-democracy leader, Aung San Suu Kyi, attracted widespread international condemnation. Both the United States and the European Union imposed sanctions,[225] and the Secretary-General expressed his grave concern and called for her release.[226] Even the Association of Southeast Asian Nations (ASEAN), which has a strong tradition of non-intervention, called for her release.[227] Some of its members argued that ASEAN should threaten Burma with expulsion if it did not release the pro-democracy leader.[228]

However, the interaction of law and politics in the international context affects the assessment of this practice. Few international law norms are consistently enforced, and the absence of enforcement is one of the structural weaknesses of international law. Thus, while attempts at enforcement are striking and suggest that the norm is considered of particular importance by the international community, the reverse is not necessarily true. A failure to act to enforce a particular rule does not strongly contradict the existence of that norm.

---

224 Carribean Net News, *Aristide Departure Is a 'Dangerous Precedent': CARICOM President* (March 4, 2004), *at* http://www.caribbeannetnews.com/2004/03/04/aristide.htm.

225 BBC, *US Approves Burma Sanctions* (July 16, 2003), *at* http://news.bbc.co.uk/2/hi/asia-pacific/3069841.stm.

226 BBC, *Burma Under Further Pressure* (July 17, 2003), *at* http://news.bbc.co.uk/2/hi/asia-pacific/3073357.stm.

227 BBC, *Burma Told to Release Suu Kyi* (July 24, 2003), *at* http://news.bbc.co.uk/2/hi/asia-pacific/3091941.stm.

228 *Id. See* comments by Malaysian Prime Minister Mahathir Mohamad, and Thai Foreign Minister Surakiart Sathirathai stating his country had drawn up a "roadmap" for establishing a democracy in Burma.

b. Analysis

Strong and repeated condemnation by the Council of rebels' attempts to overthrow a democratically elected government by violence is evidence of an emerging consensus among the Council members rejecting such use of violence and hence a principle of international policy. It is clear that the Council leads and shapes general international policy. The Council practice affects what is being condemned, rejected, and prohibited in the international community. The imposition of sanctions and binding resolutions forces individual states to change their behavior, as well as changes long-term expectations. The Council power is reinforced by the fact that its permanent members are the most powerful economic and military states. Political reality dictates that decisions are usually only taken when the majority of the General Assembly states support them—despite the limited number that officially makes the decision—and they are actually representative of a widely accepted position.

In this case, the analysis relies on the explicit and universal formulation of a principle in two prominent cases, but it is also supported by more general practice. In both Haiti and Sierra Leone, the Council rejected the coup in a robust and clear fashion. It formulated its rationale for doing so explicitly, it demanded in a binding resolution that the junta step down and reinstate the democratic government, and it sought to enforce its demands through sanctions.

Whether the Council intends to *prohibit* conduct must depend on whether it intends simply to resolve a particular threat to international peace and security or to formulate a prohibition of more general application. The initial formulation of the rule in Haiti suggested a response to an exceptional situation rather than a general rule. The Council initially emphasized that these were "unique and exceptional circumstances" when authorizing the use of force to reinstate the democratic government.[229] However, in Sierra Leone, the same rule was relied upon to justify that intervention, and there was no reference to exceptional situations.[230] This suggests that the Council now considers the prohibition to apply in a generic fashion rather than only in one particular factual situation. The Council has also repeatedly condemned coups in Burundi, Guinea Bissau, Congo (Brazzaville), Central African Republic, and Côte

---

229 S.C. Res. 841, *supra* note 204.

230 S.C. Res. 1132, *supra* note 29; S.C. Res. 1171, *supra* note 73; S.C. Res. 1181, *supra* note 73.

d'Ivoire. This repeated condemnation of conduct, and repeated demands on the parties that they behave in a certain way, must create an expectation that such conduct will continue to be condemned in the future.

This accords with the explicit formulation by the Secretary-General in 1997 that it is "an established norm" that "military coups against the democratically elected Governments by self-appointed juntas are not acceptable."[231] This statement was uncontroversial at the time it was formulated. Tying this practice back to the general debate surrounding a notion of democratic entitlement, some commentators have commented in passing that "while it might not yet be possible to identify a general obligation on States to introduce democratic government,"[232] a "forcible repudiation of the democratically expressed will of the people, the clearest manifestation of the exercise of the right to internal self-determina-

---

231 The Secretary-General, *Annual Report of the Secretary-General on the Work of the Organization*, U.N. Doc. A/52/1, ¶ 37 (Sept. 3, 1997).

232 Steven Wheatley, *Democracy in International Law: A European Perspective*, 51 INT'L & COMP. L.Q. 225, 234 (2002). *See also* the International Conferences on New or Restored Democracies in 1988, 1994, and 1997. The Secretary-General, *An Agenda for Democratization, delivered to the General Assembly*, U.N. Doc. A/51/761 (Dec. 20, 1996); Press Release, Secretary-General, Secretary-General Stresses Need for Niger's Return to Democracy and Rule of Law, U.N. Doc. SG/SM/5889 (Feb. 2, 1996); Enhancing the Effectiveness of the Principle of Periodic and Genuine Elections, G.A. Res. 48/131, U.N. Doc. A/RES/48/131 (Feb. 15, 1994); Electoral Assistance Division of the Department of Peace-Keeping Operations of the Secretariat and Department for Development Support and Management Services and Non-Governmental Organisations Colloquium on African Election Administration (Zimbabwe, 1994); Strengthening the Role of the United Nations in Enhancing the Effectiveness of the Principle of Periodic and Genuine Elections and the Promotion of Democratization, G.A. Res. 49/190, U.N. Doc. A/RES/49/190 (Mar. 9, 1995); Strengthening the Role of the United Nations in Enhancing the Effectiveness of the Principle of Periodic and Genuine Elections and the Promotion of Democratization, G.A. Res. 50/185, U.N. Doc. A/RES/50/185 (Mar. 6, 1996); The Secretary-General, *Report of the Secretary-General on Support by the United Nations System of the Efforts of Governments to Promote and Consolidate New or Restored Democracies*, U.N. Doc. A/51/512 (Oct. 18, 1996); The Secretary-General, *Report of the Secretary-General on Support by the UN System of the Efforts of Governments to Promote and Consolidate New or Restored Democracies*, U.N. Doc. A/52/513 (Oct. 21, 1997); The Secretary-General, *Report of the Secretary-General on Human Rights Questions: Enhancing the Effectiveness of the Principle of Periodic and Genuine Elections*, U.N. Doc. A/49/675 (Nov. 17, 1994); The Secretary-General, *Report of the Secretary-General on Human Rights Questions: Enhancing the Effectiveness of the Principle of Periodic and Genuine Elections*, U.N. Doc. A/50/736 (Nov. 8, 1995); The Secretary-General, *Human Rights Questions: Enhancing the Effectiveness of the Principle of Periodic and Genuine Elections*, U.N. Doc. A/52/474 (Oct. 16, 1997).

tion, will not be accepted."[233] Nonetheless, this would support the distinction between a right to democratic governance and a prohibition against the forceful overthrow of a democratic government.

In addition, the Council resolutions were not merely policy recommendations: they were formulated as being binding and were followed by sanctions or military intervention aimed at enforcing them.

In this case, it seems that through the formulation, seriousness, frequent repetition in different instances, and enforcement measures under Chapter VII, the Council can be considered to have created a quasi-legislative prohibition on violence against a democratic government conduct. This effect derives from the Council's ability to enforce its decisions and an informal precedent system within the Council. While such prohibitions are difficult to characterize under international law, they have substantial *de facto* impact.

A resolution by the Council condemning conduct must be taken seriously. The Council is the primary decision-making body responsible for international peace and security, and a failure to comply with its decisions may cause a state to become an international pariah and face sanctions or forceful intervention. While the conduct censured need not be illegal under international law, it does in practice become prohibited by the Council, which will in turn affect international opinion of the legality of the conduct.

3. An Obligation to Resolve Conflicts Peacefully?

a. *Overview of the Practice*

The Security Council has explicitly supported undertakings by parties not to use force. In Angola, the Council welcomed the Angolan government's continued disposition to reach a peaceful settlement of the conflict in conformity with the peace accords.[234] The Council highlighted the Central African Republic[235] president's commitment "to maintain

---

[233] Wheatley, *supra* note 232, at 233.

[234] S.C. Res. 864, *supra* note 115, ¶¶ 4–5.

[235] The first of two military coups against the civilian government in the Central African Republic took place in 1996. African countries mediated a truce resulting in the signature of the Bangui Agreements in 1997, which set up an inter-African force in the Central African Republic (MISAB). The second, which is relevant here, took place in May 2001 but was unsuccessful and sparked an ongoing disruption in the country.

peace in the Central African Republic through *dialogue and consultation.*"[236] In Kosovo, it noted "the clear commitment of senior representatives of the Kosovar Albanian community to non-violence."[237] In Guinea-Bissau, the Council supported both the junta and president's undertaking "never again to resort to arms."[238] Similarly, in Georgia, it welcomed the "commitment of the parties not to use force for the resolution of any disputed questions."[239] In the Former Yugoslav Republic of Macedonia, the Council supported the efforts of the government "to end the violence in a manner consistent with the rule of law"[240] and welcomed "the efforts of the Government of Albania to promote peace in the region and isolate extremists working against peace."[241]

The Council has emphasized the importance of peaceful resolution of disputes. In Afghanistan, it stressed the willingness of states "to facilitate the negotiations aimed at political settlement of the conflict." Moreover, it expressly stated that "the Afghan crisis can be settled only by peaceful means."[242] In the former Yugoslavia, it emphasized the "overwhelming importance of seeking, on the basis of the relevant resolutions of the Council, comprehensive political solutions to the conflicts in the territory of the former Yugoslavia."[243] It also affirmed "its commitment to a negotiated settlement of the conflict."[244] In the Former Yugoslav Republic of Macedonia, the Council underlined "the need for all differences to be resolved by dialogue."[245] Similarly, in Croatia, the Council stressed "the imperative need to find an urgent negotiated political solution."[246] Ultimately, it stated that its general policy was a commitment to

---

236 President of the Security Council, Statement, U.N. Doc. S/PRST/1999/7 (Feb. 18, 1999) (emphasis added).

237 S.C. Res. 1160, *supra* note 54, pmbl.

238 S.C. Res. 1233, *supra* note 219.

239 S.C. Res. 1311, *supra* note 28.

240 S.C. Res. 1345, *supra* note 63, ¶ 5.

241 *Id.*, ¶ 8.

242 S.C. Res. 1193, *supra* note 28, ¶ 1; S.C. Res. 1076, *supra* note 28, ¶ 1.

243 S.C. Res. 847, pmbl., U.N. Doc. S/RES/847 (June 30, 1993).

244 S.C. Res. 943, pmbl., U.N. Doc. S/RES/943 (Sept. 23, 1994); S.C. Res. 1022, *supra* note 137, pmbl.; S.C. Res. 1031, *supra* note 140.

245 S.C. Res. 1345, *supra* note 63, ¶ 6.

246 S.C. Res. 764, *supra* note 194, pmbl., ¶ 8.

"an overall negotiated settlement of the conflicts."[247] Other examples of similar practice include statements that parties must resolve their differences through political dialogue in Kosovo, Georgia, Lebanon, Rwanda, and Sierra Leone[248] or by national reconciliation in East Timor, Congo (Brazzaville), and the Central African Republic.[249] The Councl has stated that the seeking of "comprehensive political solutions" is of "overwhelming importance" in the former Yugoslavia, Croatia, Cyprus, and Liberia.[250] In the DRC, it has stated that it is determined to promote the peace process at the national level.[251] These statements are the equivalent of expressions of concern in that they are not binding or coercive. Nonetheless, they do highlight the policy perspective that underlies the practice.

The Council has also adopted more explicit demands that parties adopt peaceful measures. It has directly called on parties to find a negotiated political solution to the conflict. In Kosovo, it called upon the FRY, under Chapter VII, "immediately to take the further necessary steps to achieve a political solution to the issue of Kosovo through dialogue."[252] In Liberia, the Council called on the government and the rebels, under Chapter VII, "to enter without delay into bilateral ceasefire negotiations."[253] In Côte d'Ivoire, it called on the parties "to resolve the current crisis peacefully and to abstain from any actions or statements or demonstration that might jeopardize or otherwise hamper the search for a negotiated solution."[254] Similarly, in the DRC, the Council reaffirmed its

---

247 S.C. Res. 994, *supra* note 52, pmbl. *See also* S.C. Res. 981, *supra* note 51.

248 Afghanistan: S.C. Res. 1076, *supra* note 28, pmbl. Kosovo: S.C. Res. 1160, *supra* note 54, ¶ 1. *See also* S.C. Res. 1199, *supra* note 73, ¶¶ 3–4. Lebanon: S.C. Res. 542, *supra* note 80, ¶¶ 3–4. Georgia: S.C. Res. 849, *supra* note 111; S.C. Res. 896, *supra* note 111; S.C. Res. 906, *supra* note 194, ¶ 4; S.C. Res. 937, *supra* note 194, ¶ 2; S.C. Res. 1311, *supra* note 28. Rwanda: S.C. Res. 1078, ¶ 2, U.N. Doc. S/RES/1078 (Nov. 9, 1996). Sierra Leone: S.C. Res. 1162, ¶ 3, U.N. Doc. S/RES/1162 (Apr. 17, 1998).

249 Central African Republic: S.C. Res. 1271, U.N. Doc. S/RES/1271 (Oct. 22, 1999). East Timor: S.C. Res. 1264, *supra* note 29, pmbl. Congo (Brazzaville): President of the Security Council, Statement, *supra* note 73.

250 Former Yugoslavia: S.C. Res. 847, *supra* note 243, pmbl. Croatia: S.C. Res. 764, *supra* note 194, pmbl., ¶ 8. Cyprus: S.C. Res. 367, U.N. Doc. S/RES/367 (Mar. 12, 1975), ¶ 2. Liberia: S.C. Res. 788, *supra* note 135.

251 S.C. Res. 1484, *supra* note 73.

252 S.C. Res. 1160, *supra* note 54, ¶ 1. *See also* S.C. Res. 1199, *supra* note 73, ¶¶ 3–4.

253 S.C. Res. 1478, ¶ 5, U.N. Doc. S/RES/1478(May 6, 2003).

254 Press Release, President of Security Council, *Security Council Condemns Attempts*, *supra* note 178.

readiness to consider active involvement "to assist in the implementation of an effective ceasefire agreement and in an agreed process for political settlement of the conflict."[255] In Afghanistan, the Council urged "all Afghan parties to resolve their differences through peaceful means and achieve national reconciliation through political dialogue."[256] It has frequently called on parties to engage in negotiations and seek a political settlement.[257]

The Council has also called for the use of democratic elections as an alternative to violence to produce a "just and durable settlement"[258] and for the resolution of conflict through a peace agreement or a cease-fire agreement. For instance, in Croatia, acting under Chapter VII, it called for an "immediate cease-fire agreement."[259] In the FRY, it went so far as to take action to give the parties incentive to enter into a peace agreement, resolving to lift the sanctions imposed on the FRY if the it signed the Dayton Peace Agreement.[260]

Finally, in some instances, the Council has gone so far as to take measures seeking to enforce peaceful means of resolution. In the former Yugoslavia, it imposed a complete arms embargo on all parties for the purpose of establishing peace and stability.[261] Further trade sanctions were passed to ensure that parties abide by its resolutions, achieve a

---

255 S.C. Res. 1234, *supra* note 29, ¶ 15.

256 S.C. Res. 1076, *supra* note 28, pmbl.

257 Burundi: S.C. Res. 1049, *supra* note 28, ¶¶ 3–4. Georgia: S.C. Res. 849, *supra* note 111; S.C. Res. 896, *supra* note 111; S.C. Res. 906, *supra* note 194, ¶ 4; S.C. Res. 937, *supra* note 194, ¶ 2; S.C. Res. 1311, *supra* note 28. DRC: S.C. Res. 1078, *supra* note 248, ¶ 2. Congo (Brazzaville): President of the Security Council, Statement, *supra* note 73. Sierra Leone: S.C. Res. 1162, *supra* note 248, ¶ 3; S.C. Res. 1171, *supra* note 73. Côte d'Ivoire: Press Release, President of Security Council, *Security Council Condemns Attempts, supra* note 178.

258 Cambodia, S.C. Res. 745, pmbl., U.N. Doc. S/RES/745 (Feb. 28, 1995). Congo (Brazzaville): S.C. Res. 161, *supra* note 31; President of the Security Council, Statement, *supra* note 73. Mozambique: S.C. Res. 957, ¶ 3, U.N. Doc. S/RES/957 (Nov. 15, 1994). Central African Republic: S.C. Res. 1159, U.N. Doc. S/RES/1159 (Mar. 27, 1998). In adopting the 1989 resolution on Central America, the Security Council recognized and gave support to the process of democratization and reconciliation as the method for establishing firm and lasting peace in Central America, S.C. Res. 637, U.N. Doc. S/RES/637 (July 27, 1989).

259 S.C. Res. 871, *supra* note 182.

260 S.C. Res. 1022, *supra* note 137, ¶ 1.

261 S.C. Res. 713, *supra* note 37, ¶ 6.

peaceful solution, and support the efforts of the European Community to resolve the conflict through peaceful means.[262] The preamble to the resolution explained that the Council was "[d]etermined in this context to adopt certain measures with the sole objective of achieving a peaceful solution and encouraging the efforts undertaken by the European Community and its member States." Ultimately, it deployed a U.N. peacekeeping force to "create conditions of peace and security required for an . . . overall settlement of the Yugoslav crisis."[263]

b. Analysis

In addition, there is extensive Security Council practice demanding or supporting peaceful resolution of conflict. In the same way that the prohibition on recourse to force in the international context is strengthened by the corollary obligation to settle conflicts through peaceful measures under Chapter VI of the U.N. Charter, the practice supporting peaceful resolution of civil conflicts and demanding that such resolution should be non-violent supports the emergence of a norm prohibiting recourse to force for political aims in civil conflict.

The extensive Council practice demanding or supporting peaceful resolution of conflict ranges from formulations that suggest a strong policy preference, to formulations that suggest a binding obligation. For instance, in calling on parties to settle their differences by peaceful means in Afghanistan, the Council urged "all Afghan parties to resolve their differences through peaceful means and achieve national reconciliation through political dialogue,"[264] and it expressly stated that "the Afghan crisis can be settled only by peaceful means."[265] It has also welcomed the express commitments of parties to seek a peaceful resolution, such as the commitment of the Central African Republic president "to maintain peace in the Central African Republic through dialogue and consultation"[266] and the Angolan government's continued disposition to reach a peaceful settlement of the conflict in conformity with the peace

---

[262] S.C. Res. 757, *supra* note 144, pmbl.

[263] S.C. Res. 743, U.N. Doc. S/RES/743, ¶ 5 (Feb. 21, 1992). This decision followed a finding that the situation continued to present a threat to international peace and security.

[264] S.C. Res. 1076, *supra* note 28, pmbl.

[265] S.C. Res. 1193, *supra* note 28, ¶ 1; S.C. Res. 1076, *supra* note 28, ¶ 1.

[266] President of the Security Council, Statement, *supra* note 236.

accords.[267] It stated that parties must resolve their differences through political dialogue in Georgia, Lebanon, Rwanda, and Sierra Leone[268] or by national reconciliation in East Timor, Congo (Brazzaville), and the Central African Republic.[269]

Other formulations suggest that the Council increasingly considers the principle to be a binding obligation. In the Balkans, even before the Dayton Peace Accord,[270] the Council repeatedly upheld the principle of peaceful resolution of the conflicts. While it formulated its demands as arising from the Declaration of the European Community or individual peace agreements,[271] the Council did explicitly adopt the principles and attempt to enforce them under Chapter VII.

In recent practice, the Council has explicitly declared its commitment to "an overall negotiated settlement of the conflicts."[272] In Croatia, this was expressed as an "imperative need to find an urgent negotiated political solution."[273] It also called upon the government and the local Serb authorities "to refrain from the threat or use of force and to reaffirm their commitment to a peaceful resolution of their differences"[274] and backed up these demands by a statement, under Chapter VII, that parties were to comply or face coercive enforcement.[275]

---

267 S.C. Res. 864, *supra* note 115, ¶¶ 4–5.

268 Afghanistan: S.C. Res. 1076, *supra* note 28, pmbl. Kosovo: S.C. Res. 1160, *supra* note 54, ¶ 1. *See also* S.C. Res. 1199, *supra* note 73, ¶¶ 3–4. Lebanon: S.C. Res. 542, *supra* note 80, ¶¶ 3–4. Georgia: S.C. Res. 849, *supra* note 111; S.C. Res. 896, *supra* note 111; S.C. Res. 906, *supra* note 194, ¶ 4; S.C. Res. 937, *supra* note 194, ¶ 2; S.C. Res. 1311, *supra* note 28. Rwanda: S.C. Res. 1078, *supra* note 248, ¶ 2. Sierra Leone: S.C. Res. 1231, *supra* note 261, ¶ 3.

269 Central African Republic: S.C. Res. 1271, *supra* note 249. East Timor: S.C. Res. 1264, *supra* note 29, pmbl. Congo (Brazzaville): President of the Security Council, Statement, *supra* note 73.

270 Dayton Peace Accords, *supra* note 138.

271 *See* discussion of this practice in Chapter 2.

272 S.C. Res. 994, *supra* note 52, pmbl. *See also* S.C. Res. 981, *supra* note 51.

273 S.C. Res. 764, *supra* note 194, pmbl, ¶ 8.

274 S.C. Res. 981, *supra* note 51, ¶ 8.

275 *See* S.C. Res. 994, *supra* note 52, ¶ 10: "Demands that the parties refrain from taking any further military measures or actions that could lead to the escalation of the situation and warns that in the event of failure to comply with this demand it will consider further steps needed to ensure such compliance."

In Kosovo, similarly, the Council called upon the FRY, under Chapter VII, "immediately to take the further necessary steps to achieve a political solution to the issue of Kosovo through dialogue."[276] It emphasized that "all elements in the Kosovar Albanian community should pursue their goals by peaceful means only"[277] and underlined that "the way to defeat violence and terrorism in Kosovo is for the authorities in Belgrade to offer the Kosovar Albanian community a genuine political process."[278] The Council also called on the president of the FRY to implement his commitment to resolve the problems by political means and also insisted that the KLA "should pursue their goals by peaceful means only." It went on to impose an arms embargo "for the purposes of fostering peace and stability in Kosovo."[279] In the later Resolution 1203, adopted after the cease-fire agreement, it demanded compliance by both the KLA and the FRY with Resolutions 1160 and 1199, under Chapter VII.[280]

In 2001, in the Former Yugoslav Republic of Macedonia, the Council stressed "the need for all differences to be resolved by dialogue among all legitimate parties"[281] and called on all political leaders "publicly to condemn violence and ethnic intolerance and to use their influence to secure peace."[282] Similarly, in 2002, in Côte d'Ivoire, the Council called on the parties "to resolve the current crisis peacefully and to abstain from any actions or statements or demonstration that might jeopardize or otherwise hamper the search for a negotiated solution." It also emphasized that "only through a political solution can the crisis be solved."[283] In 2003, in Liberia, it called on the governments and rebels, under Chapter VII, "to enter without delay into bilateral ceasefire negotiations under the auspices of ECOWAS and the mediation of former President Abubakar of Nigeria."[284]

---

[276] S.C. Res. 1160, *supra* note 54, ¶ 1. *See also* S.C. Res. 1199, *supra* note 73, ¶¶ 3–4.

[277] S.C. Res. 1160, *supra* note 54, ¶ 2.

[278] *Id.*, ¶ 3.

[279] *Id.*, ¶ 8.

[280] S.C. Res. 1203, *supra* note 60, ¶¶ 3–4.

[281] S.C. Res. 1345, *supra* note 63, ¶ 6.

[282] *Id.*, ¶ 9.

[283] Press Release, President of Security Council, *Security Council Condemns Attempts*, *supra* note 178.

[284] S.C. Res. 1478, *supra* note 253, ¶ 5.

Thus, although the Charter obligation to resolve conflicts peacefully does not *prima facie* apply to civil conflict, unsurprisingly, in practice, the resolution of civil conflicts through non-violent means is a primary policy goal. This practice provides important evidence of the normative and moral views of the international community on recourse to force in civil conflict. In addition, the repeated support for the principle and determination with which it has been declared to apply, as well as instances of such demands being made under Chapter VII, suggest that the international community is adopting an increasingly firm position that conflict must be resolved peacefully. This bolsters the trend of emerging practice that supports a general prohibition against recourse to force for political aims.

4. Rejecting Violence Against Civilians

A fourth aspect of the practice is the rejection of violence against civilians. The protection of civilians is a serious concern of the Security Council,[285] and the Council has strongly condemned breaches of the humanitarian laws of war[286] and of human rights.[287]

---

285 Bosnia and Herzegovina: S.C. Res. 820, *supra* note 110; S.C. Res. 836, U.N. Doc. S/RES/836 (June 4, 1993). Kosovo: S.C. Res. 1199, *supra* note 73, pmbl. Haiti: S.C. Res. 917, U.N. Doc. S/RES/917 (May 6, 1994). Congo (Brazzaville): President of the Security Council, Statement, *supra* note 73. Afghanistan: S.C. Res. 1076, *supra* note 28, pmbl.; S.C. Res. 1193, *supra* note 28 (refers to human suffering and refugees); S.C. Res. 1076, *supra* note 28, ¶ 6 (deplores the creation of a great number of refugees and displaced persons). Burundi: S.C. Res. 1012, U.N. Doc. S/RES/1012 (Aug. 28, 1995); S.C. Res. 1286, U.N. Doc. S/RES/1286 (Jan. 19, 2000). Armenia, President of the Security Council, *The Situation Relating to Nagorny Karabakh*, Statement, U.N. Doc. S/PRST/1995/21 (Apr. 26, 1995).

286 Afghanistan: S.C. Res. 1193, *supra* note 28; S.C. Res. 1214, *supra* note 28. Angola S.C. Res. 811, *supra* note 73; S.C. Res. 864, *supra* note 115. Former Yugoslavia: S.C. Res. 771, *supra* note 190; S.C. Res. 780, U.N. Doc. S/RES/780 (Oct. 6, 1992); S.C. Res. 1034, *supra* note 181. Croatia: S.C. Res. 1009, *supra* note 194; S.C. Res. 1019, U.N. Doc. S/RES/1019 (Nov. 9, 1995). Bosnia and Herzegovina: S.C. Res. 764, *supra* note 194; S.C. Res. 819, *supra* note 110; S.C. Res. 820, *supra* note 110. Cambodia: S.C. Res. 880, *supra* note 29. East Timor: S.C. Res. 1272, *supra* note 29. Georgia: S.C. Res. 993, U.N. Doc. S/RES/993 (May, 12 1995). Israel: S.C. Res. 446, U.N. Doc. S/RES/446 (Mar. 22, 1979). Liberia: S.C. Res. 788, *supra* note 135; S.C. Res. 1001, U.N. Doc. S/RES/1001 (June 30, 1995). Rwanda: S.C. Res. 812, U.N. Doc. S/RES/812 (Mar. 12, 1993); S.C. Res. 846, U.N. Doc. S/RES/846 (June 22, 1993); S.C. Res. 918, *supra* note 29. Sierra Leone: S.C. Res. 1181, *supra* note 73; S.C. Res. 1231, *supra* note 261; S.C. Res. 1289, *supra* note 111. Somalia: S.C. Res. 733, *supra* note 73; S.C. Res. 794, *supra* note 194.

287 *See* East Timor, S.C. Res. 1272, *supra* note 29. In Côte d'Ivoire, it called on all parties to respect human rights "in particular with respect to civilian populations":

The protection of civilians from violence is a cardinal aspect of humanitarian law, and despite the minimal proportion of *jus in bello* treaty law applicable to civil conflicts, the prohibition on violence to life and person, murder, mutilation, and cruel treatment applies to all civil conflicts that are "armed conflicts not of an international character."[288] The applicability of the prohibition on violence against civilians in non-international conflicts has been reinforced by the decision in *Tadic*, where it was concluded that the protection of civilians from hostilities has emerged as a rule of customary law applicable in internal conflict.[289]

Massive violence against civilians has long been prohibited as a crime against humanity. This was established as early as 1915 in the declarations by the governments of France, the United Kingdom, and Russia, denouncing the massacre of Armenians taking place in Turkey, in which they

---

Press Release, President of Security Council, *Security Council Condemns Attempts, supra* note 178. In Afghanistan, it emphasized the importance of human rights standards, condemning the "discrimination against girls and women and other violations of human rights and international humanitarian law." S.C. Res. 1076, *supra* note 28, ¶ 11. *See* S.C. Res. 1193, *supra* note 28, pmbl.; S.C. Res. 1214, *supra* note 28, ¶ 12. In Croatia, it stated that full observance of human rights was essential to "the restoration of confidence between the parties and building durable peace." S.C. Res. 994, *supra* note 52, pmbl. In Kosovo, it listed as relevant the Universal Declaration of Human Rights, the international covenants and conventions on human rights, the Conventions and Protocol Relating to the Status of Refugees, the Geneva Conventions of 1949 and the Additional Protocols thereto of 1977. S.C. Res. 1239, U.N. Doc. S/RES/1239 (May 14, 1999).

[288] Common Article 3 of the Geneva Conventions, which applies to "armed conflict not of an international character," prohibits: "Violence to life and person, in particular murder of all kinds, mutilation, cruel treatment and torture; [t]aking of hostages; [o]utrages upon personal dignity, in particular humiliating and degrading treatment." Additional Protocol II, which applies to all non-international conflicts "which take place in the territory of a High Contracting Party between its armed forces and dissident armed forces or other organized armed groups which, under responsible command, exercise such control over a part of its territory as to enable them to carry out sustained and concerted military operations and to implement this Protocol." According to the Protocol, "The civilian population as such, as well as individual civilians, shall not be the object of attack. Acts or threats of violence the primary purpose of which is to spread terror among the civilian population are prohibited." Protocol Additional to the Geneva Conventions of 12 August 1949, Relating to the Protection of Victims of Non-International Armed Conflicts, art. 13, 16 I.L.M. 1442 (1977) [hereinafter Additional Protocol II].

[289] Prosecutor v. Tadic, Case No. IT-94-1-AR72, Appeal on Jurisdiction, para. 127 (Oct. 2, 1995) [hereinafter *Tadic*, Appeal on Jurisdiction]. *See* the discussion in Theodor Meron, *Editorial Comment: The Continuing Role of Custom in the Formation of International Humanitarian Law*, 90 AM. J. INT'L L. 238 (1996).

maintained that these were "crimes against humanity and civilization."[290] It is also reflected in the constitutive document of the African Union, which allows the Union to intervene in a member state "in respect of grave circumstances, namely war crimes, genocide and crimes against humanity."[291]

Before turning to the practice, the explicit restriction in Article 3 of Additional Protocol II to the Geneva Conventions must be addressed. Could this neutralize the impact of *jus in bello* on *jus ad bellum internum?* The provision states:

> Nothing in this Protocol shall be invoked for the purpose of affecting the sovereignty of a State or the responsibility of the government, by all legitimate means, to maintain or re-establish law and order in the State or to defend the national unity and territorial integrity of the State.
>
> Nothing in this Protocol shall be invoked as a justification for intervening, directly or indirectly, for any reason whatever, in the armed conflict or in the internal or external affairs of the High Contracting Party in the territory of which that conflict occurs.

However, this provision only supports the right to re-establish law and order by "by all legitimate" means. If particular means are determined to be illegitimate, this provision would not apply.

Early practice includes the arms embargo in South Africa, which was justified in response to the "large-scale killings of unarmed and peaceful demonstrators."[292] However, the practice in the former Yugoslavia is a

---

290 Egon Schwelb, *Crimes Against Humanity*, 23 BRIT. Y.B. INT'L L. 178 (1949). Interestingly, according to the trial chamber of the ICTY in *Tadic*, the "civilian population" in such crimes might include resistance movements. *Tadic*, Appeal on Jurisdiction, Case No. IT-94-1-AR72, ¶¶ 638–642. This view was also adopted in *Kupreskic*, where the tribunal stated that "the presence of those actively involved in the conflict should not prevent the characterization of a population as civilian and those actively involved in a resistance movement can qualify as victims of crimes against humanity." Prosecutor v. Kupreskic, Case No. IT-95-16-T, Judgment, para. 549 (Jan. 4, 2000).

291 Constitutive Act of the African Union, July 11, 2000, 2000 AFR. Y.B. INT'L L. 479, art. 4, *available at* http://www.au2002.gov.za/docs/key_oau/au_act.htm.

292 S.C. Res. 134, U.N. Doc. S/4300 (Apr. 1 1960), ¶¶ 2–3; S.C. Res. 181, ¶ 2, U.N. Doc. S/RES/181 (Aug. 7, 1963). The sanctions were imposed under Chapter VII in S.C. Res. 418, U.N. Doc. S/RES/418 (Nov. 4, 1977).

more typical example. The Council strongly condemned violence against civilians, both in its own right and as a breach of the humanitarian laws of war. It condemned the reports of "mass forcible expulsion and deportation of civilians, imprisonment and abuse of civilians in detention centres, deliberate attacks on non-combatants."[293] It also condemned, "in the strongest possible terms," the violations of international humanitarian law and of human rights by Bosnian Serb and paramilitary forces, especially the "summary executions, rape, mass expulsions, arbitrary detentions, forced labour and large-scale disappearances."[294] It determined that the Geneva Conventions must be abided by, at a minimum and maintained that all parties to the conflict were bound to comply with international humanitarian law.[295] Although ultimately shamefully unsuccessful, the creation of "safe areas" in the Balkans aimed to protect civilians with force if necessary.[296]

In Rwanda,[297] the peace-keeping force was sent to contribute to the security and protection of displaced persons and civilians.[298] The sanctions aimed to stop "the use of such arms and equipment in the massacres of innocent civilians."[299] In Sierra Leone, the arms and petrol embargo was imposed partly to stop the violence and loss of life.[300] Faced with the particularly brutal tactics of limb amputation of civilians, the Council also condemned the "atrocities perpetrated by the rebels on the

---

[293] S.C. Res. 771, *supra* note 190, pmbl.

[294] S.C. Res. 1034, *supra* note 181, ¶ 2.

[295] S.C. Res. 771, *supra* note 190, ¶ 3.

[296] This can be seen in Bosnia and Herzegovina where the Security Council first declared "safe areas" and authorized UNPROFOR to protect such areas from attack, including using force in the self-defense of these areas. S.C. Res. 836, *supra* note 285, ¶¶ 5, 9.

[297] The most recent civil conflict in Rwanda between the Tutsi and Hutus began in 1990. In 1993, a power-sharing agreement to end the civil war was signed, and a U.N. mission was sent to monitor the peace agreement. In April 1994, however, the presidents of Rwanda and Burundi were killed when their plane was shot down. The Rwandan Patriotic Front launched a major offensive, and extremist Hutu militia and parts of the army began a genocidal massacre of 800,000 Tutsis. When the massacre began, the Security Council was unable to contain the situation and largely withdrew its troops, although it did later reintervene.

[298] S.C. Res. 918, *supra* note 29.

[299] S.C. Res. 1011, U.N. Doc. S/RES/1011 (Aug. 16, 1995).

[300] S.C. Res. 1132, *supra* note 29.

civilian population," and urged the authorities to bring the perpetrators to justice.[301]

The aim of protecting civilians from violence can be seen directly in attempts to stop parties from killing civilians, and it is reinforced through efforts by the Council to ensure that the parties abide by humanitarian law, whose major tenets are the protection of civilians and the safeguarding of the provision of humanitarian assistance. In setting up the International Criminal Tribunals for the former Yugoslavia and Rwanda, the Council emphasized that it aimed to bring to justice those responsible for the "widespread and flagrant violations of international humanitarian law."[302] Conduct of ethnic cleansing has also been explicitly rejected.[303] In the former Yugoslavia, the Council held that "reports of mass killings" and continuance of the practice of "ethnic cleansing" amounted to a threat to international peace and security, justifying intervention under Chapter VII. Enforcement measures have been imposed with the direct aim of halting the deaths of civilians. The sanctions in Rwanda are one such example, aiming to stop "the use of such arms and equipment in the massacres of innocent civilians."[304] Another is the peace-keeping force sent to contribute to the security and protection of displaced persons and civilians.[305] The practice in Somalia emphasized the "heavy loss of human life."[306] The Security Council specified that "the international community is involved in Somalia in order to help the people of Somalia who have suffered untold miseries due to years of civil

---

301 S.C. Res. 1231, *supra* note 261, ¶ 3; S.C. Res. 1171, *supra* note 73.

302 *See* Rwanda, S.C. Res. 955, U.N. Doc. S/RES/955 (Nov. 8, 1994). *See also* the former Yugoslavia, S.C. Res. 808, U.N. Doc. S/RES/808 (May 5, 1993).

303 Croatia: S.C. Res. 779, U.N. Doc. S/RES/779 (Oct. 6, 1992), pmbl. (alarm at reports of ethnic cleansing). Bosnia and Herzegovina: S.C. Res. 752, *supra* note 46, ¶ 6; S.C. Res. 787, *supra* note 194, ¶ 2; S.C. Res. 820, *supra* note 110, ¶ 6. Georgia: S.C. Res. 876, *supra* note 28. Armenia: President of the Security Council, *The Situation Relating to Nagorny Karabakh*, Statement, *supra* note 285. Lebanon: S.C. Res. 436, *supra* note 29. *See also* S.C. Res. 490, *supra* note 29; S.C. Res. 512, *supra* note 29; S.C. Res. 542, *supra* note 80. Israel: S.C. Res. 605, U.N. Doc. S/RES/605 (Dec. 22, 1987). Georgia: S.C. Res. 876, *supra* note 28 and S.C. Res. 1036, U.N. Doc. S/RES/1036 (Jan. 12, 1996) (deep concern at the "human suffering caused by conflict in the region, and at reports of 'ethnic cleansing' and other serious violations of international humanitarian law"). Former Yugoslavia, S.C. Res. 771, *supra* note 190, pmbl.

304 S.C. Res. 1011, *supra* note 299.

305 S.C. Res. 918, *supra* note 29.

306 S.C. Res. 733, *supra* note 74.

strife in that country."[307] Moreover, in some instances, interventions have been used to secure the delivery of humanitarian assistance.[308]

It is axiomatic that massive violence against civilians is prohibited. The intertwined nature of the principles addressing civilians, humanitarian crises, and massive breaches of human rights renders this area somewhat difficult to analyze, and the international community often does not differentiate between different principles, when condemning actions, or intervening in civil conflict and imposing sanctions.

For instance, in Liberia, when the impact of the conflict on civilians became extreme, both in terms of direct civilian deaths from the conflict and in the form of a developing humanitarian crisis, the international community called on the parties to stop the fighting and negotiate a peaceful solution to the conflict. The Secretary-General called on the Council "to urgently authorise a peacekeeping force to prevent a major humanitarian tragedy and to stabilize the situation."[309] Even before the cease-fire was first brokered, the Council already expressed its concern at the "rapidly deteriorating security situation" and urged "all combatants in the strongest terms to immediately cease hostilities and agree to a ceasefire."[310]

Nonetheless, most of the rationales have been formulated in moral, not legal, terms—in statements such as, "Our collective interest and our

---

[307] S.C. Res. 837, *supra* note 111.

[308] An additional aspect of the practice to protect civilians has been the use of troops to secure the delivery of humanitarian assistance. In Albania, for instance, the protection force was specifically authorized to facilitate the safe and prompt delivery of humanitarian assistance and to help create a secure environment for the missions of international organizations. S.C. Res. 1101, *supra* note 29, ¶¶ 2–5. Similarly, in Somalia, one of the aims of UNOSOM was to protect the humanitarian relief workers. S.C. Res. 897, *supra* note 111. The force was authorized under Chapter VII and was empowered to use all necessary means to create a secure environment for humanitarian relief. S.C. Res. 794, *supra* note 194. The Council justified the mission on the basis that the provision of humanitarian assistance was an important element of its effort to restore peace and security in the region. S.C. Res. 751, *supra* note 73; S.C. Res. 794, *supra* note 194. In Rwanda, as well, UNAMIR was to provide support for and protect the humanitarian operations, as well as U.N. personnel. S.C. Res. 925, *supra* note 29; S.C. Res. 897, *supra* note 111.

[309] Letter from the Secretary-General to the President of the Security Council (June 28, 2003), U.N. Doc. S/2003/678.

[310] President of the Security Council, Statement on Liberia, U.N. Doc. SC/7787, AFR/644 (Nov. 6, 2003).

common humanity demand urgent and decisive action from the Council. We cannot be oblivious to the warning signs of an imminent possible catastrophe."[311] This is even though they ultimately led to a finding that the conflict in Liberia constituted a threat to international peace and security.

The Council decided to intervene in Liberia in light of the conflict's "effects on the humanitarian situation, including the tragic loss of countless innocent lives, in that country, and its destabilizing effect on the region."[312] It stressed "its utmost concern at the dire consequences of the prolonged conflict for the civilian population."[313] Germany maintained specifically that "the constant deaths of civilians were to be deplored and the Council must react swiftly." Chile also emphasized that "its priority was to save lives and to give an appropriate response to a humanitarian crisis that brooked no further delay."[314] This reinforces the perception that such violence has a practical impact. Massive violence against civilians is not merely a breach of *jus in bello* but can render the conflict a threat to international peace and security and justifies action to stop it.

In Sierra Leone, as well, the Council relied on widespread violence as one basis for its intervention aiming to end the conflict. When putting in place the sanctions regime, it emphasized the unacceptable violence and loss of life and the deteriorating humanitarian conditions.[315] Moreover, it authorized UNAMSIL under Chapter VII to take all necessary action to "protect civilians under imminent threat of physical violence."[316] The case of Somalia also supports such a principle. In that case the "heavy loss of human life"[317] was the key rationale leading to the intervention. The Council explained: "the international community is involved in Somalia in order to help the people of Somalia who have suffered untold miseries due to years of civil strife."[318] Resolution 794

---

311 Letter from the Secretary-General to the President of the Security Council, *supra* note 309.

312 S.C. Res. 1497, *supra* note 164, pmbl.

313 S.C. Res. 1509, *supra* note 113.

314 S.C. Res. 1497, *supra* note 164.

315 S.C. Res. 1132, *supra* note 29.

316 S.C. Res. 1270, *supra* note 73, ¶ 14; S.C. Res. 1289, *supra* note 111, ¶ 10.

317 S.C. Res. 733, *supra* note 73.

318 S.C. Res. 837, *supra* note 111.

referred to "the magnitude of the human tragedy caused by the conflict" and "the deterioration of the humanitarian situation."[319]

In the Former Yugoslav Republic of Macedonia, the Council explicitly recognized that the government was entitled to address the violence it was facing but that it should do so with "an appropriate level of restraint and to preserve the political stability of the country."[320] In Resolution 1345, it again emphasized that the government should "end the violence in a manner consistent with the rule of law."

The lack of international intervention in Rwanda could be considered a counter-example. Even in that case, however, the devastating inaction is widely viewed as the greatest failure of the international community since the creation of the Council,[321] indicating an expectation that intervention was within the proper scope of the Council mandate. This is even as the Council still strongly condemned the "large-scale violence"[322] and imposed sanctions seeking to stop "the use of such arms and equipment in the massacres of innocent civilians."[323]

In summary, therefore, the practice evidences a generalized rejection of conflicts that cause massive violence against civilians in line with the preexisting legal rules. Nonetheless, this practice remains somewhat diffuse in comparison with the practice reviewed in relation to the norm rejecting violence against a democratically elected government, lacking in explicit declaratory statements by the Council, individual states, and the Secretary-General on the policy that is being adopted and its general and binding nature. Much of the practice in this case seems to be formulated in moral, not legal, terms, and in contrast to the norm rejecting the overthrow of a democratic government discussed in Section B.2, the condemnation seems to lack a systematic, or conscious, element.

---

319 S.C. Res. 794, *supra* note 194.

320 President of the Security Council, Statement, *supra* note 61.

321 The Secretary-General, *Report of the Independent Inquiry into the Actions of the United Nations During the 1994 Genocide in Rwanda, delivered to the Security Council*, U.N. Doc S/1999/1257 (Dec. 15, 1999).

322 S.C. Res. 918, *supra* note 29; S.C. Res. 925, *supra* note 29.

323 S.C. Res. 1011, *supra* note 299.

5. Conclusion

The Security Council has typically been considered a political rather than a legal body, and its practice ranges across many resolutions in response to many conflicts. Investigating the emergence of principles in Council practice is a difficult endeavor, as Council practice seems to have developed without explicit recognition or discussion of its role in civil conflict or the implications such practice will have on international law. Nonetheless, the practice does not form *ad hoc* resolutions. If that were the case, then it would be true that Council intervention is of exclusively discretionary nature, and each conflict is of exceptional nature. Instead what emerges is that the Council has consistently supported and applied a set of recognizable principles when dealing with extreme political violence in the form of civil conflicts or coups d'état.

Complex peacekeeping frequently required the choice of sides in a conflict, thus implicating a complex system of principles. In Angola, for instance, by 1993 Council sanctions were targeted at UNITA only, rather than both parties to the conflict, and in Sierra Leone by 1998 at the RUF only. When the Security Council begins acting to enforce particular decisions against individual belligerents, it is impossible to avoid the question of what principles are being enforced. One indication that the Council must be relying on particular principles—though admittedly this does not resolve the question of the nature of these principles—can be seen in the transition from traditional peace-keeping operations to complex peace-building ones. Such operations required the peace-keeping forces to be able to enforce their Council mandate against parties that failed to abide by it. When the peace-keeping operations converted to peace-building operations, distinct normative values became incorporated into the operations. While Council neutrality was still usually maintained in the early stages of such conflicts, as these evolved and parties refused to abide by the stated principles, the Council and the peacekeepers sought to enforce them.

The Council has condemned extreme political violence in the form of civil conflicts or coups d'état in practically all cases since the 1990s, and its formulation indicates that it intends its demands to renounce such violence to be binding on the parties involved. However, the Council has not yet formulated a universal principle, and hence the analysis in favor of the emergence of such a principle relies on accumulating practice of condemnation and demands that such conduct stop. Still, the Council can be considered to have created a quasi-legislative prohibition on violence against a democratically elected government. This effect derives from the Council's formulation, seriousness, frequent repetition in different instances, and enforcement measures under Chapter VII, in relation to violence against a democratically elected government.

CHAPTER 4

THE RESPONSE OF STATES AND REGIONAL ORGANIZATIONS

Thus far, the focus has been on the Security Council practice with respect to civil conflict and coups d'état in the Balkans, Iraq, and Somalia, since that body has the power to set binding precedent for the conduct of other states, and its practice can be easily identified and collated to provide an overview of the direction of evolution of this field. This chapter turns to the response of the international community to the conflicts in Sierra Leone, Côte d'Ivoire, and Liberia, to determine whether, as could be expected, it reflects some of the principles that the Council has formulated that were identified in the previous chapter. In addition, it examines the African Union (A.U.) and Economic Community of West African States (ECOWAS) security treaties, in which the principles emerging in the Council practice are also reflected.[1]

A. SIERRA LEONE

The response of the international community to the conflict in Sierra Leone supports four principles, that echo those identified in the practice of the Security Council. The central principle in this case study is the rejection of violence to overthrow a democratically elected government. Three other principles are referred to in the practice: prohibitions on, respectively, violence to resolve political disputes, violent breach of a peace or cease-fire agreement, and violence against civilians. These latter three principles, however, are referred to less frequently, in less strongly worded statements, and are relied upon less frequently (if at all) to justify sanctions or forceful measures.

Sierra Leone's devastating civil conflict has been characterized by vested economic interests[2] and involved extreme violence against the

[1] Note that the purpose of the investigation of the response of the international community to the civil conflicts is not to determine *the legality of the interventions* or of the treaty provisions (as it was in *Nicaragua.* Military and Paramilitary Activities in and Against Nicaragua (Nicar. v. U.S.), Merits, 1986 I.C.J. 14 (June 27)). Instead, this practice is analyzed to determine whether it supports the emergence of norms of *jus ad bellum internum* prohibiting certain civil conflicts.

[2] International Crisis Group (ICG), *Sierra Leone: Time for a New Military and*

civilian population.[3] Although it began in 1991, the international community only began to pay proper attention in 1996.

From 1991 until 1996, Sierra Leone went through a period of great instability marked by a wide-ranging violent struggle between rebel forces and the military governments, which were also repeatedly overthrown in a series of coups. The civil conflict is thought to have originated as a by-product of the conflict in adjoining Liberia where the warlord Charles Taylor was fighting to overthrow the Liberian government. Sierra Leone was part of the Economic Community of West African States Monitoring Group (ECOMOG) that intervened in the Liberian conflict. In 1991, apparently in retaliation, the National Patriotic Front of Liberia began making incursions into Sierra Leone and was joined in its attacks by the Revolutionary United Front (RUF), headed by Foday Sankoh, a former corporal of the Sierra Leone Army (SLA). The rebels engaged in a vicious conflict of intimidation, attacking civilians in what became their hallmark fashion, crudely amputating limbs and ears of women, men, children, and babies. They also kidnapped children as a way of recruiting soldiers.

In 1996, with the assistance of Executive Outcomes, a mercenary company, the government pushed back the rebels and began the process of running multi-party democratic elections. The elections of March 1996 were declared free and fair by international observers, and Ahmad Kabbah was sworn in as president. On November 30, 1996, a first peace agreement, the Abidjan Peace Accord, was signed.[4] However, soon afterward, the country was again shaken by a military coup. President Kabbah fled to a neighboring country, and Major Johnny Koroma of the Armed Forces Ruling Council (AFRC) appointed himself Chairman and invited

---

Political Strategy, Africa Report No. 28, at 2 (Apr. 11, 2001); Ian Smillie et. al, *The Heart of the Matter: Sierra Leone, Diamonds, and Human Security*, PARTNERSHIP AFR. CAN. INSIGHTS (Jan. 2000), *available at* http://www.sierra-leone.org/heartmatter.html; Report of the Panel of Experts Appointed Pursuant to U.N. Security Council Resolution 1306 (2000), Paragraph 19 in Relation to Sierra Leone (Dec. 2000), *available at* http://www.sierra-leone.org/panelreport.html.

[3] Human Rights Watch, *Getting Away with Murder, Mutilation, Rape: New Testimony from Sierra Leone*, 11(3A) AFR. RTS. WATCH (1999), *available at* http://www.hrw.org/reports/1999/sierra/. *See* David Pratt, *Sierra Leone: The Forgotten Crisis*, Report to the Minister of Foreign Affairs (Apr. 23, 1999), *available at* http://www.globalsecurity.org/military/library/report/1999/crisis-e.htm, for an insightful overview of the conflict.

[4] Peace Agreement Between the Government of Sierra Leone and the Revolutionary United Front of Sierra Leone, U.N. Doc. S/1996/1034 (Nov. 30, 1996).

the RUF to join his new government. This can be considered a distinct second phase of the conflict, during which the AFRC/RUF military regime was in power in Sierra Leone.

The international community intervened intensely after this coup. Ultimately, ECOWAS sought to reinstate the government by force. In October 1997, after five months of fighting against the armed supporters of the military coup, the Conakry peace plan was signed.[5] It envisaged the reinstatement of the deposed government, the immediate cessation of hostilities, cooperation between the junta and ECOMOG to enforce sanctions peacefully, disarmament, demobilization, and reintegration of combatants, and the provision of humanitarian assistance. It also provided immunities and guarantees to the leaders of the coup.

However, it was only in March 1998 that President Kabbah was returned to power, following a strong military offensive by ECOMOG on Freetown, driving out the AFRC/RUF who had failed to abide by the Conakry Agreement and had continued fighting.[6] However, the civil conflict against the democratic government persisted despite repeated calls by the international community for rebel surrender. During this third period of the conflict, the international community continued to support the reinstated government. In July 1998, a U.N. force, UNOMSIL, was sent to monitor the military and security situation, assist with disarmament, and monitor respect for international humanitarian law.[7]

A year later, however, resolution had still not been achieved, and a compromise agreement was signed with the rebel forces. The Lomé Peace Agreement of July 7, 1999, was markedly favorable to the rebels. It provided for power to be shared between parties and gave the rebels four key government posts, including the vice presidency and effective control over the country's mineral wealth and tourism.[8] The rebels were also granted full amnesty for their actions, and the death sentence on

---

[5] ECOWAS Six Month Peace Plan for Sierra Leone, U.N. Doc. S/1997/824 (Oct. 23, 1997).

[6] Press Release, Security Council, Security Council Calls on Sierra Leone Military Junta to Fulfil Obligations Under 23 October Agreement, U.N. Doc. SC/6444 (Nov. 14, 1997).

[7] S.C. Res. 1181, U.N. Doc. S/RES/1181 (July 13, 1998).

[8] The rebels were offered the ministerial posts of trade and industry, transportation, housing, and Energy and Tourism.

Sankoh was lifted.[9] Nevertheless, the rebel forces did not abide by the agreement.[10] UNOMSIL was thus replaced by UNAMSIL, a peace-keeping and demobilizing force,[11] but the situation continued to deteriorate. In May 2000, faced with the ineffectiveness of the U.N. intervention and Sierra Leone's slide into general lawlessness, the United Kingdom intervened militarily.[12] U.K. forces, separate from the U.N. peace-keeping forces, secured the airport, trained the SLA, provided assistance to the government and the U.N. missions, and achieved the release of the forces held hostage.

Finally, by May 2001, the United Kingdom, United Nations, and SLA forces had made sufficient progress to pressure the rebels into entering into a further peace agreement.[13] This time, the agreement was largely implemented, and by January 2002 the demobilization of rebel forces had progressed substantially. In May 2002, the first democratic elections since the 1997 coup were held, returning Kabbah as president. As of November 2006, the position in Sierra Leone appears to be one of relative peace and stability.

1. Prohibition on Violence Against a Democratically Elected Government

There was little interest by the international community during the first phase of the conflict in 1991–96, although ECOMOG did assist the SLA in attempting to push the rebels back toward Liberia, apparently on the understanding that the conflict was an extension of the Liberian conflict.[14] Despite the serious violence against civilians over the next five years, the conflict still did not attract much international attention.[15] Neither did the repeated military coups cause protest. Nigeria, for instance, recognized and expressed its support for the government of

---

[9] 45(7) *Keesing's Record of World Events* (1999) (Folio Views, Infobase).

[10] They attacked UNOMSIL forces and took some hostages.

[11] S.C. Res. 1270, U.N. Doc. S/RES/1270 (Oct. 22, 1999). In February, the UNAMIL forces were doubled to fill the security vacuum left by the phasing out of the ECOWAS force. S.C. Res. 1289, U.N. Doc. S/RES/1289 (Feb. 7, 2000).

[12] 46(6) *Keesing's Record of World Events* (2000) (Folio Views, Infobase).

[13] 47(5) *Keesing's Record of World Events* (2001) (Folio Views, Infobase).

[14] 39(12) *Keesing's Record of World Events* (1993) (Folio Views, Infobase).

[15] Known as "sobels," soldiers by day, rebels by night, both forces perpetuated violence and looting. Pratt, *supra* note 3, pt. 1.

Captain Strasser within three weeks of the 1992 coup.[16] It was only in 1994 that the greater international community became involved in the conflict, and then only as an impartial negotiator, following a request to the Secretary-General to exercise his good offices in the conflict.[17]

The overturn of the democratically elected government in the 1997 coup marked a dramatic change in the response of the international community and elicited extensive and widespread condemnation, sanctions, and ultimately forceful intervention. This practice constitutes support for a prohibition on the violent overthrow of a democratically elected government.

The practice is consistent with the earlier practice of the Security Council reviewed in the last chapter, where the Council rejected a coup in Haiti by emphasizing that the government had been democratically elected. In both Haiti and Sierra Leone, the Council formulated its rationale for rejecting the violence against the democratically elected government explicitly, demanding in binding resolutions that the junta step down and reinstate the democratic government, and seeking to enforce its demands through sanctions.

a. *Condemnation of the Coup and Calls for the Junta to Step Down*

The condemnations of the rebel actions were framed in terms of the overthrow of a democratic government. Many states condemned the coup.[18] Nigeria was particularly vocal, calling for the restitution of the deposed government and intimating that it was prepared to use force to overturn the coup if necessary.[19] The OAU passed a resolution condemning the coup and endorsing military as well as diplomatic efforts to restore democracy.[20] Speaking to the Security Council on behalf of the OAU, Zimbabwe explained the decision on the basis that it had "to safeguard and defend and nurture democracy in Africa."[21] ECOWAS then

---

16 38(5) *Keesing's Record of World Events* (1992) (Folio Views, Infobase).

17 The Secretary-General, *Report of the Secretary-General on the Situation in Sierra Leone*, U.N. Doc. S/1995/975 (Nov. 21, 1995).

18 *See, e.g.*, the comments by all members of the Security Council during S.C. 3822d mtg., U.N. Doc. S/PV.3822 (Oct. 8, 1997).

19 CNN, *Sierra Leone Fighting Eases, Allowing More Evacuations* (June 3, 1997), *available at* http://www.cnn.com/WORLD/9706/03/sierra.leone/index.html.

20 OAU Summit (Harare, June 2–4, 1997).

21 S.C. 3797th mtg., U.N. Doc. S/PV.3797 (July 18, 1997).

issued a communiqué urging states not to recognize the regime installed following the coup and calling on them to make every effort to restore the lawful government.[22]

Some commentators criticized the hypocrisy of such justifications when arising from non-democratic governments. "The principle involved is not preventing military take-overs, but self-preservation,"[23] commented the *South African Weekly Mail and Guardian,* pointing out that its proponents included Zimbabwe and Nigeria, neither of which was then democratic. An alternative assessment might be that even undemocratic governments recognize the strength in the eyes of the international community of the principle rejecting violence against democratically elected governments and seek to take advantage of it—in their case—to exploit it to further their goals.

The Council reacted by repeatedly calling for the restoration of the government. It put out a presidential statement strongly deploring "this attempt to overthrow the democratically elected government" and calling "for an immediate restoration of constitutional order."[24] In the conflict that followed the coup, the Council repeatedly called for "the immediate and unconditional restoration of constitutional order in the country."[25] It demanded "the military junta take immediate steps to relinquish power in Sierra Leone and make way for the restoration of the democratically-elected Government and a return to constitutional order,"[26] calling upon the junta "to end all acts of violence and to cease all interference with the delivery of humanitarian assistance to the peo-

---

[22] ECOWAS, Final Communique (Conakry, June 26, 1997).

[23] South African Weekly Mail and Guardian, *Africa: Littered with the Debris of Democracy,* May 30, 1997.

[24] President of the Security Council, *The Situation in Sierra Leone,* Statement, U.N. Doc. S/PRST/1997/29 (May 27, 1997). *See also* statements condemning the coup of July 11, 1997, President of the Security Council, *The Situation in Sierra Leone,* Statement, S/PRST/1997/36 (July 11, 1997), President of the Security Council, *The Situation in Sierra Leone,* Statement, U.N. Doc. S/PRST/1997/42 (Aug. 6, 1997).

[25] Press Release, The Secretary-General, Secretary-General, in Statement to Security Council, Demands Unconditional Release of United Nations Peacekeepers in Sierra Leone, SG/SM/7390, AFR/226 (May 11, 2000). *See* S.C. Res. 1156, U.N. Doc. S/RES/1156 (Mar. 16, 1998) (welcomed the return of the democratic government).

[26] S.C. Res. 1132, U.N. Doc. S/RES/1132, ¶ 1 (Oct. 8, 1997), acting under Chapter VII.

ple of Sierra Leone,"[27] and went on to condemn repeatedly the resistance of the junta to the authority of the government.[28]

From the preamble of Resolution 1132, the finding of a threat to international peace and security can be seen to rely partly on the failure of the military junta to "allow the restoration of the democratically-elected Government," as well as grave concern with the "continued violence and loss of life in Sierra Leone" and at "the deteriorating humanitarian conditions in that country, and the consequences for neighbouring countries."[29] The Council did not intervene as a neutral party in Sierra Leone—it explicitly favored the deposed government,[30] seemingly on the basis of its democratic nature.[31] It also condemned the actions of the rebels, initially in relation to the coup, and later in relation to breaking peace agreements and Council resolutions.[32]

The Secretary-General played an important role in shaping the debate. He repeatedly asserted that democratic governments must not be overthrown by force: "The United Nations and the international community firmly uphold the principle that the will of the people shall be the basis for the authority of government and that governments democratically elected shall not be overthrown by force."[33] He wrote to the Council: "At stake is a great issue of principle, namely, that the efforts of the international community for democratic governance, grounded in the rule of law and respect for human rights, shall not be thwarted through illegal coups."[34] These statements were cited approvingly by many states on the Council,[35] suggesting widespread acceptance of a

---

27 *Id.*, ¶ 2.

28 S.C. Res. 1181, *supra* note 7, ¶ 1.

29 S.C. Res. 1132, *supra* note 26, preamble.

30 *See* references in *supra* note 24; S.C. Res. 1132, *supra* note 26.

31 *See* references in *supra* note 24; ; S.C. Res. 1132, *supra* note 26; S.C. Res. 1171, U.N. Doc S/RES/1171 (June 5, 1998).

32 *E.g.*, S.C. Res. 1132, *supra* note 26; S.C. Res. 1171, *supra* note 31; S.C. Res. 1270, *supra* note 11.

33 Press Release, The Secretary-General, Secretary-General Expresses Concern over Coup in Sierra Leone; Condemns Treatment of UN Staff, Looting of UN Offices, U.N. Doc. SG/SM/6241 (May 27, 1997); Letter from the Secretary-General to the Security Council 2 (Oct. 7, 1997), U.N. Doc. S/1997/776.

34 Letter from the Secretary-General to the Security Council 2, *supra* note 33.

35 *See* Kenya, France, Korea, Sweden, Guinea Bissau, and Chile at S.C. 3822d mtg., *supra* note 18.

principle rejecting the legitimacy of recourse to force against a democratically elected government.

b. Sanctions Against the Rebels

The imposition of sanctions against the rebels—a step up from mere condemnation—was clearly in response to their overthrow of the democratic government. ECOWAS imposed a total embargo on trade, petroleum products, and arms and military equipment,[36] calling on states "to restore the lawful government" by dialogue, sanctions, or force.[37]

The Security Council sanctions preventing travel of the junta members and imposing a petrol embargo were imposed a few months later under Chapter VII, and the Council strongly rejected the violent overthrow of democratic governments.[38] The Council demanded, under Chapter VII, that "the military junta take immediate steps to relinquish power in Sierra Leone and make way for the restoration of the democratically elected Government."[39] The debate prior to voting on the resolution explicitly adopted such a principle.[40] Kenya, for instance, explained: "Africa was saying, and the international community was supporting the clear statement, that military coups overthrowing democratically elected Governments were no longer going to be accepted." Similarly, the United Kingdom stated: "The international community cannot afford to acquiesce in the arbitrary and unconstitutional overthrow of a democratic Government." Egypt referred to a "new, unanimous African position regarding military coups in the countries of the continent."[41]

---

[36] ECOWAS mtg. 20th Sess. (Aug. 29, 1997).

[37] ECOWAS, Final Communique, *supra* note 22.

[38] It imposed travel embargoes on the junta and prohibited the supply to Sierra Leone of petrol and arms. S.C. Res. 1132, *supra* note 26. Later, the Security Council modified the embargo so that it only applied to the rebels and not to the Sierra Leone government or to ECOMOG. S.C. Res. 1171, *supra* note 31. It also imposed a selective arms embargo, preventing sale of arms to the rebels. S.C. Res. 1171, *supra* note 31.

[39] S.C. Res. 1132, *supra* note 26. *See also* President of the Security Council, *The Situation in Sierra Leone*, Statement, U.N. Doc. S/PRST/1997/42 (Aug. 6, 1997).

[40] Note that a number of countries emphasized that the role of the sanctions was not to punish the junta but to uphold the principles involved. *See*, for instance, the statement of Japan, S.C. 3822d mtg., *supra* note 18.

[41] Similar statements supporting the protection of democratic regimes were made by all members of the Security Council except China, which supported the resolution

c. *Forceful Intervention*

The willingness of the international community to use military intervention to enforce the principles it had formulated signifies a strong support for these principles—notwithstanding the questions regarding the legality of such interventions given the U.N. Charter's restrictions on recourse to force (an issue discussed in more depth in Chapter 5). Nigeria was particularly vocal, calling for the restitution of the deposed government and intimating that it was prepared to use force to overturn the coup if necessary.[42] Nigeria already had troops in Freetown, pursuant to a bilateral agreement with the civilian government to defend it from rebel forces,[43] and swiftly sent further troops.[44] It attempted (unsuccessfully) to reinstate the president by force on June 2, 1997.[45]

ECOWAS became involved after the coup at the invitation of the deposed president. Initially it attempted diplomatic negotiations, but it soon sent forces to join Nigeria on the ground.[46] This action was supported by the OAU, which had resolved that a Nigerian-led ECOWAS force should "take the most effective measures" to remove the military junta.[47] ECOWAS's actions included an explicit call on states to make every effort "to restore the lawful government by a combination of three measures . . . : the use of dialogue; the application of sanctions, including an embargo; and the use of force."[48] The decision to permit the use

---

but limited its statement to a more ambiguous comment: "Like other Council members, the Chinese delegation is concerned at the changes in the situation in Sierra Leone and feels deep sympathy for the sufferings experienced by the people of that country." S.C. 3822d mtg., *supra* note 18.

42 CNN, *More West African Soldiers Join Nigerians in Sierra Leone* (May 31, 1997), *available at* http://www.cnn.com/WORLD/9705/31/sierra.leone/index.html?eref=sitesearch.

43 *Id.*

44 CNN, *Mutinous Soldiers Scrap Sierra Leone Constitution* (May 28, 1997), *at* http://www.cnn.com/WORLD/9705/28/sierra.leone/index.html.

45 CNN, *Nigerians Launch Attack on Sierra Leone Mutineers* (June 2, 1997), *at* http://www.cnn.com/WORLD/9706/02/sierra.leone/index.html?eref=sitesearch.

46 The force incorporated soldiers from Ghana, Guinea, and Nigeria. CNN, *More West African soldiers Join Nigerians in Sierra Leone, supra* note 42.

47 CNN, *African Leaders Pledge to Oppose Coups, Support Democracy* (June 4, 1997), *at* http://www.cnn.com/WORLD/9706/04/zimbabwe.new.africa/index.html?eref=sitesearch.

48 ECOWAS, Final Communique, *supra* note 22.

of force did raise some concern among members but, as Nigeria explained, it was agreed to because the other two options would be ineffective without it.[49]

ECOWAS then fought the supporters of the military coup for five months before an attempt at settling the conflict by agreement. However, the Conakry Agreement providing for the return of the president was not implemented by the rebels.[50] At that point, ECOMOG reinstated the president by force, driving the AFRC/RUF out of Freetown. This is a clear indication of the aim of the military intervention. ECOWAS determinedly rejected the rebel takeover of the government and ultimately overthrew it by force. It also remained in Sierra Leone during the third phase of the conflict and supported the government while the rebels continued their struggle against it.

The United Kingdom also sent troops midway through the third phase of the conflict to assist the reinstated but beleaguered government and the ineffective U.N. forces.[51] It is thought that its intervention played a major role in bringing the conflict to a close.[52] The basis on which the intervention was justified varied over time. Initially, the United Kingdom maintained that it aimed merely to protect its nationals.[53] By October 2000, the intervention mandate included training the SLA to "build new, democratically accountable, and effective armed forces in Sierra Leone,"[54] and by February 2001, the priorities were "to repel the rebels, restore the peace and rebuild the country."[55] The legal justifications for these priorities also varied from protecting nationals to consent by the Secretary-General and the president of Sierra Leone.[56]

---

49 S.C. 3797th mtg., *supra* note 21.

50 ECOWAS, Six Month Peace Plan for Sierra Leone, S/1997/824 (Oct. 23, 1997).

51 46(6) *Keesing's Record of World Events* (2000) (Folio Views, Infobase).

52 A U.K. forceful intervention received some explicit support. *See* ICG, *Sierra Leone, supra* note 2.

53 Statement by Foreign Secretary, Robin Cook (House of Commons, May 8, 2000), *at* http://www.fco.gov.uk.

54 Speech by Foreign Secretary, Robin Cook (October 2000), *at* http://www.fco.gov.uk.

55 Speech by Foreign Commonwealth Office Minister of State, Brian Wilson, (Westminster Hall, London, Feb. 28, 2001), *at* http://www.fco.gov.uk.

56 Statement by Defense Secretary on Sierra Leone (May 15, 2000), *at* http://www.fco.gov.uk/news.

The Council did not authorize the actions by ECOWAS, OAU, or Nigeria.[57] It did not send troops until after the reinstatement of the president by ECOWAS's forceful action. When the Council did send peacekeepers, they aimed at ensuring an end to the conflict and sought to enforce the peace agreements and disarm the rebels. UNOMSIL was sent to monitor the military and security situation, assist with disarmament, and monitor respect for international humanitarian law.[58] It was replaced by UNAMSIL, a peace-keeping and demobilizing force, after the rebels repeatedly breached the Lomé Peace Accord and took UNOMSIL forces hostage.[59] UNAMSIL's mission was to disarm the rebel forces while still aiming to implement the Lomé Peace Accord.[60] It was to cooperate with the government, as well as the other parties to the accord, and assist the government in implementing the disarmament and demobilization plan.[61]

The Council had already condemned the coup and called on the junta to step down.[62] Faced with repeated breaches of the peace accord by the rebels and a deteriorating situation, including attacks on U.N. forces, the Council acted to strengthen the mandate of its peace-keeping force to support the government.[63] In this way, U.N. forces aligned more and more closely with the democratic government against the rebel forces. By the time it passed Resolution 1313, the Council unanimously denounced the widespread and serious violation of the peace accord by the RUF and mandated UNAMSIL to deter and "decisively counter the threat of RUF attack."[64]

---

[57] Although the ECOWAS and OAU actions were generally referred to positively in the Council. *See, e.g.*, President of the Security Council, *The Situation in Sierra Leone*, Statement, U.N. Doc. S/PRST/1997/36, *supra* note 24.

[58] S.C. Res. 1181, *supra* note 7.

[59] S.C. Res. 1270, *supra* note 11. In February, the UNAMIL forces were doubled to fill the security vacuum left by the phasing out of the ECOWAS force. S.C. Res. 1289, *supra* note 11.

[60] S.C. Res. 1270, *supra* note 11.

[61] *Id.*

[62] *See, e.g.*, President of the Security Council, Statement, *supra* note 30; President of the Security Council, *The Situation in Sierra Leone*, Statement, U.N. Doc. S/PRST/1997/36, *supra* note 24; President of the Security Council, *The Situation in Sierra Leone*, Statement, U.N. Doc. S/PRST/1997/42, *supra* note 24; S.C. Res. 1132, *supra* note 26; S.C. Res. 1181, *supra* note 7.

[63] S.C. Res. 1313, U.N. Doc S/RES/1313 (Aug. 4, 2000).

[64] S.C. Res. 1313, *supra* note 63.

2. Prohibition on Recourse to Violence to Resolve Political Disputes

A related principle, prohibition on the resolution of political disputes through violence, was also evident in the practice. While it is to be expected that such violence would be rejected in the context of a democracy, as one of the core features of democratic regimes is that they provide alternative methods of conflict resolution, the practice is formulated more broadly, in that it does not seem to be restricted to cases where the government is democratically elected.

The OAU intervention evidenced its will and determination "to resolve violent conflicts now plaguing the continent,"[65] and the Council repeatedly emphasized its support for the regional organizations' attempts for a peaceful resolution of the conflict and for the restoration of peace.[66] The Council also emphasized that it was gravely concerned with the conflict and violence in Sierra Leone,[67] and called, under Chapter VII, for parties to "end all acts of violence."[68] It repeatedly demanded that the junta give up arms.[69] It affirmed the importance of non-violent methods of resolution of internal disputes, particularly free and transparent elections.[70] Moreover, it emphasized the urgent need to promote peace and national reconciliation[71] and encouraged all efforts aimed at "resolving the conflict and restoring lasting peace and stability."[72] It also commended the government for its "courageous efforts to achieve peace, including through legislative and other measures already taken towards implementation of the Peace Agreement."[73] The Council repeatedly expressed support for peace agreements,[74] and called on the parties to abide by them.[75]

---

65 S.C. 3797th mtg., *supra* note 21.

66 S.C. Res. 1132, *supra* note 26, ¶ 3; S.C. Res. 1181, *supra* note 7, ¶ 5; S.C. Res. 1260, U.N. Doc. S/RES/1260 (Aug. 20, 1999).

67 S.C. Res. 1132, *supra* note 26.

68 *Id.*, ¶ 2.

69 S.C. Res. 1181, *supra* note 7, ¶ 1; S.C. Res. 1260, *supra* note 66, ¶ 8; S.C. Res. 1270, *supra* note 11, ¶ 4.

70 S.C. Res. 1400, U.N. Doc. S/RES/1400 (Mar. 28, 2002).

71 S.C. Res. 1162, ¶ 3, U.N. Doc. S/RES/1162 (Apr. 17, 1998); S.C. Res. 1171, *supra* note 31; S.C. Res. 1260, *supra* note 66, ¶ 10; S.C. Res. 1270, *supra* note 11.

72 S.C. Res. 1220, U.N. Doc. S/RES/1220 (Jan. 12, 1999).

73 S.C. Res. 1260, *supra* note 66.

74 *Id.*, ¶ 1.

75 S.C. Res. 1270, *supra* note 11, ¶ 2; S.C. Res. 1289, *supra* note 11, ¶ 3.

The use of force in support of such a principle is inherent in the U.K. intervention, which aimed to restore peace to Sierra Leone.[76] As the Foreign and Commonwealth Minister of State explained, the purpose in Sierra Leone was to help "achieve the peace that [Sierra Leonians] need, to develop their country's potential."[77] The U.N. peace-keeping missions were also sent to ensure an end to the conflict, enforce the peace agreements, and disarm the rebels.[78]

3. Prohibition on Violence Against Civilians

The conflict in Sierra Leone was particularly brutal against civilians and involved extensive torture, mutilation, rape, and the amputation of limbs of civilians.[79] The prohibition on the violence against civilians is a well-established principle in international humanitarian law, and this provided an important focus for the condemnations of the international community. The states repeatedly condemned the violence, loss of life, and human rights and humanitarian law breaches.[80] The Council was also particularly explicit; it repeatedly condemned the human rights abuses against the civilian population and demanded that the acts cease immediately.[81] It also emphasized that humanitarian law must be followed in civil conflicts.[82] The sanctions imposed by the Council empha-

---

[76] Speech by Foreign Commonwealth Office Minister of State, Brian Wilson (Westminster Hall, London, Feb. 28, 2001), *at* http://www.fco.gov.uk.

[77] *Id.*

[78] S.C. Res. 1181, *supra* note 7; S.C. Res. 1270, *supra* note 11. In February, the UNAMIL forces were doubled to fill the security vacuum left by the phasing out of the ECOWAS force. S.C. Res. 1289, *supra* note 11; S.C. Res. 1270, *supra* note 11.

[79] *See, e.g.*, Abdul Tejan-Cole, *Human Rights Under the Armed Forces Revolutionary Council in Sierra Leone: A Catalogue of Abuse*, 10 AFR. J. INT'L & COMP. L. 407 (1998); Bureau of Democracy, Human Rights, and Labor, *U.S. Department of State, Sierra Leone Country Report on Human Rights Practices for 1997* (Jan. 30 1998), *available at* http://www.sierra-leone.org/usds013098.html.

[80] The U.K. decision to intervene forcefully highlighted the brutality of the rebels and the suffering of the people. Speech by Foreign Commonwealth Office Minister of State, Brian Wilson (Westminster Hall, London, Feb. 28, 2001), *at* http://www.fco.gov.uk.

[81] S.C. Res. 1132, *supra* note 26, pmbl.; S.C. Res. 1181, *supra* note 7, pmbl.; S.C. Res. 1289, *supra* note 11; President of the Security Council, *The Situation in Sierra Leone*, Statement, U.N. Doc. S/PRST/1997/36, *supra* note 24; President of the Security Council, Statement, *supra* note 30; President of the Security Council, *The Situation in Sierra Leone*, Statement, U.N. Doc. S/PRST/1997/42, *supra* note 24; S.C. Res. 1132, *supra* note 26; S.C. Res. 1171, *supra* note 31; S.C. Res. 1231, U.N. Doc. S/RES/1231, ¶ 3 (Mar. 11, 1999); S.C. Res. 1400, *supra* note 70; S.C. Res. 1289, *supra* note 11.

[82] S.C. Res. 1181, *supra* note 7; S.C. Res. 1231, *supra* note 81, ¶ 3. Also one of

sized the unacceptable violence and loss of life in Sierra Leone and the deteriorating humanitarian conditions.[83] And UNAMSIL was authorized under Chapter VII to take all necessary action to "protect civilians under imminent threat of physical violence."[84]

4. Summary

In summary, the principles that the international community relied upon, and sought to enforce in Sierra Leone, reflect and support those identified in the practice of the Security Council in the last chapter. The principle that received the most support, and was relied upon most frequently and vehemently, was a principle rejecting the violent overthrow of a democratic government. This principle formed the core justification to actions ranging from condemnation to sanctions against the rebels to forceful intervention. This practice is in line with the earlier response of the international community in Haiti to the overthrow of the democratically elected government and can be considered a sub-category of the broader principle discussed in the last chapter rejecting all recourse to violence for political gains. This was supported by a corollary rejection of the violence of civil conflict and demand that conflicts be resolved peacefully through negotiation, reconciliation, peace agreements, and democratic elections. In this fashion, the forceful intervention by the United Kingdom and the U.N. mission both aimed to restore peace and stop the violence. However, the practice did not clearly enunciate a principle rejecting recourse to violence for political gains, in the way such a principle has been set out in the Council in some instances discussed in the last chapter. There was also a strong concern about the shocking level of violence against civilians, and condemnations, sanctions, and the peacekeeping mission aimed to protect such civilians. However, the prohibition on violence against civilians is relied upon as a secondary principle and does not on its own appear to have engendered sufficient political will to bring about action. This violence against civilians was prevalent for years before the election of the democratic government, which is when the international community began to take interest in the conflict.

UNOMSIL's key responsibilities was to monitor respect for international humanitarian law. S.C. Res. 1181, *supra* note 7.

[83] S.C. Res. 1132, *supra* note 26.

[84] S.C. Res. 1270, *supra* note 11, ¶ 14; S.C. Res. 1289, *supra* note 11, ¶ 10.

B. CÔTE D'IVOIRE

The response of the international community to the conflict in Côte d'Ivoire supports four distinct principles, which echo and, in some ways, extend those supported in the practice in Sierra Leone. The international community rejected recourse to force to bring about an unconstitutional change of government; attempts to settle the dispute through violence; violence in breach of a peace agreement; and violence against civilians. Correspondingly, it upheld an obligation to resolve conflicts peacefully, through negotiation, reconciliation, and political processes.

Two aspects of the practice are particularly interesting. First, the principle rejecting recourse to force aiming to overthrow a democratic government, at the center of the response of the international community in Sierra Leone, appears to be formulated slightly differently in this conflict—emphasizing legitimacy derived from democratic elections. This could be read as a narrowing (as well as clarification) of the principle, focusing attention on the procedural requirements of democratic elections, or alternatively, a broadening of the principle to require a constitutional (and thus non-violent) transfer of power between governments, irrespective of whether the government is democratic. An important aspect of this practice is the explicit formulation of principles by key international actors, particularly the Secretary-General, who explicitly disapproved of recourse force as a means of settling disputes.

The conflict in Côte d'Ivoire developed out of a failed violent coup on September 17, 2002. Within a few weeks, the rebel forces, who have since identified themselves as the Patriotic Movement of Côte d'Ivoire (MPCI), held half of the country and controlled two major cities, Bouake and Korhogo, although not the capital, Abidjan.[85]

President Laurent Gbagbo had come to power in October 2000 in elections marred by violence, when General Robert Guei, the winner of a successful military coup in 1999, refused to concede defeat and only left office following a violent popular uprising. Guei was found dead in the streets of Abidjan during the 2002 uprising.

The uprising in 2002 initiated a swift response by the international community. The French sent troops within nine days of the attempted coup, on September 26, 2002. These forces were initially justified as nec-

---

[85] Agence France-Presse, *Senegalese Mediator in Bid to Stave off Ivory Coast Civil War* (Oct. 11, 2002).

essary to protect the large French population in this former French colony. However, they soon took on a more complex role, separating the two armies and preventing the rebels from marching on the capital. Thus, when the rebel forces gained ground on October 1, 2002, and stated that they aimed to topple the government, the French troops warned them not to enter a broad zone that effectively cut off the route south to Abidjan, while nevertheless maintaining that the purpose of their mission was to protect their nationals.[86] The rebels responded by demanding that the French maintain strict neutrality.[87]

Other international interventions by African nations clearly supported the government. Ghana agreed to send an air squadron, and Nigeria sent warplanes to assist the government put down the rebellion.[88] ECOWAS also explicitly condemned the uprising and set up a six-member mediation group to try and bring peace and security to the country.[89]

On October 17, 2002, a cease-fire agreement was negotiated between the rebel forces and the government,[90] which provided for monitoring by the French forces until the arrival of a West African force.[91] On October 31, 2002, the government and rebels agreed to "refrain from any aggressive acts, such as exactions and extra-judicial executions, recruitment and use of mercenaries, enlisting child soldiers, and violating the ceasefire," and "to create a climate conducive to negotiations by proving our restraint through our words, actions and behavior."[92] No peace agreement was signed however, as the rebels called for President Gbagbo to step down. They maintained "that the administration of Mr Gbagbo is not a democratically elected power." The government insisted that the rebels disarm.[93]

---

[86] Agence France-Presse, *Coast Rebels Gain Ground, But French Say 'No Entry' to Evacuation Zone* (Oct. 1, 2002).

[87] *Id.*

[88] Reuters, *Exodus from Ivory Coast City Under French Guard* (Sept. 26, 2002).

[89] U.N. OCHA Integrated Regional Information Network, "Côte d'Ivoire: ECOWAS sets up mediation group" (Sept. 30, 2002), *at* http://www.reliefweb.int/.

[90] Reuters, *Ivory Coast Rebels Sign Ceasefire to End War* (Oct. 17, 2002).

[91] U.N. OCHA Integrated Regional Information Network, "Côte d'Ivoire: France to provide interim buffer force." (Oct. 18, 2002), *at* http://www.reliefweb.int/.

[92] Agence France-Presse, *Ivory Coast Government, Rebels Pledge to End 'Aggressive Acts'* (Nov. 17, 2002).

[93] Reuters, *Ivory Coast Rebels Reject Draft Peace Plan* (Nov. 14, 2002).

On November 17, 2002, the first ECOWAS troops began to arrive to take over the monitoring of the cease-fire agreement from France.[94] However, the conflict intensified in late November when two new rebel groups emerged in the west.[95] In late January 2003, France hosted negotiations that led to the Linas-Marcoussis Peace Agreement, which provided for substantial compromises on the part of the government. It created a new National Reconciliation Government that was to bring about peace and stability through a series of reforms leading to a new set of credible elections[96] and was to be supervised by France, ECOWAS, and the United Nations.

As of November 2006, the implementation of this agreement continues to face serious challenges. Nonetheless, in February 2003, the Security Council finally officially authorized, under Chapter VII, the deployment of the ECOWAS forces and the supporting French forces, whose mandate was to protect civilians threatened with physical violence, including through the use of force.[97] It also authorized a U.N. mission in Côte d'Ivoire (MINUCI), whose mandate was to facilitate the implementation by the Ivorian parties of the Linas-Marcoussis Agreement. MINUCI included a military component complementing the operations of the French and ECOWAS forces.[98] By mid-2003, the Government of

---

94 Agence France-Presse, *First West African Peacekeeping Troops Arrive in Ivory Coast, at* http://www.reliefweb.int/. France, the United States, Britain, Canada, Germany, the Netherlands, and Belgium had agreed to fund the ECOWAS operation.

95 Agence France-Presse, *Ivory Coast Belligerents Attend West African Summit to Defuse Crisis* (Dec. 16, 2002).

96 Linas-Marcoussis Accord, Jan. 24, 2003.

> a. Un gouvernement de réconciliation nationale sera mis en place dès après la clôture de la Conférence de Paris pour assurer le retour à la paix et à la stabilité.
>
> b. Il préparera les échéances électorales aux fins d'avoir des élections crédibles et transparentes et en fixera les dates.
>
> c. Le gouvernement de réconciliation nationale sera dirigé par un Premier ministre de consensus qui restera en place jusqu'à la prochaine élection présidentielle à laquelle il ne pourra se présenter. f- Le gouvernement de réconciliation nationale s'attachera dès sa prise de fonctions à refonder une armée attachée aux valeurs d'intégrité et de moralité républicaine. Il procédera à la restructuration des forces de défense et de sécurité et pourra bénéficier, à cet effet, de l'avis de conseillers extérieurs et en particulier de l'assistance offerte par la France.

97 S.C. Res. 1464, U.N. Doc. S/RES/1464 (Feb. 4, 2003).

98 S.C. Res. 1479, U.N. Doc. S/RES/1479 (May 13, 2003).

National Reconciliation had taken power, and the parties had produced a joint statement declaring that the war was over.[99]

1. Prohibition on Violence Against a Democratically Elected Government

The first principle to have received explicit support as a practical response to the conflict was the rejection of the recourse to force to overthrow a democratically elected government. France sent forces to Côte d'Ivoire rapidly after the failed coup and start of the civil conflict, initially to evacuate its nationals. From a classical legal perspective, the intervention was initially justified as a measure to protect nationals. It was also based on consent of President Gbagbo, who was calling for international intervention and later incorporated into the cease-fire.

France's troops remained in Côte d'Ivoire, and, by the end of October 2002, it emphasized that it sought to uphold a number of principles through its intervention. Dominique de Villepin, the French Minister for Foreign Affairs, explained:

> Comme nous n'avons cessé de le rappeler, notre action en Côte d'Ivoire est dictée par les principes suivants:
>
> — respect et appui résolu aux autorités légitimes, démocratiquement élues;
> — respect des frontières actuelles, de l'unité et de la souveraineté des Etats africains, de l'intégrité de leur territoire;
> — appui aux efforts de médiation et de maintien de la paix conduits par les Africains eux-mêmes;
> — condamnation ferme de toute entreprise de déstabilisation menée par des rebelles;
> — condamnation de tous les agissements susceptibles de porter atteinte à la paix civile et à la stabilité régionale.[100]

---

[99] Mr. Seydou Elimane Diarra, Prime Minister of the Government of National Reconciliation of Côte d'Ivoire, to whom I give the floor. S.C. 4793d mtg., U.N. Doc. S/PV.4793 (July 25, 2003)

[100] Entretien du Ministre des Affaires Etrangeres, M. Dominique de Villepin, avec L'Agence Algérienne de Presse «Situation en Côte d'Ivoire: rôle de la France Dernière mise à jour» (Paris, le 31 octobre 2002).

These principles were expanded upon in a later statement:

> C'est une position de principe. Nous avons des principes, la France s'y tient concernant la Côte d'Ivoire. Nous ne soutenons pas un régime, nous ne soutenons pas un homme, mais nous dénonçons les atteintes à l'unité, à l'intégrité et à la souveraineté de la Côte d'Ivoire. Nous dénonçons les violences, les exactions, les ingérences, les interférences extérieures, le recours à la force.
>
> Nous soutenons des principes qui nous paraissent particulièrement importants: le respect des élections démocratiques, le respect des droits de l'Homme, ou encore l'intégrité et la souveraineté de la Côte d'Ivoire et le soutien à tous les efforts de médiation régionale.[101]

Thus, the principles relied upon go well beyond the parameters of protection of nationals or consent of the president and highlight support for a legitimate, democratically elected government.

ECOWAS members similarly declared support for the democratically elected government. Nigeria and Ghana, in particular, immediately deployed military assistance to assist President Gbagbo after the failed coup.[102] Nigerian junior foreign minister Dubem Onyia stated: "The ECOWAS members think democracy is being threatened in Côte d'Ivoire . . . . ECOMOG is on alert and will be deployed when President Gbagbo decides."[103] He further emphasized that "ECOWAS has decided that any government that has to be changed must be changed through the ballot box" and that "[w]e are acting to prop up the elected government in Ivory Coast."[104] Interestingly, however, the ECOWAS peace-keeping force that was ultimately agreed to as a buffer force was not justified as seeking to support the government but rather to halt the fighting so that negotiations can take place.[105]

---

101 Déclaration du porte-parole du Quai d'Orsay (Paris, 13 décembre 2002).

102 U.N. OCHA Instability in Côte d'Ivoire Situation Report (Sept. 27, 2002), *at* http://www.reliefweb.int/.

103 Hugh Nevill, *Ivory Coast Prepares to Strike Rebels as Foreigners Pull Out*, AGENCE FRANCE-PRESS, Sept. 27, 2002.

104 Reuters, *Exodus from Ivory Coast City*, *supra* note 88.

105 Agence France-Presse, *West African Leaders Sending Peacekeepers to Ivory Coast* (Sept. 29, 2002).

The European Union strongly condemned the attempted coup on the grounds that it was "seriously undermining the constitutional legality and unity of the country," and it caused the "persistence of fighting and the loss of human life in Côte d'Ivoire." It reiterated its "support for the democratically elected President, Mr Laurent Gbagbo, and the government of national unity of the Republic of Côte d'Ivoire as the guarantor of democratic legitimacy and the unity of the country."[106]

Despite the above statements, the principle most clearly supported by this practice is not so much the support for legitimate democratically elected governments, as the rejection of unconstitutional changes of government, particularly through attempts to take power by force.

The Central Organ of the Mechanism for Conflict Prevention, Management and Resolution of the African Union, for instance, stressed the unconstitutional nature of the attempted change of government. It explicitly condemned "the attempt to undermine constitutional legality in Côte d'Ivoire."[107] Moreover, it recalled the provisions of the African Union and the Lomé Declaration on Unconstitutional Changes of Government in Africa[108] and "[u]rgently appealed to the parties concerned to seek, through dialogue, a lasting solution to the current problem, in strict conformity with constitutional legality, with a view to consolidating the process of reconciliation that was initiated at the Forum on National Reconciliation." In the African Union, an unconstitutional change of government includes a military coup or mercenary intervention against a democratically elected government or the replacement of a democratic government by an armed dissident group.

The ambiguity surrounding President Gbagbo's democratic legitimacy (given the violence surrounding the elections and the fact that a number of opposition members were banned from running) must nevertheless put into question whether the substantive concern was with the protection of democratically elected governments. Nonetheless, the early reactions at least nominally emphasized this principle.

---

[106] European Union, European Parliament Resolution on the Situation in Côte d'Ivoire, P5_TA-PROV(2002)0467 (Oct. 10, 2002), *at* http://www.reliefweb.int/.

[107] Press Release, African Union, Côte d'Ivoire: Communiqué of the 84th Ordinary Session (Sept. 24, 2002), *available at* http://www.reliefweb.int/rw/rwb.nsf/AllDocs ByUNID/097ed0bcfa9001a2c1256c4500578c09.

[108] Lomé Declaration on the Framework for an OAU Response to Unconstitutional Changes of Government (2000) AHG/Decl.5 (XXXVI), *available at* http://www.africanreview.org/docs/govern/govchange.pdf.

2. Prohibition on Recourse to Violence to Resolve Political Disputes

A number of international actors disapproved of the recourse to force as a means of settling disputes. The Secretary-General, in particular, expressed a general principle unequivocally condemning "any attempt to settle disputes through violence." He went on to call "on all those involved in these attacks to immediately and unconditionally cease their activities and submit to the constitutional order." He also called on all concerned parties to refrain from any action that could worsen the situation.[109] The African Union stated that it "[r]éitère également sa ferme condamnation de la tentative de prise du pouvoir par la force en Côte d'Ivoire."[110]

In addition, France made a number of statements condemning recourse to force and violence and expressing its concern at the direction the conflict was taking: "La France dénonce le recours à la force, les violences et les exactions ainsi que toute ingérence ou interférence extérieure. En liaison avec ses partenaires, elle ne manquera pas d'en tirer toutes les conclusions."[111] The violence, and its downward spiral, of itself caused serious concern—Villepin explained that what France feared was "l'engrenage de la violence, la perte des repères," and thus that it was important to recreate the basis for political and social stability.[112]

In the context of the situation in Côte d'Ivoire in general, however, these statements can only so far be considered to apply to a situation involving legitimate democratic governments, as that is the context in

---

[109] Press Release, The Secretary-General, Secretary-General Condemns Armed Attacks in Côte d'Ivoire, U.N. Doc. SG/SM/7390, AFR/226 (Sept. 20, 2002).

[110] African Union, Communiqué de l'Union Africaine: Erythrée, Soudan, Côte d'Ivoire (Oct. 12, 2002), *available at* http://wwwnotes.reliefweb.int/w/rwb.nsf/d2fc8ae9db883867852567cb0083a028/d4ca80cd5deab9b8c1256c520058c898?OpenDocument.

[111] Déclaration du porte-parole du Quai d'Orsay, (Paris, 13 décembre 2002).

> Face à la détérioration de la situation en Côte d'Ivoire, la France tient à exprimer sa préoccupation et sa conviction qu'il n'est pas de solution durable à la crise en dehors d'un règlement politique général rassemblant l'ensemble des forces politiques ivoiriennes. Les atteintes à l'unité, à l'intégrité et à la souveraineté de la Côte d'Ivoire sont inacceptables. La France dénonce le recours à la force, les violences et les exactions ainsi que toute ingérence ou interférence extérieure. En liaison avec ses partenaires, elle ne manquera pas d'en tirer toutes les conclusions.

[112] Le Quotidien «La Croix», «Entretien du ministre des affaires etrangeres, M Dominique de Villepin» (Paris, 16 décembre 2002), *at* http://www.diplomatie.gouv.fr/actu/actu.asp.

which they were formulated.[113] The Security Council formulated the key principle in these terms. It stated that it "firmly condemns attempts to use force to influence the political situation in Côte d'Ivoire and to overthrow the elected Government."[114] The European Union similarly condemned the violence perpetrated against a legitimate government and reiterated its support for the principles of the African Union condemning recourse to force to obtain unconstitutional political change.[115]

In addition, the international community explicitly and repeatedly maintained that only a peaceful resolution of the dispute was acceptable. France explained its conviction "qu'il n'est pas de solution durable à la crise en dehors d'un règlement politique général rassemblant l'ensemble des forces politiques ivoiriennes."[116] It also stated: "Notre seul objectif, c'est la recherche de la paix et de la réconciliation."[117] The European Union also reiterated its commitment to "a political solution to the crisis that encompasses all the opposing parties, pursues the course of national reconciliation embarked upon in October 2001 and respects democratic institutions and the unity of the national territory of the Republic of Côte d'Ivoire."[118] The Secretary-General explicitly supported "the Summit's call for the insurgents to cease hostilities and for all parties to work

---

[113] Déclaration du porte-parole du Quai d'Orsay (Paris, 13 décembre 2002).

C'est une position de principe. Nous avons des principes, la France s'y tient concernant la Côte d'Ivoire. Nous ne soutenons pas un régime, nous ne soutenons pas un homme, mais nous dénonçons les atteintes à l'unité, à l'intégrité et à la souveraineté de la Côte d'ivoire. Nous dénonçons les violences, les exactions, les ingérences, les interférences extérieures, le recours à la force. Nous soutenons des principes, nous soutenons des principes qui nous paraissent particulièrement importants: le respect des élections démocratiques, le respect des droits de l'Homme, ou encore l'intégrité et la souveraineté de la Côte d'Ivoire et le soutien à tous les efforts de médiation régionale.

[114] President of the Security Council, Statement, U.N. Doc. S/PRST/2002/42. *See also* Press Release, President of the Security Council, Côte d'Ivoire, U.N. Doc. AFR/506, SC/7558 (Oct. 31, 2002).

[115] EU Presidency Declaration on Côte d'Ivoire Situation (May 19, 2005), *available at* http://www.europa-eu-un.org/articles/en/article_4707_en.htm.

[116] Déclaration d'une porte-parole du Quai d'Orsay, (Paris, 12 décembre 2002).

[117] Le Quotidien «La Croix», «Entretien du ministre des affaires etrangeres, M Dominique de Villepin» (Paris, 16 décembre 2002), *at* http://www.diplomatie.gouv.fr/actu/actu.asp.

[118] Resolution on the Situation in Côte d'Ivoire, EUR. PARL. DOC. P5_TA-PROV (2002)0467 (Oct. 10, 2002).

towards a negotiated settlement to avert further violence, whose humanitarian consequences could be disastrous for Côte d'Ivoire and the entire sub-region."[119]

Finally, as reviewed in the last chapter, the Council has repeatedly emphasized the importance of peaceful resolution of disputes. In this conflict, as well, it "called on all parties to resolve the current crisis peacefully and to abstain from any actions or statements or demonstration that might jeopardize or otherwise hamper the search for a negotiated solution."[120] It also called on the parties to recognize that the crisis could only be resolved through a political solution.[121]

3. Prohibition on the Breach of a Peace or Cease-Fire Agreement

The international community also rejected recourse to force in breach of a peace or cease-fire agreement, reinforcing the practice emerging from the conflict in Sierra Leone. A number of agreements were entered into by the rebels and government during the course of the conflict,[122] and the Lomé Agreement, in particular, included an undertaking by both sides that they would refrain from "violations of the accord on cessation of hostilities." They pledged to urge "their authorities to refrain from any bellicose acts such as abuses and violence [and] extra-judicial killings."[123] The primary peace agreement, the Linas-Marcoussis Agreement,[124] explicitly provided for international supervision of the agree-

---

119 Press Release, The Secretary-General, Secretary-General Affirms UN Support for Subregional Efforts to Resolve Côte d'Ivoire Crisis, U.N. Doc. SG/SM/8408, AFR/489 (Oct. 1, 2002).

120 Press Release, President of Security Council, Security Council Condemns attempts at Force to Influence Political Situation, Overthrow Elected Government in Côte d'Ivoire, U.N. Doc. AFR/506, SC/7558 (Oct. 31, 2002).

121 *Id.*

122 The initial cease-fire brokered by ECOWAS was entered into a month into the conflict and provided for France to monitor the agreement until ECOWAS troops could be deployed. On October 31, 2002, a further accord was entered into in Lomé, which agreed to respect the cease-fire.

123 Agence France-Presse, *Ivory Coast Government, Rebels Pledge to End 'Aggressive Acts'* (Oct. 31, 2002).

124 Linas-Marcoussis Accord, *supra* note 96.

a. Un gouvernement de réconciliation nationale sera mis en place dès après la clôture de la Conférence de Paris pour assurer le retour à la paix et à la stabilité.

b. Il préparera les échéances électorales aux fins d'avoir des élections crédibles et transparentes et en fixera les dates.

ment,[125] "afin que les mesures de redressement appropriées soient prises."[126]

While there was extensive French and Nigerian intervention before any such agreements were signed, the formal intervention of the Security Council into the conflict only took place once the peace agreement was signed. The Council emphasized the binding nature of the agreement and that it expected that it would be implemented. It explicitly endorsed the accord and entrenched the agreement by calling on the parties under Chapter VII to implement it fully and without delay.[127] Moreover, the ECOWAS troops were specifically agreed on to supervise the agreement.[128]

4. Prohibition on Violence Against Civilians

The rejection of violence against civilians received repeated support. In this case, it was largely directed at the government, so the principle seems to be applicable to both the rebels (as in the case of Sierra Leone) and the government. President Gbagbo's security forces, for instance, burned down several districts that were home to immigrant workers that they felt were associated with the uprising.[129] The government also declared the rebel-held areas to be a "war zone" and indicated that its attempts to retake that territory would use all-out force.[130]

The European Union formulated the key principle in a clear and direct fashion. It stated that it "strongly condemns all acts of violence,

---

c. Le gouvernement de réconciliation nationale sera dirigé par un Premier ministre de consensus qui restera en place jusqu'à la prochaine élection présidentielle à laquelle il ne pourra se présenter. . . .

f. Le gouvernement de réconciliation nationale s'attachera dès sa prise de fonctions à refonder une armée attachée aux valeurs d'intégrité et de moralité républicaine. Il procédera à la restructuration des forces de défense et de sécurité et pourra bénéficier, à cet effet, de l'avis de conseillers extérieurs et en particulier de l'assistance offerte par la France.

[125] Supervision by the EU, AU, ECOWAS, SG, Francophonie Organization, IMF, and World Bank, G8, and France.

[126] Linas-Marcoussis Accord art. 4, *supra* note 96.

[127] S.C. Res. 1464, *supra* note 97.

[128] *Id.*, ¶ 8; S.C. Res. 1479, *supra* note 98, ¶ 2.

[129] Agence France-Presse, *Ivory Coast: A Crisis of Many Dimensions* (Sept. 27, 2002).

[130] Reuters, *Exodus from Ivory Coast City, supra* note 88.

from whatever source, against the population."[131] It also called on President Gbagbo "to urge his government and the Ivorian military to guarantee the protection of civilians, whatever their ethnic origin, and to step up their moves towards the integration and reconciliation of all the components of Ivorian society."[132] Other regional bodies, particularly the African Union, similarly condemned the violence, "the exactions against civilians," and urged the parties to observe human rights.[133]

The Security Council also called on "all parties to ensure full respect for human rights and international law, particularly with regard to the civilian population regardless of its origin, and to bring to justice all those responsible for any violation thereof."[134] The mandates of the French and ECOWAS troops incorporated the protection of civilians under the Council resolution. The Council authorized those troops "to ensure, without prejudice to the responsibilities of the Government of National Reconciliation, the protection of civilians immediately threatened with physical violence within their zones of operation."[135] It also demanded that "all Ivorian parties take all the necessary measures to prevent further violations of human rights and international humanitarian law, particularly against civilian populations whatever their origins."[136]

France had already indicated that while its prime mission did not include the protection of civilians: "[N]os soldats ne resteront évidemment pas les bras croisés s'ils étaient témoins d'exactions."[137] In response to the discovery of the mass graves, the French became resolute: "Il y a aujourd'hui des actes inacceptables qui se passent en Côte d'lvoire. C'est une question qui doit concerner et mobiliser la communauté internationale."[138]

---

[131] Press Release, European Union, Declaration by the EU Presidency Concerning the Situation in Côte d'Ivoire (Dec. 17, 2002), *available at* http://www.reliefweb.int/rw/rwb.nsf/AllDocsByUNID/c2d93086084cde80c1256c980052b8bd.

[132] Resolution on the Situation in Côte d'Ivoire, *supra* note 118.

[133] African Union, First Extraordinary Session of the Executive Council: Decision on the Situation in Côte d'Ivoire (Dec. 16, 2002), *available at* http://wwwnotes.reliefweb.int/w/rwb.nsf/d2fc8ae9db883867852567cb0083a028/6d5ee11b6d5a1a6d85256c93006b6101?OpenDocument.

[134] President of the Security Council, Statement, *supra* note 114.

[135] S.C. Res. 1464, *supra* note 97, ¶ 9.

[136] S.C. Res. 1479, *supra* note 98, ¶ 8.

[137] Déclaration du porte-parole du Quai d'Orsay (Paris, 13 décembre 2002).

[138] Le Quotidien «La Croix», «Entretien du ministre des affaires etrangeres, M

5. Summary

It may seem contradictory that the international community sought to uphold the principle of peaceful resolution by impartially demanding that both parties settle peacefully without specifying the required outcome, at the same time as it strongly condemned the recourse to force against the legitimately elected government.[139] It could have been expected that the president would be reinstalled, as had been the case in Haiti and in Sierra Leone. In this case, however, it seems that the international community did not consider that outcome to be compulsory.

Is this an indication of the predominance of the principle of preventing conflict and violence over the principle of rejecting recourse to force to bring about an unconstitutional change in government? The European Union, for instance, did not consider any particular outcome obligatory, only that the method of reaching such an agreement must not involve recourse to force. Its emphasis on a peaceful solution and a cease-fire suggests that despite its disapproval of attacks against democratic governments, when a civil conflict ensues, the conflict must nonetheless be resolved peacefully.[140] Similarly, the ECOWAS peace-keeping force was also mandated to halt the fighting to allow negotiations to take place[141] rather than to assist and reinforce the government. "President Wade of Senegal and host President John Kufuor of Ghana both made it clear the peacekeeping force would not support Ivorian government attacks on the rebels. The force's mandate, both said, is to halt the fighting to allow negotiations to take place, which would save face on both sides."[142]

On the other hand, the well-established principle prohibiting recourse to force leading to regional destabilization was only mentioned in passing in this conflict. France did comment that it rejected any actions that were likely to affect the domestic peace and security and regional stabil-

---

Dominique de Villepin» (Paris, 16 décembre 2002), *at* http://www.diplomatie.gouv.fr/actu/actu.asp.

[139] Resolution on the Situation in Côte d'Ivoire, *supra* note 118.

[140] *See also* the comments by the European Union, reinforcing the need for all parties involved in the current crisis to participate in solving the conflict by political means, cease all hostilities, and put a stop to any human rights violations European Union. Press Release, European Union, Declaration by the EU Presidency, *supra* note 131.

[141] Agence France-Presse, *West African Leaders, supra* note 106.

[142] *Id.*

ity: "Comme nous n'avons cessé de le rappeler, notre action en Côte d'Ivoire est dictée par les principes suivants . . . —condamnation de tous les agissements susceptibles de porter atteinte à la paix civile et à la stabilité régionale."[143] The African Union also commented on its concern at the threat to peace and security of the Côte d'Ivoire as well as the region.[144]

The prohibition on force leading to regional destabilization focuses narrowly on the goal of international peace, without regard for the internal character of states. In contrast, the prohibition on violence against a democratically elected government both targets the problem of regional instability, and the desirability of protecting democracy, which is expected to promote long-term regional stability.

The weak affirmative steps that were taken to uphold the principle prohibiting violence against a democratic government may be due to the discomfort surrounding President Gbagbo's legitimacy. Côte d'Ivoire's Patriotic Movement (MPCI), the political wing of mutinous Ivorian soldiers, called on France to remain neutral.[145] The release stated: "The Great France, a country of human rights, freedom and democracy, is not expected to support an autocrat, a regime tarnished by political assassinations, mass graves under the pretext of any constitutional legality. A

---

143 L'Agence Algérienne de Presse, *Entretien du Ministre des Affaires Etrangeres, M Dominique de Villepin: Situation en Côte d'Ivoire: Rôle de la France* (Oct. 31, 2002).

144 African Union, Le Conseil Exécutif de l'Union Africaine: Décision sur la situation en Côte d'Ivoire (Dec. 23, 2002), *available at* http://wwwnotes.reliefweb.int/w/rwb.nsf/d2fc8ae9db883867852567cb0083a028/351eb821cd25638bc1256c9c005c6e58?OpenDocument.

> 1. Exprime sa grave préoccupation face à la persistance de la crise, a ses graves conséquences humanitaires ainsi qu'au danger qu'elle fait peser sur la paix, la sécurité et la stabilité de la Côte d'Ivoire et de la région tout entière.
>
> 2. Souligne la nécessité de rechercher une solution négociée à la crise dans le respect de la légalité constitutionnelle et exhorte le Gouvernement de la République de Côte d'Ivoire et les Mouvements rebelles à coopérer pleinement avec la Médiation.
>
> 3. Encourage les dirigeants de la CEDEAO à poursuivre leurs efforts et à renforcer la cohésion de la région pour promouvoir une solution rapide et pacifique à la crise.

145 Pan African News Agency, *Ivorian Rebel Movement Urges France to Be Neutral* (Dec. 12, 2002).

leader who commits genocide deserves no support, he should appear before an International Criminal Tribunal."[146]

Moreover, it is interesting to note that the resolution sought more than a return to the status quo. In contrast to the traditional principle involving intra-state conflicts—the prohibition on recourse to force in international relations—where peace is preferred over justice, leading to the favoring of the status quo, here the resolution of the underlying sources of the conflict were to be addressed.[147] The Council called "upon the President of Côte d'Ivoire to involve fully all parties and to seek consensus among them."[148]

The final point that is worth considering is the extent to which consent of the state provided a legal justification for intervention.[149] President Gbagbo called for assistance to overthrow the rebels from the outset, and then called for assistance to help resolve the conflict, by military intervention if necessary. President Gbagbo's advisor in Europe, Toussaint Alain, told Reuters: "France, the United States and the European Union must get involved in the search for a peaceful solution and consider all options, even military intervention, to prevent the country and the whole region from exploding."[150]

Despite these clear requests, the legality of sending forces can be contested under traditional theory. The country was split, with rebels holding the north, and had the appearance of an insurgency or belligerency rather than a rebellion. Thus, the principle prohibiting assistance to a government, even at its request, in cases of insurgency or belligerency should have applied. The forces would be justified, however, as legitimate peacekeepers once all parties agreed to their presence to monitor the cease-fire.

Empirically, therefore, the patterns of responses during both the Sierra Leone and Côte d'Ivoire civil wars reinforce the notion of certain

---

[146] *Id.*

[147] President of Security Council, *Côte d'Ivoire*, Statement, U.N. Doc. S/PRST/2002/42 (Dec. 20, 2002).

[148] *Id.*

[149] Note once again that the legal rationale for intervention is not the focus of this enquiry.

[150] Reuters, *Ivory Coast Urges West to Help Resolve Conflict* (Dec. 10, 2002).

emerging principles rejecting recourse to violence. The principle rejecting recourse to force aiming to overthrow a democratic government is reformulated here, with the international community rejecting recourse to force attempting to bring about an unconstitutional change of government.

In addition, the review of this practice suggests that there is a complex network of principles advocated by the international community, which at times are in competition. For instance, despite condemnation of the initial attempts to overthrow the government, when the conflict became entrenched, there appeared a general condemnation of recourse to force by either party. The international community also expressed determination that the conflict should be resolved by peaceful means and peace agreements providing for power sharing. Thus, despite disapproval of the recourse to force to bring about unconstitutional changes of government, the government was not entitled to act brutally in response. As Human Rights Watch explained in condemning the conduct of the government: "the response of the government to the military revolt has not been restricted to legitimate security measures, but has rather tended, at minimum, to exacerbate existing divisions in Ivorian society and, at worst, to promote or cause human rights abuses."[151]

C. LIBERIA

The response of the international community to the conflict in Liberia echoes the principles raised in Sierra Leone and Côte d'Ivoire, though with a different emphasis. In this case, the international community not only did not emphasize the principle rejecting violence against a democratically elected government, but in fact it pressured President Charles Taylor, who was democratically elected, to step down. The primary emphasis of the international community was the condemnation of violence against civilians and the threat of a humanitarian disaster. This practice raises the question of whether procedural legitimacy is sufficient to trigger support against violent overthrow (a question that was also hinted at in the practice in Côte D'Ivoire), and the degree to which a principle prohibiting violence against civilians justifies primarily verbal condemnation, or can also justify forceful intervention. The verbal practice in support for a principle rejecting recourse to violence to resolve political disputes is particularly interesting in this case, since it

---

[151] HUMAN RIGHTS WATCH, CÔTE D'IVOIRE: GOVERNMENT ABUSES IN RESPONSE TO ARMY REVOLT (Nov. 2002).

implies that such a principle is relevant in cases where the government is not considered substantively, as opposed to procedurally, democratic. This implies that such a principle may ultimately develop to apply in a broader fashion than the principle rejecting the overthrow of democratically elected governments.

Again, the fact that the conflict in Liberia destabilized an already fragile region would be expected to play a major role in determining the response of the international community. However, it was at most referred to in passing. The International Crisis Group, for instance, stated when calling for intervention: "There is a universal cry from every voice that matters, within Liberia and internationally, for the United States to lead an effort, once and for all, to end the disastrous disintegration of Liberia and the destabilisation of the entire region to which Charles Taylor's destructive leadership has contributed so much."[152]

The 1989 civil conflict during which Taylor overthrew President Doe, who had himself come to power through a military coup, concluded in 1997 with Taylor winning the presidential elections by a landslide. International observers declared the elections free and fair. Following his election, however, Taylor proved himself to be a destabilizing influence on the region, supporting rebel wars in neighboring states, particularly Sierra Leone. Liberia was subject to arms-import and diamond-export embargos, while Taylor himself was subject to personal travel sanctions and was branded an international pariah. Within his own region of West Africa, he became shunned as a troublemaker and accused of fermenting civil wars outside his borders.[153]

The latest conflict was initiated by a rebel group in the north, the Liberians United for Reconciliation and Democracy (LURD), which was joined by the new Movement for Democracy in Liberia (MODEL) in the west in 1999. The international community maintained a stark silence on this violence, however, until June 2003, when having gained control of much of the territory of Liberia, on June 6, the rebels reached the outskirts of the capital. They began an assault and siege of Monrovia where tens of thousands of Liberian civilians had fled to escape their military campaign.

---

[152] Press Release, ICG, Liberia: ICG Urges U.S. to Lead a Robust Multinational Force (July 16, 2003).

[153] Nicole Itano, *Liberating Liberia: Charles Taylor and the Rebels Who Unseated Him*, ISS Paper 82 (2003).

The Liberian peace talks began on June 4, 2003, under the auspices of ECOWAS. They led to a cease-fire agreement on June 17, which stipulated that an interim government, from which Taylor would be excluded, would be agreed upon within 30 days.[154] However, this agreement held for less than a week before a second attack brought rebels into Monrovia's industrial area, which included the port area. After ECOWAS agreed to send peacekeepers, there was a brief period of calm before LURD again attacked and consolidated their hold on the port on July 17.[155] Large numbers of casualties resulted from these attacks, especially during intense shelling of the city.[156] As the fighting continued to intensify, ECOWAS agreed to send peacekeepers, although a substantial delay was caused by the fact that ECOWAS requested that the funding for the mission be provided by other nations.

Charles Taylor himself stepped down on August 11, 2003, and went into exile in Nigeria, in response to extensive international pressure, including an indictment issued on June 4 by the Special Court in Sierra Leone for war crimes.[157] He had agreed to a cease-fire, which anticipated an interim government without him on June 17, but had later recanted. Nonetheless, in late June 2003, President George W. Bush called for him to step down and hinted that the United States might send troops to help stabilize the situation.[158] Ultimately Taylor did resign, without recourse to further violence, and handed power to his deputy Moses Blah.

U.S. troops arrived to assist the ECOWAS peacekeepers, and a peace agreement was signed on August 18, 2003. The U.S. troops withdrew in September and were replaced by a 15,000 strong U.N. peace-keeping mission, which was mandated to protect civilians, supervise elections in 2005,

---

[154] U.N. OCHA Integrated Regional Information Network, "Liberia: Mediator threatens to end peace talks, Bush tells Taylor to quit" (June 26, 2003), *at* http://www.reliefweb.int/.

[155] Itano, *supra* note 153.

[156] *Id.* The Liberian health minister said at least 200 people had been killed and 350 injured in the latest battle for Monrovia. U.N. OCHA Integrated Regional Information Network "Liberia: Mediator threatens to end peace talks, Bush tells Taylor to quit" (June 26, 2003), *at* http://www.reliefweb.int/.

[157] U.N. News Center, *UN-Backed Sierra Leone Court indicts Liberian President Charles Taylor* (June 4, 2003), *available at* http://www.un.org/apps/news/storyAr.asp?NewsID=7305&Cr=Sierra&Cr1=Leone.

[158] Itano, *aupra* note 153.

and assist in disarming and demobilizing combatants.[159] In October, as agreed, President Blah stepped down and a National Transitional Government was created with Gyude Bryant as Chairman. The transitional government was mandated to implement the Comprehensive Peace Agreement.[160] President Ellen Johnson-Sirleaf came to power in elections in November 2005.

1. Prohibition on Violence Against a Democratically Elected Government

One of the difficulties in interpreting the response of the international community to the conflict in Liberia is that it might have been expected that the international community would have supported the government against the rebel advances as it had done in Sierra Leone—since President Taylor came to power following elections supervised and declared free and fair by the international community. However, it rapidly became clear that he was considered to be one of the causes for the ongoing violence in Liberia, as well as the region, and his departure from office was an essential element of the resolution of the conflict.

In fact, the international community put pressure on the president to resign. President Bush stated: "President Taylor needs to step down so that his country can be spared further bloodshed."[161] The European Union similarly stressed that the early deployment of an interposition/international stabilization force was essential and that this must be accompanied by Taylor immediately stepping down.[162] This does seem contrary to principles of non-intervention in the political process, and some suggested that Bush's statement had created something of a problem for the mediators at the peace talks, since his demand for Taylor to resign contravened the A.U. declaration on the removal and appointment of elected African presidents.[163] Taylor resigned reluctantly on the

---

[159] U.N. OCHA Integrated Regional Information Network, "Liberia: Disarmament of combatants to start in January" (Oct. 29, 2003), *at* http://www.reliefweb.int/.

[160] U.N. Mission in Liberia (UNMIL), National Transitional Government inaugurated in Liberia (Oct. 15, 2003), UNMIL/PIO/PR/6.

[161] U.N. OCHA Integrated Regional Information Network, "Liberia: Mediator threatens to end peace talks, Bush tells Taylor to quit" (June 26, 2003), *at* http://www.reliefweb.int/.

[162] EU Presidency Declaration on Liberia's Peace Process (July 28, 2003), *available at* http://www.europa-eu-un.org/articles/en/article_2618_en.htm.

[163] U.N. OCHA Integrated Regional Information Network, "Liberia: Ceasefire brokered, ECOWAS military chiefs to meet" (June 27, 2003), *at* http://www.reliefweb.int/.

August 11, 2003, claiming that he was a "sacrificial lamb" stepping down to spare his people more bloodshed and accusing the United States of backing his rebel foes. He said he was being "forced into exile."[164]

An additional rationale for seeking Taylor's departure was the cease-fire of June 17 in which he agreed to a transitional agreement that would exclude him. However, on June 20, he rejected the agreement and also emphasized that he reserved his "constitutional right, following the transition, to run for general elections if I decide to do so."[165]

This practice could be interpreted in a number of ways. On the one hand, it suggests that the support for democratically elected governments is one factor that must be weighed among others, such as protecting civilians and preventing humanitarian crises. In this case, the only way to do the latter involved pressuring the president to leave. Another interpretation would be to recognize that the assessment of the democratic nature of a government involves more than simply the existence of a procedurally democratic government. The fact that the international community had already condemned Taylor for his war mongering in the region, imposed sanctions on Liberia, and a travel ban on him personally, undermined his legitimacy as a democratic leader, despite being elected democratically, in the eyes of the international community.

2. Prohibition on Violence Against Civilians

The key focus in the discourse of the international community was on humanitarian disaster and large numbers of civilians being killed. The great part of the response took the form of repeated and extensive condemnation of the impact of the conflict on civilians, and it calls on the parties to stop the fighting and negotiate a peaceful solution to the conflict. Both government and rebel forces were considered to have been responsible for widespread killing, torture, sex slavery, and conscripting child fighters.[166] The only military intervention, however, was a purely peace-keeping force and was only put in place after the peace agreement providing for President Taylor's resignation.

---

164 Reuters, *Liberia's President Charles Taylor Resigns* (Aug. 11, 2003).

165 U.N. OCHA Integrated Regional Information Network, "Liberia: Taylor rejects transition government within 30 days," (June 20, 2003), *at* http://www.reliefweb.int/.

166 Agence France-Presse, *Liberia's Taylor, Rebels to Meet in Ghana for Landmark Peace Talks* (June 2, 2003).

The timing of the international community's response to the conflict correlates to the sudden increase in the threat of a humanitarian crisis following the LURD's march on Monrovia and its waves of attacks on that city beginning on June 5, 2003. Military intervention did not take place until the resignation of President Taylor under the peace agreement.

The Secretary-General explicitly called on all the parties to cease hostilities in order to give the peace negotiations a chance and allow for the safe and unhindered delivery of humanitarian assistance to Liberia's traumatized population.[167] "The combination of cholera outbreaks and food shortages in an environment of ongoing violence, disruption of life-saving services, and cessation of humanitarian aid threatens to produce a major humanitarian catastrophe."[168] The Secretary-General urgently called on the Security Council to authorize a peace-keeping force to prevent a major humanitarian tragedy and to stabilize the situation: "the consequences of allowing the situation to spiral out of control are too terrible to contemplate."[169]

The European Union also emphasized the "gravity of the humanitarian situation in Liberia and the urgent need to provide assistance."[170] ECOWAS Executive Secretary, Mohammed Chambas, told the meeting of ECOWAS military chiefs: "The situation in Liberia is grave. We need to talk about sending an international intervention force. It needs to go in now and very quickly to keep the warring factions apart, secure Monrovia and pave the way for humanitarian agencies to move in."[171]

The Council responded to these pleas and determined that the situation in Liberia constituted a threat to international peace and security.

---

[167] Press Release, The Secretary-General, Secretary-General Deeply Concerned at Renewed Fighting in Liberia, Calls for Immediate Cessation of Hostilities, U.N. Doc. SG/SM/8761, AFR/650 (June 26, 2003).

[168] Letter from the Secretary-General Addressed to the President of the Security Council (June 28, 2003), U.N. Doc. S/2003/678.

[169] *Id.*

[170] EU Presidency Declaration on the Peace Process in Liberia (July 21, 2003), *available at* http://www.europa-eu-un.org/articles/en/article_2585_en.htm.

[171] Letter from the Secretary-General Addressed to the President of the Security Council (July 29, 2003), U.N. Doc. S/2003/769. The deployment of ECOWAS troops was unfortunately repeatedly delayed for economic reasons. The members emphasized from the beginning that they needed financial assistance to undertake the operations. AllAfrica, *International Indecision as Crisis Deepens in Liberia* (July 21, 2003), *available at* http://allafrica.com/stories/200307210520.html.

It pointed to "its effects on the humanitarian situation, including the tragic loss of countless innocent lives, in that country, and its destabilizing effect on the region."[172] Thus, it authorized a multi-national force to support the implementation of the June 17, 2003, cease-fire agreement under Chapter VII and to address humanitarian aspects. Its mandate was to establish "conditions for initial stages of disarmament, demobilization and reintegration activities," "to help establish and maintain security in the period after the departure of the current President and the installation of a successor authority, taking into account the agreements to be reached by the Liberian parties," and "to secure the environment for the delivery of humanitarian assistance."[173]

Members of the Council emphasized these factors during the meeting that led to the adoption of Resolution 1497, which authorized the multi-national force.[174] The United States said that their sponsorship of the resolution "reflected the importance the United States placed on finding the right and effective means to bring peace to Liberia."[175] Germany maintained that "the constant death of civilians was to be deplored and the Council must react swiftly." Chile pointed out that it had supported the resolution "as its priority was to save lives and to give an appropriate response to a humanitarian crisis that brooked no further delay."[176] This focus by the international community was apparently also adopted by the local parties. At one point, the LURD, the main rebel group, declared a truce on the basis that it would "provide needed relief to the civil populace and subsequently avoid a grotesque humanitarian catastrophe in Monrovia."[177] Later in the conflict, Liberia's caretaker president urged the ECOWAS peacekeepers to push into the lawless interior and stop the carnage taking place.[178]

In the Liberian conflict the level of violence against the civilian population was relied upon as a primary justification for condemnation.

---

172 S.C. Res. 1497, pmbl, U.N. Doc. S/RES/1497 (Aug. 1, 2003).

173 *Id.*, ¶ 1.

174 *Id.*, adopted by 12-0-3 (France, Germany, Mexico).

175 *Id.*

176 *Id.*

177 Agence France-Presse, *Liberian Rebels Declare Truce to Prevent Humanitarian Disaster in Monrovia* (June 27, 2003).

178 Reuters, *Liberia's Blah Urges Peacekeepers to Halt Killings* (Aug. 25, 2003).

Nevertheless, it did not apparently justify the imposition of sanctions or the use of armed force that was seen in the case of Sierra Leone.

The Secretary-General called on parties to refrain from any action that might further endanger the lives of the civilian population.[179] He called on the parties to the conflict "to take all necessary measures to ensure that civilians are not targeted and are spared the effects of war." He also reminded them that violators of international humanitarian and human rights law would be held accountable for their acts.[180]

Before the cease-fire was first brokered, the Council already expressed its concern at the "rapidly deteriorating security situation" and urged "all combatants in the strongest terms to immediately cease hostilities and agree to a ceasefire." In so doing, the Council stressed "the urgent need for the combatants to spare the lives and property of innocent civilians, to maintain defensive positions well clear of Monrovia and Buchanan, and to refrain from committing further violations of human rights and international humanitarian law."[181] These concerns appear repeatedly in Council resolutions addressing the conflict.[182]

3. Prohibition on Recourse to Violence to Resolve Political Disputes

There is useful verbal practice supporting the rejection of violence to resolve political disputes. The Secretary-General formulated such a principle explicitly, condemning any attempts to resolve political differences through armed violence,[183] and rejecting attempts to seize power by force.[184] He rejected military means, maintaining that "the Liberian crisis cannot be solved by military confrontation. Such confrontation can

---

[179] Press Release, The Secretary-General, Secretary-General Deeply Concerned at Renewed Fighting in Liberia, *supra* note 169.

[180] Press Release, The Secretary-General, Secretary-General Alarmed at Impact of Fighting in Liberia, U.N. Doc. SG/SM/8740, AFR/638 (June 10, 2003).

[181] President of the Security Council, Statement on Liberia, U.N. Doc. SC/7787, AFR/644 (Nov. 6, 2003).

[182] S.C. Res. 1478, U.N. Doc. S/RES/1478, ¶ 5 (May 6, 2003); S.C. Res. 1509, U.N. Doc. S/RES/1509, ¶ 10 (Sept. 19, 2003).

[183] Press Release, The Secretary-General, Secretary-General Deeply Concerned at Renewed Fighting in Liberia, *supra* note 169.

[184] Press Release, The Secretary-General, Secretary-General Condemns Resumption of Hostilities in Liberia; Renews Call for Force Deployment to Restore Calm, U.N. Doc. SG/SM/8787, AFR/670 (July 21, 2003).

only lead to a further deterioration of an already dire humanitarian situation." In addition, he reiterated that "any attempt to seize power by force would be unacceptable to the international community."[185]

The Security Council also adopted similar principles, urging "the LURD and MODEL to refrain from any attempt to seize power by force, bearing in mind the position of the African Union on unconstitutional changes of government as stated in the 1999 Algiers Decision and the 2000 Lomé Declaration."[186] This was reinforced by statements of the African Union and ECOWAS that taking power by unconstitutional means would not be recognized. They warned rebels that they would not recognize any group that takes power in Liberia through "unconstitutional means or by force of arms."[187] ECOWAS also emphasized that a negotiated settlement was the only way to end the conflict. General Abdulsalami Abubabakar, leading ECOWAS's efforts to end the conflict, stated: "ECOWAS and the International Community will not tolerate power obtained or maintained through unconstitutional means. I remind the belligerents that dialogue remains the only avenue for ensuring permanent peace in Liberia."[188]

Similarly, the European Union condemned "the attempts by armed rebel groups to take power in Liberia by the use of force."[189] It called on all the warring parties "to put an immediate end to hostilities" and urged all the belligerents to search for a negotiated settlement of the crisis.[190]

The principle that achieving power by force is not acceptable became reflected in statements by the rebels themselves. At one time, the MODEL rebel forces reminded the LURD:

---

[185] *Id.*

[186] S.C. Res. 1497, *supra* note 172, ¶ 13.

[187] Deutsche Presse Agentur, *African, ECOWAS, Leaders Warn Liberian Rebels: No Recognition* (July 27, 2003).

[188] *Id.*

[189] Council of the European Union, Liberia, Bulletin EU 5-2002, Common Foreign and Security Policy 23/29 (2002), *available at* http://www.europa.eu/bulletin/en/200205/p106023.htm.

[190] Global News Wire, Asia Africa Intelligence Wire "European Union condemns violence in Liberia" (June 16, 2003), *at* http://web.lexis-nexis.com/executive/.

> [W]e are appealing to them to recognise the sentiments of suffering Liberians and stop the fighting now. The international community has already said it will not recognise any armed force that comes into power by the barrel of the gun. If LURD persists on their advance into Monrovia, then they will have to answer to the international community.[191]

The rejection of recourse to force to settle political disputes was explicitly adopted in the final peace agreement, which in its preamble read: "Determined to establish sustainable peace and security, and pledging forthwith to settle all past, present and future differences by peaceful and legal means and to refrain from the threat of or use of force."[192] In addition, it was agreed that the posts of chairman and vice-chairman would be open only to political parties and civil groups, not to the rebels or Blah's government.[193] ECOWAS explained: "We are trying to strike a balance. . . . [T]he stakes are very high but at the same time we cannot put out a signal that one way to power is just to take up arms and cause all-round havoc."[194] This message reflects statements by the Secretary-General that the use of means that cause suffering to the civilian population disqualifies groups from leadership roles in the future of the country: "The Secretary-General reminds those who continue to wage war in Liberia and to use means that cause so much suffering to the civilian population that they will be held individually accountable for any war crimes they commit."[195] He also stated: "By their reckless and criminal behaviour, [the warring parties] are disqualifying themselves from any leadership role in the future of their country."[196]

---

[191] U.N. OCHA Integrated Regional Information Network, "Liberia: ECOWAS and MODEL call on LURD to stop fighting" (July 21, 2003), *at* http://www.reliefweb.int/.

[192] Comprehensive Peace Agreement Between the Government of Liberia and the Liberians United for Reconciliation and Democracy (LURD) and the Movement for Democracy in Liberia (MODEL) and Political Parties, *available at* http://www.usip.org/library/pa/liberia/liberia_08182003_cpa.html.

[193] Agence France-Presse, *ECOWAS Statement: Liberian Peace Deal to Be Signed After Last-Minute Talks* (Aug. 18, 2003).

[194] *Id.*

[195] U.N. News Center, *Liberian Rebel Group "Disqualifying" Itself from Future Leadership Role—Annan* (July 28, 2003), *available at* http://www.un.org/apps/news/story.asp?NewsID=7846&Cr=Liberia&Cr1=.

[196] *Id.*

The breadth of a principle rejecting violence to gain political power, however, remains somewhat uncertain: Does it apply equally to both parties to a conflict? Does it favor the party that has democratic aspirations? In this case, President Taylor was not treated as a legitimate democratic government, and the condemnation of violence targeted both sides of the conflict. However, at the same time, President Taylor was placed under pressure by the international community to step down, implying that his opponents had greater international support.

The rejection of the use of violence to gain political power or resolve political disputes could be wider in application than the principle in Sierra Leone, which focused only on the case of violence against a democratic government. The principle here could apply in the case of a democratic, or undemocratic government, and could apply both to the government and its opposition. The degree to which this principle has emerged remains somewhat uncertain however, as the international community did not seek to enforce it through sanctions or forceful intervention, in contrast to the more limited principle prohibiting the overthrow of a democratic government formulated in Sierra Leone.

4. Prohibition on the Breach of a Peace or Cease-Fire Agreement

At a later stage of the conflict, the principle prohibiting the breach of a peace or cease-fire agreement seems to have come into play. The first cease-fire agreement was signed on June 17, 2003, and was followed by a general peace agreement on August 18, 2003. The peace agreement was signed by Liberia's interim government and the two rebel groups. It declared the end to the war and put in place a procedure to resolve the conflict peacefully through a series of reforms, particularly of the army and police, and a transitional power-sharing government leading to elections in 2006.[197] The agreement called on ECOWAS to deploy a multinational force to secure the cease-fire, create a buffer zone, and ensure free humanitarian assistance and free movement of people. It also anticipated a U.N. stabilization force under Chapter VII with the right to use force to back the proposed transitional government.

Violations of the cease-fire repeatedly attracted condemnation. The European Union expressly condemned such breaches and called on the

---

[197] Comprehensive Peace Agreement Between the Government of Liberia and the Liberians United for Reconciliation and Democracy (LURD) and the Movement for Democracy in Liberia (MODEL) and Political Parties, *available at* http://www.usip.org/library/pa/liberia/liberia_08182003_cpa.html.

parties to sign a comprehensive peace agreement.[198] The Security Council emphasized that all parties to the conflict must honor the cease-fire,[199] as did the Secretary-General, who stated that he "calls on the parties concerned and, in particular, the Liberians United for Democracy and Reconciliation, to fully observe the ceasefire."[200] He also expressed "deep concern of renewed and intensified fighting between government troops and rebel forces in Monrovia," pointing out that the development constituted a flagrant violation of the cease-fire agreement.[201]

The Council explicitly referred to the obligation of the parties to "cease hostilities throughout Liberia and fulfill their obligations under the Comprehensive Peace Agreement and the ceasefire agreement."[202] The mandate of the U.N.-authorized force explicitly referred to the implementation of the cease-fire agreement. Nigeria spoke of enforcing the cease-fire, not merely monitoring it: "Nigeria is now ready to send troops into Liberia, not only to maintain peace but also to enforce peace."[203]

5. Summary

The practice of the international community in response to the conflict in Liberia reinforces many of the principles identified in the conflicts in Sierra Leone and Côte d'Ivoire. One of the particularly interesting elements of this practice is the reliance on the prohibition on violence against civilians as the central entry point for the international community, given its reluctance to recognize President Taylor's government as democratically legitimate. However, it is clear that this principle does not have the strength of a principle prohibiting the overthrow of a democratically elected government, in that it did not result in the imposition of sanctions or the use of forceful measures.

---

198 EU Presidency Declaration on Liberia's Peace Process (July 28, 2003), *available at* http://www.europa-eu-un.org/articles/en/article_2618_en.htm.

199 Press Release, President of Security Council, Situation in Liberia, U.N. Doc. SC/7824, AFR/674 (July 24, 2003).

200 Press Release, The Secretary-General, Secretary-General Condemns Resumption of Hostilities in Liberia, *supra* note 186.

201 Press Release, The Secretary-General, Secretary-General Deeply Concerned at Renewed Fighting in Liberia, *supra* note 169.

202 S.C. Res. 1509, *supra* note 182, ¶ 4.

203 Agence France-Presse, *Statement of the Delta State Governor: Nigerian Troops Ready to "Enforce" Peace in Liberia* (July 30, 2003).

This case does provide some insight in relation to the boundaries of the principle rejecting violence to gain political power, or resolve political disputes, which can be seen to be accorded less weight than that rejecting the overthrow of a democratic government, again because the international community failed to use sanctions or forceful intervention to enforce it. This principle did however gain key support in the case of Liberia, through the explicit statements rejecting the legitimacy of parties who gained power through violence, which was carried through into the agreements that excluded rebel fighters and government fighters from the interim government.

D. THE A.U. AND ECOWAS SECURITY TREATIES

The evolution of the practice reviewed in these three case studies is also reflected in the development of the security treaties of the African Union (A.U.) and ECOWAS. It is useful to review briefly these treaties, since they set out legal norms regarding civil conflict and coup d'état that have been expressly formulated and adopted by many states in Africa and that mirror, to a large extent, the principles reflected in the practice of the greater international community. The fact that these principles have been recently adopted in a deliberate fashion by the states in Africa provides a strong indication of the direction of evolution of this field.

The A.U. constitutive documents explicitly address civil conflict,[204] whereas those of the OAU, which it replaces, did not.[205] The Constitutive Act (2000) sets out in general terms the objectives of the A.U. and some guiding principles. While it cites the usual prohibition on use of force against another state of the Union, and supports the principle of non-interference, the Constitutive Act also provides for a balance with "[t]he right of the Union to intervene in a Member State pursuant to a decision of the Assembly in respect of grave circumstances, namely war crimes, genocide and crimes against humanity"; "[r]espect for the sanctity of

---

[204] Constitutive Act of the African Union, July 11, 2000, 2000 AFR. Y.B. INT'L L. 479, *available at* http://www.au2002.gov.za/docs/key_oau/au_act.htm [hereinafter A.U. Constitutive Act]. For a discussion of the evolution and drafting of the Constitutive Act, *see* Corinne Packer and Donald Rukare, *The New African Union and Its Constitutive Act*, 96 AM. J. INT'L L. 365 (2002). *See also* Konstantinos D. Magliveras and Gino Naldi, *The African Union: A New Dawn for Africa?*, 51 INT'L & COMP. L.Q. 415 (2002).

[205] The 1993 OAU Mechanism for Conflict Prevention, Management and Resolution did not refer to civil conflicts. *See Declaration of the Assembly of Heads of State and Government on the Establishment, Within the OAU of a Mechanism for Conflict Prevention, Management and Resolution*, Cairo, Egypt, June 1993, Provision 15.

human life, condemnation and rejection of impunity and political assassination, acts of terrorism and subversive activities"; and "[c]ondemnation and rejection of unconstitutional changes of governments."[206]

The Protocol Relating to the Establishment of a Peace and Security Council focuses on conflicts. It establishes a Peace and Security Council "as a standing decision-making organ for the prevention, management and resolution of conflicts."[207] The Council is to be guided by a number of principles, including non-interference. However, of particular interest in this discussion are the "the right of the Union to intervene in a Member State pursuant to a decision of the Assembly in respect of grave circumstances, namely war crimes, genocide and crimes against humanity, in accordance with Article 4(h) of the Constitutive Act"; and "the right of Member States to request intervention from the Union in order to restore peace and security, in accordance with Article 4(j) of the Constitutive Act."[208]

The Peace and Security Council's powers include recommending intervention to the Assembly in respect of grave circumstances, "namely war crimes, genocide and crimes against humanity" and instituting sanctions "whenever an unconstitutional change of Government takes place in a Member State, as provided for in the Lomé Declaration."[209]

The member states agree that, in carrying out its duties under the Protocol, the Peace and Security Council acts on their behalf, and they agree to "accept and implement" its decisions.[210] Moreover, its decisions are binding, and states that fail to abide by them may face economic or political sanctions.[211]

The Protocol also creates an African Standby Force, whose mandate includes intervention in a member state "in respect of grave circumstances or at the request of a Member State in order to restore peace and

---

[206] A.U. Constitutive Act, *supra* note 204, art. 4.

[207] Protocol Relating to the Establishment of the Peace and Security Council of the African Union, art. 2, *available at* http://www.africa-union.org/root/au/organs/psc/Protocol_peace%20and%20security.pdf [hereinafter 2002 A.U. Protocol].

[208] *Id.*, art. 4.

[209] *Id.*, art. 7.

[210] *Id.*, art. 7.

[211] *Id.*, art. 23, para. 2.

security"; and "preventive deployment in order to prevent (i) a dispute or a conflict from escalating, (ii) an ongoing violent conflict from spreading to neighbouring areas or States, and (iii) the resurgence of violence after parties to a conflict have reached an agreement."[212]

ECOWAS's most recent Mechanism for Conflict Prevention, Management, Resolution, Peacekeeping and Security represents the most explicitly interventionist policy toward civil conflict of any regional organization. It is applicable "[i]n case of internal conflict: that threatens to trigger a humanitarian disaster, or that poses a serious threat to peace and security in the sub-region," "[i]n event of serious and massive violation of human rights and the rule of law," and "[i]n the event of an overthrow or attempted overthrow of a democratically elected government."[213]

The purpose of the Mechanism for Conflict Prevention, Management, Resolution, Peacekeeping and Security is to "prevent, manage and resolve internal and inter-State conflicts." The responsibilities of ECOWAS include intervening "to alleviate the suffering of the population and restore life to normalcy in the event of crises, conflict and disaster."[214] It is empowered "to act on all matters concerning conflict prevention, management and resolution, peace-keeping, security, humanitarian support, peace-building, control of cross-border crime, proliferation of small arms, as well as all other matters covered by the provisions of this Mechanism."[215] The Council has the power to "decide and implement all policies for conflict prevention, management and resolution, peace-keeping and security," and "authorise all forms of intervention and decide particularly on the deployment of political and military missions."[216]

This Mechanism can be seen explicitly to target civil conflict.[217] The primary focus of its provisions appears to be the protection of the popu-

---

[212] *Id.*, art. 13.

[213] ECOWAS Protocol on Democracy and Good Governance, Dec. 2001, A/SP1/12/01, art. 25, *available at* http://www.issafrica.org/AF/RegOrg/unity_to_union/pdfs/ecowas/12ProtDemocGood.pdf [hereinafter ECOWAS Protocol on Democracy and Good Governance].

[214] *Id.*, art. 40.

[215] *Id.*, art. 6.

[216] *Id.*, art. 10.

[217] This can be contrasted with the 1981 Protocol on Mutual Defence Assistance,

lation within the region. Thus, conflict that "threatens to trigger a humanitarian disaster" is open to intervention, as are "serious and massive violations of human rights and the rule of law."[218] Its Protocol on Democracy[219] includes the ability to impose sanctions where there is a massive violation of human rights by a state.[220] An internal conflict that "poses a serious threat to peace and security of the sub-region" is also subject to intervention.

1. Prohibition on Violence to Resolve Political Disputes

The security treaties do provide some support for a principle rejecting violence for political gain in the form of civil conflict. In the 2002 A.U. Protocol, conflicts, in general, are referred to as "the scourge of conflicts in Africa" and are recognized to constitute a major impediment to "the need to promote peace, security and stability as a prerequisite for the implementation of our development agenda."[221] The 2002 A.U. Protocol is explicitly applicable to civil conflicts as it expresses concern about the continued prevalence of armed conflicts "within" states.

The overall purpose of the Peace and Security Council is to prevent and resolve conflicts, including civil conflicts, and its primary power is to "anticipate and prevent disputes and conflicts, as well as policies that may lead to genocide and crimes against humanity."[222] Nevertheless, it does not explicitly condemn or prohibit recourse to force. The fact that genocide and crimes against humanity are prohibited and illegal actions, and that conflicts and "policies that lead to genocide and crimes against humanity" are listed together and are not distinguished could suggest that these are both considered prohibited conduct. However, civil con-

---

which addressed civil conflict but restricted intervention to situations where the conflict was engineered and supported from outside and was likely to endanger the peace and security of other Member States. ECOWAS, Protocol Relating to Mutual Assistance of Defence, art. 4(b) (1981), *available at* http://www.iss.co.za/af/RegOrg/unity_to_union/pdfs/ecowas/13ProtMutualDefAss.pdf. *See* Protocol Relating to the Mechanism for Conflict Prevention, Management, Resolution, Peace-Keeping and Security, art. 3 (Dec. 10, 1999), 5 J. CONFLICT & SECURITY L. 231 (2000), *available at* http://www.chr.up.ac.za/hr_docs/african/docs/other/ecowas4.doc.

[218] Protocol Relating to the Mechanism for Conflict Prevention, Management, Resolution, Peace-Keeping and Security, *supra* note 217.

[219] ECOWAS Protocol on Democracy and Good Governance, *supra* note 213.

[220] *Id.*, art. 45.

[221] 2002 A.U. Protocol, *supra* note 207, pmbl.

[222] *Id.*, art. 7.

flicts per se are not explicitly prohibited, although the purpose of the 2002 A.U. Protocol is to prevent and resolve them.[223]

Since civil conflicts are not treated separately from international conflict, the principles and mandate could be read to apply to both. However, the restatement of the principle of non-intervention in domestic affairs, which is subject to explicit exceptions in the case of genocide, crimes against humanity, and war crimes, suggests that only in those circumstances (or when a state requests assistance) are civil conflicts within the regional organization's mandate.

The mandate of the Standby Force must be interpreted within this scope. Nonetheless, its explicit listing of differing instances where it may take *preemptive action* is interesting from the point of view of differentiating various aspects of recourse to violence. The Force is mandated to take preemptive deployment to prevent escalation of a conflict, to stop violence spreading to neighbors, and to prevent the resurgence of violence after the parties to a conflict have reached an agreement. This is also indicative of different principles being applicable to different forms of violence.

Action to prevent violence spreading to neighbors implies regional destabilization and thus a threat to regional peace and security. This principle is also widely supported in the practice and ties into the general notion of preventing conduct amounting to a threat to international peace and security. The preemptive action to prevent escalation of a conflict is the broadest category of provision and supports a general rejection of violent conflict. The explicit recognition of increasing violence, or a recurrence of violence after an agreement, as matters triggering preventative deployment, are important indicators that such violence is not acceptable.

2. Prohibition on Violence Against Civilians

Under the A.U. treaties, permitting intervention into domestic affairs in relation to "war crimes, genocide and crimes against humanity" appears to regularize a form of humanitarian enforcement. Crimes against humanity, genocide, and wars crimes are illegal under well-established international law, but their prohibition is not generally enforceable or enforced.[224]

---

[223] *Id.*, art. 3.

[224] *See, e.g.*, Rwanda, but subject to the creation of the new International Criminal Court.

In the context of ECOWAS, sanctions can be applied when "there is massive violation of human rights in a member State."[225] This principle is closely linked to the doctrine of humanitarian intervention. The ECOWAS provisions have been seen by some to represent the first instance of *codification* of that controversial doctrine.[226]

3. Prohibition on Violence Against a Democratically Elected Government

Finally, a clear principle within the A.U. is the rejection and condemnation of the overthrow of a democratically elected government, formulated as unconstitutional change of government. This principle was initially stated in the Lomé Declaration on Unconstitutional Changes of Government (2000), and was defined to include "military coup d'état against a democratically elected Government," "intervention by mercenaries to replace a democratically elected Government," "replacement of democratically elected Governments by armed dissident groups and rebel movements," and "the refusal by an incumbent government to relinquish power to the winning party after free, fair and regular elections."

The Lomé Declaration provided that the OAU should "convey a clear and unequivocal warning to the perpetrators of the unconstitutional change that, under no circumstances, will their illegal action be tolerated or recognized by the OAU." In addition, after six months of suspension, "a range of limited and targeted sanctions against the regime that stubbornly refuses to restore constitutional order should be instituted, in addition to the suspension from participation in the OAU Policy Organs. This could include visa denials for the perpetrators of an unconstitutional change, restrictions of government-to government contacts, trade restrictions, etc."[227]

The A.U. Constitutive Act also lists as a key value the "[c]ondemnation and rejection of unconstitutional changes of governments," and the

---

225 ECOWAS Protocol on Democracy and Good Governance, sec. IV, art. 45, *supra* note 213.

226 Consider, for instance, Abass's argument that as the provisions were adopted post-Kosovo, they reflect the deliberate adoption of the principle of humanitarian intervention. Ademola Abass, *The New Collective Security Mechanism of ECOWAS: Innovations and Problems*, 5 J. CONFLICT & SECURITY L. 211, 211–12 (2000).

227 Lomé Declaration on the Framework for an OAU Response to Unconstitutional Changes of Government (2000) AHG/Decl.5 (XXXVI), *available at* http://www.africanreview.org/docs/govern/govchange.pdf.

2002 A.U. Protocol lists as one of the Peace and Security Council powers to "institute sanctions whenever an unconstitutional change of Government takes place in a Member State." A government refusing to relinquish power after free and fair elections falls into the same category. The formulations surrounding this principle are the closest to a declaration of illegality in the constitutive documents of the A.U. It is particularly important that such actions are declared to be "illegal," and that these actions will not be "tolerated or recognised by the OAU."[228]

In the context of ECOWAS, member states have agreed on a strong policy in relation to the overthrow of a democratically elected government and describe their response as "imposing sanctions," implying that the conduct is prohibited and illegal. According to the ECOWAS Protocol on Democracy and Good Governance, all member states agree to the constitutional principles that "[e]very accession to power must be made through free, fair and transparent elections," and there is "[z]ero tolerance for power obtained or maintained by unconstitutional means."[229] Moreover, whenever democracy "is abruptly brought to an end by any means . . . ECOWAS may impose sanctions on the State concerned."[230] The sanctions are clearly envisaged as punitive measures, listed "in increasing order of severity," and ranging from refusal to support candidates to suspension from ECOWAS decision-making bodies.[231] In addition, direct intervention is permitted in the event "of an overthrow or attempted overthrow of a democratically elected government."[232]

4. Summary

The growing interventionist response of regional organizations to civil conflict emphasizes the importance that regional organizations place on stopping such conflicts. In addition, the regional organizations are

---

[228] *Id.*

[229] ECOWAS Protocol on Democracy and Good Governance, *supra* note 213, sec. I, art. 1.

[230] *Id.*, sec. IV, art. 45.

[231] *Id.*

[232] Protocol Relating to the Mechanism for Conflict Prevention, Management, Resolution, Peace-Keeping and Security, *supra* note 217, art. 25. ECOWAS may also impose sanctions in such a situation. ECOWAS Protocol on Democracy and Good Governance, art. 45, *supra* note 213. *See also* Charter of the Organization of American States, art. 10 (Apr. 30, 1948), *available at* http://www.oas.org/juridico/English/charter.html.

increasingly prepared to address civil conflicts through resolution and prevention, as well as sanctions and intervention. While the reviewed provisions do not determine whether the intervention will support the rebels or the government, they do provide that such conduct is no longer a matter only for the state in question, and that such conflicts must be brought to an end. The most recently adopted security mechanisms have taken a particularly interventionist and bold position with respect to civil conflicts. This can be seen in the ECOWAS and A.U. provisions, which explicitly reject the forceful overthrow of a democratic government. They also foresee intervention to stop conduct causing massive violations of human rights.

E. CONCLUSION

The review of the practice of the international community in three recent conflicts and the provisions of two recent treaties support a number of principles.

1. Principles rejecting the use of force against a democratically elected government, evidenced by:
   - condemnation and action to prevent or reverse recourse to force to overthrow a democratic government;
   - condemnation and action to prevent or reverse recourse to force to take power in an unconstitutional manner.
2. Principles rejecting violence against civilians evidenced by:
   - condemnation and action to prevent or stop violence against civilians.
3. Principles rejecting recourse to force causing a threat to regional peace and security, evidenced by:
   - condemnation and action to prevent or reverse civil conflicts that threaten regional peace and security.
4. Principles supporting the importance of peaceful resolution of such disputes, evidenced by:
   - support for negotiation, peace agreements and elections as a method of resolving civil conflicts;
   - statements declaring that only peaceful methods of resolution are acceptable;
   - pressure to negotiate peace and cease-fire agreements, and support for such agreements when signed, including "entrenchment" of such agreements by the Council under Chapter VII;

- condemnation of breaches of such agreements, and action to prevent or reverse such breaches, including through sanctions or military intervention against the party breaching the agreement;
- a nascent policy denying positions in the post-conflict government to parties that persist in seeking to gain power by force.

CHAPTER 5
THE NATURE AND IMPACT OF THE EMERGING NORMS

The practice reviewed supports the emergence of two related norms. The first is a broad rejection of extreme political violence in the form of civil conflict and coup d'état. The second is the specific rejection of civil conflict and coup d'état aimed at the overthrow of a democratic government. This chapter considers the nature and impact of these two emerging norms and the direction of evolution of this field.

A. THE DOMESTIC NATURE OF CIVIL CONFLICTS?

The view that civil conflicts and coups d'état are domestic matters has been central to the position that these forms of political violence are not subject to international regulation or appropriate for Security Council intervention.[1] However, according to the Legalist perspective, at least, the question of domestic nature is a relative matter that depends on the development of international law.[2] Although most aspects of an internal conflict will remain subject to national jurisdiction, this jurisdiction may be controlled and limited by international duties through treaty or custom or, according to Brownlie, whenever a matter requires enforcing in relation to another state.[3] This view of domestic jurisdiction

---

[1] *See, e.g.*, the discussion of Northern Ireland and the Spanish Civil War. Goodrich et al. point out such arguments were raised "against the consideration of the Czech coup of 1948, the Hungarian crisis of 1956, race relations in South Africa in 1963, and various 'colonial' questions." LELAND M. GOODRICH ET AL., CHARTER OF THE UNITED NATIONS: COMMENTARY AND DOCUMENTS 273–74 (3d ed. 1969). *See also* Mary Ellen O'Connell, *Regulating the Use of Force in the 21st Century: The Continuing Importance of State Autonomy, in* POLITICS, VALUES AND FUNCTIONS: INTERNATIONAL LAW IN THE 21ST CENTURY 443, 450–51 (Jonathan I. Charney et al. eds., 1998).

[2] *See* ROSALYN HIGGINS, THE DEVELOPMENT OF INTERNATIONAL LAW THROUGH THE POLITICAL ORGANS OF THE UNITED NATIONS 58–130 (1963). Tesón also reviews these positions and assesses them, in Fernando R. Tesón, *A Symposium on Re-Envisioning the Security Council: Collective Humanitarian Intervention*, 17 MICH. J. INT'L L. 323, 327–29 (1996).

[3] IAN BROWNLIE, PRINCIPLES OF PUBLIC INTERNATIONAL LAW 293 (5th ed. 1998); Satvinder Juss, *Nationality Law, Sovereignty, and the Doctrine of Exclusive Domestic Jurisdiction*, 9 FLA. J. INT'L L. 219, 228–29 (1994). NIGEL D. WHITE, KEEPING THE

finds support in the *Nationality Decrees Case*[4] and is consistent with the exemption for Chapter VII enforcement measures. As Goodrich et al. point out, any situation that amounts to a threat to international peace and security is "patently a matter of international concern."[5] White agrees: "any finding under Article 39, whether or not combined with enforcement measures, is sufficient to internationalise the situation and to escape the grasp of Article 2(7)."[6]

The practice reviewed in the preceding chapters shows extensive involvement in civil conflicts and coups d'état by the international community, and there is an increasing assumption that such extreme political violence can amount to a threat to international peace and security and is no longer considered a domestic matter. This seems to be the case despite the numerous statements of the Council upholding state sovereignty. The formulation by the Council in such statements varies very little and is generally of the form recognizing or affirming "the sovereignty, independence, territorial integrity and national unity" of the state.[7] However, these affirmations are frequently contradicted either by direct actions of the Council or by other statements within the resolution and therefore cannot be taken to imply that the political violence is a matter exclusively for the state in question.[8] In Afghanistan, for instance, the

---

PEACE: THE UNITED NATIONS AND THE MAINTENANCE OF INTERNATIONAL PEACE AND SECURITY 56 (2d ed. 1997), *quoting* Report of the Conference held at San Francisco by the Rt Hon Frazer, Chairman of the New Zealand Delegation, NZ Dept of External Affairs Publication, No. 11, at 28 argued that Article 2(7) should be read to permit intervention where it is "proper in the interests of peace and justice, and in the preservation of human rights to interfere in the internal affairs of Member states." *Cf.* D.R. Gilmour, *The Meaning of Intervene Within Article 2(7) of the United Nations Charter*, 16 INT'L & COMP. L.Q. 330, 349 (1967), who maintains that it excludes anything internal.

4 Nationality Decrees Issued in Tunis and Morocco (French Zone) on November 8th, 1921, Advisory Opinion, 1923 P.C.I.J. (ser. B) No. 4, at 24 (Feb. 7). The notion that domestic jurisdiction is relative is also expounded there

5 GOODRICH ET AL., *supra* note 1, at 292. *See* Lois E. Fielding, *Taking a Closer Look at Threats to Peace: The Power of the Security Council to Address Humanitarian Crises*, 73 U. DET. MERCY L. REV. 551 (1996).

6 WHITE, *supra* note 3, at 56.

7 *E.g.*, S.C. Res. 696, U.N. Doc. S/RES/696 (May 30, 1991); S.C. Res. 958, U.N. Doc. S/RES/958 (Nov. 19, 1994); S.C. Res. 1101, U.N. Doc. S/RES/1101 (Mar. 28, 1997); S.C. Res. 1214, U.N. Doc. S/RES/1214 (Dec. 8, 1998); S.C. Res. 1267, U.N. Doc. S/RES/1267 (Oct. 15, 1999).

8 Resolutions of the Security Council that target the conduct of governments contradict repeated statements upholding state sovereignty. Consider, for instance, the

Council made repeated statements, "[s]tressing the importance of non-interference in the internal affairs of Afghanistan" and "[r]eaffirming its strong commitment to the sovereignty, independence, territorial integrity and national unity of Afghanistan."[9] Nonetheless, it also strongly condemned the use of force in those conflicts and repeatedly demanded that the parties stop fighting, cease armed hostilities, and renounce the use of force.[10] It also imposed a non-Chapter VII arms embargo.[11] In Sierra Leone, despite the explicit Council resolution, "[a]ffirming the commitment of all States to respect the sovereignty, political independence and territorial integrity of Sierra Leone,"[12] the extensive and varied intervention by states and the Council did not cause international outcry. Notwithstanding some prevarication regarding Nigeria's use of force, and the later use of force by the United Kingdom, no claims of illegality were made,[13] nor did ECOMOG's intervention cause outcry.[14]

---

condemnation of the South African government over "apartheid" killings; of the Serbian police for excessive use of force in Kosovo; and of the violence by both government and rebel forces in Rwanda and Burundi. In the case of the Kurds in Iraq, the Council did not defer to the Iraqi government but made explicit demands, as it did in the case of Somalia, even though these situations were classically internal matters. Even in instances where the Council has supported the government over the rebel forces, such as the wars in Angola and Sierra Leone, its intervention does not intimate that these matters are internal and entirely within the purview of the government. Rather, the implication seems to be that in the particular circumstances of those rebel wars, the Council considered the government to be worthy of support.

9 S.C. Res. 1076, U.N. Doc. S/RES/1076, pmbl. (Oct. 22, 1996); S.C. Res. 1214, *supra* note 7; S.C. Res. 1267, *supra* note 7.

10 *Id.*

11 S.C. Res. 1076, *supra* note 9.

12 S.C. Res. 1231, U.N. Doc. S/RES/1231 (Mar. 11, 1999).

13 Nigeria's intervention, despite being *prima facie* contrary to the principle of non-intervention and the prohibition on the use of force under Article 2(4) of the U.N. Charter, was not condemned by the remainder of the international community. It was initially greeted with uncertainty from some West African countries. CNN, *Sierra Leone Fighting Eases, Allowing More Evacuations* (June 3, 1997), *available at* http://www.cnn.com/WORLD/9706/03/sierra.leone/index.html. The United States opined that it would prefer to see the situation resolved politically. CNN, *More West African Soldiers Join Nigerians in Sierra Leone* (May 31, 1997), *available at* http://www.cnn.com/WORLD/9705/31/sierra.leone/index.html?eref=sitesearch. However, the Secretary-General endorsed the view that, as a last resort, force might have to be used to dislodge the coup leaders, *Annan Hints at Use of Force to Topple Sierra Leone Coup*, TIMES, June 5, 1997, *available at* http:// www.thetimes.co.uk, and the United Kingdom indicated that it would prefer a negotiated solution but recognized that force might have to be used. *Id.*

14 Similarly, there was express support for the interventions by the Economic

The International Court of Justice has emphasized that whether practice is rejected as illegal by the remainder of the international community is one important element in the determination if a norm remains valid despite inconsistent practice.[15] The lack of reaction to the interventions is indicative of an acceptance in the greater international community that such actions are not illegal. It appears that political violence of the level of a civil conflict or coup d'état is no longer considered a domestic matter and is increasingly recognized as having a severe impact on the peace and stability of the world.

B. PROHIBITION ON POLITICAL VIOLENCE AGAINST A DEMOCRATIC GOVERNMENT

The use of political violence against a democratic government in the form of a civil conflict or coup d'état has increasingly been vehemently condemned by the international community, which has gone so far as to take enforcement action to stop such violence in a number of cases. The practice of the Security Council, states, and regional organizations evidences the emergence of a new norm of international policy and international law prohibiting recourse to force to overthrow a democratically elected government. Such norms would also imply a corollary right of a democratic government to defend itself against those seeking to use force to overthrow it.

Community of West African States (ECOWAS) and Organization of African Unity (OAU), which were also unauthorized by the Security Council. *See, e.g.*, President of the Council, *The Situation in Sierra Leone*, Statement, U.N. Doc. S/PRST/1997/36 (July 11, 1997). Only Russia, during the Council debates, criticized the intervention on the basis that regional organizations' enforcement actions ought to be authorized by the Council. S.C. 3822d mtg., U.N. Doc. S/PV.3822 (Oct. 8, 1997). The U.K. government's intervention did not encounter very much condemnation either. The Secretary-General supported the presence of the U.K. troops as a stabilizing factor. Press Release, The Secretary-General, Secretary-General, in Statement to Security Council, Demands Unconditional Release of United Nations Peacekeepers in Sierra Leone, U.N. Doc. SG/SM/7390, AFR/226 (May 11, 2000). As did many states, S.C. 4139th mtg., U.N. Doc. S/PV.4139 (May 11, 1997). *See* Canada, Malaysia, Argentina, and Russia who made similar comments, as did Portugal on behalf of itself and of the European Union. Bangladesh and India dissented, on the basis that the forces should be under U.N. command. *Id.*

[15] The Court emphasized that inconsistent practice did not of itself prevent the emergence of a norm, so long as any departure was recognized as illegal. Military and Paramilitary Activities in and Against Nicaragua (Nicar. v. U.S.), Merits, 1986 I.C.J. 14, para. 186 (June 27) [hereinafter *Nicaragua*, Merits].

In both Haiti and Sierra Leone, the Council rejected the coup in a robust and clear fashion. It formulated its rationale for doing so explicitly, it demanded in a binding resolution that the junta step down and reinstate the democratically elected government, and it sought to enforce its demands through sanctions. The Council resolutions were formulated as binding and were followed by sanctions or military intervention aimed at enforcing them.

Strong and repeated condemnation by the Council of attempts by rebels to overthrow by force a democratically elected government is evidence of an emerging consensus among the Council members of the international community rejecting such use of force. Indeed, the Council practice reflects more than merely the views of its members. Its practice in this area has not caused controversy, and, hence, it must be taken to reflect a broad understanding in the international community of what principles should be followed, as well as a strong normative incentive for states to change their attitudes to accord with these principles.

The practice does not to amount to *ad hoc* decisions, but rather reflects an emerging policy position within the Council rejecting the violent overthrow of democratic governments in line with the explicit formulation by the Secretary-General in 1997 that it is "an established norm" that "military coups against the democratically elected Governments by self-appointed juntas are not acceptable."[16] The powers of enforcement of the Council ensure that this principle reflects more than a policy position, but rather an enforced *de facto* prohibition on violence seeking to overthrow a democratically elected government.

Moreover, there is a complex if intuitive link between conduct that is prohibited through Council action and illegality under traditional international law. The repeated imposition of Council sanctions on certain conduct influences the international community to view the party being sanctioned as contrary to international law.[17]

---

16 The Secretary-General, *Annual Report of the Secretary-General on the Work of the Organization*, U.N. Doc. A/52/1, ¶ 37 (Sept. 3, 1997).

17 As discussed in Chapter 3, states frequently assert non-compliance with the U.N. Charter or international law as a basis for Security Council intervention. Gowlland-Debbas, in particular, seems to consider Council sanctions to be a form of enforcement of international law, while acknowledging that the condition for the application of the sanctions is strictly not an international wrongful act. Vera Gowlland-Debbas, *The Relationship Between the International Court of Justice and the Security Council in the Light of the Lockerbie Case*, 88 AM. J. INT'L L. 643, 661 (1994). Kirgis also points out that, in

In terms of the emergence of a norm of customary law, Council resolutions, at the very least, provide evidence of *opinio juris* and verbal acts of the states members of the Council, and arguably also reflect a broader consensus. The weight of Council resolutions is greater than that of General Assembly resolutions, despite the Council's more limited membership. Moreover, they are binding, and the Council can pass sanctions. The Council's special status in the international community causes it to shape the views of the broader international community on matters on which it passes resolutions, thus creating consensus views aligned with its resolutions, and hence its practice can be considered to indicate the future direction of evolution of customary law on those matters.

Naturally, however, the emergence of a customary law norm would require reinforcing practice outside the Council. The practice of states and regional organizations provides this reinforcing practice and supports the proposition that in addition to a new international policy norm, a new international law norm rejecting the forceful overthrow of democratic governments may be emerging.

Informative in this respect is the response of states to the 1991 coup in Haiti, where a meeting of Foreign Ministers of the Member States of the Organization of American States (OAS) formally condemned the coup and called on members to impose an economic embargo[18] and to "bring about the diplomatic isolation of those who hold power illegally."[19] U.S. Secretary of State James Baker had demanded that delegates "make clear that the assault on Haiti's constitutional government has *no* legitimacy and *will not* succeed."[20] In Sierra Leone, similarly, the Economic Community of West African States (ECOWAS) urged states not to recognize the regime installed following the coup and called on them to make

many instances, the rules are self-enforcing, and that when they are not, in addition to self-help, the pressure against those that breach these rules brought by international agencies could be considered a form of enforcement. *See* Frederic L. Kirgis, Jr., *Enforcing International Law*, ASIL INSIGHTS, Jan. 1996, *at* http://www.asil.org/insights/insight1.htm.

[18] Organization of American States (OAS), Support for Democracy in Haiti, MRE/RES.2/91 (Oct. 8, 1991).

[19] *Id.*

[20] U.S. Department of State "Statement by the Honorable James A. Baker III to the OAS Meeting of Foreign Ministers on the Situation in Haiti" (Oct. 2, 1991) (emphasis in original).

every effort to restore the lawful government.[21] The Organization of African Unity (OAU) endorsed military as well as diplomatic efforts to restore democracy,[22] and ECOWAS imposed sanctions.[23] The forceful interventions authorized by ECOWAS and the OAU explicitly aimed to remove the military junta,[24] and both Nigeria and the United Kingdom sent troops to this end at different times. The statement by the Secretary-General, "The United Nations and the international community firmly uphold the principle . . . that governments democratically elected shall not be overthrown by force,"[25] was cited approvingly by many states on the Council,[26] and it is consistent with condemnation of the coup by Nigeria,[27] the OAU,[28] and ECOWAS.[29]

The situation in Côte d'Ivoire was not as clear-cut as that in Sierra Leone, because the legitimacy of the government was contested. This seems to have had an impact on the response of the international community, which did not maintain that Gbagbo should be reinstated, but rather sought to achieve a mediated solution to the conflict. For instance, although directly after the failed coup the international community had vigorously protested against the attempt to overthrow the democratically elected government,[30] the aim of the ECOWAS peace-keeping force was

---

21 ECOWAS, Final Communique (Conakry, June 26, 1997).

22 OAU Summit (Harare, June 2–4, 1997).

23 ECOWAS mtg. 20th Sess. (Aug. 29, 1997).

24 CNN, *African Leaders Pledge to Oppose Coups, Support Democracy* (June 4, 1997), *at* http://www.cnn.com/WORLD/9706/04/zimbabwe.new.africa/index.html?eref=sitesearch.

25 Press Release, The Secretary-General, Secretary-General Expresses Concern over Coup in Sierra Leone; Condemns Treatment of UN Staff, Looting of UN Offices, U.N. Doc. SG/SM/6241 (May 27, 1997).

26 *See* Kenya, France, Korea, Sweden, Guinea Bissau, Chile at S.C. 3822d mtg., *supra* note 14.

27 CNN, *More West African Soldiers, supra* note 13.

28 OAU Summit (Harare, June 2–4, 1997).

29 ECOWAS, Final Communique, *supra* note 21.

30 ECOWAS members declared support for the democratically elected government. Nigeria and Ghana, in particular, immediately deployed military assistance to assist President Gbagbo after the failed coup. Nigerian junior foreign minister Dubem Onyia, stated: "The ECOWAS members think democracy is being threatened in Cote d'Ivoire"; and, "We are acting to prop up the elected government in Ivory Coast." Hugh Nevill, *Ivory Coast Prepares to Strike Rebels as Foreigners Pull Out*, AGENCE FRANCE-

to act as a buffer and halt the fighting and allow negotiations to take place, not reinstate the government.[31] Forceful intervention was initially justified on a range of rationales—from having been requested by Gbagbo to having been incorporated into the cease-fire—to a measure to protect nationals—but it was ultimately justified in support of democratic elections[32] condemning "the attempt to undermine constitutional legality in Côte d'Ivoire."[33]

The practice supports the view that there exists a process of progressive and mutual reinforcement between the Council and states. The imposition of binding resolutions and sanctions by the Council has encouraged individual states to change their behavior and their long-term expectations. Yet, the Council would not be able to pass these resolutions without the approval of states. The adoption, acceptance, and repetition over time by states of Council principles supports the view that Council practice reflects a broad consensus and strengthens the argument that it evidences the emergence of legal norms.

In addition, the incorporation of rules into treaties contributes to the support and acceptance of the rule, rendering it more likely to crystallize as custom.[34] Moreover, treaties can evidence increasing concern over an

---

PRESSE, Sept. 27, 2002; Reuters, *Exodus from Ivory Coast City Under French Guard* (Sept. 26, 2002). The European Union resolved that the coup d'état attempt was "seriously undermining the constitutional legality and unity of the country" and strongly condemned it, as well as the "persistence of fighting and the loss of human life in Côte d'Ivoire." It reiterated its "support for the democratically elected President, Mr Laurent Gbagbo, and the government of national unity of the Republic of Côte d'Ivoire as the guarantor of democratic legitimacy and the unity of the country." Resolution on the Situation in Côte d'Ivoire, EUR. PARL. DOC. P5_TA-PROV (2002)0467 (Oct. 10, 2002).

[31] Agence France-Presse, *West African Leaders Sending Peacekeepers to Ivory Coast* (Sept. 29, 2002).

[32] Agence Algérienne de Presse, «Entretien du Ministre des Affaires Etrangeres, M Dominique de Villepin: Situation en Côte d'Ivoire: rôle de la France» (Paris, 31 octobre 2002), *at* http://www.reliefweb.int/.

[33] Press Release, African Union, Côte d'Ivoire: Communiqué of the 84th Ordinary Session (Sept. 24, 2002), *available at* http://www.reliefweb.int/rw/rwb.nsf/AllDocsBy UNID/097ed0bcfa9001a2c1256c4500578c09.

[34] See, for instance, the discussion of this matter in Legality of the Threat or Use of Nuclear Weapons, Advisory Opinion, 1996 I.C.J. 226, para. 82 (July 8):

> The extensive codification of humanitarian law and the extent of the accession to the resultant treaties, as well as the fact that the denunciation clauses that

issue and thus foreshadow that the conduct may be prohibited in the future. As the Court held in the *Nuclear Weapons Case*,[35] though the treaties in that case did not constitute a prohibition, they certainly pointed "to an increasing concern in the international community with these weapons," and could foreshadow "a future general prohibition of the use of such weapons."[36]

The A.U. and ECOWAS treaties have adopted very strong positions rejecting unconstitutional change of government that are relevant both to the prohibition on the use of force to overthrow a democratic regime and, more broadly, to a nascent principle rejecting recourse to force to gain power.[37] The Lomé Declaration, adopted by the A.U. member states, declares that unconstitutional change of government is prohibited and even illegal. The Declaration "convey[s] a clear and unequivocal warning to the perpetrators of the unconstitutional change that, under no circumstances, will their *illegal* action be tolerated or recognized by the OAU."[38]

The ECOWAS member states have formally adopted a principle of "zero tolerance" for power *obtained* or *maintained* by unconstitutional means.[39] The ECOWAS Protocol on Democracy provides for the imposition of sanctions as a punitive measure. In addition, it permits direct

---

> existed in the codification instruments have never been used, have provided the international community with a corpus of treaty rules the great majority of which had already become customary and which reflected the most universally recognized humanitarian principles.

See also Nicaragua, Merits, *supra* note 15, para. 218.

35 Legality of the Threat or Use of Nuclear Weapons, 1996 I.C.J. 226.

36 *Id.*, para. 62.

37 The Lomé Declaration defines unconstitutional change of government as including military coups against a democratically elected government, intervention by mercenaries to replace a democratically elected government, attempt by rebels and armed dissident groups to replace democratically elected governments, as well as the refusal by incumbent governments to relinquish power after free and fair regular elections.

38 Lomé Declaration on the Framework for an OAU Response to Unconstitutional Changes of Government (2000), AHG/Decl.5 (XXXVI) (emphasis added), *available at* http://www.africanreview.org/docs/govern/govchange.pdf.

39 ECOWAS Protocol on Democracy and Good Governance, Dec. 2001, A/SP1/12/01, sec. I, art. 1, *available at* http://www.issafrica.org/AF/RegOrg/unity_to_union/pdfs/ecowas/12ProtDemocGood.pdf.

intervention in the event "of an overthrow or attempted overthrow of a democratically elected government."[40]

These principles are also supported by the treaty regime of the Organization of American States, which supports the use of collective measures to restore democracy where it has been overthrown unconstitutionally.[41] This is an exception to the general policy prohibiting intervention into the internal matters of states in the OAS.[42] The Inter-American Democratic Charter provides that such a state may not participate in the OAS,[43] and it authorizes the OAS general assembly to adopt "decisions it deems appropriate" in response.[44]

---

[40] Protocol Relating to the Mechanism for Conflict Prevention, Management, Resolution, Peace-Keeping and Security, art. 25 (Dec. 10, 1999), 5 J. CONFLICT & SECURITY L. 231 (2000), *available at* http://www.chr.up.ac.za/hr_docs/african/docs/other/ecowas4.doc. ECOWAS may also impose sanctions in such a situation. ECOWAS Protocol on Democracy and Good Governance, *supra* note 39, art. 45. *See also* CHARTER OF THE ORGANIZATION OF AMERICAN STATES art. 10 (Apr. 30, 1948), *available at* http://www.oas.org/juridico/English/charter.html [hereinafter OAS CHARTER].

[41] INTER-AMERICAN DEMOCRATIC CHARTER, Sept. 11, 2001, OEA/Ser.G CP-1, *available at* http://www.oas.org/OASpage/esp/Publicaciones/CartaDemocratica_spa.pdf [hereinafter IAD CHARTER]; OAS, The Santiago Commitment to Democracy and the Renewal of the Inter-American System, G.A, 3d plen. sess. (June 4, 1991), OEA/SerP/XXIO2; OAS, Representative Democracy, G.A. Res. 1080, 5th plen. sess., OAS Doc. AG/RES. 1080 (XXI-O/91) (June 5, 1991); OAS, IAD Charter, Resolution of San Jose Costa Rica, G.A. Res. 1838, 4th plen. sess., OAS Doc. G/RES. 1838 (XXXI-O/01) (June 5, 2001). *See, e.g.*, the condemnation of the attempted coup in Venezuela in April 2003, OAS Permanent Council Emergency Meeting, Apr. 13, 2003.

[42] OAS CHARTER, *supra* note 40, art. 1, art. 2, para. b and (e); OAS, Declaration Affirming the Respect for the Personality Sovereignty and Independence of States, G.A. Declaration 14, 2d plen. sess., OAS Doc. AG/DEC. 14 14 (XXVII-O/97) (June 2, 1997).

[43] IAD CHARTER, *supra* note 43, art. 19.

[44] *Id.*, art. 20. This accords with the OAS, G.A. Res. 1080, Representative Democracy, *supra* note 41, pmbl., which had determined that "the principle, enshrined in the Charter, that the solidarity of the American states and the high aims which it pursues require the political organisation of those states to be based on effective exercise of representative democracy must be made operative," and thus that in the event of any sudden or irregular interruption of the democratic political institutional process in any of the member states, the Secretary-General must call relevant meetings "to look into the events collectively and adopt any decisions deemed appropriate, in accordance with the Charter and international law." *Id.*, arts. 1, 2.

These are indicative of an emerging consensus in Africa and Latin America rejecting the forceful overthrow of democratically elected governments. Moreover, these treaties do not occur without historical or chronological context. Given their recent adoption, they seem to represent the culmination of the earlier practice of the Council and the general practice of states.

The traditional prohibition on the use of international force except in self-defense against an aggressor state posits that states do not intervene in affairs that fall within other states' exclusive domestic jurisdiction. However, doing so repeatedly, and through forceful means, must evidence a belief of the intervener, as well as of the international community when it does not criticize the intervener's actions, that it is legally entitled to do so. In contrast with the muted criticism and condemnation to the breach of human rights conventions, which are never followed up with forceful action, the conduct of states and regional organizations in response to civil conflict is dramatic. The states that have intervened in civil conflicts have emphasized the importance of the principles relied upon and have tended to highlight that these accord with the view of the Council.[45] It would be difficult to explain such practice as deriving from a mere *ad hoc* policy choice.

1. The Impact of the Norm

Recognition of this practice as evidence of an emerging customary law norm would amount to a formal acknowledgement of an evolution of the current formal description of the relationship between international law and domestic political violence in the form of civil conflict and coup d'état.

Of course, the recognition of such a norm would not entirely regularize the practice of the international community, unless it was associated with a change in the rules governing the enforcement of international law through third-party intervention into civil conflicts where these aim at the overthrow of a democratic government. While the emergence of new customary law norm would create a binding obligation on parties, it would not, according to traditional theory, ensure their

---

45 Consider the many examples in Chapter 2 of the rationales of the A.U., ECOWAS, Nigeria, the United Kingdom, France, and the United States in intervening into various conflicts, which accorded with the explicit condemnation by the Council of the situation and the demands it made on the parties.

enforcement. A state injured by the breach of a norm of international law could seek to take the matter to the International Court of Justice, or *in extremis* take retaliatory non-forceful measures. However, other than in the case of the breach of Article 2(4) of the U.N. Charter, which can be enforced through Chapter VII measures, a breach of international law generally leads to international condemnation rather than enforcement. Nonetheless, the emergence of such a norm would provide a normative justification for much of the practice.

In part, the unevenness in response is due to the complexity of the term "democracy." While this term could have been taken to mean simply formal democracy, in the sense of any government that was brought to power through elections, this does not seem consistent with the more tentative reaction of the international community in Cote d'Ivoire, where the domestic legitimacy of the government was in question, as well as to the lack of action in Haiti, following the latest overthrow of questionably elected President Jean-Bertrand Aristide. The importance of democracy and democratization has been repeatedly recognized by the United Nations, although often it is not explicitly stated or defined.[46]

While the quality of the democracy could be evaluated on a scale of key factors,[47] such an approach is complex. Ultimately a more pragmatic

---

[46] For instance, the official mandate for the U.N. Transitional Administration in East Timor (UNTAET) stressed the need to "carry out its mandate effectively with a view to the development of local democratic institutions." S.C. Res. 1272, U.N. Doc. S/RES/1272, ¶ 8 (Oct. 25,1999). This was most clear in the later reports of the Secretary-General emphasizing that the holding of democratic elections was "no doubt, the most important, since it entails the establishment of a political system that is responsive to the citizens and a political leadership that is responsible in its decisions." The Secretary-General, *Report of the Secretary-General on the United Nations Transitional Administration in East Timor*, U.N. Doc. S/2000/738 (July 26, 2000). Note also that the role of elections and democratization as an alternative to violence to produce a "just and durable settlement" of a conflict has been emphasized by the Security Council and Secretary-General. *E.g.*, Cambodia: S.C. Res. 745, pmbl., U.N. Doc. S/RES/745 (Feb. 28, 1995). Mozambique: S.C. Res. 957, U.N. Doc. S/RES/957, ¶ 3 (Nov. 15, 1994). Central African Republic (CAR): S.C. Res. 1159, U.N. Doc. S/RES/1159 (Mar. 27, 1998). Liberia: S.C. Res. 1497, U.N. Doc. S/RES/1497, ¶ 12 (Aug. 1, 2003). *See also* The Secretary-General, *An Agenda for Democratization, delivered to the General Assembly*, U.N. Doc. A/51/761 (Dec. 20, 1996); Strengthening the Role of the United Nations in Enhancing the Effectiveness of the Principle of Periodic and Genuine Elections and the Promotion of Democratization, G.A. Res. 50/185, U.N. Doc. A/RES/50/185 (Mar. 6, 1996); The Secretary-General, *Report of the Secretary-General on Support by the United Nations System of the Efforts of Governments to Promote and Consolidate New or Restored Democracies*, U.N. Doc. A/51/512 (Oct. 18, 1996).

[47] For instance, Diamond and Morlino identify factors as the strength of the rule

operational approach may be adopted, which may rely, for instance, on a definition of democratic government as a form of government "combining three essential conditions: meaningful *competition* for political power amongst individuals and organized groups; inclusive *participation* in the selection of leaders and policies, at least through free and fair elections; and a level of *civil and political liberties* sufficient to ensure the integrity of political competition and participation."[48]

It is important also to place this norm within the broader debate on democracy in international law. During the last decade and a half, that debate has focused on the emergence of a norm of democratic governance, or the emergence of a "democratic entitlement" in international law. Much of the controversy has revolved around whether, if this norm exists, its implementation by outside actors is justified. Unsurprisingly, the logical corollary of such a right, namely the right to use "intrusive political, economic, and military measures . . . to implement democratization in a recalcitrant State" has encountered strong opposition.[49] While there is widespread support for a right to non-forceful intervention in support of democracy,[50] forceful implementation of such a norm has generally been rejected.[51]

The principle of prohibiting the recourse to force against a democratically elected government, is similar to, but distinct from, the notion of a right to democratic governance, which would provide a right to

---

of law; the level of political participation; the nature of the political competition; the extent of horizontal and vertical accountability; respect for civil and political freedoms; progressive implementation of greater political equality; and responsiveness to citizens. Larry Diamond and Leonardo Morlino, *The Quality of Democracy: An Overview*, 15 J. DEMOCRACY 19 (2004).

48 INTERNATIONAL IDEA, DEMOCRACY AND DEEP-ROOTED CONFLICT: OPTIONS FOR NEGOTIATORS (1998).

49 GREGORY H. FOX AND BRAD R. ROTH, DEMOCRATIC GOVERNANCE AND INTERNATIONAL LAW 12 (2000).

50 *See* Oscar Schachter, *The Legality of Pro-Democratic Invasion*, 78 AM. J. INT'L L. 645 (1984); Thomas M. Franck, *Intervention Against Illegitimate Regimes, in* LAW AND FORCE IN THE NEW INTERNATIONAL ORDER 159 (Lori F. Damrosch and David J. Scheffer eds., 1991).

51 Unilateral forceful intervention has been rejected in particular. W. Michael Reisman, *Coercion and Self-Determination Construing Charter Article 2(4)*, 78 AM. J. INT'L L. 642 (1984); Anthony D'Amato, *The Invasion of Panama Was a Lawful Response to Tyranny*, 4 AM. J. INT'L L. 516 (1990). Gray points out the inconsistency of Burma (1990), Algeria (1991), Nigeria (1993), Niger (1996), and Pakistan (1999). CHRISTINE GRAY, INTERNATIONAL LAW AND THE USE OF FORCE 43 (2000).

choose a government through democratic elections.[52] It could stand independent of the emergence of any norm of democratic entitlement, or it could be considered a sub-category of such a norm. It is substantially more modest than an entitlement to democracy. A prohibition against the forceful overthrow of a democracy need not presuppose a right to democracy. An alternative account would be that while international law does not recognize the right to recourse to force to obtain self-determination, it does prohibit the denial of such a right. Insofar as the overthrow of a democracy is a denial of this right to self-determination, it is prohibited.

In conclusion, the practice reviewed evidences the emergence of a policy norm and an international customary law norm prohibiting recourse to force to overthrow a democratic government. The practice also supports the implied corollary right of a democratic government to defend itself against a use of force seeking to overthrow it. Such rules would fall within a sub-category of *jus ad bellum internum*—they would prohibit civil conflict seeking to overthrow a democratic government and justify and explain a large proportion of the practice in response to such conflicts.

C. PROHIBITION ON VIOLENCE TO GAIN POLITICAL POWER?

The scope and nature of the practice, especially some of the most recent practice, which supports the emergence of a discrete norm prohibiting civil conflict and coup d'état in the circumscribed case of violence against a democratic government, also suggests a broader shift in the policy and approach of the international community to extreme political violence. There is evidence of a broad rejection of all forms of extreme political violence by the international community.[53] There are

---

[52] For a general discussion of the right to democratic governance debate, *see* Thomas F. Franck, *The Emerging Right to Democratic Governance*, 86 AM. J. INT'L L. 46 (1992); Gregory H. Fox, *The Right to Political Participation in International Law*, 17 YALE J. INT'L L. 359 (1992); GREGORY H. FOX AND BRAD R. ROTH, DEMOCRATIC GOVERNANCE AND INTERNATIONAL LAW (2000). Note *Nicaragua*, Merits, *supra* note 15, where the reasoning seems to reject such a right. Also note Thomas Carothers, *Empirical Perspectives on the Emerging Norm of Democracy in International Law*, 86 PROC. ANN. MEETING OF ASIL 261, 264 (1992); BRAD R. ROTH, GOVERNMENTAL ILLEGITIMACY IN INTERNATIONAL LAW 321 (1999).

[53] Nonetheless, any formulation of emerging norm prohibiting recourse to force for political aims would need to incorporate appropriate exceptions to reflect the legitimate rights and interests of local governments and populations, as well as international concern over the impact of violence on civilians, humanitarian concerns, and

early but crucial indications that, assuming the current trend continues, all recourse to force for political aims in civil conflicts and coups d'état (other than in self-defense against illegal overthrow or violent oppression) will, in time, become prohibited.

The practice of the Security Council, in particular, provides a useful gauge of the evolution of the view of the international community of extreme political violence. In the last decade and a half, it has become routine for the Council to condemn the recourse to force and call on the parties to stop fighting and resolve the conflict by peaceful means. Increasingly, the Council has emphasized that it is recourse to force to achieve a political outcome that it rejects. The practice can be seen to evolve from the early Balkan practice to that in Kosovo, Macedonia, Liberia, and Côte d'Ivoire. The Council has intervened in 32 civil conflicts since 1945,[54] and there is a clear trend of increasing interventionism. The majority of interventions have taken place after 1991,[55] where the Council has condemned the violence or force in at least 18 civil conflicts and has imposed enforcement measures under Chapter VII in 14 of the conflicts. Of these interventions, 13 have taken place since 1991. In addition, in many of the conflicts, quite separately from the instances of condemnation of violence listed above, the Council has expressed concern over the violence.

This practice condemns the recourse to force for political aims. The Council has expressed this explicitly in some conflicts.[56] For instance, in

---

the overthrow of a democratic government. Such exceptions (for example, a right to self-defense by a government against the use of force against it, and a right to self-defense by a people against oppressive and violent regimes and against a denial of its right to self-determination) are discussed in Section D.1.

54 According to the definition of civil conflict adopted in this text, these are: Afghanistan, Albania, Armenia, The former Yugoslavia, The Federal Republic of Yugoslavia and Kosovo, Croatia, Bosnia and Herzegovina, Burundi, Cambodia, CAR, Republic of Congo (Brazzaville), Democratic Republic of the Congo, Colombia, Côte d'Ivoire, Cyprus, East Timor, El Salvador, Georgia, Guatemala, Guinea Bissau, Haiti, Lebanon, Iraq (Kurds), Liberia, the Former Yugoslav Republic of Macedonia, Mozambique, Nicaragua, Rwanda, Sierra Leone, South Africa, Somalia, and Western Sahara.

55 The exceptions are the Republic of Congo (Brazzaville) (1961), Cyprus (1964), El Salvador (1989), Lebanon (1978), Nicaragua (1983), South Africa (1960), and Western Sahara (1975).

56 *See* Burundi, Côte d'Ivoire, CAR, Cyprus, Georgia, Haiti, Former Yugoslav Republic of Macedonia, Lebanon, and Liberia.

Georgia, it linked its demand that all parties "refrain from the use of force"[57] to its support for the "commitment of the parties not to use force for the resolution of any disputed questions," and it called on parties to refrain from "propaganda aimed at the solution of the conflict by force."[58] In Cyprus, it called on both sides to "refrain from the threat or use of force or violence as a means to resolve the Cyprus problem."[59] In Burundi, it demanded that all parties refrain from "seeking to destabilize the security situation or depose the Government by force or by other unconstitutional means."[60] In Côte d'Ivoire, it stated that it "firmly condemns attempts to use force to influence the political situation in Côte d'Ivoire."[61] In Liberia, it similarly rejected "any attempt to seize power by force," acknowledging the Lomé Declaration on unconstitutional changes of government.[62] And in Haiti, it called "upon all factions in Haiti explicitly and publicly to renounce, and to direct their supporters to renounce, violence as a means of political expression."[63]

In addition, there is extensive Council practice demanding or supporting the peaceful resolution of conflict. Although the U.N. Charter obligation to resolve conflicts peacefully does not *prima facie* apply to civil conflict, in practice resolving civil conflicts through non-violent means is a primary policy goal of the international community. The practice ranges from formulations that suggest a strong policy preference to formulations that suggest a binding obligation. In the Balkans, even before the Dayton Peace Accord,[64] the Council repeatedly upheld the principle

---

57 S.C. Res. 876, U.N. Doc. S/RES/876 (Oct. 19, 1993). *See also* S.C. Res. 881, U.N. Doc. S/RES/881, ¶ 3 (Nov. 4, 1993).

58 S.C. Res. 1311, U.N. Doc. S/RES/1311, ¶ 5 (July 28, 2000).

59 S.C. Res. 1251, U.N. Doc. S/RES/1251, ¶ 9 (June 29, 1999).

60 S.C. Res. 1049, U.N. Doc. S/RES/1049, ¶ 3 (Mar. 5, 1996).

61 President of Security Council, *Côte d'Ivoire*, Statement, U.N. Doc. S/PRST/2002/42 (Dec. 20, 2002). *See also* Press Release, President of Security Council, Security Council Condemns Attempts at Force to Influence Political Situation, Overthrow Elected Government in Côte d'Ivoire, U.N. Doc. AFR/506, SC/7558 (Oct. 31, 2002).

62 S.C. Res. 1497, *supra* note 46, ¶ 13.

63 S.C. Res. 867, U.N. Doc. S/RES/867, ¶ 8 (Sept. 23, 1993). In Cambodia, it demanded that all parties "put an end to all acts of violence and to all threats and intimidation committed on political or ethnic grounds." S.C. Res. 810, U.N. Doc. S/RES/810 (Mar. 8, 1993). *See also* the practice in Macedonia, Côte d'Ivoire, and Liberia.

64 The General Framework Agreement for Peace in Bosnia and Herzegovina

of peaceful resolution of the conflicts and attempts to enforce these under Chapter VII. In recent practice, the Council has explicitly declared its commitment to "an overall negotiated settlement of the conflicts."[65] The Council also called *upon* the government and the local Serb authorities "to refrain from the threat or use of force and to reaffirm their commitment to a peaceful resolution of their differences"[66] and backed up these demands by a statement under Chapter VII that parties were to comply or face coercive enforcement.[67]

The Council has condemned political violence in practically all of the civil conflicts in which it has intervened, particularly since the 1990s. The formulation of its condemnations suggests that the Council intends its demands on the parties to renounce such force to be binding. The frequent repetition of the rejection and the range of circumstances in which it has been adopted certainly evidences a strong policy position and, assuming the trend continues, supports the emergence of a Council-enforced principle prohibiting recourse to violence for political gain. Given the recent nature of much of the key practice, the range of circumstances in which the Council has intervened (from the former Yugoslavia, Croatia, Bosnia Herzegovina, or Albania to Somalia, the DRC, Sierra Leone, Afghanistan, or East Timor), and the fact that this issue has not been the subject of academic discussion or become incorporated into any treaties, it may be too early to establish conclusively that a binding norm has already emerged. Nonetheless, it is clear that this is the direction of evolution of this area of law, which will involve a dramatic change in the way in which civil conflict is viewed and addressed in international law. The repeated support for the principle and the determination with which it has been declared to apply, as well as instances of such demands being made under Chapter VII, suggest that the international community is adopting an increasingly firm position that conflict must be resolved peacefully. This bolsters the trend of emerging practice that supports a general prohibition against recourse to force for political aims.

(Dayton Peace Accord) (Dec. 14, 1995), *available at* http://www.ohr.int/dpa/default.asp?content_id=380.

65 S.C. Res. 994, U.N. Doc. S/RES/994, pmbl. (May 17, 1995). *See also* S.C. Res. 981, U.N. Doc. S/RES/981 (Mar. 31, 1995).

66 S.C. Res. 981, *supra* note 65, ¶ 8.

67 *See* S.C. Res. 994, *supra* note 65, ¶ 10. "Demands that the parties refrain from taking any further military measures or actions that could lead to the escalation of the situation and warns that in the event of failure to comply with this demand it will consider further steps needed to ensure such compliance."

1. A Broad Support

The practice of states and regional organizations serves as evidence that the principle has support within and across major constituent parts of the international community.

The practice in Côte d'Ivoire and Liberia is particularly illuminating. Even though the democratic legitimacy of the government was in doubt in those cases, the A.U., ECOWAS, individual states, and the Secretary-General nonetheless rejected the recourse to force. The principle was formulated as a prohibition on attempts to gain power by force—an extension on the norm rejecting recourse to force to overthrow a democratic government. In Côte d'Ivoire, the A.U. condemned the attempts to take power by force, stating that it "Reitere également sa ferme condamnation de la tentative de prise du pouvoir par la force en Côte d'Ivoire."[68] France explicitly condemned "les violences, les exactions, les ingérences, les interférences extérieures, le recours à la force," and emphasized that it supported the principle of "respect des élections démocratiques."[69] ECOWAS stated that it was prepared to act in support of the government as "any government that has to be changed must be changed through the ballot box."[70] These condemnatory statements were followed by enforcement action by France and ultimately by ECOWAS.

Similarly, in Liberia, the A.U. and ECOWAS warned rebels that that they would not recognize any group that took power in Liberia through "unconstitutional means or by force of arms."[71] The European Union also condemned "the attempts by armed rebel groups to take power in Liberia by the use of force."[72] Moreover, such a principle was explicitly adopted in the later peace agreement in Liberia, which included a pledge "forth-

---

68 African Union, Communiqué de l'Union africaine: Erythrée, Soudan, Côte d'Ivoire (Oct. 12, 2002), *available at* http://wwwnotes.reliefweb.int/w/rwb.nsf/d2fc8ae9db883867852567cb0083a028/d4ca80cd5deab9b8c1256c520058c898?OpenDocument.

69 Déclaration du porte-parole du Quai d'Orsay (Paris, 13 Décembre 2002).

70 Reuters, *Exodus from Ivory Coast, supra* note 30.

71 Deutsche Presse Agentur, *African, ECOWAS, Leaders Warn Liberian Rebels: No Recognition* (July 27, 2003).

72 Council of the European Union, Liberia, Bulletin EU 5-2002, Common Foreign and Security Policy 23/29 (2002), *available at* http://www.europa.eu/bulletin/en/200205/p106023.htm.

with to settle all past, present and future differences by peaceful and legal means and to refrain from the threat of, or use of force."[73]

The Secretary-General has made statements of a general nature both in Liberia and Côte d'Ivoire. In Liberia, he condemned "any attempts to resolve political differences through armed violence."[74] He reiterated that "any attempt to seize power by force would be unacceptable to the international community."[75] In Côte d'Ivoire, the Secretary-General stated that he "unequivocally condemns any attempt to settle disputes through violence. He calls on all those involved in these attacks to immediately and unconditionally cease their activities and submit to the constitutional order."[76]

In addition, in the Balkans, the European Community highlighted the need for "a peaceful process" and "negotiations" before they recognized the new States.[77] It also explicitly required the Federal Republic of Yugoslavia not to use force to settle questions related to the dissolution of Yugoslavia.[78] Unlike the case of Sierra Leone and the 1991 Haiti coup,

---

[73] Comprehensive Peace Agreement Between the Government of Liberia and the Liberians United for Reconciliation and Democracy (LURD) and the Movement for Democracy in Liberia (MODEL) and Political Parties, *available at* http://www.usip.org/library/pa/liberia/liberia_08182003_cpa.html.

[74] Press Release, The Secretary-General, Secretary-General Deeply Concerned at Renewed Fighting in Liberia, Calls for Immediate Cessation of Hostilities, U.N. Doc. SG/SM/8761, AFR/650 (June 26, 2003).

[75] Press Release, The Secretary-General, Secretary-General Condemns Resumption of Hostilities in Liberia; Renews Call for Force Deployment to Restore Calm, U.N. Doc. SG/SM/8787, AFR/670 (July 21, 2003).

[76] Press Release, The Secretary-General, Secretary-General Condemns Armed Attacks in Côte d'Ivoire, U.N. Doc. SG/SM/8395, AFR/485 (Sept. 20, 2002).

[77] *European Guidelines on Recognition of New States in Eastern Europe and the Soviet Union, Adopted by the European Community and Its Member States*, 92 INT'L L. REV. 174 (1991) (emphasis added). The criteria set out included a "[c]ommitment to settle by agreement, including where appropriate by recourse to arbitration, all questions concerning State succession and regional disputes." European Community Declaration on Yugoslavia, (Dec. 16, 1991). The European Community then announced recognition of Slovenia and Croatia on January 15, 1992. On April 6, 1992, the European Community recognized Bosnia as an independent state. The European Community, however, denied recognition to Macedonia. European Community Declaration on Yugoslavia, Luxembourg, (Apr. 6, 1992). The United States then recognized Slovenia, Croatia, and Bosnia as independent states on April 7, 1992.

[78] Declaration on the Formation of the Federal Republic of Yugoslavia (Apr. 27, 1992).

the aim of these interventions was not to reinstate the governments. President Taylor was pressured to leave Liberia, and President Gbagbo was encouraged to compromise with the rebels in Côte d'Ivoire.

These cases adopt a broader formulation than the prohibition on force to overthrow a democratically elected government, and the contested democratic nature of the government suggests that a broader principle may emerge. To what degree do these indications support the emergence of a new norm?

D. REALPOLITIK AND NORMATIVE TRENDS

At first glance, such a change would seem inconsistent with the geopolitics of the last few decades. During the Cold War, there was extensive covert support by the superpowers for rebel groups aiming to overthrow regimes considered unfriendly by the United States or the Soviet Union: some of these wars involved the overthrow of undemocratic or dictatorial regimes; others involved the overthrow of democratic regimes. However, that practice is largely out of step with the more recent trends in this area. From a legal standpoint, such assistance has never been accepted as legitimate. Assistance to rebels remains prohibited irrespective of the level of conflict or of the purpose of the war.[79] The International Court of Justice in *Nicaragua* rejected any exceptions to the rule of non-intervention based on the rebels' aims or political or moral values.[80] It explicitly stated that even if Nicaragua had made, and then breached, a commitment to hold elections, the United States could not use force as a remedy.[81]

Moreover, there are no international law norms authorizing rebel groups to have recourse to force to resolve internal affairs. Naturally, governments reject internal recourse to force against them for political aims, and they consider themselves to have the power to suppress such rebel-

---

[79] Rosalyn Higgins, *Internal War and International Law, in* 3 THE FUTURE OF THE INTERNATIONAL LEGAL ORDER: CONFLICT MANAGEMENT 81 (Cyril E. Black and Richard A. Falk eds., 1969); HEATHER A. WILSON, INTERNATIONAL LAW AND THE USE OF FORCE BY NATIONAL LIBERATION MOVEMENTS 30 (1988); ANTONIO CASSESE, INTERNATIONAL LAW 66–69 (2001); O'Connell, *supra* note 1, at 448; JAMES N. ROSENAU, INTERNATIONAL ASPECTS OF CIVIL STRIFE (1964). *See also* HIGGINS, *supra* note 2, at 210–11.

[80] *Nicaragua,* Merits, *supra* note 15, para. 209.

[81] *Id.* at 131–33.

lions.[82] Even in the case of wars of self-determination, where a right to self-determination is widely accepted and frequently repeated in General Assembly resolutions,[83] the use of force by such liberation movements has not been accepted as lawful under international law.[84] Similarly, recourse to force to secede is not authorized under international law.[85]

The academic literature too evidences a growing acceptance of the view that new principles addressing domestic violence are needed. Writing in 1964, in one of the leading early articles on the topic, Falk noted: "The literature of international law has been slow to respond to this aspect of the altered condition of the contemporary world. At this stage, then, an inquiry into the international legal status of intrastate violence seems dramatically appropriate."[86] This view has been taken up increasingly frequently. As Secretary-General Boutros-Ghali stated in 1992: "Civil wars are no longer civil, and the carnage they inflict will not let the world remain indifferent."[87]

In 1997, the Carnegie Commission on Conflict called on the international community to advance the fundamental principle that a state

---

[82] *See, e.g.*, U.S. CONST. art. I, § 8, which empowers Congress to declare war, raise armies and provide militia to suppress insurrections. U.S. CONST. art. I, § 9 suspends the writ of habeas corpus "when in cases of Rebellion or Invasion the public Safety may require it." The Constitution of Northern Ireland of 1937 states in Article 28(3)(3): "Nothing in this Constitution . . . shall be invoked to invalidate any law enacted . . . [by the legislature] which is expressed to be for the purpose of securing the public safety and the preservation of the State in time of war or armed rebellion." For a more general discussion of constitutional responses to political violence, particularly terrorism, *see* JOHN E. FINN, CONSTITUTIONS IN CRISIS; POLITICAL VIOLENCE AND THE RULE OF LAW (1991).

[83] *See, e.g.*, Declaration on the Inadmissibility of Intervention in the Domestic Affairs of States and the Protection of Their Independence and Sovereignty, G.A. Res. 2131(XX), U.N. Doc. A/RES/20/2131 (Dec. 21, 1965). *See also* WILSON, *supra* note 79.

[84] *See* WILSON, *supra* note 79.

[85] *See* Reference Re Secession of Quebec [1998] 2 S.C.R. 217, para. 112 (Can.). James Crawford, *State Practice and International Law in Relation to Secession*, 69 BRIT. Y.B. INT'L L. 85 (1999).

[86] Richard Falk, *Janus Tormented: The International Law of Internal Law, in* INTERNATIONAL ASPECTS OF CIVIL STRIFE 185 (James Rosenau ed., 1964).

[87] Statement by former Secretary-General Boutros Boutros-Ghali, United Nations Security Council Meeting on the Responsibility of the Security Council in the Maintenance of International Peace and Security, S.C. Mtg. 3046, U.N. Doc. S/PV. 3046 (Jan. 31, 1992).

should not be recognized if it was created through force. The focus of the report was on how to prevent and bring to an end such recourse to force.[88] Similarly, the International Commission on Intervention and State Sovereignty (ICISS) specifically included a duty to prevent all deadly conflict in its guiding principle of a responsibility to protect.[89] This duty was first the responsibility of the sovereign states and the communities within them, but then it became a duty of the international community, since the "failure of prevention can have wide international consequences and costs."[90] The ICISS's approach takes as given that civil conflict must be prevented and resolved, particularly where "full scale violence is in prospect or in occurrence."[91]

The World Bank's 2003 report on civil war upholds this trend and highlights the extent to which such conflicts are now considered problems appropriate for international resolution.[92] The report rejects the view that such conflicts should be left to resolve themselves as "foolish," given the extent to which civil wars cause civilian deaths, devastate economies, and affect the regional and global community through the spread of instability and conflict.[93] It stresses that the "question is not whether the international community has the right to intervene, but whether interventions are available that are likely to be effective at a reasonable cost."[94]

This is in line also with the view taken by some commentators that the question is no longer whether to intervene but rather how to stop conflicts. Damrosch for instance argues:

> Instead of the view that interventions in internal conflicts must be presumptively illegitimate, the prevailing trend today is to take seriously the claim that the international community

---

[88] CARNEGIE COMMISSION ON PREVENTING DEADLY CONFLICT, PREVENTING DEADLY CONFLICT: FINAL REPORT (1997).

[89] INTERNATIONAL COMMISSION ON INTERVENTION AND STATE SOVEREIGNTY, RESPONSIBILITY TO PROTECT, para. 2.24 (2001).

[90] *Id.*, para. 3.2, 3.3.

[91] *Id.*, para. 4.38.

[92] PAUL COLLIER ET AL., BREAKING THE CONFLICT TRAP: CIVIL WAR AND DEVELOPMENT POLICY SOURCE (2003).

[93] *Id.*, ch. 1, at 9.

[94] *Id.*, ch. 6, at 2.

> ought to intercede to prevent bloodshed by what ever means are available. . . . [A]rguments now focus not on condemning or justifying intervention in principle, but on how best to solve practical problems of mobilizing collective efforts to mitigate internal violence.[95]

Ramsbotham and Woodhouse claim that the basic post-Cold War conflict question is: "If internal wars cause unacceptable human suffering, should the international community develop a collective mechanism for preventing or alleviating it?"[96]

It is increasingly taken for granted that the resolution of civil conflicts is a valid aim for the international community.[97] This is in accord with Moore's prescient call in the 1970s that the value of "the maintenance of world order and the minimization of destructive violence" should replace the traditional emphasis on state sovereignty in determining the validity of intervention.[98] This view has received support, notably by former Secretary-General Javier Perez de Cuellar, who emphasized that states could not have recourse to mass slaughter or systematic campaigns of exodus of the civilian population "in the name of controlling civil strife or insurrection."[99] Or, in Falk's words:

---

[95] Lori F. Damrosch, *Concluding Reflections in Enforcing Restraint: Collective Intervention, in* INTERNAL CONFLICTS 364 (Lori F. Damrosch ed., 1993).

[96] OLIVER RAMSBOTHAM AND TOM WOODHOUSE, HUMANITARIAN INTERVENTION IN CONTEMPORARY CONFLICT: A RECONCEPTUALIZATION 139 (1996).

[97] For instance, President Bush, referring to the many thousands who died every year in conflicts in Africa, expressed support for the cease-fire in Liberia, called on President Taylor to step down, and insisted that all parties must "pursue a comprehensive peace agreement." In the same speech, President Bush claimed that the United States had an interest in "pressing forward to help end Africa's longest-running civil war in Sudan," maintaining that he had asked his Special Envoy for Peace in Sudan to "make clear that the only option on the table is peace." He also expressed support for "efforts by African governments to build effective peacekeeping forces" and supported the African Union forces in Burundi and ECOWAS forces in Ivory Coast. *President Bush Outlines His Agenda for U.S.-African Relations,* AFR. J., June 26, 2003, at 20, *available at* http://www.africacncl.org/AfricaJournal/2003_AfricaJournal_AugSept.pdf.

[98] John Norton Moore, *Introduction, in* LAW AND CIVIL WAR IN THE MODERN WORLD 18–19 (John Norton Moore ed., 1974).

[99] The Secretary-General, *Annual Report of the Secretary-General on the Work of the Organization,* U.N. Doc. A/46/1, at 11–13 (Sept. 16, 1991).

> [T]here is an urgent need to reformulate the relevance of international law to internal war. This reformulation is guided by the need to centralize authority and control with respect to internal war, to substitute community management for domestic autonomy, and to entrust supranational actors with gradually increasing competence and responsibility for the regulation of an internal war.[100]

Overall, thus, there are clear indications of increasing concern over the bloodshed and destructiveness of civil conflicts, accompanied by an emerging assumption that the regional and even global repercussions of such violence justify actions by the international community to prevent and terminate such conflicts.

1. Implied Exceptions

Any emerging norm prohibiting violence for political aims would need to incorporate appropriate exceptions to reflect the legitimate rights and interests of local governments and populations, as well as international concern over the impact of violence on civilians and the overthrow of a democratic government. Essentially this would take the form of a right to self-defense by a democratic government against the use of force against it and a right to self-defense by a people against oppressive and violent regimes and against a denial of its right to self-determination.

These exceptions already exist to some extent. When the right to self-determination is denied, it becomes an international wrong[101] and may justify the exercise of self-determination by secession[102] or the authorization of forceful assistance by the Security Council.[103] Similarly, massive violence against civilians is considered a crime against humanity and result in the loss of state immunity. As early as 1625, Grotius wrote:

---

[100] Falk, *supra* note 86, at 240.

[101] Derek Bowett, *The Interrelation of Theories of Intervention and Self-Defense*, *in* LAW AND CIVIL WAR IN THE MODERN WORLD, *supra* note 98, at 38, 43.

[102] Reference Re Secession of Quebec [1998] 2 S.C.R. 217, para. 135, 138.

[103] *Id.* at 44. *See also* ROBERT JENNINGS AND ARTHUR WATTS, OPPENHEIM'S INTERNATIONAL LAW 445–46 (9th ed. 1992), who limit the permissible assistance to humanitarian or economic.

> Though it is a rule established by the laws of nature and of social order, and a rule confirmed by all the records of history, that every sovereign is supreme judge in his own kingdom and over his own subjects, in whose disputes no foreign power can justly interfere. Yet where a Busiris, a Phalaris or a Thracian Diomede provoke their people to despair and resistance by unheard of cruelties, having themselves abandoned all the laws of nature, they lose the rights of independent sovereigns, and can no longer claim the privilege of the law of nations.[104]

The difficult question is whether force may be used to overthrow a non-violent, non-democratic government. As the practice stands, it would seem that unless a right to democratic governance emerges, recourse to force by rebels to overthrow a non-oppressive, non-democratic regime is prohibited. This follows, for instance, from the Council condemnation of recourse to force for political aims in Liberia or Côte d'Ivoire, even though the uprisings were against non-democratic or partially democratic regimes. Clearly this issue remains a controversial one. On the one hand, attempts to address issues of domestic governance or regime change through civil conflict have often led in the last few decades to devastation and extended violence, without necessarily resolving the disputes.[105] On the other hand, it is difficult to deny recourse to violence unless an alternative method of resolution of such disputes is available. A similarly difficult tension between peace and justice exists in the traditional prohibition on the international war of aggression. In that context, the value of peace was chosen as the founding principle of the United Nations—"to save succeeding generations from the scourge of war"[106]—although the debate continues in other guises (for instance, with respect to the question of humanitarian intervention).

2. Ethical and Political Rationales

The notion that violence for political purposes in civil conflict could become illegal raises fundamental ethical and political questions, as conflict has long been considered a measure of last resort to bring about political change.[107] However, the total devastation caused by most such

---

104 HUGO GROTIUS, DE JURE BELLI ET PACIS LIBRI TRES 88.

105 *See* COLLIER AT AL., *supra* note 92. Examples range from Cambodia, Sudan, Sierra Leone, Liberia, Angola, and Colombia to Western Sahara.

106 U.N. CHARTER, pmbl.

107 O'Connell, *supra* note 1, at 450–51.

conflicts, the decades of bloodshed and destruction, and the apparent rise in unjustifiable aims, such as ethnic cleansing or personal economic gain, do put into question the moral validity of this sort of violence. The notion that political violence in the form of civil conflict or coup d'etat would become prohibited under international law is consistent with the growing recognition of the impact of such violence on the international community. Civil conflicts have been seen to destabilize entire regions (spreading violence, devastating economies, and initiating massive refugee movements), and they have required the investment of substantial time, money, and energy by the international community in attempts to mitigate them.

The practice in the civil conflict context certainly establishes the emergence of moral and policy restrictions on civil conflict. This stage of development is reminiscent of the moral tradition of just war, which evolved before international aggressive war became formally illegal and sought to restrict the legitimacy of war to wars undertaken by lawful authority to defend persons and property or inflict punishment on a state that has caused injury.[108] The Just War Doctrine played a central role in the transition between the 200 years of history until World War I when international war was accepted as a valid form of international relations and the 1928 Kellogg-Briand Pact, which sought to entrench the renunciation of war as an instrument of national policy.[109]

The practice rejecting recourse to force for political aims is of a recent nature, but it is accompanied by normative changes in the perception of civil conflict. This practice provides crucial indications of the direction of evolution of this field and suggests that all recourse to force for political aims in civil conflicts (other than in self-defense against illegal overthrow or violent oppression) is increasingly being rejected by the international community as a matter of international policy and may, in time, become prohibited under international law. This would at least provide a step in the direction of addressing the distress and trauma caused by civil conflict. As Falk pointed out in 1964, "Peace exists only when the world is free from unauthorised patterns of sustained violence everywhere."[110]

---

[108] Gotius, *supra* note 104. *See* JAMES TURNER JOHNSON, JUST WAR TRADITION AND THE RESTRAINT OF WAR: A MORAL AND HISTORICAL INQUIRY (1981).

[109] This was then reformulated in Article 2(4) of the U.N. Charter as a prohibition on use or threat of force against the territorial integrity or political independence of any state, and has since become the cornerstone of the international legal system. *See* ANTHONY C. AREND AND ROBERT J. BECK, INTERNATIONAL LAW AND THE USE OF FORCE: BEYOND THE UN CHARTER PARADIGM 11–25 (1993).

[110] Falk, *supra* note 86, at 190.

APPENDIX I: SECURITY COUNCIL PRACTICE IN CIVIL CONFLICTS

AFGHANISTAN

Concern, comments, acknowledgments

1076 (1996)

Expressing concern over the continuation and recent intensification of the military confrontation in Afghanistan which have caused civilian casualties and an increase in refugees and displaced persons, and which seriously endanger the stability and peaceful development of the region,

Deeply concerned about the discrimination against women and other abuses of human rights in Afghanistan,

Stressing the need to prevent further civilian casualties, and noting in this context the proposals, inter alia, for an immediate ceasefire, exchange of prisoners of war and the demilitarization of Kabul,

Urging all Afghan parties to resolve their differences through peaceful means and achieve national reconciliation through political dialogue,

Stressing the importance of non-interference in the internal affairs of Afghanistan and the prevention of the flow of arms and ammunition to all parties to the conflict in Afghanistan,

Reaffirming its strong commitment to the sovereignty, independence, territorial integrity and national unity of Afghanistan,

Convinced that the United Nations, as a universally recognized and impartial intermediary, must continue to play the central role in international efforts towards a peaceful resolution of the Afghan conflict,

Welcoming the willingness expressed by Member States during the Security Council meeting of 16 October 1996 to support the dialogue among all the parties and to facilitate the negotiations aimed at political settlement of the conflict,

1076 (1996)

11. Denounces the discrimination against girls and women and other violations of human rights and international humanitarian law in Afghanistan, and notes with deep concern possible repercussions on international relief and reconstruction programmes in Afghanistan;

1193 (1998)

Expressing its grave concern at the continued Afghan conflict which has recently sharply escalated due to the Taliban forces' offensive in the northern parts of the country, causing a serious and growing threat to regional and international peace and security, as well as extensive human suffering, further destruction, refugee flows and other forcible displacement of large numbers of people,

Concerned also by the increasingly ethnic nature of the conflict, by reports of ethnic and religious-based persecution, particularly against the Shiites, and by the threat this poses to the unity of the Afghan State,

Deeply concerned at the serious humanitarian crisis in Afghanistan, and deploring in this regard the measures taken by the Taliban which resulted in the evacuation of the United Nations humanitarian personnel from Afghanistan and expressing hope for their early return under conditions of security,

Deeply concerned also at the continuing presence of terrorists in the territory of Afghanistan and at the production and trafficking of drugs,

Remaining deeply concerned at the continuing discrimination against girls and women and at other violations of human rights and of international humanitarian law in Afghanistan,

1214 (1998)

Expressing its grave concern at the continued Afghan conflict, which has recently sharply escalated as a result of the offensive by the Taliban forces, which is continuing despite the repeated pleas by the Security Council to cease the fighting, and causing a serious and growing threat to regional and international peace and security, as well as extensive human suffering, further destruction, refugee flows and other forcible displacement of large numbers of people,

1378 (Nov. 14, 2001)

1. Expresses its strong support for the efforts of the Afghan people to establish a new and transitional administration leading to the formation of a government, both of which:

- — should be broad-based, multi-ethnic and fully representative of all the Afghan people and committed to peace with Afghanistan's neighbours,
- — should respect the human rights of all Afghan people, regardless of gender, ethnicity or religion,
- — should respect Afghanistan's international obligations, including by cooperating fully in international efforts to combat terrorism and illicit drug trafficking within and from Afghanistan, and
- — should facilitate the urgent delivery of humanitarian assistance and the orderly return of refugees and internally displaced persons, when the situation permits;

Condemnation

1193 (1998)

Condemns the attacks on the United Nations personnel in the Taliban-held territories of Afghanistan, including the killing of the two Afghan staff-members of the World Food Programme and of the United Nations High Commissioner for Refugees in Jalalabad, and of the Military Adviser to the United Nations Special Mission to Afghanistan in Kabul, and calls upon the Taliban to investigate urgently these heinous crimes, and to keep the United Nations informed about the results of the investigation;

7. Demands that all Afghan factions and, in particular the Taliban, do everything possible to assure the safety and freedom of movement of the personnel of the United Nations and other international and humanitarian personnel;

8. Condemns also the capture of the Consulate-General of the Islamic Republic of Iran in Mazar-e-Sharif, and demands that all parties and, in particular the Taliban, do everything possible to ensure safe and dignified passage out of Afghanistan of the personnel of the Consulate-General and other Iranian nationals missing in Afghanistan;

Resolutions calling for, or demanding, particular actions or outcomes

1076 (1996)

1. Calls upon all Afghan parties immediately to cease all armed hostilities, to renounce the use of force, to put aside their differences and to engage in a political dialogue aimed at achieving national reconciliation and a lasting political settlement of the conflict and establishing a fully representative and broad-based transitional government of national unity;

2. Stresses that the main responsibility for finding a political solution to the conflict lies with the Afghan parties;

3. Calls upon all States to refrain from any outside interference in the internal affairs of Afghanistan, including the involvement of foreign military personnel, to respect the right of the Afghan people to determine their own destiny and to respect the sovereignty, independence, unity and territorial integrity of Afghanistan;

4. Calls upon all States immediately to end the supply of arms and ammunition to all parties to the conflict in Afghanistan;

5. Reiterates that the continuation of the conflict in Afghanistan provides a fertile ground for terrorism and drug trafficking which destabilize the region and beyond, and calls upon the leaders of the Afghan parties to halt such activities;

6. Expresses its regret at the civilian casualties inflicted by landmines and calls upon all parties in Afghanistan to desist from the indiscriminate use of landmines;

7. Requests the Secretary-General, in cooperation, as he deems it necessary, with interested States and international organizations, in particular the Organization of the Islamic Conference, to continue his efforts to promote the political process;

8. Reaffirms its full support for the efforts of the United Nations, in particular the activities of the United Nations Special Mission to Afghanistan in facilitating the political process towards the goals of national reconciliation and a lasting

political settlement with the participation of all parties to the conflict and all segments of Afghan society;

9. Calls upon all Afghan parties to cooperate with the United Nations Special Mission to Afghanistan, and encourages all interested States and international organizations to take all steps necessary to promote peace in Afghanistan, to support the United Nations efforts to this end and to use any influence they have to encourage the parties to cooperate fully with the United Nations Special Mission to Afghanistan;

10. Demands that all parties fulfil their obligations and commitments regarding the safety of United Nations personnel and other international personnel as well as their premises in Afghanistan, not hamper the flow of humanitarian assistance and cooperate fully with the United Nations and associated bodies as well as with other humanitarian organizations and agencies, in their efforts to respond to the humanitarian needs of the people of Afghanistan;

12. Calls upon all States and international organizations to extend all possible humanitarian assistance to the civilian population of Afghanistan;

1193 (1998)

Reiterates that the Afghan crisis can be settled only by peaceful means, through direct negotiations between the Afghan factions under United Nations auspices, aimed at achieving a solution accommodating the rights and interests of all Afghans and stresses that territorial gains through military operations will neither lead to a durable peace in Afghanistan, nor contribute to a comprehensive settlement of the conflict in this multi-cultural and multi-ethnic country;

2. Demands that all Afghan factions stop fighting, resume negotiations without delay and preconditions, and cooperate with the aim of creating a broad-based and fully representative government, which would protect the rights of all Afghans and would observe the international obligations of Afghanistan;

3. Reiterates once again that any outside interference in the internal affairs of Afghanistan should cease immediately and calls upon all States to take resolute measures to prohibit their military personnel from planning and participating in military operations in Afghanistan and immediately to end the supply of arms and ammunition to all parties to the conflict;

4. Calls upon all States neighbouring Afghanistan and other States with influence in the country to intensify their efforts under the aegis of the United Nations to bring the parties to a negotiated settlement;

1214 (1998)

1. Demands that the Taliban, as well as other Afghan factions, stop fighting, conclude a ceasefire and resume negotiations without delay and preconditions under United Nations auspices, and cooperate with the aim of creating a broad-based and fully representative government, which would protect the rights of all Afghans and observe the international obligations of Afghanistan;

12. Demands that the Afghan factions put an end to discrimination against girls and women and other violations of human rights, as well as violations of international humanitarian law, and adhere to the international norms and standards in this sphere;

13. Demands also that the Taliban stop providing sanctuary and training for international terrorists and their organizations, and that all Afghan factions cooperate with efforts to bring indicted terrorists to justice;

14. Demands further that the Taliban, as well as others, halt the cultivation, production and trafficking of illegal drugs;

1267 (1999)

Acting under Chapter VII of the Charter of the United Nations,

1. Insists that the Afghan faction known as the Taliban [. . .] comply promptly with its previous resolutions and in particular cease the provision of sanctuary and training for international terrorists and their organizations.

2. Demands that the Taliban turn over Usama bin Laden.

1333 (2000)

Acting under Chapter VII of the Charter of the United Nations,

1. Demands that the Taliban comply with resolution 1267 and, in particular, cease the provision of sanctuary and training for international terrorists and their organizations [. . .]

9. Demands that the Taliban, as well as others, halt all illegal drug activities and work to virtually eliminate the illicit cultivation of opium poppy, the proceeds of which finance Taliban terrorist activities;

1378 (Nov. 14, 2001)

2. Calls on all Afghan forces to refrain from acts of reprisal, to adhere strictly to their obligations under human rights and international humanitarian law, and to ensure the safety and security and freedom of movement of United Nations and associated personnel, as well as personnel of humanitarian organizations;

Sanctions

1267 (1999)

Acting under Chapter VII

2. Demands that the Taliban turn over Usama bin Laden without further delay to appropriate authorities in a country where he has been indicted, or to appropriate authorities in a country where he will be returned to such a country, or to appropriate authorities in a country where he will be arrested and effectively brought to justice;

3. Decides that on 14 November 1999 all States shall impose the measures set out in paragraph 4 below, unless the Council has previously decided, on the basis of a report of the Secretary-General, that the Taliban has fully complied with the obligation set out in paragraph 2 above;

4. Decides further that, in order to enforce paragraph 2 above, all States shall:

(a) Deny permission for any aircraft to take off from or land in their territory if it is owned, leased or operated by or on behalf of the Taliban as designated by the Committee established by paragraph 6 below, unless the particular flight has been approved in advance by the Committee on the grounds of humanitarian need, including religious obligation such as the performance of the Hajj;

(b) Freeze funds and other financial resources, including funds derived or generated from property owned or controlled directly or indirectly by the Taliban, or by any undertaking owned or controlled by the Taliban, as designated by the Committee established by paragraph 6 below, and ensure that neither they nor any other funds or financial resources so designated are made available, by their nationals or by any persons within their territory, to or for the benefit of the Taliban or any undertaking owned or controlled, directly or indirectly, by the Taliban, except as may be authorized by the Committee on a case-by-case basis on the grounds of humanitarian need;

5. Urges all States to cooperate with efforts to fulfil the demand in paragraph 2 above, and to consider further measures against Usama bin Laden and his associates;

1333 (2000)

Recognizing the critical humanitarian needs of the Afghan people,

Recalling the relevant international counter-terrorism conventions and in particular the obligations of parties to those conventions to extradite or prosecute terrorists,

Strongly condemning the continuing use of the areas of Afghanistan under the control of the Afghan faction known as Taliban, [. . .] for sheltering and training of terrorists and planning of terrorist acts, and reaffirming its conviction that the suppression of international terrorism is essential for the maintenance of international peace and security,

Noting the importance of the Taliban acting in accordance with the 1961 Single Convention, the 1971 Convention on Psychotropic Substances, and the 1988 Convention against Illicit Traffic in Narcotic Drugs and Psychotropic Substances [. . .]

Noting that the Taliban benefits directly from the cultivation of illicit opium by imposing a tax on its production and indirectly benefits from the processing and trafficking of such opium, and recognizing that these substantial resources strengthen the Taliban's capacity to harbour terrorists,

Noting the indictment of Usama bin Laden and his associates by the United States of America for, inter alia, the 7 August 1998 bombings of the United States embassies in Nairobi, Kenya [. . .]

Reiterating its deep concern over the continuing violations of international humanitarian law and of human rights, particularly discrimination against women and girls, over the significant rise in the illicit production of opium,

Stressing that the capture by the Taliban of the Consulate-General of the Islamic Republic of Iran and the murder of Iranian diplomats and a journalist in Mazar-e-Sharif constituted flagrant violations of established international law,

Determining that the failure of the Taliban authorities to respond to the demands in paragraph 13 of resolution 1214 (1998) and in paragraph 2 of resolution 1267 (1999) constitutes a threat to international peace and security,

Stressing its determination to ensure respect for its resolutions,

Acting under Chapter VII of the Charter of the United Nations,

5. Decides that all States shall:

   (a) Prevent the direct or indirect supply, sale and transfer to the territory of Afghanistan under Taliban control [. . .] of arms and related material of all types [. . .]

1390 (2002)

Reaffirming further that acts of international terrorism constitute a threat to international peace and security,

Acting under Chapter VII of the Charter of the United Nations,

(a) Freeze without delay the funds and other financial assets or economic resources of these individuals, groups, undertakings and entities, including funds derived from property owned or controlled, directly or indirectly, by them or by persons acting on their behalf or at their direction, and ensure that neither these nor any other funds, financial assets or economic resources are made available, directly or indirectly, for such persons' benefit, by their nationals or by any persons within their territory;

(b) Prevent the entry into or the transit through their territories of these individuals, provided that nothing in this paragraph shall oblige any State to deny entry into or require the departure from its territories of its own nationals and this paragraph shall not apply where entry or transit is necessary for the fulfilment of a judicial process or the Committee determines on a case by case basis only that entry or transit is justified;

(c) Prevent the direct or indirect supply, sale and transfer, to these individuals, groups, undertakings and entities from their territories or by their nationals outside their territories, or using their flag vessels or aircraft, of arms and related materiel of all types including weapons and ammunition, military vehicles and equipment, paramilitary equipment, and spare parts for the aforementioned and technical advice, assistance, or training related to military activities;

Observer or peace-keeping forces

1386 (2001)

Determined to ensure the full implementation of the mandate of the International Security Assistance Force, in consultation with the Afghan Interim Authority established by the Bonn Agreement, Acting for these reasons under Chapter VII of the Charter of the United Nations,

1. Authorizes, as envisaged in Annex 1 to the Bonn Agreement, the establishment for 6 months of an International Security Assistance Force to assist the Afghan Interim Authority in the maintenance of security in Kabul and its surrounding areas, so that the Afghan Interim Authority as well as the personnel of the United Nations can operate in a secure environment;

Deploring the fact that despite the readiness of the United Front of Afghanistan to conclude a durable ceasefire and to enter into a political dialogue with the Taliban, fighting continues on both sides,

Concerned also by the increasingly ethnic nature of the conflict, by reports of ethnic and religious-based persecution, particularly against the Shiites, and by the threat this poses to the unity of the Afghan State,

Authorizations of use of force

1368 (Sept. 12, 2001)

[Does not specifically refer to Chapter VII although states]

5. Expresses its readiness to take all necessary steps to respond to the terrorist attacks of 11 September 2001, and to combat all forms of terrorism, in accordance with its responsibilities under the Charter of the United Nations;

Encouragement or authorization of third-party actions

622 (1988)

Recalling the letters [. . .] from the Secretary General to the President of the Security Council concerning the agreements on the settlement of the situation relating to Afghanistan, signed at Geneva on 14 April 1988.

1. Confirms its agreement to the measures envisaged in the Secretary General's letters of 14 and 22 April 1988, in particular the arrangement for the temporary dispatch to Afghanistan and Pakistan of military officers from existing United Nations operations to assist in the mission of good offices.

647 (1990)

1. Confirms its agreement to the measures envisaged in the Secretary General's letter of 9 January 1990 concerning the arrangements for the temporary deployment in Afghanistan and Pakistan of military officers from existing United Nations operations to assist in the mission of good offices [. . .]

1378 (Nov. 14, 2001)

5. Encourages Member States to support efforts to ensure the safety and security of areas of Afghanistan no longer under Taliban control, and in particular to ensure respect for Kabul as the capital for all the Afghan people, and especially to protect civilians, transitional authorities, United Nations and associated personnel, as well as personnel of humanitarian organizations;

1386 (2001)

Supporting international efforts to root out terrorism, in keeping with the Charter of the United Nations, and reaffirming also its resolutions 1368 (2001) of 12 September 2001 and 1373 (2001) of 28 September 2001,

Welcoming developments in Afghanistan that will allow for all Afghans to enjoy inalienable rights and freedom unfettered by oppression and terror,

Applicability of humanitarian laws of war

1193 (1998)

12. Reaffirms that all parties to the conflict are bound to comply with their obligations under international humanitarian law and in particular the Geneva Conventions of 12 August 1949, and that persons who commit or order the commission of grave breaches of the Conventions are individually responsible in respect of such breaches;

13. Requests the Secretary-General to continue investigations into alleged mass killings of prisoners of war and civilians as well as ethnically-based forced displacement of large groups of the population and other forms of mass persecution in Afghanistan, and to submit the reports to the General Assembly and the Security Council as soon as they become available;

14. Urges the Afghan factions to put an end to the discrimination against girls and women and to other violations of human rights as well as violations of international humanitarian law and to adhere to the internationally accepted norms and standards in this sphere;

15. Demands the Afghan factions to refrain from harbouring and training terrorists and their organizations and to halt illegal drug activities;

16. Reminds all parties of the obligation to abide strictly by the decisions of the Security Council and expresses its firm intention, in accordance with its respon-

sibility under the Charter, to consider such further steps as may be required for the implementation of this resolution;

1214 (1998)

Reaffirming that all parties to the conflict are bound to comply with their obligations under international humanitarian law and in particular under the Geneva Conventions of 12 August 1949, and that persons who commit or order the commission of breaches of the Conventions are individually responsible in respect of such breaches,

1267 (1999)

Reiterating its deep concern over the continuing violations of international humanitarian law and of human rights, particularly discrimination against women and girls, and over the significant rise in the illicit production of opium, and stressing that the capture by the Taliban of the Consulate-General of the Islamic Republic of Iran and the murder of Iranian diplomats and a journalist in Mazar-e-Sharif constituted flagrant violations of established international law,

Sovereignty and territorial integrity

1214 (1998)

Reaffirming its strong commitment to the sovereignty, independence, territorial integrity and national unity of Afghanistan, and its respect for its cultural and historical heritage,

1267 (1999)

Reaffirming its strong commitment to the sovereignty, independence, territorial integrity and national unity of Afghanistan, and its respect for Afghanistan's cultural and historical heritage,

Threats to international peace and security

1267 (1999)

Reiterating its deep concern over the continuing violations of international humanitarian law and of human rights, particularly discrimination against women and girls, and over the significant rise in the illicit production of opium, and stressing that the capture by the Taliban of the Consulate-General of the Islamic Republic of Iran and the murder of Iranian diplomats and a journalist in Mazar-e-Sharif constituted flagrant violations of established international law,

Recalling the relevant international counter-terrorism conventions and in particular the obligations of parties to those conventions to extradite or prosecute terrorists,

Strongly condemning the continuing use of Afghan territory, especially areas controlled by the Taliban, for the sheltering and training of terrorists and planning

of terrorist acts, and reaffirming its conviction that the suppression of international terrorism is essential for the maintenance of international peace and security,

Deploring the fact that the Taliban continues to provide safe haven to Usama bin Laden and to allow him and others associated with him to operate a network of terrorist training camps from Taliban-controlled territory and to use Afghanistan as a base from which to sponsor international terrorist operations,

Determining that the failure of the Taliban authorities to respond to the demands in paragraph 13 of resolution 1214 (1998) constitutes a threat to international peace and security,

Stressing its determination to ensure respect for its resolutions,

Acting under Chapter VII of the Charter of the United Nations,

ALBANIA

Concern, comments, acknowledgments

1101 (1997)

Taking note of Decision 160 of the Permanent Council of the Organization for Security and Cooperation in Europe (OSCE) of 27 March 1997 (S/1997/259, Annex II), including to provide the coordinating framework within which other international organizations can play their part in their respective areas of competence,

Recalling the statement of the President of the Security Council on the situation in Albania of 13 March 1997 (S/PRST/1997/14), Reiterating its deep concern over the deteriorating situation in Albania,

Underlining the need for all concerned to refrain from hostilities and acts of violence, and reiterating its call to the parties involved to continue the political dialogue,

Stressing the importance of regional stability, and in this context fully supporting the diplomatic efforts of the international community to find a peaceful solution to the crisis, in particular those of the OSCE and of the European Union,

Affirming the sovereignty, independence and territorial integrity of the Republic of Albania,

Resolutions calling for or demanding particular actions or outcomes

1101 (1997)

Determining that the present situation of crisis in Albania constitutes a threat to peace and security in the region,

1. Condemns all acts of violence and calls for their immediate end;

5. Calls upon all those concerned in Albania to cooperate with the multinational protection force and international humanitarian agencies for the safe and prompt delivery of humanitarian assistance;

1114 (1997)

Underlining the need for all concerned to refrain from hostilities and acts of violence, and calling on the parties involved to continue the political dialogue and facilitate the electoral process,

Stressing the importance of regional stability and, in this context, fully supporting the diplomatic efforts of the international community, particularly the OSCE and the European Union, to find a peaceful solution to the crisis and assist in the electoral process in Albania, in cooperation with the Albanian authorities,

1. Condemns all acts of violence, and calls for their immediate end;

Authorizations of use of force

1101 (1997)

4. [. . .] acting under Chapter VII of the Charter of the United Nations, further authorizes these Member States to ensure the security and freedom of movement of the personnel of the said multinational protection force;

Encouragement or authorization of third-party actions

1101 (1997)

2. Welcomes the offer made by certain Member States to establish a temporary and limited multinational protection force to facilitate the safe and prompt delivery of humanitarian assistance, and to help create a secure environment for the missions of international organizations in Albania, including those providing humanitarian assistance;

3. Welcomes further the offer by a Member State contained in its letter (S/1997/258) to take the lead in organizing and commanding this temporary multinational protection force and takes note of all the objectives contained in that letter;

4. Authorizes the Member States participating in the multinational protection force to conduct the operation in a neutral and impartial way to achieve the objectives set out in paragraph 2 above and, acting under Chapter VII of the Charter of the United Nations, further authorizes these Member States to ensure the security and freedom of movement of the personnel of the said multinational protection force;

8. Encourages the Member States participating in the multinational protection force to cooperate closely with the Government of Albania, the United Nations, the OSCE, the European Union and all international organizations involved in rendering humanitarian assistance in Albania;

S/1997/258—Letter

In this regard, Italy has taken the initiative of promoting the creation of a multinational protection force, which will operate with full respect for the principles of the Charter of the United Nations and of the OSCE and which, to ensure security and freedom of movement of its personnel, will act under Chapter VII of the Charter. To this end, the Government of Italy has consulted with a number of Governments, in particular the Government of Albania.

The objective of the force will be to help create a safe and secure environment for the action of international organizations to provide support in areas of international assistance. The force will also ensure the protection and safety of international personnel operating in Albania. The concept of operations for the force will reflect these objectives, in particular the need to ensure early protection of ports, the Tirana airport and the main lines of communication, as well as stocks of humanitarian aid.

In this respect, a legal framework for the provision of this assistance should be envisaged. This framework should, in our view, take the form of a resolution by the Security Council authorizing Member States who are willing to participate in such a multinational force to conduct the operation to achieve the above-mentioned objectives.

Sovereignty and territorial integrity

1101 (1997)

Affirming the sovereignty, independence and territorial integrity of the Republic of Albania,

1114 (1997)

Reaffirming the sovereignty, independence and territorial integrity of the Republic of Albania

Threats to international peace and security

1101 (1997)

Reiterating its deep concern over the deteriorating situation in Albania,

Underlining the need for all concerned to refrain from hostilities and acts of violence, and reiterating its call to the parties involved to continue the political dialogue,

Stressing the importance of regional stability, and in this context fully supporting the diplomatic efforts of the international community to find a peaceful solution to the crisis, in particular those of the OSCE and of the European Union,

Determining that the present situation of crisis in Albania constitutes a threat to peace and security in the region,

ALGERIA

No relevant Security Council resolutions.

ANGOLA

Concern, comments, acknowledgments

785 (1992)

Deeply concerned at the deterioration of the political situation and the rising tension in Angola,

Deeply concerned also at the reports of recent resumption of hostilities by UNITA in Luanda and Huambo,

Affirming that any party which fails to abide by all the commitments entered into under the "Acordos de Paz para Angola" will be rejected by the international community, and that the results of use of force will not be accepted,

811 (1993)

Gravely disturbed by the recent outbreak of heavy fighting in many parts of Angola, the large number of casualties and massive loss of human life which have ensued and the further deterioration of the already dangerous political and military situation, bringing the country to the verge of the resumption of civil war,

Gravely concerned at the persistent violations by UNITA of the major provisions of the 'Acordos de Paz para Angola,'

Noting with particular concern that a humanitarian tragedy of grave proportions is developing in Angola and the need, therefore, for increased international humanitarian assistance,

Welcoming and supporting the efforts of the Secretary General and his Special Representative aimed at resolving the present crisis through negotiations,

864 (1993)

Expressing grave concern at the continuing deterioration of the political and military situation, and noting with consternation the further deterioration of an already grave humanitarian situation,

Deeply concerned that, despite its previous resolutions and the efforts undertaken by the Secretary-General and his Special Representative, the peace talks remain suspended and a cease-fire has not been established,

Welcoming the joint statement issued in Lisbon on 10 September 1993 by the representatives of Portugal, the Russian Federation and the United States of America, the three observer States to the Angolan peace process (S/26488),

4. Welcomes the continued disposition of the Government of Angola to reach a peaceful settlement of the conflict in conformity with the "Acordos de Paz" and relevant resolutions of the Security Council;

5. Reaffirms its recognition of the legitimate rights of the Government of Angola and in this regard welcomes the provision of assistance to the Government of Angola in support of the democratic process;

1173 (1998)

Expressing its grave concern at the critical situation in the peace process, which is the result of the failure by the União Nacional para a Independência Total de Angola (UNITA) to implement its obligations under the "Acordos de Paz" (S/22609, Annex), the Lusaka Protocol (S/1994/1441, Annex), relevant Security Council resolutions and the plan for the completion by 31 May 1998 of the remaining tasks of the Lusaka Protocol, which was submitted by the Special Representative of the Secretary-General to the Joint Commission on 15 May 1998

Condemnation

785 (1992)

3. Strongly condemns any such resumption of hostilities and urgently demands that such acts cease forthwith

811 (1993)

1. Strongly condemns the persistent violations by UNITA of the major provision of the "Acordos de Paz," in particular the continued rejection by UNITA of the results of the elections held on 29 and 30 September 1992 which the Special Representative of the Secretary General determined as generally free and fair, its failure to take part in the political institutions established on the basis of those elections, its failure to engage in meaningful negotiations with the Government of Angola, its withdrawal from the new Angolan armed forces, its seizure by force of provincial capitals and municipalities and the resumption of hostilities;

834 (1993)

4. Condemns UNITA for its actions and armed attacks, which have resulted in increased hostilities and which endanger the peace process, and demands that its immediately cease such actions and armed attacks,

864 (1993)

5. Reaffirms its recognition of the legitimate rights of the Government of Angola and in this regard welcomes the provision of assistance to the Government of Angola in support of democratic process,

7. Condemns UNITA for continuing military actions, which are resulting in increased suffering to the civilian population of Angola and damage to the Angolan economy and again demands that UNITA immediately cease such actions,

8. Also condemns UNITA's repeated attempts to seize additional territory and its failure to withdraw its troops from the locations which it has occupied since the

resumption of the hostilities, and demands once again that it immediately do so and agree without delay to return its troops to United Nations-monitored areas as a transitional measure pending full implementation of the "Acordos de Paz";

9. Reaffirms that such occupation is a grave violation of the "Acordos de Paz" and is incompatible with the goal of peace through agreements and reconciliation;

Resolutions calling for or demanding particular actions or outcomes

747 (1992)

5. Urges the Angolan parties to comply scrupulously with the provisions of the Accords and with the agreed deadlines; and to this end, to proceed without delay with the demobilization of their troops, formation of a unified national armed force, effective operation of joint police monitoring units, extension of the central administration and other major tasks,

6. Calls upon the Angolan authorities and parties to finalize political, legal, organizational and budgetary preparations for free and fair multi-party elections to be held in September 1992 [. . .]

785 (1992)

7. Calls upon the parties to the "Acordos de Paz" to abide by all commitments entered into under the Accords, in particular with regard to the confinement of their troops and collection of their weapons, demobilization and the formation of the unified national armed force, and to refrain from any act that might heighten tension, jeopardize the continued conduct of the electoral process and threaten the territorial integrity of Angola,

9. Reaffirms that it will hold responsible any party which refuses to take part in such a dialogue, thereby jeopardizing the entire process, and reiterates its readiness to consider all appropriate measures under the Charter of the United Nations to secure implementation of the "Acordos de Paz";

793 (1992)

4. Demands that the two parties scrupulously observe the cease-fire, immediately stop all military confrontations, and in particular offensive troop movements, and create all the conditions necessary for the completion of the peace process.

5. Strongly appeals to the two parties to engage in a continuous and meaningful dialogue aimed at national reconciliation and at the participation of all parties in the democratic process.

811 (1993)

2. Demands that UNITA accept unreservedly the results of the democratic elections of 1992 and abide fully by the "Acordos de Paz," and further demands that the two parties, particularly UNITA, produce early evidence, not later than 30

March 1993, that real progress has been made towards the implementation of the "Acordos de Paz";

3. Strongly demands an immediate cease-fire throughout the country, and further demands the resumption without delay and without preconditions of a continued and meaningful dialogue under United Nations auspices so that a clear time table for the implementation of the "Acordos de Paz" may be established;

834 (1993)

10. Calls on all States to refrain from any action which directly or indirectly could jeopardize the implementation of the "Acordos de Paz" and urges all States to refrain from providing any form of direct or indirect military assistance or other support to UNITA inconsistent with the peace process,

864 (1993)

6. Reiterates once again its demand that UNITA accept unreservedly the results of the democratic elections of 30 September 1992 and abide fully by the "Acordoz de Paz,"

1173 (1998)

1. Condemns UNITA, and holds its leadership responsible, for its failure to implement fully its obligations contained in the Lusaka Protocol, relevant Security Council resolutions, in particular resolution 1127 (1997), and the plan submitted by the Special Representative of the Secretary-General to the Joint Commission;

2. Demands that UNITA fully cooperate without conditions in the immediate extension of State administration throughout the national territory, including in particular in Andulo, Bailundo, Mungo and Nharea, and stop any attempts to reverse this process;

3. Reiterates its demand that UNITA complete its demilitarization and stop any attempts to restore its military capabilities;

Sanctions

864 (1993)

Acting under Chapter VII of the Charter of the United Nations,

17. Decides that the provisions set forth in paragraphs 19 to 25 below shall come into force ten days after the date of adoption of the present resolution unless the Secretary-General notifies the Council that an effective cease-fire has been established and that agreement has been reached on the implementation of the "Acordos de Paz" and relevant resolutions of the Security Council;

19. Decides, with a view to prohibiting all sale or supply to UNITA of arms and related matériel and military assistance, as well as petroleum and petroleum

products, that all States shall prevent the sale or supply, by their nationals or from their territories or using their flag vessels or aircraft, of arms and related matériel of all types, including weapons and ammunition, military vehicles and equipment and spare parts for the afore-mentioned, as well as petroleum and petroleum products, whether or not originating in their territory, to the territory of Angola other than through named points of entry on a list to be supplied by the Government of Angola to the Secretary-General, who shall promptly notify the Member States of the United Nations;

26. Expresses its readiness to consider the imposition of further measures under the Charter of the United Nations, including, inter alia, trade measures against UNITA and restrictions on the travel of UNITA personnel, unless by 1 November 1993 the Secretary-General has reported that an effective cease-fire has been established and that agreement has been reached on the full implementation of the "Acordos de Paz" and relevant resolutions of the Security Council;

1127 (1997)

Emphasizing the urgent need for the Government of Angola and in particular UNITA to complete without further delay the implementation of their obligations under the "Acordos de Paz" (S/22609, Annex), the Lusaka Protocol (S/1994/1441, Annex) and the relevant Security Council resolutions,

Expressing its grave concern at the serious difficulties in the peace process, which are mainly the result of delays by UNITA in the implementation of its obligations under the Lusaka Protocol,

Determining that the resulting situation in Angola constitutes a threat to international peace and security in the region,

Acting under Chapter VII of the Charter of the United Nations,

4. Decides that all States shall take the necessary measures:

(a) To prevent the entry into or transit through their territories of all senior officials of UNITA and of adult members of their immediate families, as designated in accordance with paragraph 11 (a) below, except those officials necessary for the full functioning of the Government of Unity and National Reconciliation, the National Assembly, or the Joint Commission, provided that nothing in this paragraph shall oblige a State to refuse entry into its territory to its own nationals

1173 (1998)

Determining that the current situation in Angola constitutes a threat to international peace and security in the region,

Acting under Chapter VII of the Charter of the United Nations,

11. Decides that all States, except Angola, in which there are funds and financial resources, including any funds derived or generated from property of UNITA as

an organization or of senior officials of UNITA or adult members of their immediate families designated pursuant to paragraph 11 of resolution 1127 (1997), shall require all persons and entities within their own territories holding such funds and financial resources to freeze them and ensure that they are not made available directly or indirectly to or for the benefit of UNITA as an organization or of senior officials of UNITA or adult members of their immediate families designated pursuant to paragraph 11 of resolution 1127 (1997);

Observer or peace-keeping forces

626 (1988)

Noting the decision of Angola and Cuba to conclude a bilateral agreement on 22 December 1988 for the redeployment to the north and the staged and total withdrawal of Cuban troops from Angola according to the agreed timetable,

2. Decides to establish under its authority a United Nations Angola Verification Mission [. . .]

3. Further decides that the arrangements for the establishment of the Mission shall enter into force as soon as the tripartite agreement between Angola, Cuba and South Africa on the one hand, and the bilateral agreement between Angola and Cuba on the other are signed;

696 (1991)

Welcoming the decision of the Government of the People's Republic of Angola and the National Union for the Total Independence of Angola to conclude the Peace Accords for Angola,

Stressing the importance it attaches to the signing of the Peace Accords and to the fulfilment by the parties in good faith of the obligations contained therein,

Noting with satisfaction the decision taken by the Government of the People's Republic of Angola and the Government of the Republic of Cuba to complete the withdrawal, ahead of schedule, of all Cuban troops from Angola by 25 May 1991,

2. Decides accordingly to entrust a new mandate to United Nations Verification Mission (henceforth United Nations Verification Mission II) as proposed by the Secretary General in line with the Peace Accords for Angola,

747 (1992)

1. Approves the further report of the Secretary General . . . concerning the operation plan for United Nations observation of the elections and the enlargement of the Mission;

UNAVEM III (verification mission III) was established to assist the Government and UNITA in restoring peace and achieving national reconciliation on the basis of the Peace Accords for Angola 1991 and the Lusaka Protocol 1994.

1118 (1997)

MONUA (observer mission) established to assist in consolidating peace

1229 (1999)

Reaffirming its view that a continued presence of the United Nations in Angola can contribute greatly to national reconciliation, and noting the ongoing consultations with the Government of Angola to obtain its agreement regarding the practical arrangements for this presence,

Underscoring the contribution of the United Nations to the past four years of relative peace in Angola, and expressing its deep regret that the present political and security situation in the country has prevented the United Nations Observer Mission in Angola (MONUA) from fully carrying out its mandated role,

1. Takes note that the mandate of MONUA expires on 26 February 1999;

Encouragement or authorization of third-party actions

864 (1993)

Welcoming also and supporting to that end the efforts of the Secretary-General and his Special Representative aimed at the earliest resolution of the Angolan crisis through negotiations, and stressing the importance it attaches thereto,

Welcoming further the efforts of the Ad Hoc Committee on Southern Africa of the Organization of African Unity (OAU) and of Heads of State of neighbouring countries to facilitate the resumption of the peace process in Angola,

Emphasizing the importance of a continued and effective United Nations presence in Angola with a view to fostering the peace process and advancing the full implementation of the "Acordos de Paz,"

Applicability of humanitarian laws of war

811 (1993)

11. Strongly appeals to both parties strictly to abide by applicable rules of international humanitarian law, including unimpeded access for humanitarian assistance to the civilian population in need;

864 (1993)

13. Strongly condemns the repeated attacks carried out by UNITA against the UN personnel working to provide humanitarian assistance and reaffirms that such attacks are clear violations of humanitarian law,

15. Reiterates its appeal to both parties to [. . .] strictly abide by applicable rules of international humanitarian law,

Sovereignty and territorial integrity

696 (1991)

Stressing the importance of [. . .] respecting fully the independence, sovereignty and territorial integrity of Angola

834 (1993)

Reaffirming its commitment to preserving the unity and territorial integrity of Angola.

864 (1993)

Reaffirming its commitment to preserve the unity and territorial integrity of Angola

Threats to international peace and security

864 (1993); 1221 (1999); 1237 (1999), 1127 (1997); 1130 (1997); 1135 (1997); 1173 (1998); 1176 (1998)

864 (1993)

Strongly condemning UNITA and holding its leadership responsible for not having taken the necessary measures to comply with the demands made by the Council in its previous resolutions,

Determined to ensure respect for its resolutions and the full implementation of the "Acordos de Paz,"

Urging all States to refrain from providing any form of direct or indirect assistance, support or encouragement to UNITA,

Determining that, as a result of UNITA's military actions, the situation in Angola constitutes a threat to international peace and security,

1127 (1997)

Determining that the resulting situation in Angola constitutes a threat to international peace and security in the region,

ARMENIA

Concern, comments, acknowledgments

Statement of the President S/PRST/1995/21

It expresses its satisfaction that the cease-fire in the region agreed upon on 12 May 1994 through the mediation of the Russian Federation in cooperation with the OSCE Minsk Group has been holding for almost a year.

At the same time, the Council reiterates the concern it has previously expressed at the conflict in and around the Nagorny Karabakh region of the Azerbaijani

Republic and at the tensions between the Republic of Armenia and the Azerbaijani Republic. In particular, it expresses its concern at recent violent incidents and emphasizes the importance of using the mechanism of direct contacts for the settlement of incidents as agreed upon on 6 February 1995. It strongly urges the parties to the conflict to take all necessary measures to prevent such incidents in future.

The Council reaffirms all its relevant resolutions, inter alia, on the principles of sovereignty and territorial integrity of all States in the region. It also reaffirms the inviolability of international borders and the inadmissibility of the use of force for the acquisition of territory.

The Council reiterates its full support for the efforts of the Co-Chairmen of the Minsk Conference to assist in conducting speedy negotiations for the conclusion of a political agreement on the cessation of the armed conflict, the implementation of which will eliminate major consequences of the conflict for all parties, inter alia, ensuring withdrawal of forces, and permit the convening of the Minsk Conference.

The Council stresses that the parties to the conflict themselves bear the main responsibility for reaching a peaceful settlement. It stresses the urgency of concluding a political agreement on the cessation of the armed conflict on the basis of the relevant principles of the Charter of the United Nations and of the OSCE.

Resolutions calling for or demanding particular actions or outcomes

Statement of the President S/PRST/1995/21

The Council underlines the urgency of the implementation by the parties of confidence-building measures, as agreed upon within the Minsk Group on 15 April 1994, in particular in the humanitarian field, including the release of all prisoners of war and civilian detainees by the first anniversary of the cease-fire. It calls upon the parties to prevent suffering of the civilian populations affected by the armed conflict.

In particular, it expresses its concern at recent violent incidents and emphasizes the importance of using the mechanism of direct contacts for the settlement of incidents as agreed upon on 6 February 1995. It strongly urges the parties to the conflict to take all necessary measures to prevent such incidents in future.

It strongly urges those parties to constructively conduct negotiations without preconditions or procedural obstacles and to refrain from any actions that may undermine the peace process. It emphasizes that the achievement of such an agreement is a prerequisite for the deployment of a multinational OSCE peacekeeping force.

Encouragement or authorization of third-party actions

Statement of the President S/PRST/1995/21

The Council welcomes the decision of the Budapest summit of the CSCE of 6 December 1994 on the 'Intensification of CSCE action in relation to the

Nagorny-Karabakh conflict' (S/1995/249, appendix). It confirms its readiness to provide continuing political support, inter alia, through an appropriate resolution regarding the possible deployment of a multinational OSCE peace-keeping force following agreement among the parties for cessation of the armed conflict. The United Nations also stands ready to provide technical advice and expertise.

BURMA

No relevant Security Council resolutions.

BALKAN CRISIS

This crisis includes the conflict in the former Yugoslavia, the Federal Republic of Yugoslavia and Kosovo, Croatia, and Bosnia/Herzegovina.

THE FORMER YUGOSLAVIA

Concern, comments, acknowledgments

713 (1991)

Deeply concerned about the fighting in Yugoslavia, which is causing a heavy loss of human life and material damage, and by the consequences for the countries of the region, in particular in the border areas of neighbouring countries,

Concerned that the continuation of this situation constitutes a threat to international peace and security,

Recalling the relevant principles enshrined in the Charter, and in this context taking note of the declaration of 3 September 1991 of the States participating in the Conference on Security and Cooperation in Europe that no territorial gains or changes within Yugoslavia brought about by violence are acceptable,

Alarmed by the violations of the cease-fire and the continuation of the fighting.

721 (1991)

Considering the request by the Government of Yugoslavia for the establishment of a peace-keeping operation in Yugoslavia [. . .]

Deeply concerned by the fighting in Yugoslavia and by the serious violations of earlier cease-fire agreement, which have caused heavy loss of human life and widespread material damage, and by the consequences for the countries of the region,

727 (1992)

Recalling its primary responsibility under the Charter of the United Nations for the maintenance of international peace and security,

Recalling also the provisions of Chapter VIII of the Charter, and noting the continuing role that the European community will play in achieving a peaceful solution in Yugoslavia,

771 (1992)

Expressing grave alarm at continuing reports of widespread violations of international humanitarian law occurring within the territory of the former Yugoslavia and especially in Bosnia and Herzegovina including reports of mass forcible expulsion and deportation of civilians, imprisonment and abuse of civilians in detention centres, deliberate attacks on non-combatants, hospitals and ambulances, impeding the delivery of food and medical supplies to the civilian population, and wanton devastation and destructive property,

777 (1992)

Considering that the state formerly known as the Socialist Federal Republic of Yugoslavia has ceased to exist.

1. Reaffirms that the Federal Republic of Yugoslavia (Serbia and Montenegro) cannot continue automatically the membership of the former Socialist Republic of Yugoslavia in the United Nations;

821 (1993)

Considering that the State formerly known as the Soviet Federal Republic of Yugoslavia has ceased to exist,

943 (1994)

Affirming its commitment to a negotiated settlement of the conflict in the former Yugoslavia, preserving the territorial integrity of all the States there within their internationally recognized borders,

1022 (1995)

Reaffirming its commitment to a negotiated political settlement of the conflicts in the former Yugoslavia, preserving the territorial integrity of all States there within their internationally recognized borders,

Commending the efforts of the international community, including those of the Contact Group, to assist the parties in reaching a settlement,

Praising the decision of the Governments of the Republic of Bosnia and Herzegovina, the Republic of Croatia and the Federal Republic of Yugoslavia to attend and participate constructively in proximity talks in the United States of America, and acknowledging with appreciation the efforts made by these Governments to reach a lasting peace settlement in Bosnia and Herzegovina,

Welcoming the initialling of the General Framework Agreement for Peace in Bosnia and Herzegovina and the Annexes thereto (collectively the Peace Agreement) by the Republic of Bosnia and Herzegovina, the Republic of Croatia and the Federal Republic of Yugoslavia and the other parties thereto on 21 November 1995, in Dayton, Ohio, signifying agreement between the parties to sign formally the Peace Agreement,

1031 (1995)

Reaffirming its commitment to a negotiated political settlement of the conflicts in the former Yugoslavia, preserving the territorial integrity of all States there within their internationally recognized borders,

Welcoming the signing on 14 December 1995 at the Paris Peace Conference of the General Framework Agreement for Peace in Bosnia and Herzegovina and the Annexes thereto (collectively the Peace Agreement, S/1995/999, Annex) by the Republic of Bosnia and Herzegovina, the Republic of Croatia and the Federal Republic of Yugoslavia and the other parties thereto,

Welcoming also the Dayton Agreement on implementing the Federation of Bosnia and Herzegovina of 10 November 1995 (S/1995/1021, Annex),

Condemnation

771 (1992)

2. Strongly condemns any violations of international humanitarian law, including those involved in the practice of 'ethnic cleansing';

847 (1993)

Recalling the overwhelming importance of seeking, on the basis of the relevant resolutions of the Security Council, comprehensive political solutions to the conflicts in the territory of the former Yugoslavia, and of sustaining confidence and stability in the former Yugoslav Republic of Macedonia,

Strongly condemning continuing military attacks within the territory of the Republics of Croatia and of Bosnia Herzegovina, and reaffirming its commitment to ensure respect for the sovereignty and territorial integrity of the Republic of Croatia and of the other Member States were UNPROFOR is deployed,

Resolutions calling for or demanding particular actions or outcomes

713 (1991)

4. Strongly urges all parties to abide strictly by the cease-fire agreements of 17 September 1991;

5. Appeals urgently to and encourages all parties to settle their disputes peacefully and through negotiation at the Conference on Yugoslavia, including through the mechanisms set forth within it;

7. Calls upon all States to refrain from any action which might contribute to increasing tension and to impeding or delaying a peaceful and negotiated outcome to the conflict in Yugoslavia, which would permit all Yugoslavs to decide upon and to construct their future in peace;

727 (1991)

3. Strongly urges the Yugoslav parties to comply fully with that agreement [signed in Geneva on 23 November 1991];

4. Urges all parties to honour the commitments made at Geneva and Sarajevo with a view to effecting a complete cessation of hostilities;

5. Requests all parties to take all necessary measures to ensure the safety of the personnel sent by the United Nations and of all the members of the European Community Monitoring Mission;

740 (1992)

6. Calls upon all States to continue to take all appropriate steps to ensure that the Yugoslav parties implement their unqualified acceptance of the United Nations peace-keeping plan, fulfil their commitments in good faith and cooperate fully with the Secretary General;

7. Calls upon the Yugoslav parties to cooperate fully with the Conference on Yugoslavia in its aim of reaching a political settlement consistent with the principles of the Conference on Security and Cooperation in Europe, and reaffirms that the United Nations peace-keeping plan and its implementation is in no way intended to prejudge the terms of a political settlement;

749 (1992)

5. Calls upon all parties and others concerned not to resort to violence, particularly in any area where the Force is to be based or deployed;

771 (1992)

3. Demands that all parties and others concerned in the former Yugoslavia, and all military forces in Bosnia and Herzegovina, immediately cease and desist from all breaches of international humanitarian law including from actions such as those described above;

7. Decides, acting under Chapter VII of the Charter of the United Nations, that all parties and others concerned in the former Yugoslavia, and all military forces in Bosnia and Herzegovina, shall comply with the provisions of the present resolution, failing which the Council will need to take further measures under the Charter;

Sanctions

713 (1991)

6. Decides under Chapter VII of the Charter of the United Nations, that all States shall for the purposes of establishing peace and stability in Yugoslavia, immediately implement a general and complete embargo on all deliveries of weapons and military equipment to Yugoslavia;

757 (1992)

Noting that in the very complex context of events in the former Socialist Federal Republic of Yugoslavia all parties bear some responsibility for the situation,

Reaffirming its support for the Conference on Yugoslavia including the efforts undertaken by the European Community in the framework of the discussions on constitutional arrangements for Bosnia and Herzegovina, and recalling that no territorial gains or changes brought about by violence are acceptable and that the borders of Bosnia and Herzegovina are inviolable,

Deploring the fact that the demands in resolution 752 (1992) have not been complied with, including its demands that:

All parties and others concerned in Bosnia and Herzegovina stop the fighting immediately,

All forms of interference from outside Bosnia and Herzegovina cease immediately,

All irregular forces in Bosnia and Herzegovina be disbanded and disarmed [. . .]

Deeply concerned also at developments in Croatia, including persistent cease-fire violations and the continued expulsion of non-Serb civilians, and at the obstruction of and lack of cooperation with the Force in other parts of Croatia,

Recalling its primary responsibility under the Charter of the United Nations for the maintenance of international peace and security,

Recalling also the provisions of Chapter VIII of the Charter, and the continuing role that the European Community is playing in working for a peaceful solution in Bosnia and Herzegovina, as well as in other republics of the former Socialist Federal Republic of Yugoslavia,

Recalling further its decision in resolution 752 (1992) to consider further steps to achieve a peaceful solution in conformity with its relevant resolutions, and affirming its determination to take measures against any party or parties which fail to fulfil the requirements of resolution 752 (1992) and its other relevant resolutions,

Determined in this context to adopt certain measures with the sole objective of achieving a peaceful solution and encouraging the efforts undertaken by the European Community and its member States,

Acting under Chapter VII of the Charter,

3. Decides that all States shall adopt the measures set out below which shall apply until the Council decides that the authorities of the Federal Republic of Yugoslavia (Serbia and Montenegro), including the Yugoslav People's Army, have taken effective measures to fulfil the requirements of resolution 752 (1992),

4. Decides also that all States shall prevent:

   (a) The import into their territories of all commodities and products originating in the Federal Republic of Yugoslavia [. . .]

(c) The sale or supply by their nationals or from their territories [. . .] of any commodities or products [. . .]

808 (1993)

Expressing once again its grave alarm at continuing reports of widespread violations of international humanitarian law occurring within the territory of the former Yugoslavia, including reports of mass killings and continuance of the practice of 'ethnic cleansing,'

Determining that this situation constitutes a threat to international peace and security,

Determined to put an end to such crimes and to take effective measures to bring to justice the persons who are responsible for them,

Convinced that in the particular circumstances to the former Yugoslavia the establishment of an international tribunal would enable this aim to be achieved and would contribute to the restoration and maintenance of peace,

1. Decides that an international tribunal shall be established for the prosecution of persons responsible for serious violations of international humanitarian law committed in the territory of the former Yugoslavia since 1991;

1022 (1995)

Acting under Chapter VII of the Charter of the United Nations,

1. Decides that the measures imposed by or reaffirmed in resolutions 757 (1992), 787 (1992), 820 (1993), 942 (1994), 943 (1994), 988 (1995), 992 (1995), 1003 (1995) and 1015 (1995) are suspended indefinitely with immediate effect subject to the provisions of paragraphs 2 to 5 below, and provided that if the Secretary-General reports to the Council that the Federal Republic of Yugoslavia has failed formally to sign the Peace Agreement on the date announced by the Contact Group for such purpose, and that the other parties thereto have expressed their readiness so to sign, the measures described above shall be automatically re-imposed from the fifth day following the date of such report;

2. Decides also that the suspension referred to in paragraph 1 above shall not apply to the measures imposed on the Bosnian Serb party until the day after the commander of the international force to be deployed in accordance with the Peace Agreement, on the basis of a report transmitted through the appropriate political authorities, informs the Council via the Secretary-General that all Bosnian Serb forces have withdrawn behind the zones of separation established in the Peace Agreement; and urges all parties concerned to take all necessary measures to assist in locating the two French pilots missing in Bosnia and Herzegovina, and to ensure their immediate and safe return;

3. Further decides that if at any time, with regard to a matter within the scope of their respective mandates and after joint consultation if appropriate, either the High Representative described in the Peace Agreement, or the commander of

the international force to be deployed in accordance with the Peace Agreement, on the basis of a report transmitted through the appropriate political authorities, informs the Council via the Secretary-General that the Federal Republic of Yugoslavia or the Bosnian Serb authorities are failing significantly to meet their obligations under the Peace Agreement, the suspension referred to in paragraph 1 above shall terminate on the fifth day following the Council's receipt of such a report, unless the Council decides otherwise taking into consideration the nature of the non-compliance;

4. Further decides that it will terminate the measures described in paragraph 1 above on the tenth day following the occurrence of the first free and fair elections provided for in Annex 3 of the Peace Agreement, provided that the Bosnian Serb forces have withdrawn from, and have continued to respect, the zones of separation as provided in the Peace Agreement;

5. Further decides that so long as the measures referred to in paragraph 1 above remain suspended, or are terminated by a subsequent Council decision in accordance with paragraph 4 above, all funds and assets previously frozen or impounded pursuant to resolutions 757 (1992) and 820 (1993) may be released by States in accordance with law, provided that any such funds and assets that are subject to any claims, liens, judgements, or encumbrances, or which are the funds or assets of any person, partnership, corporation, or other entity found or deemed insolvent under law or the accounting principles prevailing in such State, shall remain frozen or impounded until released in accordance with applicable law, and decides further that obligations of States related to freezing or impounding funds and assets contained in such resolutions shall be suspended pursuant to paragraph 1 above with respect to all funds and assets not currently frozen or impounded until the measures concerned are terminated by a subsequent Council decision;

Observer or peace-keeping forces

721 (1991)

Considering further the fact, as conveyed in the above mentioned letter of the Secretary General, that each one of the Yugoslav participants in the meeting with his Personal Envoy stated that they wanted to see the deployment of a United Nations peace-keeping operation as soon as possible,

2. Endorses the statement made by the Personal Envoy of the Secretary General to the parties that the deployment of a United Nations peace-keeping operation cannot be envisaged without, inter alia, full compliance by all parties with the agreement signed in Geneva on 23 November 1991 [. . .]

740 (1992)

Taking note of the further report of the Secretary General of 4 February 1992 [. . .] and welcoming his report that the ceasefire has been generally observed thus removing one of the obstacles to the deployment of a peace-keeping operation,

3. Approves the proposal by the Secretary General to increase the authorized strength of the military liaison mission to a total of seventy-five officers.

5. Expresses its concern that the United Nations peacekeeping plan has not yet been fully and unconditionally accepted by all in Yugoslavia on whose cooperation its success depends;

743 (1992)

Concerned that the situation in Yugoslavia continues to constitute a threat to international peace and security as determined in resolution 713 (1991),

2. Decides to establish, under its authority, a United Nations Protection Force in accordance with the above-mentioned report and the United Nations peace-keeping plan,

5. Recalls that, in accordance with paragraph 1 of the United Nations peacekeeping plan, the Force should be an interim arrangement to create the conditions of peace and security required for the negotiation of an overall settlement of the Yugoslav Crisis.

749 (1992)

Full deployment of the peacekeeping force.

Encouragement or authorization of third-party actions

713 (1991)

Commending the efforts undertaken by the European Community in its member States, with the support of the States participating in the Conference on Security and Cooperation in Europe, to restore peace and dialogue in Yugoslavia through, inter alia, the implementation of a cease-fire including the sending of observers, the convening of a conference on Yugoslavia, including the mechanisms set forth within it, and the suspension of the delivery of all weapons and military equipment to Yugoslavia,

1. Expresses its full support for the collective efforts for peace and dialogue in Yugoslavia undertaken under the auspices of the member States of the European Community [. . .]

2. Supports fully all arrangements and measures resulting from such collective efforts as those described above, in particular with regard to assistance and support to the cease-fire observers, and to consolidate an effective end to hostilities in Yugoslavia and to assure the smooth functioning of the process instituted within the framework of the Conference on Yugoslavia;

943 (1994)

Expressing appreciation for the efforts of the representatives of the United Nations, the European Union, the United States of America and the Russian Federation to assist the parties in reaching a settlement,

Applicability of humanitarian laws of war

771 (1992)

Expressing grave alarm at continuing reports of widespread violations of international humanitarian law occurring within the territory of the former Yugoslavia and especially in Bosnia and Herzegovina including reports of mass forcible expulsion and deportation of civilians, imprisonment and abuse of civilians in detention centres, deliberate attacks on non-combatants [. . .]

1. Reaffirms that all parties to the conflict are bound to comply with their obligations under international humanitarian law and in particular the Geneva Conventions of 12 August 1949, and that persons who commit or order the commission of grave breaches of the Conventions are individually responsible in respect of such breaches;

1034 (1995)

1. Strongly condemns all violations of international humanitarian law and of human rights in the territory of the former Yugoslavia and demands that all concerned comply fully with their obligations in this regard and reiterates that all those who commit violations of international humanitarian law will be held individually responsible in respect of such acts;

2. Condemns in particular in the strongest possible terms the violations of international humanitarian law and of human rights by Bosnian Serb and paramilitary forces in the areas of Srebrenica, Zepa, Banja Luka and Sanski Most as described in the report of the Secretary-General of 27 November 1995 and showing a consistent pattern of summary executions, rape, mass expulsions, arbitrary detentions, forced labour and large-scale disappearances;

Threats to international peace and security

713 (1991); 724 (1991); 757 (1992); 760 (1992); 771 (1992); 787 (1992); 808 (1993) 827 (1993); 908 (1994); 914 (1994); 947 (1994); 967 (1994); 992 (1995); 1074 (1996); 1166 (1998); 1207 (1998)

713 (1991)

Deeply concerned about the fighting in Yugoslavia, which is causing a heavy loss of human life and material damage, and by the consequences for the countries of the region, in particular in the border areas of neighbouring countries,

Concerned that the continuation of this situation constitutes a threat to international peace and security,

808 (1993)

Expressing once again its grave alarm at continuing reports of widespread violations of international humanitarian law occurring within the territory of the former Yugoslavia, including reports of mass killings and continuance of the practice of 'ethnic cleansing,'

Determining that this situation constitutes a threat to international peace and security,

FEDERAL REPUBLIC OF YUGOSLAVIA AND KOSOVO

Concern, comments, acknowledgments

855 (1993)

Deeply concerned at the refusal of the authorities in the Federal Republic of Yugoslavia (Serbia and Montenegro) to allow the CSCE missions of long duration to continue their activities,

Bearing in mind that the CSCE missions of long duration are an example of preventative diplomacy undertaken within the framework of the CSCE, and have greatly contributed to promoting stability and counteracting the risk of violence in Kosovo, Sandjak and Vojvodina, the Federal Republic of Yugoslavia (Serbia and Montenegro),

Reaffirming its relevant resolutions aimed at putting an end to conflict in the former Yugoslavia,

Determined to avoid any extension of the conflict in the former Yugoslavia and, in this context, attaching great importance to the work of the CSCE missions and to the continued ability of the international community to monitor the situation in Kosovo [. . .]

943 (1994)

Welcoming the decision by the authorities of the Federal Republic of Yugoslavia (Serbia and Montenegro) to support the proposed territorial settlement (S/1994/1081) for the Republic of Bosnia and Herzegovina which has been put to the Bosnian parties,

Also welcoming the decision by the authorities of the Federal Republic of Yugoslavia (Serbia and Montenegro) to close the international border between the Federal Republic of Yugoslavia (Serbia and Montenegro) and the Republic of Bosnia and Herzegovina with respect to all goods except foodstuffs, medical supplies and clothing for essential humanitarian needs,

1160 (1998)

Noting also the clear commitment of senior representatives of the Kosovar Albanian community to non-violence,

1199 (1998)

Noting further the communication by the Prosecutor of the International Tribunal for the Former Yugoslavia to the Contact Group on 7 July 1998, expressing the view that the situation in Kosovo represents an armed conflict within the terms of the mandate of the Tribunal,

Gravely concerned at the recent intense fighting in Kosovo and in particular the excessive and indiscriminate use of force by Serbian security forces and the Yugoslav Army which have resulted in numerous civilian casualties and, according to the estimate of the Secretary-General, the displacement of over 230,000 persons from their homes,

Deeply concerned by the flow of refugees into northern Albania, Bosnia and Herzegovina and other European countries as a result of the use of force in Kosovo, as well as by the increasing numbers of displaced persons within Kosovo, and other parts of the Federal Republic of Yugoslavia, up to 50,000 of whom the United Nations High Commissioner for Refugees has estimated are without shelter and other basic necessities,

Reaffirming the right of all refugees and displaced persons to return to their homes in safety, and underlining the responsibility of the Federal Republic of Yugoslavia for creating the conditions which allow them to do so,

Deeply concerned by the rapid deterioration in the humanitarian situation throughout Kosovo, alarmed at the impending humanitarian catastrophe as described in the report of the Secretary-General, and emphasizing the need to prevent this from happening,

Deeply concerned also by reports of increasing violations of human rights and of international humanitarian law, and emphasizing the need to ensure that the rights of all inhabitants of Kosovo are respected,

Reaffirming the objectives of resolution 1160 (1998), in which the Council expressed support for a peaceful resolution of the Kosovo problem which would include an enhanced status for Kosovo, a substantially greater degree of autonomy, and meaningful self-administration,

1239 (1999)

Bearing in mind the provisions of the Charter of the United Nations and guided by the Universal Declaration of Human Rights, the international covenants and conventions on human rights, the Conventions and Protocol relating to the Status of Refugees, the Geneva Conventions of 1949 and the Additional Protocols thereto of 1977, as well as other instruments of international humanitarian law,

Expressing grave concern at the humanitarian catastrophe in and around Kosovo, Federal Republic of Yugoslavia, as a result of the continuing crisis,

Deeply concerned by the enormous influx of Kosovo refugees into Albania, the former Yugoslav Republic of Macedonia, Bosnia and Herzegovina, and other countries, as well as by the increasing numbers of displaced persons within Kosovo, the Republic of Montenegro and other parts of the Federal Republic of Yugoslavia,

4. Reaffirms the right of all refugees and displaced persons to return to their homes in safety and in dignity;

5. Emphasizes that the humanitarian situation will continue to deteriorate in the absence of a political solution to the crisis consistent with the principles adopted by the Foreign Ministers of Canada, France, Germany, Italy, Japan, the Russian Federation, the United Kingdom of Great Britain and Northern Ireland and the United States of America on 6 May 1999 (S/1999/516), and urges all concerned to work towards this aim;

Condemnation

1160 (1998)

Condemning the use of excessive force by Serbian police forces against civilians and peaceful demonstrators in Kosovo, as well as all acts of terrorism by the Kosovo Liberation Army or any other group or individual and all external support for terrorist activity in Kosovo, including finance, arms and training,

1199 (1998)

Condemning all acts of violence by any party, as well as terrorism in pursuit of political goals by any group or individual, and all external support for such activities in Kosovo, including the supply of arms and training for terrorist activities in Kosovo.

1244 (1999)

Condemning all acts of violence against the Kosovo population as well as all terrorist acts by any party,

Resolutions calling for or demanding particular actions or outcomes

855 (1993)

2. Calls upon the authorities in the Federal Republic of Yugoslavia (Serbia and Montenegro) to reconsider their refusal to allow the continuation of the activities of the CSCE missions in Kosovo, Sandjak and Vojvodina [. . .]

1160 (1998)

Acting under Chapter VII of the Charter of the United Nations,

1. Calls upon the Federal Republic of Yugoslavia immediately to take the further necessary steps to achieve a political solution to the issue of Kosovo through dialogue and to implement the actions indicated in the Contact Group statements of 9 and 25 March 1998;

2. Calls also upon the Kosovar Albanian leadership to condemn all terrorist action, and emphasizes that all elements in the Kosovar Albanian community should pursue their goals by peaceful means only;

3. Underlines that the way to defeat violence and terrorism in Kosovo is for the authorities in Belgrade to offer the Kosovar Albanian community a genuine political process;

4. Calls upon the authorities in Belgrade and the leadership of the Kosovar Albanian community urgently to enter without preconditions into a meaningful dialogue on political status issues, and notes the readiness of the Contact Group to facilitate such a dialogue;

5. Agrees, without prejudging the outcome of that dialogue, with the proposal in the Contact Group statements of 9 and 25 March 1998 that the principles for a solution of the Kosovo problem should be based on the territorial integrity of the Federal Republic of Yugoslavia and should be in accordance with OSCE standards, including those set out in the Helsinki Final Act of the Conference on Security and Cooperation in Europe of 1975, and the Charter of the United Nations, and that such a solution must also take into account the rights of the Kosovar Albanians and all who live in Kosovo, and expresses its support for an enhanced status for Kosovo which would include a substantially greater degree of autonomy and meaningful self-administration;

1199 (1998)

Acting under Chapter VII of the Charter of the United Nations,

1. Demands that all parties, groups and individuals immediately cease hostilities and maintain a ceasefire in Kosovo, Federal Republic of Yugoslavia, which would enhance the prospects for a meaningful dialogue between the authorities of the Federal Republic of Yugoslavia and the Kosovo Albanian leadership and reduce the risks of a humanitarian catastrophe;

2. Demands also that the authorities of the Federal Republic of Yugoslavia and the Kosovo Albanian leadership take immediate steps to improve the humanitarian situation and to avert the impending humanitarian catastrophe;

3. Calls upon the authorities in the Federal Republic of Yugoslavia and the Kosovo Albanian leadership to enter immediately into a meaningful dialogue without preconditions and with international involvement, and to a clear timetable, leading to an end of the crisis and to a negotiated political solution to the issue of Kosovo, and welcomes the current efforts aimed at facilitating such a dialogue;

4. Demands further that the Federal Republic of Yugoslavia, in addition to the measures called for under resolution 1160 (1998), implement immediately the following concrete measures towards achieving a political solution to the situation in Kosovo as contained in the Contact Group statement of 12 June 1998:

(a) cease all action by the security forces affecting the civilian population and order the withdrawal of security units used for civilian repression;

(b) enable effective and continuous international monitoring in Kosovo by the European Community Monitoring Mission and diplomatic missions accredited to the Federal Republic of Yugoslavia, including access and complete freedom of movement of such monitors to, from and within Kosovo unimpeded by government authorities, and expeditious issuance of appropriate travel documents to international personnel contributing to the monitoring;

(c) facilitate, in agreement with the UNHCR and the International Committee of the Red Cross (ICRC), the safe return of refugees and displaced persons to their homes and allow free and unimpeded access for humanitarian organizations and supplies to Kosovo;

(d) make rapid progress to a clear timetable, in the dialogue referred to in paragraph 3 with the Kosovo Albanian community called for in resolution 1160 (1998), with the aim of agreeing confidence-building measures and finding a political solution to the problems of Kosovo;

5. Notes, in this connection, the commitments of the President of the Federal Republic of Yugoslavia, in his joint statement with the President of the Russian Federation of 16 June 1998:

(a) to resolve existing problems by political means on the basis of equality for all citizens and ethnic communities in Kosovo;

(b) not to carry out any repressive actions against the peaceful population;

(c) to provide full freedom of movement for and ensure that there will be no restrictions on representatives of foreign States and international institutions accredited to the Federal Republic of Yugoslavia monitoring the situation in Kosovo;

(d) to ensure full and unimpeded access for humanitarian organizations, the ICRC and the UNHCR, and delivery of humanitarian supplies;

(e) to facilitate the unimpeded return of refugees and displaced persons under programmes agreed with the UNHCR and the ICRC, providing State aid for the reconstruction of destroyed homes,

(f) and calls for the full implementation of these commitments;

6. Insists that the Kosovo Albanian leadership condemn all terrorist action, and emphasizes that all elements in the Kosovo Albanian community should pursue their goals by peaceful means only;

1203 (1998)

Affirming that the unresolved situation in Kosovo, Federal Republic of Yugoslavia, constitutes a continuing threat to peace and security in the region,

Acting under Chapter VII of the Charter of the United Nations,

1. Endorses and supports the agreements signed in Belgrade on 16 October 1998 between the Federal Republic of Yugoslavia and the OSCE, and on 15 October 1998 between the Federal Republic of Yugoslavia and NATO, concerning the verification of compliance by the Federal Republic of Yugoslavia and all others concerned in Kosovo with the requirements of its resolution 1199 (1998),

and demands the full and prompt implementation of these agreements by the Federal Republic of Yugoslavia;

2. Notes the endorsement by the Government of Serbia of the accord reached by the President of the Federal Republic of Yugoslavia and the United States Special Envoy (S/1998/953, Annex), and the public commitment of the Federal Republic of Yugoslavia to complete negotiations on a framework for a political settlement by 2 November 1998, and calls for the full implementation of these commitments;

3. Demands that the Federal Republic of Yugoslavia comply fully and swiftly with resolutions 1160 (1998) and 1199 (1998) and cooperate fully with the OSCE Verification Mission in Kosovo and the NATO Air Verification Mission over Kosovo according to the terms of the agreements referred to in paragraph 1 above;

4. Demands also that the Kosovo Albanian leadership and all other elements of the Kosovo Albanian community comply fully and swiftly with resolutions 1160 (1998) and 1199 (1998) and cooperate fully with the OSCE Verification Mission in Kosovo;

1244 (1999)

Welcoming the general principles on a political solution to the Kosovo crisis adopted on 6 May 1999 (S/1999/516, Annex 1 to this resolution) and welcoming also the acceptance by the Federal Republic of Yugoslavia of the principles set forth in points 1 to 9 of the paper presented in Belgrade on 2 June 1999 (S/1999/649, Annex 2 to this resolution), and the Federal Republic of Yugoslavia's agreement to that paper,

[. . .] acting for these purposes under Chapter VII of the Charter of the United Nations,

1. Decides that a political solution to the Kosovo crisis shall be based on the general principles in Annex 1 [concluded in the G8 Foreign Ministers meeting—end of violence and repression, withdrawal of military forces from Kosovo, deployment of international civil and security presence] and as further elaborated in the principles and other required elements in Annex 2;

3. Demands in particular that the Federal Republic of Yugoslavia put an immediate and verifiable end to violence and repression in Kosovo, and begin and complete verifiable phased withdrawal from Kosovo of all military, police and paramilitary forces according to a rapid timetable, with which the deployment of the international security presence in Kosovo will be synchronized;

1244 (1999)

[. . .] acting for these purposes under Chapter VII

15. Demands that the KLA and other armed Kosovo Albanian groups end immediately all offensive actions and comply with the requirements for demilitarization as laid down by the head of the international security presence in consultation with the Special Representative of the Secretary-General;

Sanctions

1160 (1998)

8. Decides that all States shall, for the purposes of fostering peace and stability in Kosovo, prevent the sale or supply to the Federal Republic of Yugoslavia, including Kosovo, by their nationals or from their territories or using their flag vessels and aircraft, of arms and related matériel of all types, such as weapons and ammunition, military vehicles and equipment and spare parts for the aforementioned, and shall prevent arming and training for terrorist activities there;

Observer or peace-keeping forces

1244 (1999)

5. Decides on the deployment in Kosovo, under United Nations auspices, of international civil and security presences, with appropriate equipment and personnel as required, and welcomes the agreement of the Federal Republic of Yugoslavia to such presences;

6. Requests the Secretary-General to appoint, in consultation with the Security Council, a Special Representative to control the implementation of the international civil presence, and further requests the Secretary-General to instruct his Special Representative to coordinate closely with the international security presence to ensure that both presences operate towards the same goals and in a mutually supportive manner;

7. Authorizes Member States and relevant international organizations to establish the international security presence in Kosovo as set out in point 4 of Annex 2 with all necessary means to fulfil its responsibilities under paragraph 9 below;

8. Affirms the need for the rapid early deployment of effective international civil and security presences to Kosovo, and demands that the parties cooperate fully in their deployment;

Encouragement or authorization of third-party actions

1160 (1998)

Welcoming the decision of the Permanent Council of the Organization for security and Cooperation in Europe (OSCE) of 11 March (S/1998/246).

7. Expresses its support for the efforts of the OSCE for a peaceful resolution of the crisis in Kosovo, including through the Personal Representative of the Chairman-in-Office for the Federal Republic of Yugoslavia, who is also the Special Representative of the European Union, and the return of the OSCE long-term missions;

1203 (1998)

Welcoming the agreement signed in Belgrade on 16 October 1998 by the Minister of Foreign Affairs of the Federal Republic of Yugoslavia and the

Chairman-in-Office of the Organization for Security and Cooperation in Europe (OSCE) providing for the OSCE to establish a verification mission in Kosovo (S/1998/978), including the undertaking of the Federal Republic of Yugoslavia to comply with resolutions 1160 (1998) and 1199 (1998),

Welcoming also the agreement signed in Belgrade on 15 October 1998 by the Chief of General Staff of the Federal Republic of Yugoslavia and the Supreme Allied Commander, Europe, of the North Atlantic Treaty Organization (NATO) providing for the establishment of an air verification mission over Kosovo

(S/1998/991, Annex), complementing the OSCE Verification Mission, Acting under Chapter VII of the Charter of the United Nations,

1. Endorses and supports the agreements signed in Belgrade on 16 October 1998 between the Federal Republic of Yugoslavia and the OSCE, and on 15 October 1998 between the Federal Republic of Yugoslavia and NATO, concerning the verification of compliance by the Federal Republic of Yugoslavia and all others concerned in Kosovo with the requirements of its resolution 1199 (1998), and demands the full and prompt implementation of these agreements by the Federal Republic of Yugoslavia;

2. Notes the endorsement by the Government of Serbia of the accord reached by the President of the Federal Republic of Yugoslavia and the United States Special Envoy (S/1998/953, Annex), and the public commitment of the Federal Republic of Yugoslavia to complete negotiations on a framework for a political settlement by 2 November 1998, and calls for the full implementation of these commitments;

1244 (1999)

7. Authorizes Member States and relevant international organizations to establish the international security presence in Kosovo as set out in point 4 of Annex 2 with all necessary means to fulfil its responsibilities under paragraph 9 below;

9. Decides that the responsibilities of the international security presence to be deployed and acting in Kosovo will include:

(a) Deterring renewed hostilities, maintaining and where necessary enforcing a ceasefire, and ensuring the withdrawal and preventing the return into Kosovo of Federal and Republic military, police and paramilitary forces, except as provided in point 6 of Annex 2;

(b) Demilitarizing the Kosovo Liberation Army (KLA) and other armed Kosovo Albanian groups as required in paragraph 15 below;

(c) Establishing a secure environment in which refugees and displaced persons can return home in safety, the international civil presence can operate, a transitional administration can be established, and humanitarian aid can be delivered;

(d) Ensuring public safety and order until the international civil presence can take responsibility for this task;

(e) Supervising demining until the international civil presence can, as appropriate, take over responsibility for this task;

(f) Supporting, as appropriate, and coordinating closely with the work of the international civil presence;

(g) Conducting border monitoring duties as required;

(h) Ensuring the protection and freedom of movement of itself, the international civil presence, and other international organizations;

Applicability of humanitarian laws of war

1199 (1998)

Deeply concerned also by reports of increasing violations of human rights and of international humanitarian law, and emphasizing the need to ensure that the rights of all inhabitants of Kosovo are respected,

Under Chap VII

13. Calls upon the authorities of the Federal Republic of Yugoslavia, the leaders of the Kosovo Albanian community and all others concerned to cooperate fully with the Prosecutor of the International Tribunal for the Former Yugoslavia in the investigation of possible violations within the jurisdiction of the Tribunal;

14. Underlines also the need for the authorities of the Federal Republic of Yugoslavia to bring to justice those members of the security forces who have been involved in the mistreatment of civilians and the deliberate destruction of property;

Sovereignty and territorial integrity

1160 (1998)

Affirming the commitment of all Member States to the sovereignty and territorial integrity of the Federal Republic of Yugoslavia,

1199 (1998)

Reaffirming also the commitment of all Member States to the sovereignty and territorial integrity of the Federal Republic of Yugoslavia,

Threats to international peace and security

1160 (1998); 1199 (1998); 1203 (1998); 1244 (1999)

1199 (1998)

Affirming that the deterioration of the situation in Kosovo, Federal Republic of Yugoslavia, constitutes a threat to peace and security in the region,

1244 (1999)

Condemning all acts of violence against the Kosovo population as well as all terrorist acts by any party,

Recalling the statement made by the Secretary-General on 9 April 1999, expressing concern at the humanitarian tragedy taking place in Kosovo,

Reaffirming the right of all refugees and displaced persons to return to their homes in safety,

Determining that the situation in the region continues to constitute a threat to international peace and security,

CROATIA

Concern, comments, acknowledgments

753 (1992)

[Admitted the Republic of Croatia to the UN.]

762 (1993)

Welcoming the progress made as a result of the assumption of responsibilities by the United Nations Protection Force in Sectors East and West, and concerned about the difficulties encountered by the Force in Sectors North and South,

779 (1992)

Expressing grave alarm at continuing reports of "ethnic cleansing" in the UNPAs and of forcible expulsion of civilians and deprivation of their rights of residence and property,

802 (1993)

Reaffirming in particular its commitment to the United Nations peace-keeping plan (S/23280, Annex III),

Deeply concerned by the information provided by the Secretary-General to the Security Council on 25 January 1993 on the rapid and violent deterioration of the situation in Croatia as a result of military attacks by Croatian armed forces on the areas under protection of the United Nations Protection Force (UNPROFOR)

Deeply concerned also by the lack of cooperation in recent months by the Serb local authorities in the areas under the protection of UNPROFOR, by the recent seizure by them of heavy weapons under UNPROFOR control, and by threats to widen the conflict,

871 (1993)

Deeply concerned that the United Nations peace-keeping plan for the Republic of Croatia [. . .] and all relevant Security Council resolutions, in particular resolution 769 (1992), have not yet been fully implemented,

994 (1995)

Emphasizing that full observance of human rights, including appropriate international monitoring thereof, in particular in the area of Western Slavonia known as Sector West, is an essential step towards restoration of confidence between the parties and building a durable peace,

Condemnation

802 (1993)

Strongly condemning those attacks which have led to casualties and loss of life in UNPROFOR, as well as among the civilian population,

871 (1993)

3. Condemns once again continuing military attacks within the territory of the Republic of Croatia and the Republic of Bosnia and Herzegovina and the former Yugoslav Republic of Macedonia, where UNPROFOR is deployed;

Resolutions calling for or demanding particular actions or outcomes

762 (1993)

2. Urges all parties and others concerned to honour their commitments to effect a complete cessation of hostilities and to implement the United Nations peace-keeping plan;

802 (1993)

1. Demands the immediate cessation of hostile activities by Croatian armed forces within or adjacent to the United Nations Protected Areas and the withdrawal of the Croatian armed forces from these areas;

807 (1993)

Determined to ensure the security of UNPROFOR and to this end, acting under Chapter VII of the Charter of the United Nations,

1. Demands that the parties and others concerned comply fully with the United Nations peace-keeping plan in Croatia and with other commitments they have undertaken and in particular with their cease-fire obligations;

2. Demands further that the parties and others concerned refrain from positioning their forces in the proximity of UNPROFOR's units in the United Nations Protected Areas (UNPAs) and in the pink zones;

871 (1993)

Acting under Chapter VII

6. Calls for an immediate cease-fire agreement between the Croatian Government and local Serb authorities in the UNPAs,

981 (1995)

8. Calls upon the Government of the Republic of Croatia and the local Serb authorities to refrain from the threat or use of force and to reaffirm their commitment to a peaceful resolution of their differences;

994 (1995)

10. Demands that the parties refrain from taking any further military measures or actions that could lead to the escalation of the situation and warns that in the event of failure to comply with this demand it will consider further steps needed to ensure such compliance;

1009 (1995)

Acting under Chapter VII

2. Demands further that the Government of the Republic of Croatia, in conformity with internationally recognized standards and in compliance with the agreement of 6 August 1995 between the Republic of Croatia and the United Nations Peace Forces (a) respect fully the rights of the local Serb population including their rights to remain, leave or return in safety, (b) allow access to this population by international humanitarian organizations, and (c) create conditions conducive to the return of those persons who have left their homes;

Observer or peace-keeping forces

762 (1993)

7. Authorizes the strengthening of the Force by the addition of up to sixty military observers and on hundred and twenty civilian police to perform the functions envisaged in paragraph 16 of the report of the Secretary-General, with the agreement of the Government of Croatia and others concerned;

779 (1992)

Reaffirming its resolution 743 (1992) of 21 February 1992 and all subsequent resolutions relating to the activities of the United Nations Protection Force in Croatia,

Concerned about the difficulties encountered by the United Nations Protection Force in the implementation of resolution 762 (1992) due to cease-fire violations and in particular the creation of paramilitary forces in the United Nations protected areas in violation of the United Nations peace-keeping plan,

2. Authorizes the United Nations Protection Force to assume responsibility for monitoring the arrangements agreed for the complete withdrawal of the Yugoslav Army from Croatia, the demilitarisation of the Prevlaka peninsula and the removal of heavy weapons from neighbouring areas of Croatia and Montenegro, in cooperation, as appropriate, with the European Community Monitoring Mission, looks forward to the report of the Secretary-General on how this is implemented, and calls on all parties and others to cooperate fully with UNPROFOR in its performance of this new task;

4. Urges all parties and others concerned in Croatia to comply with their obligations under the United Nations peace-keeping plan, especially with regard to the withdrawal and disarming of all forces, including paramilitary forces;

981 (1995)

2. Decides to establish under its authority the United Nations Confidence Restoration Operation in Croatia, which shall be known as UNCRO, in accordance with paragraph 84 of the above-mentioned report for a period terminating on 30 November 1995 and requests the Secretary-General to take the measures necessary to ensure its earliest possible deployment;

Authorizations of use of force

871 (1993)

Acting under Chapter VII
9. Authorizes UNPROFOR, in carrying out its mandate in the Republic of Croatia, acting in self-defence, to take the necessary measures, including use of force, to ensure its security and freedom of movement;

958 (1994)

Acting under Chapter VII of the Charter of the United Nations,

Decides that the authorization given in paragraph 10 of its resolution 836 (1993) to Member States, acting nationally or through regional organizations or arrangements, to take, under the authority of the Security Council and subject to close coordination with the Secretary-General and the United Nations Protection Force (UNPROFOR), all necessary measures, through the use of air power, in an around the safe areas in the Republic of Bosnia and Herzegovina referred to in resolution 824 (1993) of 6 May 1993, to support UNPROFOR in the performance of its mandate set out in paragraphs 5 and 9 of resolution 836 (1993) shall apply also to such measures taken in the Republic of Croatia.

Encouragement or authorization of third-party actions

762 (1993)

Commending again the efforts undertaken by the European Community and its member States, with the support of States participating in the Conference on Security and Cooperation in Europe, through the convening of a Conference on Yugoslavia, including the mechanisms set forth within it, to ensure a peaceful political settlement,

981 (1995)

Welcoming also the continuing efforts of representatives of the United Nations, the European Union, the Russian Federation and the United States of America to facilitate a negotiated solution to the conflict in the Republic of Croatia, and reaffirming its call upon the Government of the Republic of Croatia and the local Serb authorities to enter into the negotiations, urgently and without preconditions, for such a settlement, making full use of the plan presented to them by those representatives,

Applicability of humanitarian laws of war

780 (1992) [applying to entire former Yugoslavia]

Recalling paragraph 10 of its resolution 764 (1992) of 13 July 1992, in which it reaffirmed that all parties are bound to comply with the obligations under international humanitarian law and in particular the Geneva Conventions of 12 August 1949,

Recalling also its resolution 771 (1992) of 13 August 1992, in which, inter alia, it demanded that all parties and others concerned in the former Yugoslavia, and all military forces in Bosnia and Herzegovina, immediately cease and desist from all breaches of international humanitarian law,

Expressing once again its grave alarm at continuing reports of widespread violations of international humanitarian law occurring within the territory of the former Yugoslavia and especially in Bosnia and Herzegovina, including reports of mass killings and the continuance of the practice of 'ethnic cleansing,'

2. Requests the Secretary General to establish, as a matter of urgency, an impartial commission of Experts to examine and analyse the information submitted pursuant to resolution 771 (1992) and the present resolution together with its own investigations or efforts, of other persons or bodies pursuant to resolution 771 (1992), with a view to providing the Secretary-General with its conclusions on the evidence of grave breaches of the Geneva Conventions and other violations of international humanitarian law committed to the territory of the former Yugoslavia.

1009 (1995)

4. Reiterates that all those who commit violations of international humanitarian law will be held individually responsible in respect of such acts;

5. Requests the Secretary-General in cooperation with the United Nations High Commissioner for Refugees, the United Nations High Commissioner for Human Rights, the International Committee of the Red Cross and other relevant international humanitarian institutions to assess the humanitarian situation of the local Serb population including the problem of refugees and displaced persons, and to report thereon as soon as possible;

1019 (1995)

Expressing its strong support for the work of the International Tribunal established pursuant to its resolution 827 (1993) of 25 May 1993,

1. Condemns in the strongest possible terms all violations of international humanitarian law and of human rights in the territory of the former Yugoslavia and demands that all concerned comply fully with their obligations in this regard;

Sovereignty and territorial integrity

958 (1994)

Reaffirming its commitment to the sovereignty and territorial integrity of the Republic of Croatia,

981 (1995)

Affirming its commitment to the search for an overall negotiated settlement of the conflicts in the former Yugoslavia ensuring the sovereignty and territorial integrity of all the States there within their internationally recognized borders, and stressing the importance it attaches to the mutual recognition thereof,

994 (1995)

Affirming its commitment to the search for an overall negotiated settlement of the conflicts in the former Yugoslavia ensuring the sovereignty and territorial integrity of all the States there within their internationally recognized borders and stressing the importance it attaches to the mutual recognition thereof, and in this context welcoming all international efforts to facilitate a negotiated solution to the conflict in the Republic of Croatia,

Threats to international peace and security

807 (1993); 815 (1993); 847 (1993); 869 (1993); 870 (1993); 871 (1993); 981 (1995); 990 (1995); 994 (1995); 1009 (1995); 1025 (1995); 1037 (1996); 1079 (1996); 1120 (1997)

743 (1992)

Concerned that the situation in Yugoslavia continues to constitute a threat to international peace and security as determined in resolution 713 (1991),

2. Decides to establish, under its authority, a United Nations Protection Force in accordance with the above-mentioned report and the United Nations peace-keeping plan,

5. Recalls that, in accordance with paragraph 1 of the United Nations peace-keeping plan, the Force should be an interim arrangement to create the conditions of peace and security required for the negotiation of an overall settlement of the Yugoslav Crisis.

807 (1993)

Deeply concerned by the lack of cooperation of the parties and others concerned in implementing the United Nations peace-keeping plan in Croatia,

Deeply concerned also by the recent and repeated violations by the parties and others concerned of their cease-fire obligations,

Determining that the situation thus created constitutes a threat to peace and security in the region,

958 (1994)

Determining that the situation in the former Yugoslavia continues to constitute a threat to international peace and security, and determined to support UNPROFOR in the performance of its mandate set out in paragraphs 5 and 9 of resolution 836 (1993), and to this end, acting under Chapter VII of the Charter of the United Nations,

BOSNIA/HERZEGOVINA

Concern, comments, acknowledgments

752 (1992)

Deeply concerned about the serious situation in certain parts of the former Socialist Federal Republic of Yugoslavia, and in particular about the rapid and violent deterioration of the situation in Bosnia and Herzegoniva.

Recalling also the provisions of Chapter VIII of the Charter, and the continuing role that the European Community is playing in achieving a peaceful solution.

755 (1992)

Admits Bosnia and Herzegovina as a new member of the United Nations

819 (1993)

Concerned by the pattern of hostilities by Bosnian Serb paramilitary units against towns and villages in eastern Bosnia.

Deeply alarmed at the information provided by the Secretary-General to the Security Council on 16 April 1993 on the rapid deterioration of the situation in Srebrenica and its surrounding areas as a result of the continued deliberate armed attacks on and shelling of the innocent civilian population by Bosnian Serb paramilitary units.

820 (1993)

Deeply alarmed and concerned about the magnitude of the plight of innocent victims of the conflict in the Republic of Bosnia and Herzegovina,

836 (1993)

Deeply concerned by the continuing armed hostilities in the territory of the Republic of Bosnia and Herzegovina which run totally counter to the Peace plan,

Alarmed by the resulting plight of the civilian population in the territory of the Republic of Bosnia and Herzegovina,

Condemning the obstruction, primarily by the Bosnian Serb party, of the delivery of humanitarian assistance,

Determined to ensure the protection of the civilian population in safe areas and to promote a lasting political solution,

1004 (1995)

Recalling the Agreement for the demilitarization of Srebrenica of 18 April 1993 (S/25700, Annex) by the Government of the Republic of Bosnia and Herzegovina and the Bosnian Serb party, and regretting that it has not been implemented in full by either party,

Stressing the importance of renewed efforts to achieve an overall peaceful settlement, and the unacceptability of any attempt to resolve the conflict in the Republic of Bosnia and Herzegovina by military means,

Condemnation

757 (1992)

Acting under Chapter VII

Condemns the failure of the authorities of the Federal Republic of Yugoslavia to take effective measures to fulfil the requirements in resolution 752 (1992)

820 (1993)

Reaffirming once again that any taking of territory by force or any practice of 'ethnic cleansing' is unlawful and totally unacceptable, and insisting that all displaced persons be enabled to return in peace to their former homes,

1034 (1995)

Condemning the failure of the Bosnian Serb party to comply with their commitments in respect of giving access to displaced persons and to persons detained or reported missing,

1. Strongly condemns all violations of international humanitarian law and of human rights in the territory of the former Yugoslavia and demands that all concerned comply fully with their obligations in this regard and reiterates that all those who commit violations of international humanitarian law will be held individually responsible in respect of such acts;

2. Condemns in particular in the strongest possible terms the violations of international humanitarian law and of human rights by Bosnian Serb and paramilitary forces in the areas of Srebrenica, Zepa, Banja Luka and Sanski Most as described in the report of the Secretary-General of 27 November 1995 and showing a consistent pattern of summary executions, rape, mass expulsions, arbitrary detentions, forced labour and large-scale disappearances;

6. Affirms that the violations of humanitarian law and human rights in the areas of Srebrenica, Zepa, Banja Luka and Sanski Most from July to October 1995 must be fully and properly investigated by the relevant United Nations and other international organizations and institutions;

Resolutions calling for or demanding particular actions or outcomes

752 (1992)

1. Demands that all parties and others concerned in Bosnia and Herzegovina stop the fighting immediately, respect immediately and fully the cease-fire signed on 12 April 1992 and cooperate with the efforts of the European Community to bring about urgently a negotiated political solution respecting the principle that any change of borders by forces is not acceptable,

6. Calls on all parties and others concerned to ensure that forcible expulsions of persons from the areas where they live and any attempts to change the ethnic composition of the population, anywhere in the former Socialist Federal Republic of Yugoslavia, cease immediately,

764 (1992)

Stressing once again the imperative need to find an urgent negotiated political solution for the situation in Bosnia and Herzegoniva.

8. Calls again on all parties concerned to resolve their differences through a negotiated political solution to the problems of that region

770 (1992)

Acting under Chapter VII:

1. Reaffirms its demand that all parties and others concerned in Bosnia and Herzegovina stop the fighting immediately.

787 (1992)

1. Calls upon the parties in the Republic of Bosnia and Herzegovina to consider the draft outline constitution as a basis for negotiating a political settlement of the conflict in that country.

2. Reaffirms that any taking of territory by force or any practice of 'ethnic cleansing' is unlawful and unacceptable, and will not be permitted to affect the outcome of the negotiations on constitutional arrangements.

819 (1993)

Demands [. . .] the immediate cessation of armed attacks by Bosnian Serb paramilitary units against Srebrenica and their immediate withdrawal from the areas surrounding Srebrenica.

820 (1993)

4. Demands that all parties and others concerned continue to observe the cease-fire and refrain from any further hostilities,

824 (1993)

Acting under Chapter VII:

2. Demands that any taking of territory by force cease immediately

1004 (1995)

Acting under Chapter VII of the Charter of the United Nations,

1. Demands that the Bosnian Serb forces cease their offensive and withdraw from the safe area of Srebrenica immediately;

2. Demands also that the parties respect fully the status of the safe area of Srebrenica in accordance with the Agreement of 18 April 1993;

3. Demands further that the parties respect fully the safety of UNPROFOR personnel and ensure their complete freedom of movement, including resupply;

4. Demands that the Bosnian Serb forces immediately and unconditionally release unharmed all detained UNPROFOR personnel;

1031 (1995)

Acting under Chapter VII of the Charter of the United Nations,

1. Welcomes and supports the Peace Agreement and calls upon the parties to fulfil in good faith the commitments entered into in that Agreement;

30. Affirms the need for the implementation of the Peace Agreement in its entirety and, in this context, stresses the importance it attaches to the urgent implementation of Annex 11 of the Peace Agreement, decides to act expeditiously on the report of the Secretary-General recommending the establishment of a United Nations Civilian Police Force with the tasks set out in that Annex, together with a civilian office with the responsibilities described in the report of the Secretary-General

39. Recognizes the unique, extraordinary and complex character of the present situation in Bosnia and Herzegovina, requiring an exceptional response;

1034 (1995)

6. Affirms that the violations of humanitarian law and human rights in the areas of Srebrenica, Zepa, Banja Luka and Sanski Most from July to October 1995 must be fully and properly investigated by the relevant United Nations and other international organizations and institutions;

7. Takes note that the International Tribunal established pursuant to resolution 827 (1993) of 25 May 1993 issued on 16 November 1995 indictments against the Bosnian Serb leaders Radovan Karadzic and Ratko Mladic for their direct and individual responsibilities for the atrocities committed against the Bosnian Muslim population of Srebrenica in July 1995;

8. Reaffirms its demand that the Bosnian Serb party give immediate and unrestricted access to the areas in question, including for the purpose of the investigation of the atrocities, to representatives of the relevant United Nations and other international organizations and institutions, including the Special Rapporteur of the Commission on Human Rights;

10. Stresses the obligations of all the parties to cooperate with and provide unrestricted access to the relevant United Nations and other international organizations and institutions so as to facilitate their investigations and takes note of their commitment under the Peace Agreement in this regard;

11. Reiterates its demand that all parties, and in particular the Bosnian Serb party, refrain from any action intended to destroy, alter, conceal or damage any evidence of violations of international humanitarian law and that they preserve such evidence;

12. Reiterates further its demand that all States, in particular those in the region of the former Yugoslavia, and all parties to the conflict in the former Yugoslavia, comply fully and in good faith with the obligations contained in paragraph 4 of resolution 827 (1993) to cooperate fully with the International Tribunal and calls on them to create the conditions essential for the Tribunal to perform the task for which it has been created, including the establishment of offices of the Tribunal when the latter deems it necessary;

Sanctions

757 (1992)

[Imposes trade sanctions on the Republic of Yugoslavia, under Chapter VII for its failure to comply with resolution 752].

Observer or peace-keeping forces

819 (1993)

3. Acting under Chapter VII: Declares that the capital city [. . .] and other such threatened areas [. . .] should be treated as safe areas by all the parties concerned and should be free from armed attacks and from any other hostile acts.

7. Declares its readiness, in the event of failure by any part to comply with the present resolution, to consider immediately the adoption of any additional measures necessary with a view to its full implementation.

836 (1993)

5. Decides to extend [. . .] the mandate of UNPROFOR in order to enable it [. . .] to deter attacks against the safe areas, to monitor the cease-fire, to promote the withdrawal of military or paramilitary units other than those of the Government of the Republic of Bosnia and Herzegovina and to occupy some key points on the ground, in addition to participating in the delivery of humanitarian relief to the population,

6. Affirms that these safe areas are a temporary measure and that the primary objective remains to reverse the consequences of the use of force and to allow all persons displaced from their homes [to remain there] in peace.

1031 (1993)

14. Authorizes the Member States acting through or in cooperation with the organization referred to in Annex 1-A of the Peace Agreement [NATO] to establish a multinational implementation force (IFOR) under unified command and control in order to fulfil the role specified in Annex 1-A and Annex 2 of the Peace Agreement;

1088 (1996)

18. Authorizes the Member States acting through or in cooperation with [NATO] to establish for a planned period of 18 months a multinational stabilization force (SFOR) as the legal successor to IFOR under unified command and control in order to fulfil the role specified in Annex 1-A and Annex 2 of the Peace Agreement;

Authorizations of use of force

836 (1993)

9. Authorizes UNPROFOR [. . .] acting in self-defence, to take the necessary measures, including the use of force, in reply to bombardments against the safe areas by any of the parties or to armed incursion into them or in the event of any deliberate obstruction in or around those areas to the freedom of movement of UNPROFOR or of protected humanitarian convoys.

1031 (1998)

15. Authorizes the Member States acting under paragraph 14 above to take all necessary measures to effect the implementation of and to ensure compliance with Annex 1-A of the Peace Agreement, stresses that the parties shall be held equally responsible for compliance with that Annex, and shall be equally subject to such enforcement action by IFOR as may be necessary to ensure implementation of that Annex and the protection of IFOR, and takes note that the parties have consented to IFOR's taking such measures

1088 (1996)

19. Authorizes the Member States acting under paragraph 18 above to take all necessary measures to effect the implementation of and to ensure compliance with Annex 1-A of the Peace Agreement, stresses that the parties shall continue to be held equally responsible for compliance with that Annex and shall be equally subject to such enforcement action by SFOR as may be necessary to ensure implementation of that Annex and the protection of SFOR, and takes note that the parties have consented to SFOR's taking such measures;

20. Authorizes Member States to take all necessary measures, at the request of SFOR, either in defence of SFOR or to assist the force in carrying out its mission, and recognizes the right of the force to take all necessary measures to defend itself from attack or threat of attack;

21. Authorizes the Member States acting under paragraph 18 above, in accordance with Annex 1-A of the Peace Agreement, to take all necessary measures to ensure compliance with the rules and procedures, to be established by the Commander of SFOR, governing command and control of airspace over Bosnia and Herzegovina with respect to all civilian and military air traffic.

Encouragement or authorization of third-party actions

770 (1992)

2. Calls upon States to take nationally or through regional agencies or arrangements all measures necessary to facilitate in coordination with the United Nations the delivery by relevant United Nations humanitarian organizations and others of humanitarian assistance to Sarajevo and wherever needed in other parts of Bosnia and Herzegovina.

1031 (1995)

6. Welcomes the agreement by the Organization for Security and Cooperation in Europe (OSCE) to adopt and put in place a programme of elections for Bosnia and Herzegovina, at the request of the parties to Annex 3 of the Peace Agreement;

Applicability of humanitarian laws of war

764 (1992)

Reaffirms that all parties are bound to comply with the obligations under international humanitarian law and in particular the Geneva Conventions of 12 August 1949.

819 (1993)

Reaffirming its condemnation of all violations of international humanitarian law.

820 (1993)

6. Condemns once again all violations of international humanitarian law, including in particular the practice of 'ethnic cleansing,' and the massive, organized and systematic detention and rape of women, and reaffirms that those who commit or have committed or have ordered the commission of such acts will be held individually responsible in respect of such acts;

Sovereignty and territorial integrity

787 (1992)

Deeply concerned at the threats to the territorial integrity of the Republic of Bosnia and Herzegovina, which, as a State Member of the United Nations, enjoys the rights provided for in the Charter of the United Nations,

3. Strongly reaffirms its call on all parties and others concerned to respect strictly the territorial integrity of the republic of Bosnia and Herzegovina

819 (1993)

Reaffirming the sovereignty, territorial integrity and political independence of the republic of Bosnia and Herzegovina

Threats to international peace and security

770 (1992); 816 (1993); 819 (1993); 820 (1993); 824 (1993); 836 (1993); 844 (1993); 859 (1993); 900 (1994); 913 (1994); 941 (1994); 942 (1994); 943 (1994); 958 (1994); 970 (1995); 982 (1995); 987 (1995); 988 (1995); 998 (1995); 1003 (1995); 1004 (1995); 1015 (1995); 1021 (1995); 1022 (1995); 1026 (1995); 1031 (1995); 1088 (1996); 1174 (1998); 1247 (1999)

770 (1992)

Recognizing that the situation in Bosnia and Herzegovina constitutes a threat to international peace and security

BURUNDI

Concern, comments, acknowledgments

1012 (1995)

Expressing once again its grave concern at reports indicating that systematic, widespread and flagrant violations of international humanitarian law have been committed in Burundi,

Reiterating its profound concern over the resumption of radio broadcasts inciting ethnic hatred and violence and recognizing the need for ending such broadcasts,

1. Requests the Secretary-General to establish, as a matter of urgency, an international commission of inquiry, with the following mandate:

(a) To establish the facts relating to the assassination of the President of Burundi on 21 October 1993, the massacres and other related serious acts of violence which followed;

(b) To recommend measures of a legal, political or administrative nature, as appropriate, after consultation with the Government of Burundi, and measures with regard to the bringing to justice of persons responsible for those acts, to prevent any repetition of deeds similar to those investigated by the commission and, in general, to eradicate impunity and promote national reconciliation in Burundi;

1040 (1996)

Deeply concerned at the continued deterioration in the situation in Burundi, and at the threat this poses to the stability of the region as a whole,

Stressing the importance it attaches to the continuation and intensification of efforts by the international community to avert a further worsening of the situation in Burundi, and to promote dialogue and national reconciliation there,

1049 (1996)

Deeply concerned also at all acts of violence in Burundi and at the continued incitement to ethnic hatred and violence by radio stations and the growth of calls for exclusion and genocide,

Deeply disturbed that the persistence of the conflict has had a negative impact on the humanitarian situation and on the capacity of the international community to continue to assist the people of Burundi,

1072 (1996)

Recalling the statement by its President of 24 July 1996 (S/PRST/1996/31) in which the Council strongly condemned any attempt to overthrow the legitimate Government of Burundi by force or coup d'état, and recalling also the statement by its President of 29 July 1996 (S/PRST/1996/32) in which the Council condemned the actions that led to the overthrow of constitutional order in Burundi,

Deeply concerned at the continued deterioration in the security and humanitarian situation in Burundi that has been characterized in the last years by killings, massacres, torture and arbitrary detention, and at the threat that this poses to the peace and security of the Great Lakes Region as a whole

Condemnation

1040 (1996)

Condemning in the strongest terms those responsible for the increasing violence, including against refugees and international humanitarian personnel

1049 (1996)

2. Condemns in the strongest terms all acts of violence perpetrated against civilians, refugees and international humanitarian personnel and the assassination of government officials;

1072 (1996)

1. Condemns the overthrow of the legitimate government and constitutional order in Burundi and condemns also all those parties and factions which resort to force and violence to advance their political objectives;

1286 (2000)

Expressing deep concern at the ongoing violence and insecurity in Burundi marked by increased attacks by armed groups on the civilian population in and around the capital,

2. Reiterates its strong support for the renewed Arusha peace process, endorses the call at the Eighth Arusha Regional Summit for all parties to the conflict in Burundi to extend maximum cooperation to the new peace process Facilitator, and calls for increased efforts to build an internal political partnership in Burundi;

6. Condemns continuing violence perpetrated by all parties, and in particular by those non-State actors who refuse to participate in the Arusha peace process, and strongly urges all parties to end the ongoing armed conflict and to resolve their differences peacefully;

Resolutions calling for or demanding particular actions or outcomes

1040 (1996)

1. Demands that all concerned in Burundi exercise restraint and refrain from acts of violence;

1049 (1996)

3. Demands that all concerned in Burundi refrain from all acts of violence, incitement to violence and from seeking to destabilize the security situation or depose the Government by force or by other unconstitutional means;

4. Calls upon all concerned in Burundi to engage, as a matter of urgency, in serious negotiations and mutual accommodation within the framework of the National Debate agreed upon by the signatories to the Convention and to increase efforts towards national reconciliation;

1072 (1996)

3. Calls upon the regime to ensure a return to constitutional order and legality, to restore the National Assembly and to lift the ban on all political parties;

4. Demands that all sides in Burundi declare a unilateral cessation of hostilities, call an immediate halt to violence and assume their individual and collective responsibilities to bring peace, security and tranquillity to the people of Burundi;

Encouragement or authorization of third-party actions

1049 (1996)

8. Expresses strong support for the efforts of the Secretary-General of the United Nations and his Special Representative, the Organization of African Unity, the European Union, former Presidents Nyerere and Carter and the other facilitators appointed by the Cairo Conference, and others seeking to facilitate political dialogue in Burundi and encourages the international community to extend political and financial support to the National Debate;

10. Encourages the Organization of African Unity to increase the size of its Observer Mission in Burundi, as formally requested by the Government of Burundi, and stresses the need for the military observers to operate without any restrictions on their movement to any part of the country;

1072 (1996)

Determined to support the efforts and initiatives of the countries in the region, which were also supported by the Central Organ of the Organization of African Unity (OAU) Mechanism for Conflict Prevention, Management and Resolution aimed at returning Burundi to a democratic path and contributing to stability in the region,

2. Expresses its strong support for the efforts of regional leaders, including at their meeting in Arusha on 31 July 1996, of the OAU and of former President Nyerere, to assist Burundi to overcome peacefully the grave crisis which it is undergoing, and encourages them to continue to facilitate the search for a political solution

CAMBODIA

Concern, comments, acknowledgments

668 (1991)

Convinced of the need to find an early, just and lasting peaceful solution to the Cambodia conflict.

745 (1992)

Convinced that free and fair elections are essential to producing a just and durable settlement to the Cambodia conflict, thereby contributing to regional and international peace and security

810 (1993)

Concerned by the increasing number of acts of violence perpetrated on political grounds

Condemnation

766 (1992)

Deplores the continuing violations of the cease-fire and urges all parties to cease all hostilities forthwith, to cooperate fully with the Authority

Resolutions calling for or demanding particular actions or outcomes

810 (1993)

Demands that all Cambodian parties take the necessary measures to put an end to all acts of violence and to all threats and intimidation committed on political or ethnic grounds [. . .]

880 (1993)

5. Demands the cessation of all illegal acts of violence, on whatever grounds, and the cessation of military activities directed against the democratically elected government of Cambodia, as well as against the personnel of UNTAC and other United Nations and international agencies

Observer or peace-keeping forces

717 (1992)

Decides to establish, under its authority, a United Nations Advance Mission in Cambodia immediately after the signing of agreements for a comprehensive political settlement of the Cambodia conflict.

745 (1992)

[Establishes the UNTA]

Encouragement or authorization of third-party actions

668 (1990)

Taking note with appreciation of the continuing efforts of China, France, the Union of Soviet Socialist Republics, the United Kingdom and the United States of America, which have resulted in the framework for a comprehensive political settlement of the Cambodia conflict.

Applicability of humanitarian laws of war

880 (1993)

6. Affirms the importance, particularly in view of the recent tragic history of Cambodia, of ensuring respect for international humanitarian law in that country

Sovereignty and territorial integrity

880 (1993)

4. Calls upon all States to respect the sovereignty, independence, territorial integrity and inviolability, neutrality and national unity of Cambodia

CENTRAL AFRICAN REPUBLIC

Concern, comments, acknowledgments

1125 (1997)

Concerned by the grave crisis facing the Central African Republic.

Concerned by the fact that, in the Central African Republic, former mutineers, members of militias and other persons continue to bear arms in contravention of the Bangui Agreements,

1271 (1999)

Recalling the importance of the process of national reconciliation, and urging all the political forces of the Central African Republic to continue their efforts towards cooperation and understanding,

Presidential Statement—S/PRST/1999/7

[. . .] takes note with satisfaction of the commitment expressed by the President of the Central African Republic to maintain peace in the Central African Republic through dialogue and consultation. In this context, it strongly reaffirms that the complete implementation of the Bangui Agreements (S/1997/561, appendices III–VI) and of the National Reconciliation Pact (S/1998/219) is essential to peace and national reconciliation in the Central African Republic.

Condemnation

Presidential Statement—S/PRST/2001/18 (2001)

The Security Council reiterates its condemnation of the recent attempted coup in the Central African Republic. It recognizes the importance of the Central African Republic to subregional stability.

It expresses its deep concern at the precarious situation in the country and the persisting acts of violence, in particular against certain ethnic groups.

The Council notes that such a climate is not conducive to encouraging the continuation of the return home of the thousands of Central Africans that were displaced or took refuge in neighbouring countries as a result of the events at the end of May.

Resolutions calling for or demanding particular actions or outcomes

1152 (1998)

Calls upon the parties in the Central African Republic to complete the implementation without delay of the provisions of the Bangui Agreements and also calls for the fulfilment of the commitments expressed in the letter of 8 January 1998 to the Secretary-General from the President of the Central African Republic (S/1998/61, Annex);

Presidential Statement—S/PRST/2001/18 (2001)

It calls upon the Government of the Central African Republic to take urgent steps to bring an end to all acts of violence.

Presidential Statement—S/PRST/1999/7

The Security Council calls upon the Government of the Central African Republic to continue to take concrete steps to implement political, economic, social and security reforms as referred to in the report of the Secretary-General of 23 February 1998 (S/1998/148) and to fulfil the commitments expressed in the letters of 8 January 1998 (S/1998/61, Annex) and of 23 January 1999 (S/1999/98, Annex) to the Secretary-General by the President of the Central African Republic. It recalls that the success, the future mandate and the ongoing presence of the United Nations Mission in the Central African Republic are closely linked to the fulfilment of these commitments, in particular the immediate resumption of a constructive political dialogue.

Observer or peace-keeping forces

1159 (1998)

Stressing the importance of regional stability and the need to consolidate the progress achieved by MISAB, and in particular to assist the people of the Central African Republic to consolidate the process of national reconciliation and help to sustain a secure and stable environment conducive to the holding of free and fair elections.

Stressing also the need for all signatories to the Bangui Agreements to continue to implement these Agreements, and for the authorities of the Central African Republic to take concrete steps to implement political, economic, social and security reforms as referred to in the report of the Secretary-General of 23 February 1998 including the establishment of an electoral code and preparations for legislative elections scheduled for August/September 1998,

Acting under Chapter VII

9. Decides to establish a United Nations Mission in the Central African Republic (MINURCA) with effect from 15 April 1998, and decides also that the military component of MINURCA will not exceed 1,350 personnel;

10. Decides that, taking into account the recommendations of the Secretary-General in his report of 23 February 1998, MINURCA shall have the following initial mandate:

(a) To assist in maintaining and enhancing security and stability, including freedom of movement, in Bangui and the immediate vicinity of the city;

(b) To assist the national security forces in maintaining law and order and in protecting key installations in Bangui;

(c) To supervise, control storage, and monitor the final disposition of all weapons retrieved in the course of the disarmament exercise;

Encouragement or authorization of third-party actions

1125 (1997)

Approves the continued conduct by Member States participating in MISAB of the operation in a neutral and impartial way to achieve its objective to facilitate the return to peace and security by monitoring the implementation of the Bangui Agreements in the Central African Republic as stipulated in the mandate of MISAB (S/1997/561, Appendix I), including through the supervision of the surrendering of arms of former mutineers, militias and all other persons unlawfully bearing arms;

Taking note with appreciation of the signing of the Bangui Agreements (S/1997/561, Appendixes III-VI) of 25 January 1997 and the creation of the Inter-African Mission to Monitor the Implementation of the Bangui Agreements (MISAB),

Determining that the situation in the Central African Republic continues to constitute a threat to international peace and security in the region,

1. Welcomes the efforts of the Member States which participate in MISAB and of those Member States which support them;

3. Acting under Chapter VII of the Charter of the United Nations, authorizes the Member States participating in MISAB and those States providing logistical support to ensure the security and freedom of movement of their personnel;

1159 (1998)

Reiterating its appreciation for the neutral and impartial way in which the Inter-African Mission to Monitor the Implementation of the Bangui Agreements (MISAB) has carried out its mandate, in close cooperation with the Central African authorities and noting with satisfaction that MISAB has contributed significantly to stabilizing the situation in the Central African Republic, in particular through the supervision of the surrendering of arms.

6. Acting under Chapter VII of the Charter of the United Nations, authorizes the Member States participating in MISAB and those States providing logistical support to ensure security and freedom of movement of their personnel

Sovereignty and territorial integrity

1271 (1999)

Affirming the commitment of all States to respect the sovereignty, political independence and territorial integrity of the Central African Republic,

Threats to international peace and security

1125 (1997); 1136 (1997); 1152 (1998); 1155 (1998); 1159 (1998)

1125 (1997)

Determining that the situation in the Central African Republic continues to constitute a threat to international peace and security in the region

CHAD

Observer or peace-keeping forces

915 (1994)

Establishes the United Nations Aouzou Strip Observer Group (UNASOG) in relation to the settlement of the dispute between Chad and Libya.

Encouragement or authorization of third party actions

504 (1982)

Bearing in mind the relevant resolutions of the General Assembly on co-operation between the United Nations and the Organization of African Unity

Takes note of the decision of the Organization of African Unity to establish, in agreement with the Government of the Republic of Chad, a peace-keeping force for the maintenance of peace and security in Chad.

CHECHNYA

No relevant Security Council resolutions.

THE REPUBLIC OF CONGO (BRAZZAVILLE)

Concern, comments, acknowledgments

161 (1961)

Having learned with deep regret of the announcement of the killing of the Congolese leaders,

Deeply concerned at the grave repercussions of these crimes and the danger of widespread civil war and bloodshed in Congo and the threat to international peace and security,

Gravely concerned at the continuing deterioration of the situation in the Congo and the prevalence of conditions which seriously imperil peace and order and territorial integrity of the Congo and threaten international peace and security,

Noting with deep regret and concern the systematic violations of human rights and fundamental freedoms and the general absence of the rule of law in the Congo;

Recognizing the imperative necessity for the restoration of parliamentary institutions in the Congo in accordance with the fundamental law of the country, so that the will of the people should be reflected through the freely elected Parliament,

Convinced that the solution of the problem of the Congo lies in the hands of the Congolese people themselves without any interference from outside, and that there can be no solution without conciliation,

169 (1961)

Recognizing the Government of the Republic of the Congo as exclusively responsible for the conduct of the external affairs of the Congo,

1. Strongly deprecates the secessionist activities illegally carried out by the provincial administration of Katanga with the aid of external resources and manned by foreign mercenaries;

2. Insists that all such activities shall cease forthwith and calls upon all concerned to desist therefrom,

Resolutions calling for or demanding particular actions or outcomes

161 (1961)

1. Urges that the United Nations take immediately all appropriate measures to prevent the occurrence of civil war in the Congo, including arrangements for

cease-fires, the halting of all military operations, the prevention of clashes and the use of force if necessary in the last resort;

B. 1. Urges the convening of the Parliament and the taking of necessary protective measures in that connexion;

2. Urges that Congolese armed units and personnel should be reorganized and brought under discipline and control, and arrangements made on and equitable bases to that end and with a view to the elimination of any possible interference by such units and personnel in the political life of the Congo;

169 (1961)

9. Declares that all secessionist activities against the Republic of Congo are contrary to the Loi Fondamentale and Security Council decisions and specifically demands that such activities which are now taking place in Katanga shall cease forthwith;

S/PRST/1997/43 (1997)

Statement by President of the Council

The Security Council expresses its grave concern at the recent recurrence of fighting in Brazzaville, calls upon the two parties to the conflict to halt all acts of violence immediately and underlines the need to respect the ceasefire agreement signed on 14 July 1997. It also calls upon the two parties to resolve the crisis on the basis of the proposals submitted by the President of Gabon currently under discussion in Libreville, including agreement on an interim government of national unity and a timetable for the holding of Presidential elections.

S/PRST/1997/47 (1997)

The Security Council is deeply concerned about the grave situation in the Republic of the Congo and calls for an immediate end to all hostilities. It deplores the loss of life and the deteriorating humanitarian situation and calls upon all parties to ensure the safety of the civilian population and the safe and unrestricted delivery of humanitarian assistance.

The Security Council calls upon all States in the region to support a peaceful resolution of the conflict and to avoid any actions which could exacerbate the situation. It condemns all external interference in the Republic of the Congo, including the intervention of foreign forces, in violation of the Charter of the United Nations, and calls for the immediate withdrawal of all foreign forces including mercenaries.

The Security Council reiterates the importance of a political settlement and national reconciliation and calls upon the parties to cooperate with the International Mediation Committee chaired by the President of Gabon and with the Joint United Nations/Organization of African Unity Special Envoy in reaching rapid agreement on peaceful transitional arrangements leading to the holding of democratic and free and fair elections with the participation of all parties.

Observer or peace-keeping forces

143 (1960)

2. Decides to authorize the Secretary-General to take the necessary steps, in consultation with the Government of the Republic of the Congo, to provide the Government with such military assistance as might be necessary until, through the efforts of the Congolese Government efforts with technical assistance of the United Nations, the national security forces may be able, in the opinion of the Government, to meet fully their tasks.

146 (1960)

2. Calls upon the Government of Belgium to withdraw immediately its troops from the province of Katanga.

4. Reaffirms that the United Nations Force in the Congo will not be a party to or in any way intervene in or be used to influence the outcome of any internal conflict, constitutional or otherwise;

169 (1961)

Reaffirming the policies and purposes of the United Nations with respect to Congo

(b) To assist the Central Government of Congo in the restoration and maintenance of law and order,

(c) To prevent the occurrence of civil war in the Congo

(d) To secure the immediate withdrawal and evacuation from the Congo of all foreign military, paramilitary and advisory personnel not under the United Nations Command, and all mercenaries,

S/PRST/1997/43 (1997)

Statement by President of the Council

The Security Council recalls the letter of 20 June 1997 to its President from the Secretary-General (S/1997/483) drawing attention to the request of the President of Gabon for deployment of an appropriate force to Brazzaville, and the relevant letters to the Secretary-General from the President of the Republic of the Congo and the Secretary-General of the OAU (S/1997/495, annexes I and II). The Council endorses the three conditions for the establishment of such a force set by the Secretary-General, namely complete adherence to an agreed and viable ceasefire, agreement to the international control of Brazzaville airport and a clear commitment to a negotiated settlement covering all political and military aspects of the crisis

Authorizations of use of force

169 (1961)

4. Authorizes the Secretary-General to take vigorous action, including the use of the requisite measure of force, if necessary, for the immediate apprehension,

detention pending legal action and/or deportation of all foreign military and paramilitary personnel and political advisers not under the United Nations Command, and mercenaries;

5. Further requests the Secretary-General to take all necessary measures to prevent the entry or return of such elements under whatever guise, and also of arms, equipment or other material in support of such activities;

Sovereignty and territorial integrity

169 (1961)

Reaffirming the policies and purposes of the United Nations with respect to Congo

(a) To maintain territorial integrity and the political independence of the Republic of Congo

Threats to international peace and security

S/PRST/1997/43 (1997)

Statement by President

The Security Council is deeply concerned about the situation in the Republic of the Congo following the outbreak of factional fighting in Brazzaville on 5 June 1997.

The Council is particularly concerned at the plight of civilians caught up in the fighting, which has resulted in widespread loss of life, displacement of the population and severe humanitarian conditions in Brazzaville. The Council considers that the situation in the Republic of the Congo is likely to endanger peace, stability and security in the region

DEMOCRATIC REPUBLIC OF CONGO

Concern, comments, acknowledgments

1078 (1996)

Gravely concerned at the deteriorating situation in the Great Lakes region, in particular eastern Zaire, and at the effect of the continued fighting on the inhabitants of the region,

Particularly concerned at the humanitarian situation and the large-scale movements of refugees and internally displaced persons,

Deeply concerned at the obstacles to the efforts of all international humanitarian agencies to provide relief and assistance to those in need,

Stressing the need to address, as a matter of urgency, the humanitarian situation, and in this context, underlining the necessity to adopt, in consultation with the States concerned, measures necessary in order to enable the return in the region of humanitarian agencies and to secure the prompt and safe delivery of humanitarian assistance to those in need,

Taking note of the request addressed to the Council by the regional leaders at their meeting in Nairobi on 5 November 1996, to take urgent measures to ensure the establishment of safe corridors and temporary sanctuaries by deploying a neutral force,

Underlining the urgent need for an international conference on peace, security and development in the Great Lakes region under the auspices of the United Nations and the OAU to address the problems of the region in a comprehensive way,

1080 (1996)

Gravely concerned at the continuing deteriorating situation in the Great Lakes region, in particular eastern Zaire,

Taking note of the communiqué issued by the Fourth Extraordinary Session of the Central Organ of the Organization of African Unity Mechanism for Conflict Prevention, Management and Resolution held at the level of Ministers in Addis Ababa on 11 November 1996 (S/1996/922) as well as a communication dated 13 November 1996 from the Permanent Observer Mission of the Organization of African Unity (OAU) to the United Nations,

Recognizing that the current situation in eastern Zaire demands an urgent response by the international community,

Reiterating the urgent need for an international conference on peace, security and development in the Great Lakes region under the auspices of the United Nations and the OAU to address the problems of the region in a comprehensive way,

1097 (1997)

Gravely concerned at the deteriorating situation in the Great Lakes region, in particular eastern Zaire, and expressing serious concern over the safety of refugees and displaced persons whose lives are in danger,

Underlining the obligation of all concerned to respect strictly the relevant provisions of international humanitarian law,

1. Endorses the following five-point peace plan for eastern Zaire, as set out in the letter from the Secretary-General of 18 February 1997:

- Immediate cessation of hostilities;
- Withdrawal of all external forces, including mercenaries;
- Reaffirmation of respect for the national sovereignty and the territorial integrity of Zaire and other States of the Great Lakes region;
- Protection and security for all refugees and displaced persons and facilitation of access to humanitarian assistance;
- Rapid and peaceful settlement of the crisis through dialogue, the electoral process and the convening of an international conference on peace, security and development in the Great Lakes region;

S/PRST/1997/11 (1997)

The Security Council welcomes the declaration of the Government of Zaire of 5 March 1997 (S/1997/197, Annex) regarding its acceptance of the United Nations peace plan endorsed by the Security Council in its resolution 1097 (1997).

S/PRST/1997/19 (1997)

The Security Council reiterates its deep concern about the alarming situation of refugees and displaced persons in eastern Zaire.

S/PRST/1997/31 (1997)

The Security Council expresses its support for the people of the Democratic Republic of the Congo as they begin a new period in their history. The Council respects the legitimate national aspirations of the people of the Democratic Republic of the Congo to achieve peace, national reconciliation and progress in the political, economic and social fields to the benefit of all, and opposes any interference in its internal affairs.

The Security Council welcomes the end of the fighting and expresses its satisfaction that stability has begun to return to the country.

The Security Council, in accordance with the United Nations five point peace plan, calls for the rapid and peaceful settlement of the crisis through dialogue and the convening of an international conference on peace, security and development in the Great Lakes region. The Council also reaffirms the statement of its President of 30 April 1997 (S/PRST/1997/24) calling for rapid agreement on peaceful transitional arrangements leading to the holding of democratic and free elections with the participation of all parties.

The Security Council believes that the convening of an international conference on peace, security and development in the Great Lakes region under the auspices of the United Nations and the Organization of African Unity will be essential in promoting regional peace and stability.

The Security Council, in accordance with the United Nations fivepoint peace plan, calls for protection and security for all refugees and displaced persons and facilitation of access to humanitarian assistance.

It reiterates its call for full respect for the rights of refugees and displaced persons, and for access and safety for humanitarian relief workers. It also reiterates in the strongest terms its call for complete cooperation with the United Nations mission investigating reports of massacres, other atrocities and violations of international humanitarian law in the country, including to provide it full and immediate access and to ensure its security. It is particularly concerned by reports that refugees in the east of the country are being systematically killed. It calls for an immediate end to the violence against refugees in the country.

1234 (1999)

Expressing its concern at the further deterioration of the situation in the Democratic Republic of the Congo and the continuation of hostilities,

Expressing its concern at all violations of human rights and international humanitarian law in the territory of the Democratic Republic of the Congo, including acts of and incitement to ethnic hatred and violence by all parties to the conflict

1258 (1999)

1. Welcomes the signing of the Ceasefire Agreement on the conflict in the Democratic Republic of the Congo by the States concerned in Lusaka on 10 July 1999 (S/1999/815) which represents a viable basis for a resolution of the conflict in the Democratic Republic of the Congo;

2. Also welcomes the signing of the Ceasefire Agreement on 1 August 1999 by the Movement for the Liberation of the Congo, expresses deep concern that the Congolese Rally for Democracy has not signed the Agreement and calls upon the latter to sign the Agreement without delay in order to bring about national reconciliation and lasting peace in the Democratic Republic of the Congo;

1279 (1999)

Reaffirming also that the Lusaka Ceasefire Agreement (S/1999/815) represents the most viable basis for a resolution of the conflict in the Democratic Republic of the Congo, and noting the role it requests the United Nations to play in the implementation of the ceasefire,

Expressing its concern at the alleged violations of the Ceasefire Agreement and urging all parties to refrain from any declarations or action that could jeopardize the peace process,

Expressing its concern at the severe consequences of the conflict for the security and well-being of the civilian population throughout the territory of the Democratic Republic of the Congo,

Expressing also its concern at the adverse impact of the conflict on the human rights situation in the Democratic Republic of the Congo, particularly in the eastern parts of the country, and the continuing violations of human rights and international humanitarian law committed throughout the territory of the Democratic Republic of the Congo,

1484 (2003)

Determined to promote the peace process at the national level, and in particular to facilitate the early establishment of an inclusive transitional government in the Democratic Republic of the Congo,

Expressing its utmost concern at the fighting and atrocities in Ituri, as well as the gravity of the humanitarian situation in the town of Bunia,

Taking note of the request of the Secretary-General to the Council in his letter dated 15 May 2003 (S/2003/574) and taking note also of the support for this request expressed in the letter to the Secretary-General from the President of the Democratic Republic of the Congo and also by the Ituri parties on 16 May 2003 in Dar es Salaam, as well as the support expressed in the letters to the Secretary-General from the President of Rwanda and from the Minister of State for Foreign Affairs of Uganda, as requested by the Secretary-General, for the deployment of a multinational force in Bunia,

Condemnation

1078 (1996)

Determining that the magnitude of the present humanitarian crisis in eastern Zaire constitutes a threat to peace and security in the region,

1. Condemns all acts of violence, and calls for an immediate ceasefire and a complete cessation of all hostilities in the region;

S/PRST/1997/11 (1997)

The Security Council calls upon the Alliance of Democratic Forces for the Liberation of Congo/Zaire to declare publicly their acceptance of resolution 1097 (1997) in all its provisions, in particular an immediate cessation of hostilities, and calls on all parties to implement its provisions without delay.

1234 (1999)

7. Condemns all massacres carried out on the territory of the Democratic Republic of the Congo and calls for an international investigation into all such events,

8. Condemns the continuing activity of and support to all armed groups, including the ex-Rwandese Armed Forces, Interahamwe, and others in the Democratic Republic of the Congo;

1279 (1999)

1. Calls upon all parties to the conflict to cease hostilities, to implement fully the provisions of the Ceasefire Agreement, and to use the JMC to resolve disputes over military issues;

2. Stresses the need for a continuing process of genuine national reconciliation, encourages all Congolese to participate in the national dialogue to be organized in coordination with the Organization of African Unity (OAU), and calls upon all Congolese parties and the OAU to finalize agreement on the facilitator for the national dialogue;

1304 (2000)

2. Reiterates its unreserved condemnation of the fighting between Ugandan and Rwandan forces in Kisangani in violation of the sovereignty and territorial integrity of the Democratic Republic of the Congo, and demands that these forces and those allied to them desist from further fighting;

1399 (2002)

1. Condemns the resumption of fighting in the Moliro pocket, and the capture of Moliro by RCD-Goma, and stresses that this is a major violation of the ceasefire;

Resolutions calling for or demanding particular actions or outcomes

1078 (1996)

2. Calls upon all States in the region to create the conditions necessary for the speedy and peaceful resolution of the crisis and to desist from any act that may further exacerbate the situation, and urges all parties to engage in a process of political dialogue and negotiation without delay;

1080 (1996)

Determining that the present situation in eastern Zaire constitutes a threat to international peace and security in the region,

Bearing in mind the humanitarian purposes of the multinational force as specified below,

Acting under Chapter VII of the Charter of the United Nations,

1. Reiterates its condemnation of all acts of violence, and its call for an immediate ceasefire and a complete cessation of all hostilities in the region;

1234 (1999)

2. Deplores the continuing fighting and the presence of forces of foreign States in the Democratic Republic of the Congo in a manner inconsistent with the principles of the Charter of the United Nations, and calls upon those States to bring to an end the presence of these uninvited forces and to take immediate steps to that end;

3. Demands an immediate halt to the hostilities;

15. Reaffirms its readiness to consider the active involvement of the United Nations, in coordination with the Organization of African Unity, including through concrete sustainable and effective measures, to assist in the implementation of an effective ceasefire agreement and in an agreed process for political settlement of the conflict;

1258 (1999)

4. Calls upon all parties to the conflict, in particular the rebel movements, to cease hostilities, to implement fully and without delay the provisions of the Ceasefire Agreement, to cooperate fully with the OAU and the United Nations in the implementation of the Agreement and to desist from any act that may further exacerbate the situation;

1279 (1999)

1. Calls upon all parties to the conflict to cease hostilities, to implement fully the provisions of the Ceasefire Agreement, and to use the JMC to resolve disputes over military issues;

2. Stresses the need for a continuing process of genuine national reconciliation, encourages all Congolese to participate in the national dialogue to be organized in coordination with the Organization of African Unity (OAU), and calls upon all Congolese parties and the OAU to finalize agreement on the facilitator for the national dialogue;

1304 (2000)

Acting under Chapter VII of the Charter of the United Nations,

1. Calls on all parties to cease hostilities throughout the territory of the Democratic Republic of the Congo and to fulfil their obligations under the Ceasefire Agreement and the relevant provisions of the 8 April 2000 Kampala disengagement plan;

3. Demands that Ugandan and Rwandan forces as well as forces of the Congolese armed opposition and other armed groups immediately and completely withdraw from Kisangani, and calls on all parties to the Ceasefire Agreement to respect the demilitarization of the city and its environs;

1484 (2003)

Acting under Chapter VII

5. Demands that all the parties to the conflict in Ituri and in particular in Bunia cease hostilities immediately and reiterates that international humanitarian law must be respected, and that there will be no impunity for violators;

Observer or peace-keeping forces

1080 (1996)

Acting under Chapter VII

3. Welcomes the offers made by Member States, in consultation with the States concerned in the region, concerning the establishment for humanitarian purposes of a temporary multinational force to facilitate the immediate return of humanitarian organizations and the effective delivery by civilian relief organizations of humanitarian aid to alleviate the immediate suffering of displaced persons, refugees and civilians at risk in eastern Zaire, and to facilitate the voluntary, orderly repatriation of refugees by the United Nations High Commissioner for Refugees as well as the voluntary return of displaced persons, and invites other interested States to offer to participate in these efforts;

4. Welcomes further the offer by a Member State (S/1996/941, Annex) to take the lead in organizing and commanding this temporary multinational force;

5. Authorizes the Member States cooperating with the Secretary-General to conduct the operation referred to in paragraph 3 above to achieve, by using all necessary means, the humanitarian objectives set out therein;

1258 (1999)

8. Authorizes the deployment of up to 90 United Nations military liaison personnel, together with the necessary civilian, political, humanitarian and administrative staff

1279 (1999)

5. Decides also that MONUC, led by the Special Representative of the Secretary-General, consistent with resolutions 1258 (1999) and 1273 (1999), shall carry out the following ongoing tasks:

(a) To establish contacts with the signatories to the Ceasefire Agreement at their headquarters levels, as well as in the capitals of the States signatories;

(b) To liaise with the JMC and provide technical assistance in the implementation of its functions under the Ceasefire Agreement, including in the investigation of ceasefire violations;

(c) To provide information on security conditions in all areas of its operation, with emphasis on local conditions affecting future decisions on the introduction of United Nations personnel;

(d) To plan for the observation of the ceasefire and disengagement of forces;

(e) To maintain liaison with all parties to the Ceasefire Agreement to facilitate the delivery of humanitarian assistance to displaced persons, refugees, children, and other affected persons, and assist in the protection of human rights, including the rights of children;

1291 (2000)

4. Authorizes the expansion of MONUC to consist of up to 5,537 military personnel, including up to 500 observers, or more, provided that the Secretary-General determines that there is a need and that it can be accommodated within the overall force size and structure, and appropriate civilian support staff in the areas, inter alia, of human rights, humanitarian affairs, public information, child protection, political affairs, medical support and administrative support, and requests the Secretary-General to recommend immediately any additional force requirements that might become necessary to enhance force protection;

8. Acting under Chapter VII of the Charter of the United Nations, decides that MONUC may take the necessary action, in the areas of deployment of its infantry battalions and as it deems it within its capabilities, to protect United Nations and co-located JMC personnel, facilities, installations and equipment, ensure the security and freedom of movement of its personnel, and protect civilians under imminent threat of physical violence;

Authorizations of use of force

1484 (2003)

4. Authorizes the Member States participating in the Interim Emergency Multinational Force in Bunia to take all necessary measures to fulfil its mandate;

Encouragement or authorization of third-party actions

S/PRST/1997/11

The Security Council reiterates, in that respect, its full support for the five-point peace plan for eastern Zaire contained in its resolution 1097 (1997) of 18 February 1997 and welcomes the endorsement of that plan by the Organization of African Unity (OAU) at its 65th ordinary session of the Council of Ministers held in Tripoli from 24 to 28 February 1997.

1234 (1999)

11. Expresses its support for the regional mediation process by the OAU and Southern African Development Community to find a peaceful settlement to the conflict in the Democratic Republic of the Congo and calls upon the international community to continue to support these efforts;

14. Reaffirms the importance of holding, at the appropriate time, an international conference on peace, security and stability in the Great Lakes region under the auspices of the United Nations and the Organization of African Unity, with the participation of all the Governments of the region and all others concerned;

15. Reaffirms its readiness to consider the active involvement of the United Nations, in coordination with the Organization of African Unity, including through concrete sustainable and effective measures, to assist in the implementation of an effective ceasefire agreement and in an agreed process for political settlement of the conflict;

1258 (1999)

3. Commends the Organization of African Unity (OAU) and the Southern African Development Community for their efforts to find a peaceful settlement to the conflict in the Democratic Republic of the Congo and in particular the President of the Republic of Zambia, and also the Secretary-General, the Special Envoy of the Secretary-General for the peace process in the Democratic Republic of the Congo, the Representative of the Secretary-General to the Great Lakes Region and all those who contributed to the peace process

1484 (2003)

1. Authorizes the deployment until 1 September 2003 of an Interim Emergency Multinational Force in Bunia in close coordination with MONUC, in particular its contingent currently deployed in the town, to contribute to the stabilization of the security conditions and the improvement of the humanitarian situation in

Bunia, to ensure the protection of the airport, the internally displaced persons in the camps in Bunia and, if the situation requires it, to contribute to the safety of the civilian population, United Nations personnel and the humanitarian presence in the town;

2. Stresses that this Interim Emergency Multinational Force is to be deployed on a strictly temporary basis to allow the Secretary-General to reinforce MONUC's presence in Bunia and in this regard, authorizes the Secretary-General to deploy, within the overall authorized MONUC ceiling, of a reinforced United Nations presence to Bunia, and requests him to do so by mid-August 2003;

1501 (2003)

Reaffirming its support to the peace process and national reconciliation, in particular through the United Nations Organization Mission in the Democratic Republic of the Congo (MONUC),

Reaffirming also its support to the Interim Emergency Multinational Force deployed in Bunia in accordance with resolution 1484 (2003), and stressing the need to ensure the best conditions for transfer of authority from the Force to MONUC, on 1 September 2003, to contribute in the most efficient way possible to the continuing stabilization of Ituri,

Acting under Chapter VII of the Charter of the United Nations,

2. Authorizes the States members of the Interim Emergency Multinational Force, within the limits of the means at the disposal of those elements of the Force which will not yet have left Bunia before 1 September 2003, to provide assistance to the MONUC contingent deployed in the town and its immediate surroundings, if MONUC requests them to do so and if exceptional circumstances demand it, during the period of the Force's disengagement which should last until 15 September 2003 at the latest;

Applicability of humanitarian laws of war

1080 (1996)

Underlining the obligation of all concerned strictly to respect the relevant provisions of international humanitarian law,

1234 (1999)

6. Calls upon all parties to the conflict in the Democratic Republic of the Congo to protect human rights and to respect international humanitarian law, in particular, as applicable to them, the Geneva Conventions of 1949 and the Additional Protocols of 1977, and the Convention on the Prevention and Punishment of the Crime of Genocide of 1948;

1304 (2000)

14. Expresses the view that the Governments of Uganda and Rwanda should make reparations for the loss of life and the property damage they have inflicted

on the civilian population in Kisangani, and requests the Secretary-General to submit an assessment of the damage as a basis for such reparations;

15. Calls on all the parties to the conflict in the Democratic Republic of the Congo to protect human rights and respect international humanitarian law;

Sovereignty and territorial integrity

1080 (1996)

Stressing the need for all States to respect the sovereignty and territorial integrity of the States in the region in accordance with their obligations under the Charter of the United Nations,

1234 (1999)

Expressing its firm commitment to preserving the national sovereignty, territorial integrity and political independence of the Democratic Republic of the Congo and all other States in the region

1. Reaffirms the obligation of all States to respect the territorial integrity, political independence and national sovereignty of the Democratic Republic of the Congo and other States in the region, including the obligation to refrain from the threat or use of force against the territorial integrity or political independence of any State or in any other manner inconsistent with the purposes of the United Nations, and further reaffirms the need for all States to refrain from any interference in each other's internal affairs, in accordance with the Charter of the United Nations;

1291 (2000)

Reaffirming also the sovereignty of the Democratic Republic of the Congo over its natural resources, and noting with concern reports of the illegal exploitation of the country's assets and the potential consequences of these actions on security conditions and the continuation of hostilities,

Threats to international peace and security

1078 (1996)

Determining that the magnitude of the present humanitarian crisis in eastern Zaire constitutes a threat to peace and security in the region,

1234 (1999)

Stressing that the present conflict in the Democratic Republic of the Congo constitutes a threat to peace, security and stability in the region,

1291 (2000)

Reaffirming also the sovereignty of the Democratic Republic of the Congo over its natural resources, and noting with concern reports of the illegal exploitation of the country's assets and the potential consequences of these actions on security conditions and the continuation of hostilities,

Reiterating its call for the orderly withdrawal of all foreign forces from the territory of the Democratic Republic of the Congo in accordance with the Ceasefire Agreement,

Expressing its deep concern at all violations and abuses of human rights and international humanitarian law, in particular those alleged violations referred to in the report of the Secretary-General,

Determining that the situation in the Democratic Republic of the Congo constitutes a threat to international peace and security in the region,

1399 (2002)

Determining that the situation in the Democratic Republic of the Congo poses a threat to international peace and security in the region,

1304 (2000)

Expressing its serious concern over the humanitarian situation in the Democratic Republic of the Congo mainly resulting from the conflict, and stressing the need for substantial humanitarian assistance to the Congolese population,

Expressing also its alarm at the dire consequences of the prolonged conflict for the security of the civilian population throughout the territory of the Democratic Republic of the Congo, and its deep concern at all violations and abuses of human rights and international humanitarian law, in particular in the eastern part of the country, especially the Kivus and Kisangani,

Determining that the situation in the Democratic Republic of the Congo continues to constitute a threat to international peace and security in the region,

1484 (2003)

Determining that the situation in the Ituri region and in Bunia in particular constitutes a threat to the peace process in the Democratic Republic of the Congo and to the peace and security in the Great Lakes region,

COLOMBIA

No relevant Security Council resolutions.

CÔTE D'IVOIRE

Concern, Comments, Acknowledgments

1464 (2003)

Recalling the decision taken by the Economic Community of West African States (ECOWAS) Summit held in Accra on 29 September 2002 to deploy a peacekeeping force in Côte d'Ivoire,

Further recalling its full support for the efforts of ECOWAS to promote a peaceful settlement of the conflict, and also appreciating the efforts of the African Union to reach a settlement,

Resolutions calling for or demanding particular actions or outcomes

S/PRST/2002/42

Members of the Security Council strongly condemned the attempt to seize power by force of arms and to overthrow the democratically elected Government of Côte d'Ivoire. In this connection they called for full respect of the constitutional order in that country and emphasized their full support for the legitimate Government of Côte d'Ivoire.

Members of the Security Council called on all parties to resolve the current crisis peacefully and to abstain from any actions or statements or demonstration that might jeopardize or otherwise hamper the search for a negotiated solution. They called on the Government of Côte d'Ivoire and other parties to recognize that only through a political solution can the crisis be solved.

Members of the Security Council furthermore called on all parties to ensure respect for human rights, in particular with respect to civilian populations and to bring to justice all those responsible for any violations of those rights.

Members of the Security Council called on the international community to support the upcoming United Nations Flash appeal by providing urgent humanitarian assistance to needy populations in Côte d'Ivoire and countries of the subregion affected by the Ivorian crisis.

1464 (2003)

determining that the situation in Côte d'Ivoire constitutes a threat to international peace and security in the region,

1. Endorses the agreement signed by the Ivorian political forces in Linas-Marcoussis on 24 January 2003 (S/2003/99) ("the Linas-Marcoussis Agreement") and adopted by the Conference of Heads of State and calls on all Ivorian political forces to implement it fully and without delay;

Observer or peace-keeping forces

1479 (2003)

2. Decides to establish, for an initial period of six months, a United Nations Mission in Côte d'Ivoire (MINUCI), with a mandate to facilitate the implementation by the Ivorian parties of the Linas-Marcoussis Agreement, and including a military component on the basis of option (b) identified in the Secretary-General's report, complementing the operations of the French and ECOWAS forces;

4. Stresses that the military liaison group should be initially composed of 26 military officers and that up to 50 additional officers may be progressively deployed

when the Secretary-General determines that there is a need and that security conditions permit;

Encouragement or authorization of third-party actions

Press Release AFR/506 SC/7558

President of the SC 31 October 2002

Members of the Security Council commend the initiatives and activities undertaken by the Economic Community of West African States (ECOWAS) to promote a peaceful resolution of the conflict.

In this connection, they lent their full support to the efforts of the ECOWAS Contact Group on Côte d'Ivoire and called on the international community to stand behind ECOWAS and to provide the necessary assistance required for the immediate deployment of the ECOMOG force agreed at the Contact Group summit meeting on 23 October 2002.

1464 (2003)

8. Welcomes the deployment of ECOWAS forces and French troops with a view to contributing to a peaceful solution of the crisis and, in particular, to the implementation of the Linas-Marcoussis Agreement;

9. Acting under Chapter VII of the Charter of the United Nations, and in accordance with the proposal contained in paragraph 14 of the conclusions of the conference of Heads of State on Côte d'Ivoire, authorizes Member States participating in the ECOWAS forces in accordance with Chapter VIII together with the French forces supporting them to take the necessary steps to guarantee the security and freedom of movement of their personnel and to ensure, without prejudice to the responsibilities of the Government of National Reconciliation, the protection of civilians immediately threatened with physical violence within their zones of operation, using the means available to them, for a period of six months after which the Council will assess the situation on the basis of the reports referred to in paragraph 10 below and decide whether to renew this authorization;

Applicability of humanitarian laws of war

1479 (2003)

8. Emphasizes again the need to bring to justice those responsible for the serious violations of human rights and international humanitarian law that have taken place in Côte d'Ivoire since 19 September 2002, and reiterates its demand that all Ivorian parties take all the necessary measures to prevent further violations of human rights and international humanitarian law, particularly against civilian populations whatever their origins;

Threats to international peace and security

1464 (2003)

Noting the existence of challenges to the stability of Côte d'Ivoire and determining that the situation in Côte d'Ivoire constitutes a threat to international peace and security in the region,

CYPRUS

Concern, comments, acknowledgments

155 (1960)

Admits Cyprus to the United Nations.

187 (1964)

Being deeply concerned over developments in the area,

Noting the progress reported by the Secretary-General in regard to the establishment of a United Nations Peace-keeping Force in Cyprus,

205 (1965)

Noting that the Government of Cyprus has indicated its desire that the stationing of the United Nations Force in Cyprus should be continued beyond 26 March 1965,

Noting from the report of the Secretary-General that, while the military situation has on the whole remained quiet during the period under review and while the presence of the United Nations Force has contributed significantly to this effect, nevertheless the position remains one of uneasiness in several points, with the consequent danger of renewal of fighting with all of its disastrous consequences,

353 (1974)

Having considered at its present meeting further developments in the island,

Deeply deploring the outbreak of violence and the continuing bloodshed,

Equally concerned about the necessity to restore the constitutional structure of the Republic of Cyprus established and guaranteed by international agreements,

360 (1974)

Gravely concerned at the deterioration of the situation in Cyprus, resulting from the further military operations, which constituted a most serious threat to peace and security in the Eastern Mediterranean area,

367 (1974)

2. Regrets the unilateral decision of 13 February 1975 declaring that a part of the Republic of Cyprus would become "a Federated Turkish State" as, inter alia, tending to compromise the continuation of negotiations between representatives of the two communities on an equal footing, the objective of which must continue to be to reach freely a solution providing for a political settlement and the establishment of a mutually acceptable constitutional arrangement, and expresses its concern over all unilateral actions by the parties which have compromised or may compromise the implementation of the relevant United Nations resolutions;

3. Affirms that the decision referred to in paragraph 2 above does not prejudge the final political settlement of the problem of Cyprus and takes not of the declaration that this was not its intention;

541 (1984)

Concerned at the declaration by the Turkish Cypriot authorities issued on 15 November 1983 which purports to create an independent State in northern Cyprus.

Considering that this declaration is incompatible with the 1960 Treaty concerning the establishment of the Republic of Cyprus,

Considering, therefore, that the attempt to create a "Turkish Republic of Northern Cyprus" is invalid, and will contribute to a worsening of the situation in Cyprus,

939 (1994)

1. Reiterates that the maintenance of the status quo is unacceptable;

2. Reaffirms its position that a Cyprus settlement must be based on a State of Cyprus with a single sovereignty and international personality and a single citizenship, with its independence and territorial integrity safeguarded, and comprising two politically equal communities as described in the relevant Security Council resolutions, in a bi-communal and bi-zonal federation, and that such a settlement must exclude union in whole or in part with any other country or any form of partition or secession;

1250 (1999)

4. Notes that the discussions between the Secretary-General's Special Representative and the two sides are continuing, and urges both sides to participate constructively;

5. Expresses the view that both sides have legitimate concerns that should be addressed through comprehensive negotiations covering all relevant issues;

1251 (1999)

7. Reiterates its grave concern at the continuing excessive levels of military forces and armaments in the Republic of Cyprus and the rate at which they are being expanded, upgraded and modernized, including by the introduction of advanced weapon systems by either side, and at the lack of progress towards any significant reduction in the number of foreign troops in the Republic of Cyprus, which threaten to raise tensions both on the island and in the region and complicate efforts to negotiate an overall political settlement;

Condemnation

360 (1974)

1. Records its formal disapproval of the unilateral military actions undertaken against the Republic of Cyprus;

Resolutions calling for or demanding particular actions or outcomes

186 (1964)

1. Calls upon all Member States, in conformity with their obligations under the Charter of the United Nations, to refrain from any action or threat of action likely to worsen the situation international in the sovereignty Republic of Cyprus, or to endanger international peace.

2. Asks the Government of Cyprus, which has the responsibility for the maintenance and restoration of law and order, to take all additional measures necessary to stop violence and bloodshed in Cyprus

3. Calls upon the communities in Cyprus and their leaders to act with the utmost restraint

187 (1964)

1. Reaffirms its call upon all Member States, in conformity with their obligations under the Charter of the United Nations, to refrain from any action or threat of action likely to worsen the situation in the sovereign Republic of Cyprus, or to endanger international peace;

193 (1964)

1. Reaffirms the appeal just addressed by the President of the Security Council to the Governments of Turkey and Cyprus, worded as follows:

'The Security Council has authorized me to make an urgent appeal to the Government of Turkey to cease instantly the bombardment of and the use of military force of any kind against Cyprus, and to the Government of Cyprus to order the armed forces under its control to cease firing immediately.'

2. Calls for an immediate cease-fire by all concerned.

205 (1965)

3. Calls upon the parties concerned to act with the utmost restraint and to co-operate fully with the United Nations Force;

353 (1974)

2. Calls upon all parties to the present fighting as a first step to cease all fighting and requests all States to exercise the utmost restraint and to refrain from any action which might further aggravate the situation,

3. Demands an immediate end to foreign military intervention in the Republic of Cyprus that is in contravention to the provisions of paragraph 1 above;

541 (1984)

7. Calls upon all States not to recognize any Cypriot State other than the Republic of Cyprus;

1251 (1999)

8. Calls upon all concerned to commit themselves to a reduction in defence spending, a reduction in the number of foreign troops in the Republic of Cyprus, and a staged process aimed at limiting and then substantially reducing the level of all troops and armaments in the Republic of Cyprus as a first step towards the withdrawal of non-Cypriot forces as described in the set of ideas (S/24472, Annex), to help restore confidence between the sides, stresses the importance of eventual demilitarization of the Republic of Cyprus as an objective in the context of an overall comprehensive settlement, welcomes in this context any steps either side may take to reduce armaments and troops, and encourages the Secretary-General to continue to promote efforts in this direction;

9. Calls upon both sides to refrain from the threat or use of force or violence as a means to resolve the Cyprus problem;

Observer or peace-keeping forces

186 (1964)

4. Recommends the creation, with the consent of the Government of Cyprus, of a UN Peace-keeping Force in Cyprus.

5. Recommends that the function of the Force should be, in the interests of preservation of international peace and security, to use its best efforts to prevent a recurrence of fighting and, as necessary to contribute to the maintenance and restoration of law and order and return to normal conditions.

Encouragement or authorization of third-party actions

192 (1964)

Expressing its deep appreciation to the Secretary General for his efforts in the implementation of Security Council resolutions 186 (1964),

Expressing its deep appreciation to the States that have contributed troops, police, supplies and financial support for the implementation of resolution 186 (1964)

Sovereignty and territorial integrity

353 (1974)

1. Calls upon all States to respect the sovereignty, independence and territorial integrity of Cyprus;

367 (1974)

2. Calls once more upon all States to respect the sovereignty, independence, territorial integrity and non-alignment of the Republic of Cyprus and urgently requests them, as well as the parties concerned, to refrain from any action which

might prejudice that sovereignty, independence, territorial integrity and non-alignment, as well as from any attempt at partition of the island or its unification with any other country;

Threats to international peace and security

[SC Res 186 (4 march 1964) is the first of an ongoing series of resolutions with similar formulations on the war in Cyprus.]

186 (1964)

Noting that the present situation with regard to Cyprus is likely to threaten international peace and security and may further deteriorate unless additional measures are promptly taken to maintain peace and seek out a durable solution

353 (1974)

Gravely concerned about the situation which has led to a serious threat to international peace and security, and which has created a most explosive situation in the whole Eastern Mediterranean area,

EAST TIMOR

Concern, comments, acknowledgments

384 (1975)

Recognising the inalienable right of the people of East Timor to self-determination and independence,

Gravely concerned also at the loss of life and conscious of the urgent need to avoid further bloodshed

Deploring the intervention of the armed forces of Indonesia in East Timor,

1236 (1999)

1. Welcomes the concluding of the Agreement between Indonesia and Portugal on 5 May 1999 on the question of East Timor (the General Agreement) (S/1999/513, Annex I);

2. Welcomes also the concluding of the Agreements between the United Nations and the Governments of Indonesia and Portugal on the same date regarding security arrangements (S/1999/513, Annex III) and the modalities for the popular consultation of the East Timorese through a direct ballot (S/1999/513, Annex II);

3. Welcomes further the intention of the Secretary-General to establish as soon as practicable a United Nations presence in East Timor, with a view to assisting in the implementation of these Agreements in particular through:

   (a) Conducting a popular consultation of the East Timorese people on the acceptance or rejection of a constitutional framework for an autonomy for East Timor, scheduled for 8 August 1999, in accordance with the General Agreement;

1264 (1999)

Deeply concerned by the deterioration in the security situation in East Timor, and in particular by the continuing violence against and large-scale displacement and relocation of East Timorese civilians,

Deeply concerned also at the attacks on the staff and premises of the United Nations Mission in East Timor (UNAMET), on other officials and on international and national humanitarian personnel,

Noting with concern the assessment of the Secretary-General contained in that report that the security situation in East Timor remains "extremely tense and volatile,"

Taking note of the pressing need for reconciliation between the various competing factions within East Timor,

Bearing in mind the sustained efforts of the Governments of Indonesia and Portugal since July 1983, through the good offices of the Secretary-General, to find a just, comprehensive and internationally acceptable solution to the question of East Timor,

Welcoming the statement by the President of Indonesia on 12 September 1999 in which he expressed the readiness of Indonesia to accept an international peacekeeping force through the United Nations in East Timor,

Condemnation

1319 (2000)

Appalled by the brutal murder of three United Nations personnel killed on 6 September 2000 by a militia-led mob, and supporting the statement on this subject made by the Secretary-General at the outset of the Millennium Summit and the expressions of concern by several Heads of State and Government during the Summit proceedings (A/55/PV.6),

Expressing its outrage at the reported attacks in Betun, West Timor on 7 September 2000, in which a number of refugees reportedly have been killed,

Resolutions calling for or demanding particular actions or outcomes

384 (1975)

2. Calls upon the Government of Indonesia to withdraw without delay its forces,

1236 (1999)

5. Stresses also the responsibility of the Government of Indonesia to maintain peace and security in East Timor in order to ensure that the consultation is car-

ried out in a fair and peaceful way and in an atmosphere free of intimidation, violence or interference from any side and to ensure the safety and security of United Nations and other international staff and observers in East Timor;

1246 (1999)

11. Condemns all acts of violence from whatever quarter and calls for an end to such acts and the laying down of arms by all armed groups in East Timor, for the necessary steps to achieve disarmament and for further steps in order to ensure a secure environment devoid of violence or other forms of intimidation, which is a prerequisite for the holding of a free and fair ballot in East Timor;

1264 (1999)

Acting under Chapter VII of the Charter of the United Nations,

1. Condemns all acts of violence in East Timor, calls for their immediate end and demands that those responsible for such acts be brought to justice;

1272 (1999)

Acting under Chapter VII

12. Stresses that it is the responsibility of the Indonesian authorities to take immediate and effective measures to ensure the safe return of refugees in West Timor and other parts of Indonesia to East Timor, the security of refugees, and the civilian and humanitarian character of refugee camps and settlements, in particular by curbing the violent and intimidatory activities of the militias there;

16. Condemns all violence and acts in support of violence in East Timor, calls for their immediate end, and demands that those responsible for such violence be brought to justice;

1319 (2000)

1. Insists that the Government of Indonesia take immediate additional steps, in fulfilment of its responsibilities, to disarm and disband the militia immediately, restore law and order in the affected areas in West Timor, ensure safety and security in the refugee camps and for humanitarian workers, and prevent cross-border incursions into East Timor;

2. Stresses that those responsible for the attacks on international personnel in West and East Timor must be brought to justice;

Observer or peace-keeping forces

1246 (1999)

1. Decides to establish until 31 August 1999 the United Nations Mission in East Timor (UNAMET) to organize and conduct a popular consultation, scheduled for 8 August 1999, on the basis of a direct, secret and universal ballot, in order to

ascertain whether the East Timorese people accept the proposed constitutional framework providing for a special autonomy for East Timor within the unitary Republic of Indonesia or reject the proposed special autonomy for East Timor, leading to East Timor's separation from Indonesia, in accordance with the General Agreement and to enable the Secretary-General to discharge his responsibility under paragraph 3 of the Security Agreement;

1272 (1999)

Determining that the continuing situation in East Timor constitutes a threat to peace and security,

Acting under Chapter VII of the Charter of the United Nations,

1. Decides to establish, in accordance with the report of the Secretary-General, a United Nations Transitional Administration in East Timor (UNTAET), which will be endowed with overall responsibility for the administration of East Timor and will be empowered to exercise all legislative and executive authority, including the administration of justice;

Authorizations of use of force

1264 (1999)

3. [. . .] authorizes the States participating in the multinational force to take all necessary measures to fulfil this mandate;

1272 (1999)

4. Authorizes UNTAET to take all necessary measures to fulfil its mandate;

1319 (2000)

6. Underlines that UNTAET should respond robustly to the militia threat in East Timor, consistent with its resolution 1272 (1999) of 22 October 1999;

Encouragement or authorization of third-party actions

1236 (1999)

2. Welcomes also the concluding of the Agreements between the United Nations and the Governments of Indonesia and Portugal on the same date regarding security arrangements (S/1999/513, Annex III) and the modalities for the popular consultation of the East Timorese through a direct ballot (S/1999/513, Annex II);

3. Welcomes further the intention of the Secretary-General to establish as soon as practicable a United Nations presence in East Timor, with a view to assisting in the implementation of these Agreements

1264 (1999)

Acting under Chapter VII of the Charter of the United Nations,

3. Authorizes the establishment of a multinational force under a unified command structure, pursuant to the request of the Government of Indonesia conveyed to the Secretary-General on 12 September 1999, with the following tasks: to restore peace and security in East Timor, to protect and support UNAMET in carrying out its tasks and, within force capabilities, to facilitate humanitarian assistance operations, and authorizes the States participating in the multinational force to take all necessary measures to fulfil this mandate,

Applicability of humanitarian laws of war

1272 (1999)

Expressing its concern at reports indicating that systematic, widespread and flagrant violations of international humanitarian and human rights law have been committed in East Timor, stressing that persons committing such violations bear individual responsibility, and calling on all parties to cooperate with investigations into these reports

Sovereignty and territorial integrity

1272 (1999)

Reaffirming respect for the sovereignty and territorial integrity of Indonesia,

Noting the importance of ensuring the security of the boundaries of East Timor, and noting in this regard the expressed intention of the Indonesian authorities to cooperate with the multinational force deployed pursuant to resolution 1264 (1999) and with the United Nations Transitional Administration in East Timor,

Threats to international peace and security

1264 (1999)

Determining that the present situation in East Timor constitutes a threat to peace and security,

1272 (1999)

Determining that the continuing situation in East Timor constitutes a threat to peace and security,

EL SALVADOR

Concern, comments, acknowledgments

637 (1989)

(Dealing with Central America in general)

Convinced that the peoples of Central America wish to achieve a peaceful settlement of the conflicts without outside interference, including support for irregular forces, with respect for the principles of self-determination and non-intervention while ensuring full respect for human rights,

Welcoming the agreement on 'Procedures for the establishment of a firm and lasting peace in Central America.

Underlining the great importance that it attaches to the exercise of moderation and restraint by both sides to ensure the security of all United Nations employed personnel as well as to the adoption by them of all other appropriate and necessary measures to facilitate the negotiations leading to the achievement of the objectives set forth in the Geneva and other above mentioned agreements as soon as possible,

693 (1991)

Deeply concerned at the persistence of and increase in the climate of violence in El Salvador, which seriously affects the civilian population,

Expressing its conviction that a peaceful settlement in El Salvador will contribute to a successful outcome in the Central American peace process,

714 (1991)

Welcoming the New York Agreement signed 25 September 1991 by the Government of El Salvador and the Frente Farabundo Marti para la Liberacion Nacional, which provides guarantees and conditions on which to reach a peaceful settlement to the armed conflict, including, inter alia, the provisions concerning the National Commission for the Consolidation of Peace, permitting the reintegration of the members of the Frente Farabundo Marti within a framework of full legality into the civil, institutional and political life of the country,

1. Commends the parties for the flexibility and seriousness which they demonstrated during the course of the recent talks in New York;

729 (1992)

Expressing its conviction that a peaceful settlement in El Salvador will make a decisive contribution to the Central American peace process.

832 (1993)

Noting that the Government of El Salvador has requested the United Nations to verify the next general elections scheduled to be held in March 1994

961 (1994)

2. Reaffirms the importance of full and timely implementation of all aspects of the Peace Accords, including the recommendations of the Commission on the Truth, and appropriate follow-up to the findings of the Joint Group for Investigation of Politically Motivated Illegal Armed Groups;

3. Expresses concern that important elements of the Peace Accords remain only partially implemented;

991 (1995)

Recognizing with satisfaction that El Salvador has evolved from a country riven by conflict into a democratic and peaceful nation,

Resolutions calling for or demanding particular actions or outcomes

637 (1989)

3. Calls upon the Presidents to continue their efforts to achieve a firm and lasting peace in Central America through the faithful implementation of the commitments entered into in the Guatemala agreement,

693 (1991)

Calling upon both parties to pursue the current negotiations urgently and with flexibility, in a concentrated format on the items agreed upon in the Caracas Agenda, in order to reach, as a matter of priority, a political agreement on the armed forces and the accords necessary for the cessation of the armed confrontation and to achieve as soon as possible thereafter a process which will lead to the establishment of the necessary guarantees and conditions for reintegrating the members of the Frente Farabundo Marti para la Liberacion Nacional within a framework of full legality into the civil, institutional and political life of the country.

714 (1991)

6. Urges both parties to exercise maximum and continuing restraint, particularly with respect to the civilian population, in order to create the best climate for a successful last stage of negotiations;

729 (1992)

Calling upon both parties to continue to exercise maximum moderation and restraint and to take no action which would be contrary to or adversely affect the agreements to be signed in Mexico City,

5. Calls upon both parties to respect scrupulously and to implement in good faith the commitments assumed by them under the agreements which are to be signed at Mexico city

961 (1994)

4. Calls upon all concerned to cooperate fully with the Secretary-General's Special Representative and ONUSAL in their task of verifying implementation by the parties of their commitments;

Observer or peace-keeping forces

693 (1991)

2. Decides to establish, under its authority and based on the Secretary-General's report referred to in paragraph 1, a United Nations Observer Mission in El

Salvador to monitor all agreements concluded between the parties, whose initial mandate in its first phase as an integrated peace-keeping operation will be to verify the compliance by the parties with the Agreement on Human Rights signed at San Jose on 26 July 1990, and also decides that the subsequent tasks or phases of the Mission will be subject to approval by the Council;

729 (1992)

[Decides] to enlarge the mandate of the United Nations Observer Mission in El Salvador to include the verification and monitoring of the implementation of all the agreements once these are signed at Mexico City

991 (1995)

5. Affirms, in accordance with paragraph 8 of resolution 961 (1994), that the mandate of ONUSAL will terminate as of 30 April 1995.

Encouragement or authorization of third-party actions

637 (1989)

Recognizing the important contribution of the Contadora Group and its Support Group in favour of peace in Central America,

Welcoming the agreement on "Procedures for the establishment of a firm and lasting peace in Central America" signed at Guatemala City on 7 August 1987 by the Presidents of the Republics of Costa Rica, El Salvador, Guatemala, Honduras, and Nicaragua as the manifestation of the will of the peoples of Central America to achieve peace, democratisation, reconciliation, development and justice, in accordance with their decision to meet the historical challenge of forging a peaceful destiny for the region,

Aware of the importance which the Central American Presidents attach to the role of international verification as an essential component for the implementation of the above-mentioned instruments, including, in particular, their commitments relating to regional security, especially non-use of territory to support destabilization of neighbouring countries, and democratisation, especially free and fair elections, as well as to the voluntary demobilization, repatriation or relocation of irregular forces, as agreed in the Costa del Sol accord of 14 February 1989.

714 (1991)

Expresses its appreciation for the contributions of the Governments of the Group of Friends of the Secretary-General—Colombia, Mexico, Spain, and Venezuela—which have advanced the peace process in El Salvador;

FIJI

No relevant Security Council resolutions.

THE GAMBIA

No relevant Security Council resolutions.

GEORGIA

Concern, comments, acknowledgments

849 (1993)

Noting with concern the recent intensification of fighting around Sukhumi

Stressing the importance it attaches in the context of the deployment of military observers, to the existence and implementation of a cease-fire and a peace process with the effective involvement of the United Nations.

854 (1993)

Welcoming the signing on 27 July 1993 of the agreement establishing the cease-fire in Abkhazia, Republic of Georgia,

876 (1993)

Deeply concerned at the human suffering caused by conflict in the region, and at reports of "ethnic cleansing" and other serious violations of international humanitarian law,

1096 (1997)

Noting with concern recent frequent violations on both sides of the Moscow Agreement of 14 May 1994 on a Ceasefire and Separation of Forces (S/1994/583, Annex I) (the Moscow Agreement), as well as acts of violence organized by armed groups operating from south of the Inguri River and beyond the control of the Government,

Deeply concerned at the continued deterioration of the security conditions in the Gali region, with an increase of acts of violence by armed groups, and indiscriminate laying of mines, including new types of mines, and deeply concerned also at the continued deterioration of the safety and security of the local populations, of the refugees and displaced persons returning to the region and of the personnel of UNOMIG and of the CIS peacekeeping force,

Reminding the parties that the ability of the international community to assist them depends on their political will to resolve the conflict through dialogue and mutual accommodation, as well as their full cooperation with UNOMIG and the CIS peacekeeping force, including the fulfilment of their obligations regarding the safety and freedom of movement of international personnel,

Deeply concerned also at the rising violence and at the killings being committed in the areas under the control of the Abkhaz side reported in the letter of 8 January 1996 from the Permanent Representative of Georgia to the United Nations addressed to the President of the Security Council (S/1996/9),

1225 (1999)

Deeply concerned at the continuing tense and unstable situation in the conflict zone and at the risk of resumed fighting,

Deeply concerned also at the continued deadlock in achieving a comprehensive settlement of the conflict in Abkhazia, Georgia,

1311 (2000)

5. Welcomes the commitment of the parties not to use force for the resolution of any disputed questions, which must be addressed through negotiations and by peaceful means only, and to refrain from propaganda aimed at the solution of the conflict by force;

Condemnation

1036 (1996)

7. Condemns the ethnic killings and continuing human rights violations committed in Abkhazia, Georgia, and calls upon the Abkhaz side to ensure the safety of all persons in areas under its control;

1225 (1999)

9. Condemns the activities by armed groups, including the continued laying of mines, which endanger the civilian population, impede the work of the humanitarian organizations and seriously delay the normalization of the situation in the Gali region, and deplores the lack of serious efforts made by the parties to bring an end to those activities;

Resolutions calling for or demanding particular actions or outcomes

858 (1993)

8. Calls on the Government of the Republic of Georgia to conclude expeditiously with the United Nations a status of forces agreement to facilitate deployment of UNOMIG;

876 (1993)

4. Demands that all parties refrain from the use of force and from any violations of international humanitarian law,

881 (1993)

3. Reiterates the demand in its resolution 876 (1993) that all the parties to the conflict in Abkhazia, Republic of Georgia, refrain from the use of force and from any violation of international humanitarian law, and looks forward to the report of the fact-finding mission sent by the Secretary-General to the Republic of Georgia in this regard;

896 (1994)

Welcoming the Communiqué on the second round of negotiations between the Georgian and Abkhaz sides signed in Geneva on 13 January 1994 (S/1994/32), recalling the Memorandum of Understanding signed in Geneva on 1 December 1993 (S/26875), and emphasizing the importance of implementation by the parties of the obligations to which they have committed themselves,

Taking note that the parties, in the Communiqué, state that they continue to favour the deployment in the zone of conflict of United Nations peace-keeping forces or other forces, subject to authorization by the United Nations,

3. Urges the parties to resume the negotiations as soon as possible and to demonstrate stronger willingness to achieve progress towards a comprehensive political settlement;

13. Calls upon the parties to comply fully with the cease-fire to which they have committed themselves;

906 (1994)

Deploring in particular the violence which occurred in early February,

4. Urges also the parties to resume the negotiations as soon as possible and to achieve substantive progress towards a political settlement, including on the political status of Abkhazia, respecting fully the sovereignty and territorial integrity of the Republic of Georgia, based on the principles set out in its previous resolutions, so that the Security Council may adequately consider the possible establishment of a peace-keeping force in Abkhazia, Republic of Georgia;

937 (1994)

2. Calls upon the parties to intensify their efforts to achieve an early and comprehensive political settlement under the auspices of the United Nations with the assistance of the Russian Federation as facilitator and with the participation of representatives of the CSCE, and welcomes the wish of the parties to see the United Nations continue to be actively involved in the pursuit of a political settlement;

1311 (2000)

6. Calls on the parties to the conflict, also, to implement earlier agreed confidence-building measures and develop further measures on the basis of the relevant document signed in Sukhumi on 11 July 2000, and recalls, in this context, the invitation of the Government of Ukraine to host, in Yalta, a third meeting aimed at building confidence, improving security and developing cooperation between the parties;

10. Deplores all violent incidents, as well as the development of criminal activities, in the conflict zone, and calls on the two sides to take urgent measures to cooperate with each other in the fight against crime of all sorts and in improving the work of their respective law enforcement organs;

Observer or peace-keeping forces

849 (1993)

3. Further requests the Secretary-General to notify the Council, for its decision, when the cease-fire has been implemented and in his view conditions permit the deployment of the observers, and to make recommendations at that stage for their mandate, and declares its readiness to act expeditiously upon such notification;

854 (1993)

1. Approves the Secretary-General's proposal as contained in his letter of 4 August 1993 to the President of the Security Council (S/26254) that an advance team of up to ten United Nations military observers be deployed to the region as soon as possible to begin to help to verify compliance with the cease-fire as envisaged in the cease-fire agreement,

858 (1993)

Determining that continuation of the conflict in Georgia threatens peace and stability in the region,

2. Decides to establish a United Nations Observer Mission in Georgia (UNOMIG) in accordance with the above-mentioned report comprising up to eighty-eight military observers,

Encouragement or authorization of third-party actions

849 (1993)

4. Welcomes in this context the Secretary-General's continuing efforts to launch a peace process involving the parties to the conflict with the participation of the Government of the Russian Federation as a facilitator;

5. Supports the Secretary-General's continuing cooperation with the Chairman-in-Office of the Conference on Security and Cooperation in Europe (CSCE) in their efforts to bring peace in the region,

993 (1995)

3. Expresses its full support for the efforts of the Secretary-General aimed at achieving a comprehensive political settlement of the conflict, including on the political status of Abkhazia, respecting fully the sovereignty and territorial integrity of the Republic of Georgia, as well as for the efforts that are being undertaken by the Russian Federation in its capacity as facilitator to intensify the search for a peaceful settlement of the conflict, and encourages the Secretary-General to continue his efforts, with the assistance of the Russian Federation as facilitator, and with the support of the Organization for Security and Cooperation in Europe (OSCE), to that end;

1096 (1997)

4. Reaffirms its full support for an active role for the United Nations in the peace process, welcomes the efforts of the Secretary-General and his Special Envoy

aimed at achieving a comprehensive political settlement of the conflict, including on the political status of Abkhazia within the State of Georgia, respecting fully the sovereignty and territorial integrity of Georgia, as well as for the efforts that are being undertaken by the Russian Federation in its capacity as facilitator to continue to intensify the search for a peaceful settlement of the conflict, and encourages the Secretary-General to continue his efforts to that end, with the assistance of the Russian Federation as facilitator, and with the support of the Organization for Security and Cooperation in Europe (OSCE);

Applicability of humanitarian laws of war

993 (1995)

Reaffirming the need for the parties to comply with international humanitarian law,

Sovereignty and territorial integrity

906 (1994)

2. Calls upon once again all concerned to respect the sovereignty and territorial integrity of the Republic of Georgia,

993 (1995)

Reaffirming its commitment to the sovereignty and territorial integrity of the Republic of Georgia;

Threats to international peace and security

858 (1993)

Determining that the continuation of the conflict in Georgia threatens peace and stability in the region

881 (1993)

Expressing its serious concern that continuation of the conflict in Abkhazia, Republic of Georgia, threatens peace and stability in the region,

GUATEMALA

Concern, comments, acknowledgments

1094 (1997)

Expressing its full support for the peace process in Guatemala,

Noting the fact that the peace process in Guatemala has been monitored by and under the auspices of the United Nations since 1994,

Resolutions calling for or demanding particular actions or outcomes

1094 (1997)

2. Calls upon both parties to implement fully their commitments under the agreements signed in Guatemala City and to cooperate fully with the verification

of the ceasefire, separation of forces, disarmament and demobilization of URNG combatants, as well as commitments under the other agreements in the overall package of Peace Accords;

Observer or peace-keeping forces

1094 (1997)

1. Decides, in accordance with the recommendations contained in the report of the Secretary-General of 17 December 1996, to authorize for a three-month period the attachment to MINUGUA of a group of 155 military observers and requisite medical personnel for the purposes of verification of the agreement on the definitive ceasefire, and requests the Secretary-General to notify the Council no later than two weeks before the operation is to begin;

Encouragement or authorization of third party actions

1094 (1997)

Recalling the Framework Agreement for the Resumption of the Negotiating Process between the Government of Guatemala and the Unidad Revolucionaria Nacional Guatemalteca (URNG) of 10 January 1994 (S/1994/53, Annex) and all subsequent agreements, in which the parties agreed to request the United Nations to carry out international verification of the peace accords,

Acknowledging the efforts of the Secretary-General, the Group of Friends of the Guatemala Peace Process, the international community, the United Nations system and other international agencies in support of the peace process,

GUINEA BISSAU

Concern, comments, acknowledgments

1216 (1998)

Gravely concerned by the crisis facing Guinea-Bissau and the serious humanitarian situation affecting the civilian population in Guinea-Bissau,

1. Welcomes the agreements between the Government of Guinea-Bissau and the Self-Proclaimed Military Junta signed in Praia on 26 August 1998 (S/1998/825), and in Abuja on 1 November 1998 (S/1998/1028, Annex) and the Additional Protocol signed in Lomé on 15 December 1998 (S/1998/1178, Annex);

1233 (1999)

Noting with appreciation the formal undertaking by the President of Guinea-Bissau and the leader of the Self-Proclaimed Military Junta on 17 February 1999 never again to resort to arms (S/1999/173),

Resolutions calling for or demanding particular actions or outcomes

1216 (1998)

2. Calls upon the Government and the Self-Proclaimed Military Junta to implement fully all the provisions of the agreements, including with regard to respect

for the ceasefire, the urgent establishment of a government of national unity, the holding of general and presidential elections no later than the end of March 1999, and the immediate opening of the airport and seaport in Bissau, and, in cooperation with all concerned, the withdrawal of all foreign troops in Guinea-Bissau and the simultaneous deployment of the interposition force of the Military Observer Group (ECOMOG) of the Economic Community of West African States (ECOWAS);

1233 (1999)

Reiterating the need to conduct general and presidential elections pursuant to the Abuja Agreement and in accordance with national constitutional requirements as soon as possible, and noting the expression by the parties of their firm interest in having elections held as soon as possible,

Encouragement or authorization of third-party actions

1233 (1999)

Welcoming the deployment of troops constituting the Interposition Force of the Military Observer Group of the Economic Community of West African States (ECOMOG) by States in the region to implement their peacekeeping mandate and the withdrawal of all foreign forces from Guinea-Bissau pursuant to the Abuja Agreement of 1 November 1998 (S/1998/1028, Annex),

Sovereignty and territorial integrity

1216 (1998)

Expressing its firm commitment to preserve the unity, sovereignty, political independence and territorial integrity of Guinea-Bissau,

HAITI

Concern, comments, acknowledgments

841 (1993)

Recognising the urgent need for an early, comprehensive and peaceful settlement of the crisis in Haiti in accordance with the provisions of the Charter of the United Nations and international law,

Deploring the fact that, despite the efforts of the international community, the legitimate Government of President Jean-Bertrand Aristide has not been reinstated,

Concerned that the persistence of this situation contributes to a climate of fear and persecution and economic dislocation which could increase the number of Haitians seeking refuse in neighbouring Member states and convinced that reversal of this situation is needed to prevent its negative repercussions on the region.

862 (1993)

Reaffirming the international community's commitment to a resolution of the crisis in Haiti, including a restoration of democracy.

867 (1993)

Concerned about the escalation of politically motivated violence in Haiti at this time of critical political transition, and recalling in this respect the statement of the President of the Security Council of 17 September 1993 (S/26460),

875 (1993)

Taking note of the letter of President Jean-Bertrand Aristide to the Secretary-General of 15 October 1993 (S/26587), in which he requested the Council to call on Member States to take the necessary measures to strengthen the provisions of Security Council resolution 873 (1993),

940 (1994)

Recalling the terms of the Governors Island Agreement (S/26063) and the related Pact of New York (S/26297),

Condemning the continuing disregard of those agreements by the illegal de facto regime, and the regime's refusal to cooperate with efforts by the United Nations and the Organization of American States (OAS) to bring about their implementation,

Gravely concerned by the significant further deterioration of the humanitarian situation in Haiti, in particular the continuing escalation by the illegal de facto regime of systematic violations of civil liberties, the desperate plight of Haitian refugees and the recent expulsion of the staff of the International Civilian Mission (MICIVIH), which was condemned in its Presidential statement of 12 July 1994 (S/PRST/1994/32),

Reaffirming that the goal of the international community remains the restoration of democracy in Haiti and the prompt return of the legitimately elected President, Jean-Bertrand Aristide, within the framework of the Governors Island Agreement,

948 (1994)

1. Welcomes with great satisfaction the return to Haiti of President Jean-Bertrand Aristide on 15 October 1994 and expresses its confidence that the people of Haiti can now begin to rebuild their country with dignity and consolidate democracy in a spirit of national reconciliation;

Condemnation

875 (1993)

Deeply disturbed by the continued obstruction to the dispatch of the United Nations Mission in Haiti (UNMIH), pursuant to resolution 867 (1993), and the failure of the Armed Forces of Haiti to carry out their responsibilities to allow the mission to begin its work,

Condemning the assassination of officials of the legitimate Government of President Jean-Bertrand Aristide,

917 (1994)

Strongly condemning the numerous instances of extra-judicial killings, arbitrary arrests, illegal detentions, abductions, rape and enforced disappearances, the continued denial of freedom of expression, and the impunity with which armed civilians have been able to operate and continue operating,

Resolutions calling for or demanding particular actions or outcomes

867 1993)

7. Notes that such safety and freedoms are a prerequisite for the successful implementation of the Mission, and requests the Secretary-General to report to the Council in the event such conditions do not exist;

8. Calls upon all factions in Haiti explicitly and publicly to renounce, and to direct their supporters to renounce violence as a means of political expression;

Sanctions

841 (1993)

Under Chapter VII imposes a trade embargo on petrol and arms consistent with that recommended by the OAS.

861 (1993)

[Having received the report of the Secretary General indicating that the Prime Minister of Haiti has been confirmed and has assumed office in Haiti, the UN suspends the sanctions.]

873 (1993)

Having received the report of the Secretary-General (S/26573) informing the Council that the military authorities of Haiti, including the police, have not complied in good faith with the Governors Island Agreement,

[The UN re-imposes the sanctions.]

Observer or peace-keeping forces

867 (1993)

1. Approves the recommendation of the Secretary-General contained in his report of 21 September 1993 (S/26480) and his report of 25 August 1993 (S/26352) to authorize the establishment and immediate dispatch of the United Nations Mission in Haiti (UNMIH) for a period of six months subject to the proviso that it will be extended beyond seventy-five days only upon a review by the Council to be based on a report from the Secretary-General on whether or not substantive progress has been made towards the implementation of the Governors Island Agreement and the political accords contained in the New York Pact;

940 (1994)

4. Acting under Chapter VII of the Charter of the United Nations, authorizes Member States to form a multinational force under unified command and control

Approves the establishment, upon adoption of this resolution, of an advance team of UNMIH of not more than sixty personnel, including a group of observers, to establish the appropriate means of coordination with the multinational force, to carry out the monitoring of the operations of the multinational force and other functions described in paragraph 23 of the report of the Secretary-General of 15 July 1994 (S/1994/828), and to assess requirements and to prepare for the deployment of UNMIH upon completion of the mission of the multinational force;

8. Decides that the multinational force will terminate its mission and UNMIH will assume the full range of its functions described in paragraph 9 below when a secure and stable environment has been established and UNMIH has adequate force capability and structure to assume the full range of its functions; the determination will be made by the Security Council, taking into account recommendations from the Member States of the multinational force, which are based on the assessment of the commander of the multinational force, and from the Secretary-General;

1123 (1996)

1. Affirms the importance of a professional, self-sustaining, fully functioning national police force of adequate size and structure, able to conduct the full spectrum of police functions, to the consolidation of democracy and the revitalization of Haiti's system of justice;

2. Decides further to paragraph 1 above, and at the request of the President of the Republic of Haiti, to establish the United Nations Transition Mission in Haiti (UNTMIH) with a mandate limited to a single four-month period ending on 30 November 1997 in order to assist the Government of Haiti by supporting and contributing to the professionalization of the Haitian National Police, as set out in paragraphs 32 to 39 of the Secretary-General's report of 19 July 1997;

3. Further decides that UNTMIH be composed of up to 250 civilian police, and 50 military personnel to form the headquarters of a security element;

Authorizations of use of force

940 (1994)

3. Determines that the illegal de facto regime in Haiti has failed to comply with the Governors Island Agreement and is in breach of its obligations under the relevant resolutions of the Security Council;

4. Acting under Chapter VII of the Charter of the United Nations, authorizes Member States to form a multinational force under unified command and con-

trol and, in this framework, to use all necessary means to facilitate the departure from Haiti of the military leadership, consistent with the Governors Island Agreement, the prompt return of the legitimately elected President and the restoration of the legitimate authorities of the Government of Haiti, and to establish and maintain a secure and stable environment that will permit implementation of the Governors Island Agreement,

Encouragement or authorization of third-party actions

841 (1993)

Strongly supportive of the continuing leadership by the Secretary General of the United Nations and the Secretary General of the Organization of American States and the efforts of the international community to reach a political solution to the crisis in Haiti,

867 (1993)

13. Expresses its appreciation for the constructive role of the Organization of American States in cooperation with the United Nations in promoting the solution of the political crisis and the restoration of democracy in Haiti and, in this context, stresses the importance of ensuring close coordination between the United Nations and the Organization of American States in their work in Haiti;

1048 (1996)

Underlining the importance of the peaceful transfer of power to the new democratically elected President of Haiti,

Welcoming and supporting the efforts of the Organization of American States to promote in cooperation with the United Nations consolidation of peace and democracy in Haiti,

Stressing the need to ensure that the Government of Haiti will be able to maintain the secure and stable environment established by the Multinational Force in Haiti (MNF) and maintained with the assistance of the United Nations,

Sovereignty and territorial integrity

1123 (1996)

Recognizing that the people of Haiti bear the ultimate responsibility for national reconciliation, the maintenance of a secure and stable environment, the administration of justice, and the reconstruction of their country,

Threats to international peace and security

841 (1993)

Also recalling the statement of 26 February 1993 (S/25344), in which the Council noted with concern the incidence of humanitarian crises, including mass displacements of population, becoming or aggravating threats to international peace and security,

Concerned that the persistence of this situation contributes to a climate of fear and persecution and economic dislocation which could increase the number of Haitians seeking refuge in neighbouring Member States and convinced that a reversal of this situation is needed to prevent its negative repercussions in the region,

Recalling, in this respect, the provisions of Chapter VIII of the Charter of the United Nations, and stressing the need for effective cooperation between regional organisations and the United Nations,

Determining that, in these unique and exceptional circumstances, the continuation of this situation threatens international peace and security in the region

873 (1993)

Having received the report of the Secretary-General (S/26573) informing the Council that the military authorities of Haiti, including the police, have not complied in good faith with the Governors Island Agreement,

Determining that their failure to fulfil obligations under the Agreement constitutes a threat to peace and security in the region,

Considering that the above-mentioned request of the Permanent Representative of Haiti, made within the context of the related actions previously taken by the Organisation of American States and by the General Assembly of the United Nations, defines a unique and exceptional situation warranting extraordinary measures by the Security Council in support of the efforts undertaken within the framework of the Organization of American States

IRELAND

No relevant Security Council resolutions.

ISRAEL AND PALESTINE

Concern, comments, acknowledgments

72 (1949)

2. Finds that the Armistice Agreements constitute an important step toward the establishment of permanent peace in Palestine and considers that these agreements supersede the truce provided for in Security Council resolutions 50 (1948) of 29 May and 54 (1948) of 15 July 1948;

468 (1980)

At the same meeting, the Council also decided, by a vote, that an invitation should be accorded to the representative of the Palestine Liberation Organization to participate in the debate

Deeply concerned at the expulsion by the Israeli military occupation authorities of the Mayors of Hebron and Halhoul and of the Sharia Judge of Hebron,

592 (1986)

Seriously concerned about the situation in the Palestinian and other Arab territories occupied by Israel since 1967, including Jerusalem,

2. Strongly deplores the opening of fire by the Israeli army resulting in the death and the wounding of defenceless students;

5. Also calls on all concerned parties to exercise maximum restraint, to avoid violent acts and to contribute towards the establishment of peace;

605 (1987)

Taking into account the need to consider measures for the impartial protection of the Palestinian civilian population under Israeli occupation,

Considering that the current policies and practices of Israel, the occupying Power, in the occupied territories are bound to have grave consequences for the endeavours to achieve comprehensive, just and lasting peace in the Middle East,

1. Strongly deplores those policies and practices of Israel, the occupying Power, which violate the human rights, of the Palestinian people in the occupied territories, and in particular the opening of fire by the Israeli army, resulting in the killing and wounding of defenceless Palestinian civilians;

1397 (2002)

Affirming a vision of a region where two States, Israel and Palestine, live side by side within secure and recognized borders,

Expressing its grave concern at the continuation of the tragic and violent events that have taken place since September 2000, especially the recent attacks and the increased number of casualties,

Stressing the need for all concerned to ensure the safety of civilians,

1402 (2002)

Expressing its grave concern at the further deterioration of the situation, including the recent suicide bombings in Israel and the military attack against the headquarters of the President of the Palestinian Authority,

1405 (2002)

Concerned by the dire humanitarian situation of the Palestinian civilian population, in particular reports from the Jenin refugee camp of an unknown number of deaths and destruction,

1435 (2002)

Reiterating its grave concern at the tragic and violent events that have taken place since September 2000 and the continuous deterioration of the situation,

Condemnation

1322 (2000)

2. Condemns acts of violence, especially the excessive use of force against Palestinians, resulting in injury and loss of human life;

Resolutions calling for or demanding particular actions or outcomes

43 (1948)

In the exercise of its primary responsibility for the maintenance of international peace and security,

1. Notes the increasing violence and disorder in Palestine and believes it is of the utmost urgency that an immediate truce be effected in Palestine;

2. Calls upon the Jewish Agency for Palestine and the Arab Higher Committee to make representatives available to the Security Council for the purpose of arranging a truce between the Arab and Jewish communities of Palestine; and emphasizes the heavy responsibility which would fall upon any party failing to observe such a truce;

3. Calls upon Arab and Jewish armed groups in Palestine to case acts of violence immediately.

46 (1948)

Considering that, as stated in that resolution, it is of the utmost urgency to bring about the immediate cessation of acts of violence in Palestine and to establish conditions of peace in that country,

Considering that the United Kingdom Government, so long as it remains the Mandatory Power, is responsible for the maintenance of peace and order in Palestine and should continue to take all steps necessary to that end,

1. Calls upon all persons and organisations in Palestine, and especially upon the Arab Higher Committee and the Jewish Agency, to take immediately, without prejudice to their rights, claims, or positions, and as a contribution to the well-being and permanent interests of Palestine, the following measures:

   (a) Cease all activities of a military or paramilitary nature, as well as acts of violence, terrorism and sabotage;

   (b) Refrain from bringing and from assisting and encouraging the entry into Palestine of armed bands and fighting personnel, groups and individuals, whatever their origin;

50 (1948)

Desiring to bring about a cessation of hostilities in Palestine without prejudice to the rights, claims and positions of either Arabs or Jews,

1. Call upon all Governments and authorities concerned to order a cessation of all acts of armed force for a period of four weeks;

2. Call upon all Governments and authorities concerned to undertake that they will not introduce fighting personnel into Palestine, Egypt, Iraq, Lebanon, Saudi Arabia, Syria, Transjordan and Yemen during the cease-fire;

4. Calls upon all Governments and authorities concerned to refrain from importing or exporting war material into or to Palestine, Egypt, Iraq, Lebanon, Saudi Arabia, Syria, Transjordan and Yemen during the cease-fire;

54 (1948)

Finds a threat to international peace and security:

2. Orders the Governments and authorities concerned, pursuant to Article 40 of the Charter, to desist from further military action and to this end to issue cease-fire orders to their military and paramilitary forces

3. Declares that failure by any of the Governments or authorities concerned to comply with the preceding paragraph of this resolution would demonstrate the existence of a breach of the peace within the meaning of Article 39 of the Charter requiring immediate consideration by the Security Council

5. Orders as a matter of special and urgent necessity an immediate and unconditional cease-fire in the City of Jerusalem to take effect twenty four hours from the time of the adoption of this resolution, and instructs the Truce Commission to take any necessary steps to make this cease-fire effective;

6. Instructs the Mediator to continue to bring about the demilitarisation of the City of Jerusalem, without prejudice to the future political status of Jerusalem, and to assure the protection of and access to the Holy Places, religious buildings and sites in Palestine

62 (1948)

1. Decides that, in order to eliminate the threat to the peace in Palestine and to facilitate the transition from the present truce to permanent peace in Palestine, an armistice shall be established in all sectors of Palestine;

2. Calls upon the parties directly involved in the conflict in Palestine, as a further provisional measure under Article 40 of the Charter, to seek agreement forthwith, by negotiations conducted either directly or through the Acting Mediator, with a view to the immediate establishment of the armistice,

66 (1948)

Having considered the report of the Acting Mediator on the hostilities which broke out in southern Palestine on 22 December 1948,

Calls upon the Governments concerned:

i) To order an immediate cease-fire

242 (1967)

Regarding Israel's withdrawal from the territories, the Sinai Peninsula, Gaza Strip, Golan Heights, West Bank, and East Jerusalem:

Emphasising the inadmissibility of the acquisition of territory by war and the need for a just and lasting peace in which every State in the area can live in security.

Affirms that the fulfilment of Charter principles requires the establishment of a just and lasting peace in the Middle East which should include the application of both the following principles

(i) Withdrawal of Israel armed forces from territories occupied in the recent conflict

(ii) Termination of all claims or state of belligerency and respect for and acknowledgement of the sovereignty, territorial integrity and political independence of every state in the area and their right to live in peace within secure and recognized boundaries free from threats or acts of force

338 (1973)

1. Calls upon all parties to the present fighting to cease all firing and terminate all military activity immediately, no later than 12 hours after the moment of the adoption of this decision, in the positions they now occupy.

3. Decides that, immediately and concurrently with the cease-fire, negotiations shall state between parties concerned under appropriate auspices aimed at establishing a just and durable peace in the Middle East.

446 (1979)

1. Determines that the policy and practices of Israel in establishing settlements in the Palestinian and other Arab territories occupied since 1967 have no legal validity and constitute a serious obstruction to achieving a comprehensive, just and lasting peace in the Middle East.

468 (1980)

1. Calls upon the Government of Israel, as the occupying Power, to rescind these illegal measures and to facilitate the immediate return of the expelled Palestinian leaders so that they can resume the functions for which they were elected and appointed;

1322 (2000)

4. Calls for the immediate cessation of violence, and for all necessary steps to be taken to ensure that violence ceases, that new provocative actions are avoided and that the situation returns to normality in a way which promotes the prospects for the Middle East process;

1397 (2002)

1. Demands immediate cessation of all acts of violence, including all acts of terror, provocation, incitement and destruction;

2. Calls upon the Israeli and Palestinian sides and their leaders to cooperate in the implementation of the Tenet work plan and Mitchell Report recommendations with the aim of resuming negotiations on a political settlement;

1402 (2002)

1. Calls upon both parties to move immediately to a meaningful ceasefire; calls for the withdrawal of Israeli troops from Palestinian cities, including Ramallah; and calls upon the parties to cooperate fully with Special Envoy Zinni, and others, to implement the Tenet security work plan as a first step towards implementation of the Mitchell Committee recommendations, with the aim of resuming negotiations on a political settlement;

2. Reiterates its demand in resolution 1397 (2002) of 12 March 2002 for an immediate cessation of all acts of violence, including all acts of terror, provocation, incitement and destruction;

1435 (2002)

1. Reiterates its demand for the complete cessation of all acts of violence, including all acts of terror, provocation, incitement and destruction;

2. Demands that Israel immediately cease measures in and around Ramallah including the destruction of Palestinian civilian and security infrastructure;

3. Demands also the expeditious withdrawal of the Israeli occupying forces from Palestinian cities towards the return to the positions held prior to September 2000;

Observer or Peacekeeping forces

48 (1948)

Establishes a Truce Commission for Palestine composed of representatives of those members of the Security Council which have career consular officers in Jerusalem, noting, however, that the representative of Syria has indicated that his Government is not prepared to serve on the Commission. The function of the Commission shall be to assist the Security Council in supervising the implementation by parties of resolution 46 (1948).

50 (1948)

6. Instructs the United Nations Mediator in Palestine, in concert with the Truce Commission, to supervise the observance of the above provisions, and decides that they shall be provided with a sufficient number of military observers;

Encouragement or authorization of third-party actions

1397 (2002)

3. Expresses support for the efforts of the Secretary-General and others to assist the parties to halt the violence and to resume the peace process;

Applicability of humanitarian laws of war

56 (1948)

2. Decides pursuant to resolution 54 (1948), and so informs the Governments and authorities concerned, that:

(a) Each party is responsible for the actions of both regular and irregular forces operating under its authority or in territory under its control;

(b) Each party has the obligation to use all means at its disposal to prevent action violating the truce by individuals or groups who are subject to its authority

(e) No party is entitled to gain military or political advantage through violation of the truce.

446 (1979)

Affirming once more that the Geneva Conventions relative to the Protection of Civilian Persons in Time of War, of 12 August 1949, is applicable to the Arab territories occupied by Israel since 1967, including Jerusalem,

1. Determines that the policy and practices of Israel in establishing settlements in the Palestinian and other Arab territories occupied since 1967 have no legal validity and constitute a serious obstruction to achieving a comprehensive, just and lasting peace in the Middle East,

452 (1979)

Considering that the policy of Israel in establishing settlements in the occupied Arab territories has no legal validity and constitutes a violation of the Geneva Convention relative to the Protection of Civilian Persons in Time of War, of 12 August 1949,

1. Call upon the Government and people of Israel to cease, on an urgent basis, the establishment, construction and planning of settlements in the Arab territories since 1967, including Jerusalem;

1397 (2002)

Stressing also the need to respect the universally accepted norms of international humanitarian law,

1405 (2002)

Calling for the lifting of restrictions imposed, in particular in Jenin, on the operations of humanitarian organizations, including the International Committee of the Red Cross and United Nations Relief and Works Agency for Palestine Refugees in the Near East,

Stressing the need for all concerned to ensure the safety of civilians, and to respect the universally accepted norms of international humanitarian law,

1. Emphasizes the urgency of access of medical and humanitarian organizations to the Palestinian civilian population;

Threats to international peace and security

50 (1948)

11. Decides that if the present resolution is rejected by either party or by both, or if, having been accepted, it is subsequently repudiated or violated, the situation in Palestine will be considered with a view to action under Chapter VII of the Charter of the United Nations;

54 (1948)

Taking into consideration that the Provisional Government of Israel has indicated its acceptance in principle of a prolongation of the truce in Palestine, that the States members of the Arab League have rejected successive appeals of the United Nations Mediator, and of the Security Council in its resolution 53 (1948) of 7 July 1948, for the prolongation of the truce in Palestine; and that there has consequently developed a renewal of hostilities in Palestine,

1. Determines that the situation in Palestine constitutes a threat to the peace within the meaning of Article 39 of the Charter of the United Nations,

LEBANON

Concern, comments, acknowledgments

436 (1978)

Noting with grave concern the deteriorating situation in Beirut and its surroundings,

Deeply grieved at the consequent loss of life, human suffering and physical destruction,

490 (1981)

Reaffirming the urgent appeal made by the President and the members of the Security Council on 17 July 1981, which reads as follows:

'The President of the Security Council and the members of the Council, after hearing the report of the Secretary-General, express their deep concern at the extent of the loss of life and the scale of the destruction caused by the deplorable events that have been taking place for several days in Lebanon.'

'They launch an urgent appeal for an immediate end to all armed attacks and the greatest restraint so that peace and quiet may be established in Lebanon and a just and lasting peace in the Middle East as a whole.'

512 (1982)

Deeply concerned at the sufferings of the Lebanese and Palestinian civilian populations,

513 (1982)

Alarmed by the continued sufferings of the Lebanese and Palestinian civilian populations in southern Lebanon and in West Beirut.

542 (1983)

Having considered the situation prevailing in Northern Lebanon,

Deeply concerned by the intensification of the fighting, which continues to cause great suffering and loss of human life,

1. Deplores the loss of human life caused by the events taking place in Northern Lebanon;

Condemnation

520 (1982)

Condemning the murder of Bashir Gemayel, the constitutionally elected President-elect of Lebanon, and every effort to disrupt by violence the restoration of a strong, stable government in Lebanon,

521 (1982)

Appalled at the massacre of Palestinian civilians in Beirut,

Noting that the Government of Lebanon has agreed to the dispatch of United Nations observers to the sites of greatest human suffering and losses in and around the city,

1. Condemns the criminal massacre of Palestinian civilians in Beirut,

Resolutions calling for or demanding particular actions or outcomes

436 (1978)

1. Calls upon all those involved in hostilities in Lebanon to put an end to acts of violence and observe scrupulously an immediate and effective cease-fire and cessation of hostilities so that internal peace and national reconciliation may be restored based on the preservation of Lebanese unity, territorial integrity, independence and national sovereignty;

490 (1981)

1. Calls for an immediate cessation of all armed attacks

512 (1982)

1. Calls upon all the parties to the conflict to respect the rights of the civilian populations, to refrain from all acts of violence against those populations and to

take all appropriate measures to alleviate the suffering caused by the conflict, in particular, by facilitating the dispatch and distribution of aid provided by United Nations agencies and by non-governmental organizations

513 (1982)

Referring to the humanitarian principles of the Geneva Conventions of 1949 and to the obligations arising from the regulations annexed to The Hague Conventions of 1907.

Reaffirming its resolutions 508 (1982), 509 (1982) and 512 (1982)

1. Calls for respect for the rights of the civilian populations without any discrimination and repudiates all acts of violence against those populations;

2. Calls further for the restoration of the normal supply of vital facilities such as water, electricity, food and medical provisions, particularly in Beirut;

520 (1982)

Taking note of the determination of Lebanon to ensure the withdrawal of all non-Lebanese forces from Lebanon,

5. Reaffirms its resolutions 512 (1982) and 513 (1982), which call for respect for the rights of the civilian population without any discrimination, and repudiates all acts of violence against those populations,

542 (1983)

Having considered the situation prevailing in Northern Lebanon,

3. Requests the parties concerned immediately to accept a cease-fire and scrupulously to observe the cessation of hostilities;

4. Invites the parties concerned to settle their differences exclusively by peaceful means and to refrain from the threat or use of force;

Observer or peace-keeping forces

128 (1958)

Having heard the charges of the representative of Lebanon concerning interference by the United Arab Republic in the internal affairs of Lebanon and the reply to the representatives of the United Arab Republic,

1. Decides to dispatch urgently an observation group to proceed to Lebanon so as to ensure that there is no illegal infiltration of personnel or supply of arms or other material across the Lebanese borders.

425 (1978)

Gravely concerned at the deterioration of the situation in the Middle East and its consequences for the maintenance of international peace

3. Decides, in the light of the request of the Government of Lebanon, to establish immediately under its authority a United Nations interim force for Southern

Lebanon for the purpose of confirming the withdrawal of Israeli forces, restoring international peace and security and assisting the Government of Lebanon in ensuring the return of its effective authority in the area,

521 (1982)

2. Requests the Secretary-General, in consultation with the Government of Lebanon, to ensure the rapid deployment of those observers in order that they may contribute in every way possible within their mandate to the effort to ensure full protection for the civilian populations;

523 (1982)

3. Authorizes the Force during that period to carry out, with the consent of the Government of Lebanon, interim tasks in the humanitarian and administrative fields, as indicated in resolutions 511 (1982) and 519 (1982), and to assist the Government of Lebanon in ensuring the security of all the inhabitants of the area without any discrimination;

Sovereignty and territorial integrity

490 (1981)

2. Reaffirms its commitment to the sovereignty, territorial integrity and the independence of Lebanon within its internationally recognized boundaries,

IRAQ KURDS 1991

Condemnation

688 (1991)

1. Condemns the repression of the Iraqi civilian population in many parts of Iraq, including most recently in Kurdish populated areas, the consequences of which threaten international peace and security in the region.

Resolutions calling for or demanding particular actions or outcomes

688 (1991)

Demands that Iraq as a contribution to removing the threat to international peace and security in the region immediately end this repression

Sovereignty and territorial integrity

688 (1991)

Reaffirming the commitment of all Member States to respect the sovereign, territorial integrity and political independence of Iraq

Threats to international peace and security

688 (1991)

Gravely concerned by the repression of the Iraqi civilian population in many parts of Iraq, including most recently in Kurdish-populated areas, which led to a massive flow of refugees towards and across international frontiers and to cross-border incursions, which threaten international peace and security in the region

LIBERIA

Concern, comments, acknowledgments

856 (1993)

Welcoming the signing under the auspices of ECOWAS, on 25 July 1993, at Cotonou, Benin, of a Peace Agreement

Considering that the signing of the Peace Agreement constitutes a major achievement and an important contribution to the restoration of peace and security in Liberia and in this region of West Africa, and creates the opportunity to bring an end to the conflict,

911 (1994)

Expressing its concern over renewed fighting between the Liberian parties and the negative impact that this fighting has had on the disarmament process, the effort to provide humanitarian relief, and the plight of displaced persons,

972 (1995)

Deeply concerned that the humanitarian situation in Liberia has worsened due to the lack of security in the country and the resulting inability of national and international relief organizations to function effectively,

3. Expresses deep concern at the failure of the Liberian parties so far to reach agreement on the composition of the Council of State as stipulated in the Accra Agreement at the recent talks in Accra and calls upon them to work together to implement the Accra Agreement by upholding the cease-fire, resuming disarmament and demobilization of combatants and implementing the other relevant aspects of the agreement in accordance with the timetable, including the prompt installation of the New Council of State;

1001 (1995)

Emphasizing that the people of Liberia bear the ultimate responsibility for achieving peace and national reconciliation, Noting that a further concerted and harmonized effort by all concerned, including the ECOWAS States, would be helpful to advance the peace process,

Concerned that the Liberian parties have so far failed to install the Council of State, re-establish an effective cease-fire and take concrete steps towards the implementation of the other provisions of the Accra Agreement,

Deeply concerned also at the continuing inter- and intra-factional fighting in parts of Liberia, which has further worsened the plight of the civilian population, particularly in rural areas, as well as affected the ability of humanitarian agencies to provide relief,

Expressing great concern over the continued flow of arms into Liberia in violation of Security Council resolution 788 (1992),

2. Stresses that continued international community support for the peace process in Liberia, including the continued presence of UNOMIL, is contingent on immediate actions by the Liberian parties to peacefully resolve their differences and achieve national reconciliation;

1020 (1995)

9. Reiterates that continued support by the international community for the peace process in Liberia is contingent on the continued commitment by the Liberian parties to achieve national reconciliation in line with the peace process;

Concerned that the Liberian parties have so far failed to install the Council of State, re-establish an effective cease-fire and take concrete steps towards the implementation of the other provisions of the Accra Agreement,

1497 (2003)

Deeply concerned over the conflict in Liberia and its effects on the humanitarian situation, including the tragic loss of countless innocent lives, in that country, and its destabilizing effect on the region,

Condemnation

788 (1992)

3. Condemns the violation of the cease-fire of 28 November 1990 by any party to the conflict.

4. Condemns the continuing armed attacks against the peace-keeping forces of ECOWAS in Liberia by one of the parties to the conflict;

1041 (1995)

4. Condemns the recent armed attacks against personnel of ECOMOG and against civilians, and demands that such hostile acts cease forthwith;

Resolutions calling for or demanding particular actions or outcomes

788 (1992)

6. Calls upon all parties to the conflict to respect and implement the cease-fire and the various accords of the peace process.

856 (1993)

4. Calls upon all parties to the conflict to respect and implement the cease-fire provided for the Peace Agreement and to cooperate fully with the advance mission and ensure the safety to all United Nations personnel and all other peace-keeping and humanitarian personnel within Liberia,

911 (1994)

5. Urges all Liberian parties to cease hostilities immediately and to cooperate with ECOMOG forces to complete the disarmament process expeditiously;

1020 (1995)

5. Calls upon all the Liberian parties to respect and implement fully and expeditiously all the agreements and commitments they have entered into, in particular with regard to the maintenance of the cease-fire, disarmament and demobilization of combatants, and national reconciliation, taking into account that the restoration of peace and democracy in Liberia is primarily the responsibility of those parties which signed the Abuja Agreement on 19 August 1995 (S/1995/742)

1116 (1997)

2. Calls upon the Liberian parties to implement fully all the agreements and commitments they have entered into, and urges all Liberians to participate peacefully in the electoral process;

1478 (2003)

Deeply concerned by the deteriorating humanitarian situation and widespread human rights violations in Liberia, and by the serious instability in Liberia and neighbouring countries, including Côte d'Ivoire,

Determining that the active support provided by the Government of Liberia to armed rebel groups in the region, including to rebels in Côte d'Ivoire and former Revolutionary United Front (RUF) combatants who continue to destabilize the region, constitutes a threat to international peace and security in the region,

Acting under Chapter VII of the Charter of the United Nations,

4. Calls upon all States in the region, particularly the Government of Liberia, to participate actively in all regional peace initiatives, particularly those of ECOWAS, the International Contact Group, the Mano River Union and the Rabat Process, and expresses its strong support for these initiatives;

5. Calls upon the Government of Liberia and the LURD to enter without delay into bilateral ceasefire negotiations under the auspices of ECOWAS and the mediation of former President Abubakar of Nigeria;

1497 (2003)

12. Stresses the urgent need for all Liberian parties who are signatories to the 17 June ceasefire agreement, in particular the LURD and MODEL leadership, immediately and scrupulously to uphold the 17 June ceasefire agreement, to cease using violent means and to agree as soon as possible to an all-inclusive political framework for a transitional government until such a time when free and fair elections can be held and notes that critical to this endeavour is the fulfilment of the commitment to depart from Liberia made by President Charles Taylor;

13. Urges the LURD and MODEL to refrain from any attempt to seize power by force, bearing in mind the position of the African Union on unconstitutional changes of government as stated in the 1999 Algiers Decision and the 2000 Lomé Declaration;

Sanctions

788 (1992)

8. Decides under Chapter VII of the Charter of the United Nations that all States shall, for the purpose of establishing peace and stability in Liberia, immediately implement a general and complete embargo on all deliveries of weapons and military equipment to Liberia

1343 (2001)

Acting under Chapter VII of the Charter of the United Nations,

Noting that the conflict in Liberia has been resolved, that national elections have taken place within the framework of the Yamoussoukro IV Agreement of 30 October 1991 (S/24815, Annex) and that the Final Communiqué of the informal consultative group meeting of ECOWAS Committee of Five on Liberia issued in Geneva on 7 April 1992 (S/23863) has been implemented, and determining therefore that the embargo imposed by paragraph 8 of resolution 788 (1992) should be terminated,

1. Decides to terminate the prohibitions imposed by paragraph 8 of resolution 788 (1992) and to dissolve the Committee established under resolution 985 (1995);

2. Demands that the Government of Liberia immediately cease its support for the RUF in Sierra Leone

5. (a) Decides that all States shall take the necessary measures to prevent the sale or supply to Liberia, by their nationals or from their territories or using their flag vessels or aircraft, of arms and related materiel of all types, including weapons and ammunition, military vehicles and equipment, paramilitary equipment and spare parts for the aforementioned, whether or not originating in their territories;

(b) Decides that all States shall take the necessary measures to prevent any provision to Liberia by their nationals or from their territories of technical training or assistance related to the provision, manufacture, maintenance or use of the items in subparagraph (a) above;

(c) Decides that the measures imposed by subparagraphs (a) and (b) above shall not apply to supplies of non-lethal military equipment intended solely for humanitarian or protective use, and related technical assistance or training, as approved in advance by the Committee established by paragraph 14 below;

(d) Affirms that the measures imposed by subparagraph (a) above do not apply to protective clothing, including flak jackets and military helmets, temporarily exported to Liberia by United Nations personnel, representatives of the media and humanitarian and development workers and associated personnel, for their personal use only;

6. Decides further that all States shall take the necessary measures to prevent the direct or indirect import of all rough diamonds from Liberia, whether or not such diamonds originated in Liberia;

1478 (2003)

Acting under Chapter VII of the Charter of the United Nations,

1. Decides that the Government of Liberia has not complied fully with the demands in resolution 1343 (2001);

3. Stresses that the demands referred to in paragraph 1 above are intended to help consolidate and assure peace and stability in Sierra Leone and to build and strengthen peaceful relations among the countries of the region;

5. Calls upon the Government of Liberia and the LURD to enter without delay into bilateral ceasefire negotiations under the auspices of ECOWAS and the mediation of former President Abubakar of Nigeria;

8. Calls upon the Government of Liberia and all parties, particularly the LURD and other armed rebel groups, to ensure unimpeded and safe movement for the personnel of United Nations humanitarian agencies and non-governmental organizations, to end the use of child soldiers and to prevent sexual violence and torture;

10. Decides that the measures imposed by paragraphs 5 to 7 of resolution 1343 (2001) shall remain in force for a further period of 12 months

17. Decides that

(a) all States shall take the necessary measures to prevent, for a period of 10 months, the import into their territories of all round logs and timber products originating in Liberia;

Observer or peace-keeping forces

788 (1992)

Noting the request of 29 July 1992 from ECOWAS for the United Nations to dispatch an observer group to Liberia to very and monitor the electoral process,

Taking note of the invitation of ECOWAS of 20 October 1992, in Cotonou, Benin, for the Secretary-General to consider, if necessary, the dispatch of a group to observe the encampment and disarmament of the warring parties,

Convinced that it is vital to find a peaceful, just and lasting solution to the conflict in Liberia,

866 (1993)

Recognizing that United Nations involvement would contribute significantly to the effective implementation of the Peace Agreement and would serve to underline the international community's commitment to conflict resolution in Liberia,

2. Decides to establish UNOMIL under its authority and under the direction of the Secretary-General

3. Decides that UNOMIL shall comprise military observers as well as medical, engineering, communications, transportation and electoral components, in the

numbers indicated in the Secretary General's report, together with minimal staff necessary to support it, and shall have the following mandate:

(a) To receive and investigate all reports on alleged incidents of violations of the cease-fire agreement

(b) To monitor compliance with other elements of the Peace Agreement, including at points on Liberia's borders with Sierra Leone and other neighbouring countries, and to verify its impartial application, and in particular to assist in the monitoring of compliance with the embargo on delivery of arms and military equipment to Liberia and the cantonment, disarmament and demobilization of combatants;

(c) To observe and verify the election process,

(f) To report on any major violations of international humanitarian law to the Secretary-General;

1116 (1997)

Emphasizing that the holding of free and fair elections is an essential stage of Liberia's peace process and that the United Nations Observer Mission in Liberia (UNOMIL) is mandated to observe and verify the election process, including the legislative and presidential elections, as stated in resolution 866 (1993) of 23 September 1993

1497 (2003)

Acting under Chapter VII of the Charter of the United Nations,

1. Authorizes Member States to establish a Multinational Force in Liberia to support the implementation of the 17 June 2003 ceasefire agreement, including establishing conditions for initial stages of disarmament, demobilization and reintegration activities, to help establish and maintain security in the period after the departure of the current President and the installation of a successor authority, taking into account the agreements to be reached by the Liberian parties, and to secure the environment for the delivery of humanitarian assistance, and to prepare for the introduction of a longer-term United Nations stabilization force to relieve the Multinational Force;

2. Declares its readiness to establish such a follow-on United Nations stabilization force to support the transitional government and to assist in the implementation of a comprehensive peace agreement for Liberia and requests the Secretary-General to submit to the Council recommendations for the size, structure, and mandate of this force, preferably by 15 August 2003, and subsequent deployment of the United Nations force no later than 1 October 2003;

3. Authorizes UNAMSIL to extend the necessary logistical support, for a limited period of up to 30 days, to the forward ECOWAS elements of the Multinational Force, without prejudicing UNAMSIL's operational capability with respect to its mandate in Sierra Leone;

4. Requests the Secretary-General, pending a decision by the Security Council on the establishment of a United Nations peacekeeping operation in Liberia, to take the necessary steps, including the necessary logistical support to the ECOWAS elements of the Multinational Force, and pre-positioning critical logistical and personnel requirements to facilitate the rapid deployment of the envisaged operation;

5. Authorizes the Member States participating in the Multinational Force in Liberia to take all necessary measures to fulfil its mandate;

11. Further calls on all Liberian parties and Member States to cooperate fully with the Multinational Force in Liberia in the execution of its mandate and to respect the security and freedom of movement of the Multinational Force, as well as to ensure the safe and unimpeded access of international humanitarian personnel to populations in need in Liberia;

Encouragement or authorization of third-party actions

788 (1992)

Welcoming the continued commitment of the Economic Community of West African States (ECOWAS) to and the efforts towards a peaceful resolution of the Liberian conflict,

Further welcoming the endorsement and support by the Organization of African Unity of these efforts,

1. Commends ECOWAS for its efforts to restore peace, security and stability in Liberia

972 (1995)

Commending also those African States that have contributed troops to the ECOWAS Monitoring Group (ECOMOG), and those Member States that have provided assistance in support of the peace negotiations and the peace-keeping forces, including contributions to the Trust Fund for Liberia,

Applicability of humanitarian laws of war

788 (1992)

5. Calls upon all parties to the conflict and all others concerned to respect strictly the provisions of international humanitarian Law;

1001 (1995)

Calling on the Liberian factions, especially the combatants, to respect the human rights of the civilian population and to respect international humanitarian law,

Sovereignty and territorial integrity

1001 (1995)

Emphasizing that the people of Liberia bear the ultimate responsibility for achieving peace and national reconciliation,

1116 (1997)

Reiterating that the people of Liberia and their leaders bear the ultimate responsibility for achieving peace and national reconciliation,

Threats to international peace and security

788 (1992)

Determining that the deterioration of the situation in Liberia constitutes a threat to international peace and security, particularly in West Africa as a whole,

2. Reaffirms its belief that the Yamoussoukro IV accord offers the best possible framework for a peaceful resolution of the Liberian conflict by creating the necessary conditions for free and fair elections in Liberia, and calls upon ECOWAS to continue its efforts to assist in the peaceful implementation of this Accord;

Regretting that parties to the conflict in Liberia have not respected or implemented the various accords to date.

8. Decides, under Chapter VII of the Charter of the United Nations, [. . .]

1497 (2003)

Deeply concerned over the conflict in Liberia and its effects on the humanitarian situation, including the tragic loss of countless innocent lives, in that country, and its destabilizing effect on the region,

Determining that the situation in Liberia constitutes a threat to international peace and security, to stability in the West Africa subregion, and to the peace process for Liberia,

THE FORMER YUGOSLAV REPUBLIC OF MACEDONIA

Concern, comments, acknowledgments

S/PRST/2001/7

The Security Council expresses its deep concern at those events, which constitute a threat to the stability and security not only of the former Yugoslav Republic of Macedonia but also of the entire region. It calls on all political leaders in the former Yugoslav Republic of Macedonia and Kosovo, Federal Republic of Yugoslavia, who are in a position to do so to isolate the forces behind the violent incidents and to shoulder their responsibility for peace and stability in the region.

The Security Council underlines the responsibility of the Government of the former Yugoslav Republic of Macedonia for the rule of law in its territory. It supports actions by the Government of the former Yugoslav Republic of Macedonia to address the violence with an appropriate level of restraint and to preserve the political stability of the country and foster harmony between all ethnic components of the population.

1345 (2001)

Also welcoming the plan put forward by the Government of the Federal Republic of Yugoslavia to resolve peacefully the crisis in certain municipalities in southern Serbia, and expressing encouragement for the implementation of political and economic reforms designed to reintegrate the ethnic Albanian population as full members of civil society,

1345 (2001)

5. Supports the Government of the former Yugoslav Republic of Macedonia and the Federal Republic of Yugoslavia in their efforts to end the violence in a manner consistent with the rule of law;

6. Underlines the need for all differences to be resolved by dialogue among all legitimate parties;

7. Further underlines the requirement for all parties to act with restraint and full respect for international humanitarian law and human rights;

8. Welcomes the efforts of the Government of Albania to promote peace in the region and isolate extremists working against peace, and encourages it and all States to take all possible concrete steps to prevent support for extremists, taking also into account resolution 1160 (1998);

1371 (2001)

Welcoming the steps taken by the Government of The former Yugoslav Republic of Macedonia to consolidate a multi-ethnic society within its borders, and expressing its full support for the further development of this process,

Welcoming international efforts, including those of the Organization for Security and Cooperation in Europe, the European Union and the North Atlantic Treaty Organization, in cooperation with the Government of The former Yugoslav Republic of Macedonia, and other States, to prevent the escalation of ethnic tensions in the area and to facilitate the full implementation of the Framework Agreement, thus contributing to peace and stability in the region,

Condemnation

S/PRST/2001/7

The Security Council strongly condemns recent violence by ethnic Albanian armed extremists in the north of the former Yugoslav Republic of Macedonia, in particular the killing of three soldiers of the armed forces of the former Yugoslav Republic of Macedonia in the area of Tanusevci. The Council regrets that the violence continues and calls for an immediate end to it.

1345 (2001)

1. Strongly condemns extremist violence, including terrorist activities, in certain parts of the former Yugoslav Republic of Macedonia and certain municipalities

in southern Serbia, Federal Republic of Yugoslavia, and notes that such violence has support from ethnic Albanian extremists outside these areas and constitutes a threat to the security and stability of the wider region;

Resolutions calling for or demanding particular actions or outcomes

1345 (2001)

3. Reiterates its strong support for the full implementation of resolution 1244 (1999);

4. Demands that all those who are currently engaged in armed action against the authorities of those States immediately cease all such actions, lay down their weapons and return to their homes;

9. Calls on Kosovo Albanian political leaders, and leaders of the ethnic Albanian communities in the former Yugoslav Republic of Macedonia, southern Serbia and elsewhere, publicly to condemn violence and ethnic intolerance and to use their influence to secure peace, and calls on all those who have contact with the extremist armed groups to make clear that they have no support from any quarter in the international community;

10. Welcomes the efforts of KFOR to implement resolution 1244 (1999) in cooperation with the authorities of the former Yugoslav Republic of Macedonia and the Federal Republic of Yugoslavia, and calls on KFOR to continue further to strengthen its efforts to prevent unauthorized movement and illegal arms shipments across borders and boundaries in the region, to confiscate weapons within Kosovo, Federal Republic of Yugoslavia, and to continue to keep the Council informed in accordance with resolution 1160 (1998);

1371 (2001)

2. Calls for the full implementation of resolution 1345 (2001);

3. Supports the full and timely implementation of the Framework Agreement, rejects the use of violence in pursuit of political aims and stresses that only peaceful political solutions can assure a stable and democratic future for The former Yugoslav Republic of Macedonia;

Encouragement or authorization of third-party actions

S/PRST/2001/7

The Security Council welcomes the steps taken by the international security presence (KFOR) to control the border between Kosovo, Federal Republic of Yugoslavia and the former Yugoslav Republic of Macedonia in accordance with the military-technical agreement signed in Kumanovo on 9 June 1999. It welcomes the ongoing dialogue between the Government of the former Yugoslav Republic of Macedonia and KFOR on practical steps to address the immediate security situation and to prevent crossing of the border by extremists as well as possible violations of resolution 1160 (1998) of 31 March 1998. It welcomes the efforts of all relevant international organizations in cooperation with the Government of the former Yugoslav Republic of Macedonia to promote stability and to create conditions for a return of the inhabitants to their homes.

1345 (2001)

Further welcoming the contribution of the European Union to a peaceful solution to the problems in certain municipalities in southern Serbia, its decision substantially to increase the presence of the European Union Monitoring Mission there on the basis of its existing mandate, and its wider contribution to the region,

Welcoming the cooperation between the North Atlantic Treaty Organization and the authorities of the former Yugoslav Republic of Macedonia and the Federal Republic of Yugoslavia in addressing the security problems in parts of the former Yugoslav Republic of Macedonia and certain municipalities in southern Serbia,

1371 (2001)

4. Welcomes the efforts of the European Union and the Organization for Security and Cooperation in Europe to contribute to the implementation of the Framework Agreement, in particular through the presence of international observers;

5. Endorses the efforts of Member States and relevant international organizations to support the implementation of the Framework Agreement and strongly supports in that regard the establishment of a multinational security presence in The former Yugoslav Republic of Macedonia at the request of its Government to contribute towards the security of the observers, and invites the Government of The former Yugoslav Republic of Macedonia to keep the Council informed;

Sovereignty and territorial integrity

S/PRST/2001/7

The Security Council recalls the need to respect the sovereignty and territorial integrity of the former Yugoslav Republic of Macedonia. In this context it emphasizes that the border demarcation agreement, signed in Skopje on 23 February 2001, and ratified by the Parliament of the former Yugoslav Republic of Macedonia on 1 March 2001, must be respected by all.

1345 (2001)

2. Reaffirms its commitment to the sovereignty and territorial integrity of the Federal Republic of Yugoslavia, the former Yugoslav Republic of Macedonia and the other States of the region, as set out in the Helsinki Final Act;

1371 (2001)

1. Reaffirms its commitment to the sovereignty and territorial integrity of The former Yugoslav Republic of Macedonia and other States of the region;

Threats to international peace and security

1345 (2001)

1. Strongly condemns extremist violence, including terrorist activities, in certain parts of the former Yugoslav Republic of Macedonia and certain municipalities in southern Serbia, Federal Republic of Yugoslavia, and notes that such violence has support from ethnic Albanian extremists outside these areas and constitutes a threat to the security and stability of the wider region;

MOZAMBIQUE

Concern, comments, acknowledgments

782 (1992)

Welcoming the signature, on 4 October 1992 in Rome, of a General Peace Agreement between the Government of Mozambique and the Resistencia Nacional Mocambicana (RENAMO)

Considering that the signature of the Agreement constitutes an important contribution to the restoration of peace and security in the region,

916 (1994)

Reiterating the importance it attaches to the General Peace Agreement for Mozambique (S/24635, Annex), and the timely fulfilment in good faith by all parties of their obligations under the Agreement,

6. Welcomes the announcement by the President of Mozambique on 11 April 1994 that elections will take place on 27 and 28 October 1994, the inauguration of the National Elections Commission and the establishment of its provincial offices throughout the country; and reiterates the importance it attaches to the elections taking place on these dates with electoral registration commencing on 1 June 1994;

8. Expresses its concern, however, at continuing delays in the implementation of major aspects of the General Peace Agreement, in particular assembly and demobilization of troops, militia and paramilitary forces, and the formation of the new Mozambican Defence Force in accordance with the revised timetable and in line with paragraph 10 of resolution 882 (1993) of 5 November 1993, and calls upon the parties to comply fully with all the provisions of the General Peace Agreement;

957 (1994)

1. Welcomes the elections that took place in Mozambique on 27, 28 and 29 October 1994 in accordance with the General Peace Agreement;

960 (1994)

1. Welcomes the elections that took place in Mozambique on 27, 28 and 29 October 1994 in accordance with the General Peace Agreement;

2. Welcomes also the statement of the Special Representative of the Secretary-General of 19 November 1994 (SG/SM/5488) on the results of the elections, declaring them free and fair;

3. Endorses the results of these elections;

Resolutions calling for or demanding particular actions or outcomes

797 (1992)

4. Calls upon the Government of Mozambique and the resistencia Nacional Mocambicana to cooperate fully with the interim Special Representative of the Secretary-General and with the United Nations Operation in Mozambique and to respect scrupulously the cease-fire and all the commitments entered into under the Agreement.

898 (1994)

10. Notes the recent acceleration in the assembly of the troops of the Government of Mozambique, and calls upon the Government to redouble its efforts to achieve balance between the parties in the cantonment of troops and an expeditious and timely conclusion of this process as called for in the revised timetable;

11. Underlines the need for the troops of the Government of Mozambique and RENAMO to hand over all weapons to the United Nations at the assembly areas and for the parties to come to an immediate agreement on the transfer of all weapons to regional depots so as to ensure security in the assembly areas;

12. Reiterates the vital importance it attaches to the holding of general elections no later than October 1994 and to the early commencement of electoral registration and other electoral preparations, and urges the parties to agree promptly on a specific election date;

957 (1994)

2. Reiterates its intention to endorse the results of the elections should the United Nations declare them free and fair and calls upon all Mozambican parties to accept and fully abide by the results of the elections;

3. Also calls upon all Mozambican parties to complete the process of national reconciliation based, as provided for in the General Peace Agreement, on a system of multi-party democracy and the observance of democratic principles which will ensure lasting peace and political stability;

960 (1994)

4. Calls upon all Mozambican parties to stand by their obligation to accept and fully abide by the results of the elections;

Observer or peace-keeping forces

782 (1992)

1. Approves the appointment by the Secretary-General of an interim Special Representative, and the despatch to Mozambique of a team of up to 25 military observers

797 (1992)

2. Decides to establish a United Nations Operation in Mozambique as proposed by the Secretary-General and in line with the General Peace Agreement for Mozambique,

Encouragement or authorization of third-party actions

916 (1994)

Commending also the role played by the Organization of African Unity (OAU) Emphasizing the need for the fullest possible cooperation by the Government of Mozambique and RENAMO with ONUMOZ, including with its police component,

NICARAGUA

Concern, comments, acknowledgments

530 (1983)

Deeply concerned, on the one hand, at the situation prevailing on and inside the northern border of Nicaragua and, on the other hand, at the consequent danger of a military confrontation between Honduras and Nicaragua, which could further aggravate the existing critical situation in Central America,

1. Reaffirms the right of Nicaragua and of all the other countries of the area to live in peace and security, free from outside interference;

562 (1985)

2. Reaffirms once again its firm support to the Contadora Group and urges it to intensify its efforts; it also expresses its conviction that only with genuine political support from all interested States will those peace efforts prosper;

4. Calls upon the Governments of the United States of America and Nicaragua to resume the dialogue they had been holding in Manzanillo, Mexico with a view to reaching accords favourable for normalizing their relations and regional détente;

650 (1990)

Reiterating its support for the Central American peace process and commending the efforts made by the Central American Presidents, represented by the agreements they have concluded,

Resolutions calling for or demanding particular actions or outcomes

650 (1990)

Urging all parties to comply with their undertakings under those agreements, including in particular the commitments relating to regional security, and reiterating its full support for the Secretary General's mission of good offices in the region,

656 (1990)

Expressing its concern that the process of demobilization has not yet been fully completed, [. . .]

2. Urges all those directly involved in the demobilization process to take all necessary measures to maintain and, if possible, increase the rate of demobilization

Observer or peace-keeping forces

650 (1990)

2. Decides to authorize, on a contingency basis in accordance with that report, an enlargement of the mandate of the United Nations Observer Group in Central America and the addition of armed personnel to its strength, in order to enable it to play a part in the voluntary demobilization of the members of the Nicaraguan resistance;

RWANDA

Concern, comments, acknowledgments

812 (1993)

Gravely concerned by the fighting in Rwanda and its consequences regarding international peace and security,

Alarmed by the humanitarian consequences of the latest resumption of the fighting in Rwanda, in particular the increasing number of refugees and displaced persons and the threats to the civilian populations,

Taking note of the statements by the Government of Rwanda and the Rwandese Patriotic Front [. . .] by which the Rwandese armed forces would remain in the current positions, the army of the RPF would pull back to the positions it occupied before 7 February 1993 and the buffer zone between the forces would be considered as a neutral demilitarised zone used to monitor the implementation of the cease-fire by an international force,

Determined that the United Nations, in consultation with the OAU, and in support of its ongoing efforts, should consider how a United Nations contribution might assist the process towards a political settlement in Rwanda, in particular by preventing the resumption of fighting and monitoring the cease-fire,

846 (1993)

Emphasizing the need to prevent the resumption of fighting in Rwanda that could have adverse consequences on the situation in Rwanda and on international peace and security,

Stressing the need of a negotiated political solution, in the framework of the agreements to be signed by the parties in Arusha, in order to put an end to the conflict in Rwanda,

Taking note of the joint request of the Government of Rwanda and the Rwandese Patriotic Front concerning the establishment of a neutral international force in Rwanda

912 (1994)

Appalled at the ensuing large-scale violence in Rwanda, which has resulted in the death of thousands of innocent civilians, including women and children, the displacement of a significant number of the Rwandese population, including those who sought refuge with UNAMIR, and the significant increase in refugees to neighbouring countries,

Deeply concerned by continuing fighting, looting, banditry and the breakdown of law and order, particularly in Kigali,

918 (1994)

Deeply concerned that the situation in Rwanda, which has resulted in the death of many thousands of innocent civilians, including women and children, the internal displacement of a significant percentage of the Rwandan population, and the massive exodus of refugees to neighbouring countries, constitutes a humanitarian crisis of enormous proportions,

Deeply disturbed by the magnitude of the human suffering caused by the conflict and concerned that the continuation of the situation in Rwanda constitutes a threat to peace and security in the region.

925 (1994)

Noting with concern that, to date, the parties have not ceased hostilities, agreed to a cease-fire, or brought an end to the violence and carnage affecting civilians,

Noting with the gravest concern the reports indicating that acts of genocide have occurred in Rwanda and recalling in this context that genocide constitutes a crime punishable under international law,

Expressing its outrage that the perpetrators of these killings have been able to operate and continue operating within Rwanda with impunity,

929 (1994)

Deeply concerned by the continuation of systematic and widespread killings of the civilian population in Rwanda,

Condemnation

912 (1994)

4. Condemns the ongoing violence in Rwanda, particularly in Kigali, which endangers the lives and safety of the civilian population;

5. Strongly condemns the attacks against UNAMIR and other United Nations personnel leading to the deaths of and injury to several UNAMIR personnel and

calls upon all concerned to put an end to these acts of violence and to respect fully international humanitarian law;

918 (1994)

Strongly condemning the ongoing violence in Rwanda and particularly condemning the very numerous killings of civilians which have taken place in Rwanda and the impunity with which armed individuals have been able to operate and continue operating therein,

925 (1994)

Reiterating its strong condemnation of the ongoing violence in Rwanda and, in particular, the systematic killing of thousands of civilians,

Resolutions calling for or demanding particular actions or outcomes

812 (1994)

1. Calls upon the Government of Rwanda and the RPF to respect the cease-fire which took effect on 9 March 1993, to allow the delivery of humanitarian supplies and the return of displaced persons, to fulfil the obligations they have accepted in the agreements they have signed and to implement the commitments they have undertaken

846 (1993)

9. Urges the Government of Rwanda and the RPF to conclude quickly a comprehensive peace agreement;

872 (1993)

Welcoming the signing of the Arusha Peace Agreement (including its Protocols) on 4 August 1993 and urging the parties to continue to comply fully with it,

912 (1994)

6. Demands an immediate cessation of hostilities between the forces of the Government of Rwanda and the Rwandese Patriotic Front and for an end to the mindless violence and carnage which are engulfing Rwanda;

918 (1994)

Stressing the importance of the Arusha Peace Agreement to the peaceful resolution of the conflict in Rwanda and the necessity for all parties to recommit themselves to its full implementation.

Demands that all parties to the conflict immediately cease hostilities, agree to a cease-fire, and bring an end to the mindless violence and carnage engulfing Rwanda

925 (1994)

6. Demands that all parties to the conflict cease hostilities, agree to a cease-fire and immediately take steps to bring an end to systematic killings in areas under their control;

Sanctions

918 (1994)

Determining that the situation in Rwanda constitutes a threat to peace and security in the region,

Acting under Chapter VII of the Charter of the United Nations,

13. Decides that all States shall prevent the sale or supply to Rwanda by their nationals or from their territories or using their flag vessels or aircraft of arms and related matériel of all types, including weapons and ammunition, military vehicles and equipment, paramilitary police equipment and spare parts;

1011 (1995)

Recalling that the prohibition on the delivery of arms and matériel to Rwanda was originally aimed at stopping the use of such arms and equipment in the massacres of innocent civilians,

7. Decides that, with immediate effect and until 1 September 1996, the restrictions imposed by paragraph 13 of resolution 918 (1994) shall not apply with regard to the sale or supply of arms and related matériel to the Government of Rwanda

Observer or peace-keeping forces

846 (1993)

2. Decides to establish the United Nations observer Mission Uganda-Rwanda that will be deployed on the Ugandan side of the border, for an initial period of six months, as set out in the report of the Secretary-General

3. Decides that UNOMUR shall monitor the Uganda/Rwanda border to verify that no military assistance reaches Rwanda

872 (1993)

2. Decides to establish a peace-keeping operation under the name 'United Nations Assistance Mission for Rwanda' (UNAMIR)

3. Decides that, drawing from the Secretary-General's recommendations, UNAMIR shall have the following mandate:

(a) To contribute to the security of the city of Kigali

(b) To monitor observance of the cease-fire agreement,

(c) To monitor the security situation during the final period of transitional government's mandate, leading up to the elections;

918 (1994)

3. Decides to expand UNAMIR's mandate under resolution 912 (1994) to include the following additional responsibilities within the limits of the resources available to it:

(a) To contribute to the security and protection of displaced persons, refugees and civilians at risk in Rwanda, including through the establishment and maintenance, where feasible, of secure humanitarian areas;

(b) To provide security and support for the distribution of relief supplies and humanitarian relief operations;

Authorizations of use of force

925 (1994)

5. Recognizes that UNAMIR may be required to take action in self-defence against persons or groups who threaten protected sites and populations, United Nations and other humanitarian personnel or the means of delivery and distribution of humanitarian relief;

Encouragement or authorization of third-party actions

812 (1993)

Paying tribute to the efforts of the Organization of African Unity (OAU) in order to promote a political solution,

846 (1993)

Paying tribute to the efforts of the Organization of African Unity (OAU) and the Government of the Republic of Tanzania to promote such a political solution,

912 (1994)

10. Reiterates the crucial importance of the full implementation of the Arusha Peace Agreement to the settlement of the Rwandan conflict and invites the Organization of African Unity (OAU) to continue to cooperate fully with the United Nations in this regard;

872 (1993)

Welcoming the signing of the Arusha Peace Agreement (including its Protocols) on 4 August 1993 and urging the parties to continue to comply fully with it,

929 (1994)

1. Welcomes the Secretary-General's letter dated 19 June 1994 and agrees that a multinational operation may be set up for humanitarian purpose in Rwanda until UNAMIR is brought up to the necessary strength;

3. Acting under Chapter VII of the Charter of the United Nations, authorizes the Member States [France and Senegal] cooperating with the Secretary-General to conduct the operation referred to in paragraph 2 above using all necessary means to achieve the humanitarian objectives set out

955 (1994)

Expressing once again its grave concern at the reports indicating that genocide and other systematic, widespread and flagrant violations of international humanitarian law have been committed in Rwanda,

Determining that this situation continues to constitute a threat to international peace and security,

Determined to put an end to such crimes and to take effective measures to bring to justice the persons who are responsible for them,

Convinced that in the particular circumstances of Rwanda, the prosecution of persons responsible for serious violations of international humanitarian law would enable this aim to be achieved and would contribute to the process of national reconciliation and to the restoration and maintenance of peace,

Acting under Chapter VII of the Charter of the United Nations,

1. Decides hereby, having received the request of the Government of Rwanda (S/1994/1115), to establish an international tribunal for the sole purpose of prosecuting persons responsible for genocide and other serious violations of international humanitarian law committed in the territory of Rwanda and Rwandan citizens responsible for genocide and other such violations committed in the territory of neighbouring States, between 1 January 1994 and 31 December 1994 and to this end to adopt the Statute of the International Criminal Tribunal for Rwanda annexed hereto;

Applicability of humanitarian laws of war

812 (1993)

8. Urges both parties to strictly respect the rules of international humanitarian law

846 (1993)

Urges the Government of Rwanda and the RPF strictly to respect the rules of international humanitarian law

912 (1994)

5. Strongly condemns the attacks against UNAMIR and other United Nations personnel leading to the deaths of and injury to several UNAMIR personnel and calls upon all concerned to put an end to these acts of violence and to respect fully international humanitarian law;

918 (1994)

Expressing once again its alarm at continuing reports of systematic widespread and flagrant violations of international humanitarian law in Rwanda as well as other violations of the rights to life and property.

Recalling in this context that the killing of member of an ethnic group with the intention of destroying such a group [. . .] constitutes a crime punishable under international law.

18. Requests the Secretary-General to present a report as soon as possible on the investigation of serious violations of international humanitarian law committed in Rwanda during the conflict.

Sovereignty and territorial integrity

912 (1994)

14. Affirms its commitment to preserving the unity and territorial integrity of Rwanda;

918 (1994)

Reaffirming its commitment to the unity and territorial integrity of Rwanda,

Recognizing that the people of Rwanda bear ultimate responsibility for national reconciliation and reconstruction of their country

Threats to international peace and security

918 (1994); 929 (1994); 955 (1994); 1005 (1995); 1011 (1995); 1165 (1998)

918 (1994)

Determining that the situation in Rwanda constitutes a threat to peace and security in the region

929 (1994)

Recognizing that the current situation in Rwanda constitutes a unique case which demands an urgent response by the international community,

Determining that the magnitude of the humanitarian crisis in Rwanda constitutes a threat to peace and security in the region,

SIERRA LEONE

Concern, comments, acknowledgments

1132 (1997)

Recalling the statements of its President of 27 May 1997 (S/PRST/1997/29), 11 July 1997 (S/PRST/1997/36) and 6 August 1997 (S/PRST/1997/42) condemning the military coup in Sierra Leone,

Taking note of the decision of the thirty-third summit of the Organization of African Unity (OAU) held in Harare, Zimbabwe, from 2 to 4 June 1997 concerning the situation in Sierra Leone,

Deploring the fact that the military junta has not taken steps to allow the restoration of the democratically-elected Government and a return to constitutional order,

Gravely concerned at the continued violence and loss of life in Sierra Leone following the military coup of 25 May 1997, the deteriorating humanitarian conditions in that country, and the consequences for neighbouring countries,

Reaffirming its view that the Abidjan Agreement (S/1996/1034) continues to serve as a viable framework for peace, stability and reconciliation in Sierra Leone.

1156 (1998)

Acting under Chapter VII of the Charter of the United Nations,

1. Welcomes the return to Sierra Leone of its democratically elected President on 10 March 1998;

1162 (1998)

3. Emphasizes the need to promote national reconciliation in Sierra Leone, and encourages all parties in the country to work together towards this objective;

1171 (1998)

Welcoming the efforts of the Government of Sierra Leone to restore peaceful and secure conditions in the country, to re-establish effective administration and the democratic process, and to promote national reconciliation,

Deploring the continued resistance to the authority of the legitimate Government of Sierra Leone and stressing the urgency for all rebels to put an end to the atrocities, cease their resistance and lay down their arms,

1181 (1993)

Gravely concerned at the loss of life and immense suffering undergone by the people of Sierra Leone, including refugees and displaced persons, as a result of the continuing rebel attacks, and in particular at the plight of children affected by the conflict,

1220 (1999)

Expressing its deep concern over the recent deterioration of the situation in Sierra Leone, and encouraging all efforts aimed at resolving the conflict and restoring lasting peace and stability,

1260 (1999)

1. Welcomes the signing of the Peace Agreement between the Government of Sierra Leone and the Revolutionary United Front of Sierra Leone (RUF) in Lomé on 7 July 1999 (S/1999/777), and commends the President of Togo, the Special Representative of the Secretary-General, the Economic Community of West African States (ECOWAS) and all those involved in facilitating the negotiations in Lomé on their contribution to this achievement;

2. Commends the Government of Sierra Leone for its courageous efforts to achieve peace, including through legislative and other measures already taken towards implementation of the Peace Agreement, commends also the leadership of the RUF for taking this decisive step towards peace, and calls upon them both to ensure that the provisions of the Agreement are fully implemented;

10. Stresses the urgent need to promote peace and national reconciliation and to foster accountability and respect for human rights in Sierra Leone

1270 (1999)

6. Deplores the recent taking of hostages, including UNOMSIL and ECOMOG personnel, by rebel groups and calls upon those responsible to put an end to such practices immediately and to address their concerns about the terms of the Peace Agreement peacefully through dialogue with the parties concerned;

1346 (2001)

6. Expresses its deep concern at the reports of human rights abuses committed by the Revolutionary United Front (RUF) and others, including other military groups, against the civilian population, in particular the harassment and forced recruitment of adults and children for fighting and forced labour, demands that these acts cease immediately, and requests the Secretary-General to ensure all human rights monitoring positions within UNAMSIL are filled in order to address the concerns raised in paragraphs 44 to 51 of the report of the Secretary-General;

7. Expresses also its deep concern that the Ceasefire Agreement signed in Abuja on 10 November 2000 (S/2000/1091) between the Government of Sierra Leone and the RUF has not been fully implemented, and demands that the RUF take immediate steps to fulfil its commitments under that Agreement to ensure full liberty for the United Nations to deploy its troops throughout the country, the free movement of persons and goods, unimpeded movement of humanitarian agencies, refugees and displaced persons and the immediate return of all seized weapons, ammunition and other equipment, and to recommence active participation in the disarmament, demobilization and reintegration programme;

1400 (2002)

Emphasizing the importance of free, fair, transparent and inclusive elections, and welcoming the progress made by the Government of Sierra Leone and the National Electoral Commission of Sierra Leone in preparing for elections, particularly with voter registration,

Reiterating the importance of the effective extension of State authority throughout the country, the reintegration of ex-combatants, voluntary and unhindered return of refugees and internally displaced persons, full respect for human rights and the rule of law, and effective action on impunity and accountability, paying special attention to the protection of women and children, and stressing continued United Nations support for the fulfilment of these objectives,

Welcoming the Agreement between the United Nations and the Government of Sierra Leone on the Establishment of a Special Court for Sierra Leone,

6. Welcomes the formal completion of the disarmament process, expresses concern at the serious financial shortfall in the multi-donor Trust Fund for the disarmament, demobilization and reintegration programme, and urges the Government of Sierra Leone to seek actively the urgently needed additional resources for reintegration;

12. Expresses its serious concern at the violence, particularly sexual violence, suffered by women and children during the conflict in Sierra Leone, and emphasizes the importance of addressing these issues effectively;

13. Expresses its serious concern at the evidence UNAMSIL has found of human rights abuses and breaches of humanitarian law set out in paragraphs 38 to 40 of the Secretary-General's report of 14 March 2002 (S/2002/267), encourages UNAMSIL to continue its work and in this context requests the Secretary-General to provide a further assessment in his September report, particularly regarding the situation of women and children who have suffered during the conflict;

Condemnation

1181 (1998)

1. Condemns the continued resistance of remnants of the ousted junta and members of the Revolutionary United Front (RUF) to the authority of the legitimate government and the violence they are perpetrating against the civilian population of Sierra Leone, and demands that they lay down their arms immediately;

1231 (1999)

3. Condemns the atrocities perpetrated by the rebels on the civilian population of Sierra Leone, including in particular those committed against women and children, deplores all violations of human rights and international humanitarian law which have occurred in Sierra Leone during the recent escalation of violence as referred to in paragraphs 21 to 28 of the report of the Secretary-General, including the recruitment of children as soldiers, and urges the appropriate authorities to investigate all allegations of such violations with a view to bringing the perpetrators to justice;

Resolutions calling for or demanding particular actions or outcomes

1132 (1997)

Acting under Chapter VII of the Charter of the United Nations,

1. Demands that the military junta take immediate steps to relinquish power in Sierra Leone and make way for the restoration of the democratically-elected Government and a return to constitutional order;

2. Reiterates its call upon the junta to end all acts of violence and to cease all interference with the delivery of humanitarian assistance to the people of Sierra Leone;

1260 (1999)

8. Calls upon the RUF and all other armed groups in Sierra Leone to begin immediately to disband and give up their arms in accordance with the provisions of the Peace Agreement, and to participate fully in the disarmament, demobilization and reintegration programme in Sierra Leone;

10. Stresses the urgent need to promote peace and national reconciliation and to foster accountability and respect for human rights in Sierra Leone and, in this context, takes note of the views contained in paragraph 54 of the report of the Secretary-General, welcomes the provisions in the Peace Agreement on the establishment of the Truth and Reconciliation Commission and the Human Rights Commission in Sierra Leone, and calls upon the Government of Sierra Leone and the RUF to ensure these Commissions will be established promptly within the time-frame provided for in the Peace Agreement;

1270 (1999)

2. Calls upon the parties to fulfil all their commitments under the Peace Agreement to facilitate the restoration of peace, stability, national reconciliation and development in Sierra Leone;

4. Calls upon the RUF, the Civil Defence Forces, former Sierra Leone Armed Forces/Armed Forces Revolutionary Council (AFRC) and all other armed groups in Sierra Leone to begin immediately to disband and give up their arms in accordance with the provisions of the Peace Agreement, and to participate fully in the disarmament, demobilization and reintegration programme;

5. Welcomes the return to Freetown of the leaders of the RUF and AFRC, and calls upon them to engage fully and responsibly in the implementation of the Peace Agreement and to direct the participation of all rebel groups in the disarmament and demobilization process without delay;

1289 (2000)

3. Reiterates its call upon the parties to fulfil all their commitments under the Peace Agreement to facilitate the restoration of peace, stability, national reconciliation and development in Sierra Leone, and stresses that the responsibility for the success of the peace process ultimately lies with the people and leaders of Sierra Leone;

Sanctions

1132 (1997)

[Acting under Chapter VII, the Security Council imposes a petrol and arms embargo on Sierra Leone.]

5. Decides that all States shall prevent the entry into or transit through their territories of members of the military junta and adult members of their families, as designated in accordance with paragraph 10 (f) below, provided that the entry into or transit through a particular State of any such person may be authorized by the Committee established by paragraph 10 below for verified humanitarian purposes or purposes consistent with paragraph 1 above, and provided that nothing in this paragraph shall oblige a State to refuse entry into its territory to its own nationals;

6. Decides that all States shall prevent the sale or supply to Sierra Leone, by their nationals or from their territories, or using their flag vessels or aircraft, of petroleum and petroleum products and arms and related matériel of all types, including weapons and ammunition, military vehicles and equipment, paramilitary equipment and spare parts for the aforementioned, whether or not originating in their territory;

1156 (1998)

2. Decides to terminate, with immediate effect, the prohibitions on the sale or supply to Sierra Leone of petroleum and petroleum products referred to in paragraph 6 of resolution 1132 (1997);

1171 (1998)

Acting under Chapter VII of the Charter of the United Nations,

1. Decides to terminate the remaining prohibitions imposed by paragraphs 5 and 6 of resolution 1132 (1997);

2. Further decides, with a view to prohibiting the sale and supply of arms and related matériel to non-governmental forces in Sierra Leone, that all States shall prevent the sale or supply, by their nationals or from their territories, or using their flag vessels or aircraft, of arms and related matériel of all types, including weapons and ammunition, military vehicles and equipment, paramilitary equipment and spare parts for the aforementioned, to Sierra Leone other than to the Government of Sierra Leone

5. Decides that all States shall prevent the entry into or transit through their territories of leading members of the former military junta and of the Revolutionary United Front (RUF),

1306 (2000)

Under Chapter VII

1. Decides that all States shall take the necessary measures to prohibit the direct or indirect import of all rough diamonds from Sierra Leone to their territory;

2. Requests the Government of Sierra Leone to ensure, as a matter of urgency, that an effective Certificate of Origin regime for trade in diamonds is in operation in Sierra Leone;

Observer or peace-keeping forces

1162 (1998)

5. Authorizes the deployment, with immediate effect, of up to ten United Nations military liaison and security advisory personnel in accordance with paragraph 44 of the report of the Secretary-General of 18 March 1998 to Sierra Leone for a period of up to 90 days, to work under the authority of the Special Envoy of

the Secretary-General, to coordinate closely with the Government of Sierra Leone and ECOMOG, to report on the military situation in the country, to ascertain the state of and to assist in the finalization of planning by ECOMOG for future tasks, such as the identification of the former combatant elements to be disarmed and the design of a disarmament plan, as well as to perform other related security tasks as identified in paragraphs 42, 45 and 46 of the report of the Secretary-General of 18 March 1998;

1181 (1998)

6. Decides to establish UNOMSIL for an initial period of six months until 13 January 1999, and further decides that it shall include up to 70 military observers as well as a small medical unit, with the necessary equipment and civilian support staff, with the following mandate:

(a) To monitor the military and security situation in the country as a whole, as security conditions permit, and to provide the Special Representative of the Secretary-General with regular information thereon in particular with a view to determining when conditions are sufficiently secure to allow subsequent deployments of military observers beyond the first phase described in paragraph 7 below;

(b) To monitor the disarmament and demobilization of former combatants concentrated in secure areas of the country, including monitoring of the role of ECOMOG in the provision of security and in the collection and destruction of arms in those secure areas;

1270 (1999)

8. Decides to establish the United Nations Mission in Sierra Leone (UNAMSIL) with immediate effect for an initial period of six months and with the following mandate:

(a) To cooperate with the Government of Sierra Leone and the other parties to the Peace Agreement in the implementation of the Agreement;

(b) To assist the Government of Sierra Leone in the implementation of the disarmament, demobilization and reintegration plan;

(c) To that end, to establish a presence at key locations throughout the territory of Sierra Leone, including at disarmament/reception centres and demobilization centres;

(d) To ensure the security and freedom of movement of United Nations personnel;

(e) To monitor adherence to the ceasefire in accordance with the Ceasefire Agreement of 18 May 1999 (S/1999/585, Annex) through the structures provided for therein;

(f) To encourage the parties to create confidence-building

Authorizations of use of force

1270 (1999)

14. Acting under Chapter VII of the Charter of the United Nations, decides that in the discharge of its mandate UNAMSIL may take the necessary action to ensure the security and freedom of movement of its personnel and, within its capabilities and areas of deployment, to afford protection to civilians under imminent threat of physical violence, taking into account the responsibilities of the Government of Sierra Leone and ECOMOG;

1289 (2000)

10. Acting under Chapter VII of the Charter of the United Nations, [. . .] authorizes UNAMSIL to take the necessary action to fulfil the additional tasks set out above, and affirms that, in the discharge of its mandate, UNAMSIL may take the necessary action to ensure the security and freedom of movement of its personnel and, within its capabilities and areas of deployment, to afford protection to civilians under imminent threat of physical violence, taking into account the responsibilities of the Government of Sierra Leone;

Encouragement or authorization of third-party actions

1132 (1997)

3. Expresses its strong support for the efforts of the ECOWAS Committee to resolve the crisis in Sierra Leone and encourages it to continue to work for the peaceful restoration of the constitutional order, including through the resumption of negotiations;

4. Encourages the Secretary-General, through his Special Envoy, in cooperation with the ECOWAS Committee, to assist the search for a peaceful resolution of the crisis and, to that end, to work for a resumption of discussions with all parties to the crisis;

8. Acting also under Chapter VIII of the Charter of the United Nations, authorizes ECOWAS, cooperating with the democratically-elected Government of Sierra Leone, to ensure strict implementation of the provisions of this resolution relating to the supply of petroleum and petroleum products, and arms and related matériel of all types, including, where necessary and in conformity with applicable international standards, by halting inward maritime shipping in order to inspect and verify their cargoes and destinations, and calls upon all States to cooperate with ECOWAS in this regard;

1181 (1998)

5. Commends the positive role of ECOWAS and ECOMOG in their efforts to restore peace, security and stability throughout the country at the request of the Government of Sierra Leone, and notes the role of ECOMOG in assisting the implementation of the disarmament, demobilization and reintegration plan

adopted by the Government of Sierra Leone, including the provision of security and responsibility for arms collection and destruction

1260 (1999)

3. Commends also the Military Observer Group of ECOWAS (ECOMOG) on the outstanding contribution which it has made to the restoration of security and stability in Sierra Leone, the protection of civilians and the promotion of a peaceful settlement of the conflict,

1270 (1999)

Determining that the situation in Sierra Leone continues to constitute a threat to international peace and security in the region,

1. Welcomes the important steps taken by the Government of Sierra Leone, the leadership of the Revolutionary United Front of Sierra Leone (RUF), the Military Observer Group (ECOMOG) of the Economic Community of West African States (ECOWAS) and the United Nations Observer Mission in Sierra Leone (UNOMSIL) towards implementation of the Peace Agreement (S/1999/777) since its signing in Lomé on 7 July 1999,

1289 (2000)

8. Expresses its appreciation to ECOMOG for its indispensable contribution towards the restoration of democracy and the maintenance of peace, security and stability in Sierra Leone, commends highly the forces and the Governments of its contributing States for their courage and sacrifice, and encourages all States to assist the contributing States further in meeting the costs they have incurred in making possible the deployment of ECOMOG forces in Sierra Leone;

Applicability of humanitarian laws of war

1181 (1998)

12. Demands that all factions and forces in Sierra Leone strictly respect the status of UNOMSIL personnel, as well as organizations and agencies delivering humanitarian assistance throughout Sierra Leone, and that they respect human rights and abide by applicable rules of international humanitarian law;

1231 (1999)

4. Calls upon all parties to the conflict in Sierra Leone fully to respect human rights and international humanitarian law and the neutrality and impartiality of humanitarian workers, and to ensure full and unhindered access for humanitarian assistance to affected populations;

1289 (2000)

5. Notes also with concern the continuing human rights violations against the civilian population of Sierra Leone, and emphasizes that the amnesty extended

under the Peace Agreement does not extend to such violations committed after the date of its signing;

Sovereignty and territorial integrity

1231 (1999)

Affirming the commitment of all States to respect the sovereignty, political independence and territorial integrity of Sierra Leone,

1306 (2000)

Affirming the commitment of all States to respect the sovereignty, political independence and territorial integrity of Sierra Leone.

Threats to international peace and security

1132 (1997)

Deploring the fact that the military junta has not taken steps to allow the restoration of the democratically-elected Government and a return to constitutional order,

Gravely concerned at the continued violence and loss of life in Sierra Leone following the military coup of 25 May 1997, the deteriorating humanitarian conditions in that country, and the consequences for neighbouring countries,

Determining that the situation in Sierra Leone constitutes a threat to international peace and security in the region,

1270 (1999)

Determining that the situation in Sierra Leone continues to constitute a threat to international peace and security in the region,

1299 (2000)

Convinced that the deterioration in security conditions on the ground necessitates the rapid reinforcement of the military component of the United Nations Mission in Sierra Leone (UNAMSIL) to provide the mission with additional resources to fulfil its mandate,

1. Decides that the military component of UNAMSIL shall be expanded to a maximum of 13,000 military personnel, including the 260 military observers already deployed;

SOUTH AFRICA

Concern, comments, acknowledgments

182 (1963)

Deploring the refusal of the Government of the Republic of South Africa, as confirmed in the reply of the Minister of Foreign Affairs

Noting with deep satisfaction the overwhelming support for resolution 1881 (XVIII) adopted by the General Assembly on 11 October 1963,

Taking into account the serious concern of the Member States with regard to the policy of Apartheid,

Being strengthened in its conviction that the situation in South Africa is seriously disturbing international peace and security, and strongly deprecating the policies of the Government of South Africa in its perpetuation of racial discrimination in the Charter of the United Nations and with its obligations as a Member of the United Nations,

Expressing the firm conviction that the policies of Apartheid and racial discrimination as practiced by the Government of the Republic of South Africa are abhorrent to the conscience of mankind and that therefore a positive alternative to these policies must be found in peaceful means,

190 (1964)

Noting with great concern that the arbitrary Rivonia trial instituted against the leaders of the anti-Apartheid movement has been resumed, and that the imminent verdict to be delivered under arbitrary laws prescribing long terms of imprisonment and the death sentence may have very serious consequences,

191 (1964)

Convinced that the situation in South Africa is continuing seriously to disturb international peace and security,

5. Endorses and subscribes in particular to the main conclusion of the Group of Experts that "all the people of South Africa should be brought into consultation and should thus be enabled to decide the future of their country at the national level";

282 (1970)

Recognizing the legitimacy of the struggle of the oppressed people of South Africa in pursuance of their human and political rights set forth in the Charter of the United Nations and the Universal Declaration of Human Rights,

418 (1977)

Gravely concerned that South Africa is at the threshold of producing nuclear weapons,

473 (1980)

Gravely concerned by the aggravation of the situation in South Africa, in particular the repression and the killings of schoolchildren protesting against Apartheid as well as the repression directed against churchmen and workers.

Reaffirming its recognition of the legitimacy of the struggle of the South African people for the elimination of Apartheid and the establishment of a democratic society in accordance with their inalienable human and political rights as set forth in the Charter of the United Nations and the Universal Declaration of Human Rights

473 (1980)

2. Expresses its profound sympathy with the victims of this violence

3. Reaffirms that the policy of Apartheid is a crime against the conscience and dignity of mankind and is incompatible with the rights and dignity of man, the Charter of the United nations and the Universal Declaration of Human Rights, and seriously disturbs international peace and security.

554 (1984)

Convinced that the so-called "new constitution" endorsed on 2 November 1983 by the exclusively white electorate in South Africa would continue the process of denationalisation of the indigenous African majority

Welcoming the massive united resistance of the oppressed people of South Africa against these 'constitutional' manoeuvres,

Reaffirming the legitimacy of the struggle of the oppressed people of South Africa for the elimination of Apartheid and for the establishment of a society in which all the people of South Africa as a whole, irrespective of race, colour, sex or creed, will enjoy equal and full political and other rights and participate freely in the determination of their destiny,

Firmly convinced that the so-called 'elections' to be organized by the Pretoria regime in the current month of August for the 'coloured' people and people of Asian origin and the implementation of this 'new constitution' will inevitably aggravate tension in South Africa and in southern Africa as a whole,

2. Strongly rejects and declares null and void the so-called 'new constitution' and the 'elections'

3. Further rejects any so-called 'negotiated settlement' based on Bantustan structures or on the so-called 'new constitution';

4. Solemnly declares that only the total eradication of Apartheid and the establishment of a non-racial democratic society based on majority rule, through the full and free exercise of the universal adult suffrage by all the people in a united and unfragmented South Africa, can lead to a just and lasting solution to the explosive situation in South Africa;

765 (1992)

Gravely concerned by the escalating violence in South Africa which is causing a heavy loss of human life and by its consequences for the peaceful negotiations aimed at creating a democratic, non racial and united South Africa

Recalling the Declaration on Apartheid and its Destructive Consequences in Southern Africa adopted by consensus by the General Assembly at its sixteenth special session, on 14 December 1989, which called for negotiations in South Africa to take place in a climate free of violence,

Emphasizing the responsibility of the South African authorities to take all necessary measures to stop the violence immediately and protect the life and property of all South Africans,

Emphasising also the need for all parties to cooperate in combating violence and to exercise restraint,

1. Condemns the escalating violence in South Africa and in particular the massacre at Boipatong township on 17 June 1992, as well as subsequent incidents of violence, including the shooting of unarmed protesters;

3. Calls upon all the parties to cooperate in combating violence and to ensure the effective implementation of the National Peace Accord

Condemnation

134 (1960)

2. Deplores the policies and actions of the Government of the Union of South Africa which have given rise to the present situation;

3. Deplores the policies and actions of the Government of the Union of South Africa which have given rise to the present situation;

181 (1963)

Finds that the situation in South Africa is disturbing international peace and security

1. Strongly deprecates the policies of South Africa in its perpetuation of racial discrimination as being inconsistent with the principles contained in the Charter of the United Nations and contrary to its obligations as a Member of the United Nations;

182 (1963)

3. Condemns the non-compliance by the Government of the Republic of South Africa with the appeals contained in the above-mentioned resolutions of the General Assembly and the Security Council;

191 (1964)

1. Condemns the Apartheid policies of the Government of the Republic of South Africa and the legislation supporting these policies,

282 (1970)

Reiterating its condemnation of the evil and abhorrent policies of Apartheid and the measures being taken by the Government of South Africa to enforce and extend those policies beyond its borders,

311 (1972)

Convinced that urgent measures must be taken by the Security Council to secure implementation of its resolutions and thereby promote a solution to the grave situation in South Africa and southern Africa,

1. Condemns the Government of South Africa for continuing its policies of Apartheid in violation of its obligations under the Charter of the United Nations;

2. Reiterates its total opposition to the policies of Apartheid of the Government of South Africa;

417 (1977)

Recalling its resolution 392 (1976) of 19 June 1976, strongly condemning the racist regime of South Africa for its resort to massive violence against and wanton killings of the African people, including schoolchildren and students and others opposing racial discrimination, and calling upon the South African racist regime urgently to tend violence against the African people and take urgent steps to eliminate Apartheid and racial discrimination,

Noting with deep anxiety and indignation that the South African racist regime has continued violence and massive repression against the black people and all opponents of Apartheid in defiance of the resolutions of the Security Council

473 (1980)

1. Strongly condemns the racist regime of South Africa for further aggravating the situation and its massive repression against all opponents of Apartheid, for killings of peaceful demonstrators and for its defiance of General Assembly and Security Council resolutions.

560 (1985)

1. Strongly condemns the Pretoria regime for the killing of defenceless African people protesting against their forced removal from Crossroads and other places;

2. Strongly condemns the arbitrary arrests by the Pretoria regime of members of the United Democratic Front

Resolutions calling for or demanding particular actions or outcomes

134 (1960)

4. Calls upon the Government of the Union of South Africa to initiate measures aimed at bringing about racial harmony based on equality in order to ensure that the present situation does not continue or recur, and to abandon its policies of Apartheid and racial discrimination;

181 (1963)

2. Calls upon the Government of South Africa to abandon the policies of Apartheid and discrimination, as called for in Security Resolution 134 (1960),

and to liberate all persons imprisoned, interned or subjected to other restrictions for having opposed the policy of Apartheid;

182 (1963)

2. Urgently requests the Government of the Republic of South Africa to cease forthwith its continued imposition of discriminatory and repressive measures which are contrary to the principles and purposes of the Charter and which are in violation of its obligations as a Member of the United Nations and of the provisions of the Universal Declaration of Human Rights;

4. Again calls upon the Government of the Republic of South Africa to liberate all persons imprisoned interned or subjected to other restrictions for having opposed the policy of Apartheid;

190 (1964)

1. Urges the Government of South Africa:
   (a) To renounce the execution of the persons sentenced to death for acts resulting from their opposition to the policy of Apartheid;
   (b) To end forthwith the trial in progress, instituted within the framework of the arbitrary laws of Apartheid;
   (c) To grant an amnesty to all persons already imprisoned, interned or subjected to other restrictions for having opposed the policy of Apartheid, and particularly to the defendants of the Rivonia trial;

191 (1964)

2. Urgently reiterates its appeal to the Government of the Republic of South Africa to liberate all persons imprisoned, interned or subjected to other restrictions for having opposed the policies of Apartheid;

311 (1972)

4. Urgently calls upon the Government of South Africa to release all persons imprisoned, interned or subjected to other restrictions as a result of the policies of Apartheid;

417 (1977)

Demands that the racist regime of South Africa

(a) Ends violence and repression against the black people and other opponents of Apartheid

(b) Release all persons imprisoned under arbitrary security laws and all those detained for their opposition to Apartheid

765 (1992)

Emphasizing the responsibility of the South African authorities to take all necessary measures to stop the violence immediately and protect the life and property of all South Africans

Emphasizing the need for all parties to cooperate in combating violence and to exercise restraint

473 (1980)

5. Calls upon the Government of South Africa urgently to end violence against the African people and to take urgent measures to eliminate Apartheid;

Sanctions

181 (1963)

3. Solemnly calls upon all States to cease forthwith the sale and shipment of arms, ammunition of all types and military vehicles to South Africa;

182 (1963)

5. Solemnly calls upon all states to cease forthwith the sale and shipment of equipment and materials for the manufacture and maintenance of arms and ammunitions in South Africa

282 (1970)

Convinced of the need to strengthen the arms embargo

Convinced further that the situation resulting from the continued application of the policies of Apartheid and the constant build-up of the South African military and police forces, made possible by the continued acquisition of arms, military vehicles and other equipment, and of spare parts for military equipment from a number of Member States and by local manufacture of arms and ammunition under licences granted by some Member States, constitutes a potential threat to international peace and security,

4. Calls on all States to strengthen the arms embargo

418 (1977)

Convinced that a mandatory arms embargo needs to be universally applied against South Africa in the first instance,

Acting under Chapter VII of the Charter of the United Nations,

2. Decides that all States shall cease forthwith any provision to South Africa of arms and related material of all types,

Observer or peace-keeping forces

191 (1964)

8. Decides to establish an expert committee, composed of representatives of each present member of the Security Council, to undertake a technical and practical study and report to the Council as to the feasibility, effectiveness and impli-

cations of measures which could, as appropriate, be taken by the Council under the Charter of the United Nations;

10. Authorises the expert committee to request all States Members of the United Nations to co-operate with it and submit to it their views on such measures no later than 30 November 1964

772 (1992)

Authorises the Secretary-General to deploy, as a matter of urgency, United Nations observers in South Africa

Encouragement or authorization of third party actions

182 (1963)

6. Requests the Secretary-General to establish under his direction and reporting to him a small group of recognized experts to examine methods of resolving the present situation in South Africa through full, peaceful and orderly application of human rights and fundamental freedoms to all inhabitants of the territory as a whole, regardless of race, colour or creed, and to consider what part the United Nations might play in achievement of that end;

190 (1964)

2. Invites all States to exert all their influence in order to induce the Government of South Africa to comply with the provisions of the present resolution;

554 (1984)

5. Urges all Governments and organizations not to accord recognition to the results of the so-called 'elections' and to take appropriate action, in cooperation with the United Nations and the Organization of African Unity and in accordance with the present resolution, to assist the oppressed people of South Africa in their legitimate struggle for a non-racial, democratic society;

Threats to international peace and security

418 (1977); 421 (1977)

134 (1960)

Having considered the complaint of twenty-nine Member States contained in document S/4279 and Add.1 concerning "the situation arising out of the large-scale killings of unarmed and peaceful demonstrators against racial discrimination and segregation in the Union of South Africa,"

Taking into account the strong feelings and grave concern aroused among Governments and peoples of the world by the happenings in the Union of South Africa,

1. Recognises that the situation in the Union of South Africa is one that has led to international friction and if continued might endanger international peace and security;

181 (1963)

Taking into account that world public opinion has been reflected in General Assembly resolution 1761 (XVII)

Noting with concern the recent arms build-up by the Government of South Africa, some of which arms are being used in furtherance of that Government's racial policies

Regretting that some States are indirectly providing encouragement in various ways to the government of South Africa to perpetuate, by force, its policy of Apartheid

Being convinced that the situation in South Africa is seriously disturbing international peace and security

182 (1963)

Being strengthened in its conviction that the situation in South Africa is seriously disturbing international peace and security, and strongly deprecating the policies of the Government of South Africa in its perpetuation of racial discrimination in the Charter of the United Nations and with its obligations as a Member of the United Nations

418 (1977)

Strongly condemning the South African government for its resort to massive violence against and killings of the African people [. . .] and calling upon that government urgently to end violence against African people and to take urgent steps to eliminate Apartheid and racial discrimination

Recognising that the military build up by South Africa and its persistent acts of aggression against neighbouring states seriously disturb the security of those states

Further recognising that the existing arms embargo must be strengthened and universally applied

Gravely concerned that South Africa is at the threshold of producing nuclear weapons

Considering that the policies and acts of the South African government are fraught with danger to international peace and security

[Acting under Chapter VII—the Security Council imposes an arms embargo.]

765 (1992)

Concerned that the continuation of this situation would seriously jeopardize peace and security in the region

SUDAN

Recent Security Council resolutions have dealt with the civil war although up until recently there were only a series dealing with the harbouring of terrorists.

Condemnation

1044 (1996)

Deeply disturbed by the world-wide persistence of acts of international terrorism in all its forms which endanger or take innocent lives, have a deleterious effect on international relations and jeopardize the security of States,

Gravely alarmed at the terrorist assassination attempt on the life of the President of the Arab Republic of Egypt, in Addis Ababa, Ethiopia, on 26 June 1995, and convinced that those responsible for that act must be brought to justice,

Taking note that the Third Extraordinary Session of the Organization of African Unity (OAU) Mechanism for Conflict Prevention, Management and Resolution of 11 September 1995, considered that attack as aimed, not only at the President of the Arab Republic of Egypt, and not only at the sovereignty, integrity and stability of Ethiopia, but also at Africa as a whole,

4. Calls upon the Government of the Sudan to comply with the requests of the Organization of African Unity without further delay to:

(a) Undertake immediate action to extradite to Ethiopia for prosecution the three suspects sheltering in the Sudan and wanted in connection with the assassination attempt on the basis of the 1964 Extradition Treaty between Ethiopia and the Sudan;

(b) Desist from engaging in activities of assisting, supporting and facilitating terrorist activities and from giving shelter and sanctuaries to terrorist elements and act in its relations with its neighbours and with others in full conformity with the Charter of the United Nations and with the Charter of the Organization of African Unity;

1556 (2004)

Condemning all acts of violence and violations of human rights and international humanitarian law by all parties to the crisis, in particular by the Janjaweed, including indiscriminate attacks on civilians, rapes, forced displacements, and acts of violence especially those with an ethnic dimension, and expressing its utmost concern at the consequences of the conflict in Darfur on the

civilian population, including women, children, internally displaced persons, refugees

Resolutions calling for or demanding particular actions or outcomes

1556 (2004)

Under Chapter VII

1. *Calls on* the Government of Sudan to fulfil immediately all of the commitments it made in the 3 July 2004 Communiqué, including particularly by facili-

tating international relief for the humanitarian disaster by means of a moratorium on all restrictions that might hinder the provision of humanitarian assistance and access to the affected populations, by advancing independent investigation in cooperation with the United Nations of violations of human rights and international humanitarian law, by the establishment of credible security conditions for the protection of the civilian population and humanitarian actors, and by the resumption of political talks with dissident groups from the Darfur region, specifically the Justice and Equality Movement (JEM) and the Sudan Liberation Movement and Sudan Liberation Army (SLM/A) on Darfur;

6. Demands that the Government of Sudan fulfil its commitments to disarm the Janjaweed militias and apprehend and bring to justice Janjaweed leaders and their associates who have incited and carried out human rights and international humanitarian law violations and other atrocities, and *further requests* the Secretary-General to report in 30 days, and monthly thereafter, to the Council on the progress or lack thereof by the Government of Sudan on this matter and *expresses its intention* to consider further actions, including measures as provided for in Article 41 of the Charter of the United Nations on the Government of Sudan, in the event of non-compliance;

Sanctions

1054 (1996)

3. Decides that all States shall:

   (a) Significantly reduce the number and the level of the staff at Sudanese diplomatic missions and consular posts and restrict or control the movement within their territory of all such staff who remain;

   (b) Take steps to restrict the entry into or transit through their territory of members of the Government of Sudan, officials of that Government and members of the Sudanese armed forces;

1070 (1996)

3. Decides that all States shall deny aircraft permission to take off from, land in, or overfly their territories if the aircraft is registered in Sudan, or owned, leased or operated by or on behalf of Sudan Airways or by any undertaking, wherever located or organized, which is substantially owned or controlled by Sudan Airways, or owned, leased or operated by the Government or public authorities of Sudan, or by an undertaking, wherever located or organized, which is substantially owned or controlled by the Government or public authorities of Sudan;

1372 (2001)

Noting the steps taken by the Government of the Sudan to comply with the provisions of resolutions 1044 (1996) and 1070 (1996),

Welcoming the accession of the republic of Sudan to the relevant international conventions for the elimination of terrorism,

Acting under Chapter VII of the Charter of the United Nations,

1. Decides to terminate, with immediate effect, the measures referred to in paragraphs 3 and 4 of resolution 1054 (1996) and paragraph 3 of resolution 1070 (1996).

1556 (2004)

7. Decides that all states shall take the necessary measures to prevent the sale or supply, to all non-governmental entities and individuals, including the Janjaweed, operating in the states of North Darfur, South Darfur and West Darfur, by their nationals or from their territories or using their flag vessels or aircraft, of arms and related materiel of all types, including weapons and ammunition, military vehicles and equipment, paramilitary equipment, and spare parts for the aforementioned, whether or not originating in their territories;

Applicability of humanitarian laws of war

1556 (2004)

Urging all the parties to take the necessary steps to prevent and put an end to violations of human rights and international humanitarian law and underlining that there will be no impunity for violators, Welcoming the commitment by the Government of Sudan to investigate the atrocities and prosecute those responsible,

Threats to international peace and security

1054 (1996); 1070 (1996)

1054 (1996)

Determining that the non-compliance by the Government of Sudan with the requests set out in paragraph 4 of resolution 1044 (1996) constitutes a threat to international peace and security

SOMALIA

Concern, comments, acknowledgments

733 (1992)

Gravely alarmed at the rapid deterioration of the situation in Somalia and the heavy loss of human life and widespread material damage resulting from the conflict in the region and aware of its consequences on the stability and peace in the region,

Recalling its primary responsibility under the Charter for the maintenance of international peace and security,

746 (1992)

Taking note of the signing at Mogadishu on 3 March 1992 of the cease-fire agreements, including agreements for the implementation of measures aimed at stabilizing the cease-fire through a United Nations monitoring mission,

Deeply regretting that the factions have not yet abided by their commitment to implement the cease-fire and thus have still not permitted the unimpeded provision and distribution of humanitarian assistance to the people in need in Somalia,

Deeply disturbed by the magnitude of human suffering caused by the conflict and concerned that the continuation of the situation in Somalia constitutes a threat to international peace and security,

767 (1992)

Deeply concerned about the availability of arms and ammunitions in the hands of civilians and the proliferation of armed banditry throughout Somalia.

Alarmed by the sporadic outbreak of hostilities in several parts of Somalia leading to continued loss of life and destruction of property, and putting at risk the personnel of the United Nations, non-governmental organizations and other international humanitarian organizations, as well as disrupting their operations,

Deeply disturbed by the magnitude of the human suffering caused by the conflict and concerned that the situation in Somalia constitutes a threat to international peace and security.

Responding to the urgent calls by the parties in Somalia for the international community to take measures in Somalia to ensure the delivery of humanitarian assistance in Somalia,

794 (1992)

Recognizing the unique character of the present situation in Somalia and mindful of its deteriorating, complex and extraordinary nature, requiring an immediate and exceptional response,

Determining that the magnitude of the human tragedy caused by the conflict in Somalia, further exacerbated by the obstacles being created to the distribution of humanitarian assistance, constitutes a threat to international peace and security,

Determined also to restore peace, stability and law and order with a view to facilitating the process of a political settlement under the auspices of the United Nations, aimed at national reconciliation in Somalia,

837 (1993)

Gravely alarmed at the premeditated armed attacks launched by forces apparently belonging to the United Somali Congress (USC/SNA) against the personnel of the United Nations Operation in Somalia (UNOSOM II)

Expressing outrage at the loss of life as a result of these criminal attacks,

Reaffirming its commitment to assist the people of Somalia in re-establishing conditions of normal life,

Stressing that the international community is involved in Somalia in order to help the people of Somalia who have suffered untold miseries due to years of civil strife in that country,

886 (1993)

Stressing the commitment of the international community to continue helping Somalia in its efforts to accelerate the process of national reconstruction and to promote stability, rehabilitation and political reconciliation and to regain a normal, peaceful life,

Recalling that the highest priority of UNOSOM II continues to be to support the efforts of the Somali people in promoting the process of national reconciliation and the establishment of democratic institutions,

897 (1994)

Stressing the importance the Council attaches to the Somali parties fulfiling in good faith all obligations and agreements to which they commit themselves, and affirming once again that the General Agreement signed in Addis Ababa on 8 January 1993 and the Addis Ababa Agreement of the First Session of the Conference on National Reconciliation in Somalia signed on 27 March 1993 ("the Addis Ababa Agreements") constitute the basis for the resolution of the problems in Somalia,

Affirming the importance of establishing, by the Somali people, of representative district and regional councils and of a transitional national council, as well as the importance of a re-established police force and a judicial system for the restoration of public order throughout Somalia,

923 (1994)

Emphasizing in this context that the people of Somalia bear the ultimate responsibility for achieving national reconciliation and for rebuilding their country,

Stressing the importance the Council attaches to the Somali parties working seriously to achieve peace and national reconciliation in their country and to their fulfiling in good faith all obligations and agreements to which they commit themselves,

Condemnation

837 (1993)

Strongly condemning such actions, which directly undermine international efforts aimed at the restoration of peace and normalcy in Somalia,

Acting under Chapter VII

1. Strongly condemns the unprovoked armed attacks against the personnel of UNOSOM II on 5 June 1993, which appear to have been part of a calculated and premeditated series of cease-fire violations to prevent by intimidation UNOSOM II from carrying out its mandate,

897 (1994)

Expressing serious concern at reports that Somali factions are re-arming and that a troop build-up is taking place in some regions of Somalia,

Condemning the continued incidents in Somalia of fighting and banditry and in particular condemning violence and armed attacks against persons engaged in humanitarian and peace-keeping efforts,

923 (1994)

Condemning the continuing incidents of fighting and banditry and, in particular, violence and armed attacks against persons engaged in humanitarian and peace-keeping efforts,

Resolutions calling for or demanding particular actions or outcomes

733 (1992)

4. Strongly urges all parties to the conflict immediately to cease hostilities and agree to a ceasefire and to promote the process of reconciliation and of political settlement in Somalia;

746 (1992)

2. Urges the Somali factions to honour their commitment under the cease-fire agreements signed at Mogadishu on 3 March 1992,

751 (1992)

9. Calls upon all parties, movements and factions in Somalia immediately to cease hostilities and to maintain a cease-fire throughout the country in order to promote the process of reconciliation and political settlement in Somalia;

767 (1992)

9. Calls upon all parties, movements and factions in Somalia immediately to cease hostilities and to maintain a cease-fire throughout the country;

794 (1992)

1. Reaffirms its demand that all parties, movements and factions in Somalia immediately cease hostilities,

837 (1993)

Acting under Chapter VII

4. Demands once again that all Somali parties, including movements and factions, comply fully with the commitments they have undertaken in the agreements they concluded at the informal Preparatory Meeting on Somali Political Reconciliation in Addis Ababa,

886 (1993)

Acting under Chapter VII

6. Urges all parties in Somalia, including movements and factions, to accelerate their efforts to achieve political reconciliation, peace and security, and immediately to abide by the cease-fire and disarmament agreements reached in Addis Ababa, particularly the immediate cantonment of all heavy weapons;

897 (1994)

Acting under Chapter VII

7. Calls upon all parties in Somalia to cooperate fully with UNOSOM II and respect the cease-fire arrangements and other commitments entered into by them;

Sanctions

733 (1992)

5. Decides under Chapter VII of the Charter of the United Nations, that all States shall for the purposes of establishing peace and stability in Somalia, immediately implement a general and complete embargo on all deliveries of weapons and military equipment to Somalia until the Council decides otherwise;

Observer or peace-keeping forces

751 (1992)

Taking note of the signing of the cease-fire agreements in Mogadishu;

Deeply disturbed by the magnitude of the human suffering by the conflict and concerned that the continuation of the situation in Somalia constitutes a threat to international peace and security.

2. Decides to establish under its authority, and in support of the Secretary-General in accordance with paragraph 7 below, a United Nations Operation in Somalia;

3. Requests the Secretary-General immediately to deploy a unit of fifty United Nations observers to monitor the cease-fire in Mogadishu

4. Agrees, in principle, also to establish under the overall direction of the Special Representative of the Secretary-General a United Nations security force to be deployed as soon as possible,

794 (1992)

Noting the offer by Member States (US) aimed at establishing a secure environment for humanitarian relief operations in Somalia as soon as possible,

6. Decides that the operations and the further deployment of the three thousand five hundred personnel of the United Nations Operation in Somalia authorized by paragraph 3 of resolution 775 (1992) should proceed at the discretion of the Secretary-General

9. Welcomes the offer by a Member State described in the Secretary-General's above mentioned letter concerning the establishment of an operation to create such a secure environment;

897 (1994)

2. Approves the Secretary-General's recommendation for the continuation of UNOSOM II, as set out in particular in paragraph 57 of his report, with a revised mandate for the following:

(a) Encouraging and assisting the Somali parties in implementing the "Addis Ababa Agreements," in particular in their cooperative efforts to achieve disarmament and to respect the cease-fire;

(b) Protecting major ports and airports and essential infrastructure and safeguarding the lines of communications vital to the provision of humanitarian relief and reconstruction assistance;

(c) Continuing its efforts to provide humanitarian relief to all in need throughout the country;

(d) Assisting in the reorganization of the Somali police and judicial system;

(e) Helping with the repatriation and resettlement of refugees and displaced persons;

(f) Assisting also in the ongoing political process in Somalia, which should culminate in the installation of a democratically elected government;

(g) Providing protection for the personnel, installations and equipment of the United Nations and its agencies, as well as of non-governmental organizations providing humanitarian relief and reconstruction assistance;

954 (1994)

Recognizing that the lack of progress in the Somali peace process and in national reconciliation, in particular the lack of sufficient cooperation from the Somali parties over security issues, has fundamentally undermined the United Nations objectives in Somalia and, in these circumstances, continuation of UNOSOM II beyond March 1995 cannot be justified

Authorizations of use of force

794 (1992)

10. Acting under Chapter VII of the Charter of the United Nations, authorises the Secretary-General and Member States cooperating to implement the offer referred to in paragraph 8 above to use all necessary means to establish as soon as possible a secure environment for humanitarian relief operations in Somalia;

837 (1993)

5. Reaffirms that the Secretary-General is authorized under resolution 814 (1993) to take all necessary measures against all those responsible for the armed

attacks referred to in paragraph 1 above, including against those responsible for publicly inciting such attacks, to establish the effective authority of UNOSOM II throughout Somalia, including to secure the investigation of their actions and their arrest and detention for prosecution, trial and punishment;

Encouragement or authorization of third-party actions

733 (1992)

2. Requests the Secretary-General of the United Nations in cooperation with the Secretary-General of the Organization of African Unity and the Secretary-General of the League of Arab States immediately to contact all parties involved in the conflict, to seek their commitment to the cessation of hostilities in order to permit the humanitarian assistance to be distributed, to promote a cease-fire and compliance therewith, and to assist in the process of a political settlement of the conflict in Somalia

746 (1992)

Expressing its appreciation to the regional organizations including the Organisation of African Unity, the League of Arab States and the Organization of the Islamic Conference for their cooperation with the United Nations in the effort to resolve the Somali problem,

751 (1992)

Expressing its appreciation to the regional organizations including the Organization of African Unity, the League of Arab states and the Organization of the Islamic Conference for their cooperation with the United Nations in the effort to resolve the Somali problem.

954 (1994)

Acting under Chapter VII

10. Invites the Organization of African Unity, the League of Arab States and the Organization of the Islamic Conference to continue their efforts in cooperation with the United Nations in the search for lasting peace in Somalia;

11. Calls upon all Member States, in particular the neighbouring States, to continue to provide support for all Somali efforts towards genuine peace and national reconciliation and to refrain from any action capable of exacerbating the conflict situation in Somalia;

Applicability of humanitarian laws of war

733 (1992)

8. Urges all parties to take all the necessary measures to ensure the safety of personnel sent to provide humanitarian assistance, to assist them in their tasks and to ensure full respect for the rules and principles of international law regarding the protection of civilian populations;

794 (1992)

Expressing grave alarm at continuing reports of widespread violations of international humanitarian law occurring in Somalia, including reports of violence and threats of violence against personnel participating lawfully in impartial humanitarian relief activities; deliberate attacks on non-combatants, relief consignments and vehicles and medical and relief facilities; and the impeding of the delivery of food and medical supplies essential for the survival of the civilian population,

5. Strongly condemns all violations of international humanitarian law occurring in Somalia

Sovereignty and territorial integrity

794 (1992)

Recognising that the people of Somalia bear ultimate responsibility for national reconciliation and the reconstruction of their own country,

897 (1994)

Bearing in mind respect for the sovereignty and territorial integrity of Somalia in accordance with the Charter of the United Nations and recognizing that the people of Somalia bear the ultimate responsibility for setting up viable national political institutions and for reconstructing their country.

Threats to international peace and security

733 (1992); 794 (1992); 814 (1993); 837 (1993); 878 (1993); 886 (1993); 897 (1994); 923 (1994); 954 (1994)

733 (1992)

Concerned that the continuation of this situation constitutes, as stated in the report of the Secretary-General, a threat to international peace and security,

767 (1992)

Recognizing that the provision of humanitarian assistance in Somalia is an important element in the effort of the Council to restore international peace and security in the area.

794 (1992)

Recognising the unique character of the present situation in Somalia and mindful of its deteriorating, complex and extraordinary nature, requiring an immediate and exceptional response,

Determining that the magnitude of human tragedy caused by the conflict further exacerbated by the obstacles being created to the distribution of humanitarian constitutes a threat to international peace and security.

Responding to the urgent calls from Somalia for the international community to take measures to ensure delivery of humanitarian assistance in Somalia,

SPAIN

Franco's Civil War in Spain did not attract Security Council intervention although the matter was debated in the Security Council in 1946. The question was discussed in the Security Council in 1946 from the perspective of intervention only being permissible on the basis of a threat to international peace and security. No resolution was passed, and no intervention permitted. Although Poland and Russia suggested that there was a threat to international peace and security, this was rejected by the UK and the US. S/32 and S/34 SCOR, 1.1 Supp 2 at 54–55, Security Council, April 17, 1946, SCOR 1.1 N2, 167.

Invoking articles 2(6), 34, and 35 of the Charter, the representative of Poland placed on the Council's agenda 'the situation arising from the existence and activities of the Franco regime in Spain' [S/32 and s/34 SCOR, 1.1 Supp 2 at 54–55] he proposed a resolution which declared that Franco 'endangered international peace and security.' The Soviet Union's ambassador [. . .] took the position that sanctions would not violate Article 2(7) since that provision envisaged 'circumstances' in which 'the United Nations both can and should take certain measures required by the situation arising even out of the internal affairs of a State when these internal affairs constitute a menace to international peace and security' [Security Council, April 17, 1946, SCOR 1.1 N2, 167]. Although British and American representatives challenged the view that the nature of Franco's regime in itself constituted a threat to peace.

SRI LANKA

No relevant Security Council resolutions.

WESTERN SAHARA

Concern, comments, acknowledgments

377 (1975)

1. Acting in accordance with Article 34 of the Charter of the United Nations and without prejudice to any action which the General Assembly might take under the terms of resolution 3292 (XXIX) of 13 December 1974 or to negotiations that the parties concerned and interested might undertake under Article 33 of the Charter, requests the Secretary-General to enter into immediate consultations with the parties concerned and interested and to report to the Security Council as soon as possible on the results of his consultations in order to enable the Council to adopt appropriate measures to deal with the present situation concerning Western Sahara;

379 (1975)

Having noted with concern that the situation in the area remains grave,

380 (1975)

Noting with grave concern that the situation concerning Western Sahara has seriously deteriorated,

621 (1988)

Having heard a report by the Secretary-General of the United Nations on his mission of good offices, pursued jointly with the current Chairman of the Assembly of Heads of States and Government of the Organization of African Unity, in conformity with the General Assembly resolution 40/50 of 2 December 1985, with a view to settling the question of Western Sahara,

Taking note of the agreement in principle given by the Kingdom of Morocco and the Frente Popular para la Liberacion de Saguia el-Hamra y de Rio de Oro on 30 August 1988 to the joint proposals of the Secretary-General and the current Chairman of the Organization of African Unity,

Anxious to support these efforts with a view to the holding of a referendum for self-determination of the people of Western Sahara, organized and supervised by the United Nations in co-operation with the Organization of African Unity,

2. Requests the Secretary-General to transmit to it as soon as possible a report on the holding of a referendum for self-determination of the people of Western Sahara

995 (1995)

1. Reiterates its commitment to holding, without further delay, a free, fair and impartial referendum for self-determination of the people of Western Sahara in accordance with the Settlement Plan which has been accepted by the two parties;

2. Commends the progress in identifying potential voters since the beginning of the year;

1042 (1996)

4. Expresses deep concern about the stalemate which has been hindering the identification process and the consequent lack of progress towards completion of the Settlement Plan

1084 (1996)

Reaffirming its commitment to assist the parties to achieve a just and lasting solution to the question of Western Sahara,

Welcoming the reiteration by the Kingdom of Morocco of its commitment to the Settlement Plan,

Welcoming also the reiteration by the Polisario Front of its commitment to the Settlement Plan,

Stressing the importance it attaches to the maintenance of the ceasefire, as an integral part of the Settlement Plan,

Stressing also the importance and usefulness of the resumption of exploratory talks between the parties, without prejudice to their respective positions, in order to create an atmosphere of mutual confidence conducive to a speedy and effective implementation of the Settlement Plan,

1429 (2002)

Reaffirming its commitment to assist the parties to achieve a just and lasting solution to the question of Western Sahara,

Welcoming the reiteration by the Kingdom of Morocco of its commitment to the Settlement Plan,

Welcoming also the reiteration by the Polisario Front of its commitment to the Settlement Plan,

Stressing the importance it attaches to the maintenance of the ceasefire, as an integral part of the Settlement Plan,

Stressing also the importance and usefulness of the resumption of exploratory talks between the parties, without prejudice to their respective positions, in order to create an atmosphere of mutual confidence conducive to a speedy and effective implementation of the Settlement Plan,

Noting also the fundamental differences with regard to the four options contained in the report of the Secretary-General of 19 February 2002,

1. Continues to support strongly the efforts of the Secretary-General and his Personal Envoy to find a political solution to this long-standing dispute, invites the Personal Envoy to pursue these efforts taking into account the concerns expressed by the parties and expresses its readiness to consider any approach which provides for self-determination that may be proposed by the Secretary-General and the Personal Envoy, consulting, as appropriate, others with relevant experience;

Resolutions calling for or demanding particular actions or outcomes

377 (1975)

2. Appeals to the parties concerned and interested to exercise restraint and moderation;

379 (1975)

1. Urges all the parties concerned and interested to avoid any unilateral or other action which might further escalate the tension in the area;

380 (1975)

2. Calls on Morocco immediately to withdraw from the Territory of Western Sahara all the participants in the march;

3. Calls upon Morocco and all other parties concerned and interested, without prejudice to any action

690 (1991)

3. Calls upon the two parties to cooperate fully with the Secretary-General in the implementation of his plan as described in his report of 18 June 1990;

Observer or Peacekeeping forces

690 (1991)

4. Decides to establish, under its authority, a United Nations Mission for the Referendum in Western Sahara in accordance with the report of 19 April 1991;

APPENDIX 2: TABLE OF SECURITY COUNCIL INTERVENTIONS AND CONSENT

	Demands and statements	Economic sanctions and military embargoes	Forceful measures
Consensual Interventions: Direct Consent	The Council has not suggested that any of its demands that parties stop fighting or renounce force, for instance, derive its authority from the consent of parties.	The Council has not suggested that economic sanctions or military embargoes were imposed on the basis of consent.	The former Yugoslavia: the Council emphasized the invitation of the parties to send peace-keeping troops. SC Res 721 (1991) set up in SC Res 743 (1992). Kosovo: it similarly welcomed the agreement of the FRY to a peace-keeping force. SC Res 1244 (1999). Cyprus: it emphasized the consent of the government. SC Res 186 (1964). East Timor: it emphasized consent in relation to the multi-national force. SC Res 1264 (1999). Lebanon: forces were sent in light of a request by the government. SC Res 521 (1982).
Consensual Interventions: **Peace agreements**			Angola: UNAVEM I was to be sent once the agreements were signed, SC Res 626 (1988) and UNAVEM II was stated to be "in line with the Peace Accords for Angola," SC Res 696 (1991). Bosnia: the multi-lateral force IFOR was authorized in accordance with peace accords. SC Res 1031 (1993).

APPENDIX 2: TABLE OF SECURITY COUNCIL INTERVENTIONS AND CONSENT *(continued)*

	Demands and statements	Economic sanctions and military embargoes	Forceful measures
			El Salvador: the forces were sent to monitor the agreements concluded by the parties. SC Res 693 (1991). Guatemala: the forces were sent to monitor the agreements concluded by the parties. SC Res 1094 (1997). Liberia: the Council practice took place following the signing of a cease-fire agreement that called on the United Nations and ECOMOG to assist in its implementation. SC Res 866 (1993). Mozambique, it was stated to be in line with the General Peace Agreement. SC Res 797 (1992). Sierra Leone: the rebels rejected the peace-keeping forces sent "To cooperate with the Government of Sierra Leone and the other parties to the Peace Agreement in the imple mentation of the Agreement" (SC Res 1270 (1999) para 8a) and went so far as to attack them.

APPENDIX 2: TABLE OF SECURITY COUNCIL INTERVENTIONS AND CONSENT *(continued)*

	Demands and statements	Economic sanctions and military embargoes	Forceful measures
			Acting beyond peace agreements While ostensibly relying on agreements to justify its intervention, however, the Council appears to be acting beyond the scope agreed in these agreements. In Angola, the Peace Accords, accepted as binding by both the government and the rebels, provided for U.N. monitoring, and the Fundamental Principles for the Establishment of Peace in Angola included a commitment to "free and fair elections" conducted "under the supervision of international election observers," (Point 4, Fundamental Principles for the Establishment of Peace in Angola, Peace Accords). Nevertheless, the practice of the Council went much further than overseeing the ceasefire or the elections. It essentially sought to enforce the agreements, sending repeated UNAVEM missions to do so, imposing punitive sanctions for breaches, (SC Res 864 (1993), SC Res 1127 (1997)), and declaring that the parties must abide by the agreements, stop military confrontation (SC Res 793 (1992) para 4) and engage in a meaningful dialogue aimed at reconciliation (SC Res 793 (1992) para 5).

APPENDIX 2: TABLE OF SECURITY COUNCIL INTERVENTIONS AND CONSENT *(continued)*

	Demands and statements	Economic sanctions and military embargoes	Forceful measures
Chapter VII Interventions with Consent			In some instances the Council has relied on both consent and Chapter VII in authorising the force. East Timor: the Council only intervened once the consent of Indonesia was secured, SC Res 1236 (1999) paras 1–3, however it authorized the force on the basis of a finding of a threat to international peace and security. SC Res 1264 (1999). Liberia: the cease-fire agreement was mentioned but the intervention was in fact authorized on the basis of the deterioration of the situation, which constituted a threat to international peace and security. SC Res 866 (1993).
Chapter VII Interventions	Afghanistan: in SC Res 1267 (1999) and SC Res 1333 (2000) the Security Council acted under Chapter VII when it insisted that the Afghan faction known as the Taliban "comply with its previous resolutions." Albania: the situation was found to be a threat to international peace and security	Sanctions have practically uniformly been passed under Chapter VII. The sanctions in Afghanistan, Angola, former Yugoslavia, Kosovo, Bosnia and Herzegovina, Haiti, Liberia, Rwanda, Sierra Leone, and Somalia where passed under Chapter VII.	A non-negligible proportion of the peace-keeping forces have been authorized under Chapter VII without reference to the consent of the parties. Croatia: UNPROFOR was authorized to use force in self-defense under Chapter VII, SC Res 871 (1993). Bosnia: its mandate was extended to the

APPENDIX 2: TABLE OF SECURITY COUNCIL INTERVENTIONS AND CONSENT *(continued)*

	Demands and statements	Economic sanctions and military embargoes	Forceful measures
	and was followed by a call for the end of all acts of violence in SC Res 1101 (1997) para 1, but the reliance on Chapter VII only related to the authorization of the multi-lateral force (para 4). Kosovo: SC Res 1004 (1995), the demands were made directly under Chapter VII (paras 1–4). In SC Res 1160 (1998) again the Security Council specified it was acting under Chapter VII when it called upon the FRY to achieve a political solution and the Kosovar leadership to condemn terrorism. In this resolution as well it went on to impose a military embargo. Similarly, SC Res 1199 (1998), SC Res 1203 (1998), and SC Res 1244 (1999) all specified that the situations amounted to a threat to peace and security and that it was acting pursuant to Chapter VII. Croatia: SC Res 807 (1993) the demands were made under Chapter VII. SC Res 871 (1993) relied on Chapter VII as did SC Res 1009 (1995). Bosnia: SC Res 757 (1992) the condemnation of the FRY was expressed to be pursuant to Chapter VII, and went on to		protection of the safe areas under Chapter VII. SC Res 836 (1993). Rwanda: the mandate was authorized under Chapter VII. SC Res 929 (1994). Central African Republic: SC Res 1159 (1998). Georgia: observer force authorized under Chapter VII, SC Res 854 (1993) para 1, SC Res 858 (1993) para 2, SC Res 858 (1993), see also SC Res 881 (1993). Finally, the most enforcement-like interventions have been explicitly authorized under Chapter VII. Haiti: involved troops that were authorized to "use all necessary means to facilitate the departure from Haiti of the military leadership." SC Res 940 (1994) para 4. Somalia: the force was authorized under Chapter VII to use all necessary means to establish a safe environment for humanitarian relief. SC Res 794 (1992). Albania: The multi-national protection

APPENDIX 2: TABLE OF SECURITY COUNCIL INTERVENTIONS AND CONSENT *(continued)*

	Demands and statements	Economic sanctions and military embargoes	Forceful measures
	impose trade sanctions. In SC Res 770 (1992) the demands to stop fighting were made pursuant to Chapter VII. In SC Res 787 (1992), SC Res 819 (1993), SC Res 820 (1993) relating to cessation of hostilities and the unacceptable practice of taking territory by force, no reference to Chapter VII was made, but in SC Res 824 (1993) the demand that the taking of territory by force stop was made under Chapter VII. East Timor: SC Res 1272 (1999) acting under Chapter VII calling for the end of violence and demanding that those responsible be brought to justice. Georgia: SC Res 858 (1993) and SC Res 881 (1993) contain findings that the situation amounts to a threat to international peace and security. Iraq/Kurds: SC Res 688 (1991) was not passed under Chapter VII but did demand that Iraq make a contribution to removing the threat to international peace and security in the region.		force was authorized under Chapter VII to take measures to ensure its security and freedom of movement as it set out to achieve the objectives of restoring order and overseeing elections. SC Res 1101 (1997).

APPENDIX 2: TABLE OF SECURITY COUNCIL INTERVENTIONS AND CONSENT *(continued)*

	Demands and statements	Economic sanctions and military embargoes	Forceful measures
	Sierra Leone: acting under Chapter VII demanded that the junta step down, SC Res 1132 (1997), but the remaining calls and demands were not passed under Chapter VII, SC Res 1260 (1999), SC Res 1270 (1999), SC Res 1289 (2000). Somalia: SC Res 751 (1992), SC Res 767 (1992), SC Res 794 (1992) did not refer to Chapter VII, but the demands and calls in SC Res 837 (1993), SC Res 886 (1993), and SC Res 897 (1994) were formulated under Chapter VII.		
Neither consent nor Chapter VII interventions	The demands in the following conflicts were not made under Chapter VII: Angola: repeated demands and calls on parties in SC Res 747 (1992), SC Res 785 (1992), SC Res 793 (1992), SC Res 811 (1993), SC Res 834 (1993) without resorting to Chapter VII. In SC Res 864 (1993) and SC Res 1173 (1998) it did make a Chapter VII finding but acted under it only in relation to sanctions SC Res 864 (1993) paras 17, 19, 26, SC Res 1173 (1998) para 11. In the former Yugoslavia under SC Res 713 (1991) paras 6–7 calls on parties, and unusually on states, were made without relying on	One exception is South Africa where a military embargo was initially formulated without reliance on Chapter VII (SC Res 181 (1963)) but was later reimposed under Chapter VII (SC Res 418 (1977).) One other possible exception occurred in Afghanistan, where the Council called on "all states immediately to end the supply of arms and ammunition to all parties to the conflict in Afghanistan." (SC Res 1076 (1996) para 4). Ultimately, however, the Council	

APPENDIX 2: TABLE OF SECURITY COUNCIL INTERVENTIONS AND CONSENT *(continued)*

	Demands and statements	Economic sanctions and military embargoes	Forceful measures
	Chapter VII, although the military embargo was imposed under Chapter VII. SC Res 721 (1991), SC Res 740 (1992), SC Res 749 (1992) and SC Res 771 (1992) are further examples of calls outside Chapter VII. In Burundi none of the demands for restraint and end to violence under SC Res 1040 (1996) and SC Res 1049 (1996) and for return to constitutional order under SC Res 1072 (1996) were made under Chapter VII. Also: Cambodia SC Res 880 (1993), CAR SC Res 1152 (1998), Cyprus SC Res 193 (1964), SC Res 205 (1965), SC Res 353 (1974), SC Res 541 (1984), SC Res 1251 (1999), El Salvador SC Res 637 (1989), SC Res 693 (1991), SC Res 714 (1991), SC Res 129 (1992), SC Res 961 (1994), Guatemala SC Res 1094 (1997), Guinea Bissau SC Res 1216 (1998), Haiti SC Res 867 (1993), Israel SC Res 43 (1948), SC Res 46 (1948), SC Res 50 (1948), SC Res 468 (1980), SC Res 1322 (2000), SC Res 1397 (2002), SC Res 1402 (2002), Lebanon SC Res 512 (1982), SC Res 513 (1982), SC Res 520 (1982), Liberia SC		did specifically impose an arms embargo under Chapter VII. (SC Res 1333 (2000))

APPENDIX 2: TABLE OF SECURITY COUNCIL INTERVENTIONS AND CONSENT *(continued)*

	Demands and statements	Economic sanctions and military embargoes	Forceful measures
	Res 788 (1992), SC Res 856 (1993), SC Res 1020 (1995), SC Res 1116 (1997), although in SC Res 788 (1992) it did impose an arms embargo under Chapter VII, para 7, Mozambique SC Res 797 (1992), SC Res 957 (1994), SC Res 960 (1994), South Africa SC Res 134 (1960), SC Res 181 (1963), SC Res 182 (1963), SC Res 190 (1964), SC Res 191 (1964), SC Res 417 (1977), SC Res 473 (1980), Western Sahara SC Res 377 (1975), SC Res 380 (1975), SC Res 690 (1991).		

APPENDIX 3: RATIONALE FOR NON-INTERVENTION IN CONFLICTS

NON-INTERVENTION BY STATES

Country	Situation	Response	Possible explanation
Aceh	The recent Indonesian military intervention into Aceh in May 2003 followed the collapse of the December 2002 peace agreement, which offered autonomy in exchange for the disarming of the rebels of the Free Aceh Movement.[1]	Very little international attention. EU expressed concern at the "outbreak of violence" and appealed to both sides to return to the negotiating table and to implement the obligations they entered into by signing the peace agreement.[2]	None given. Likely geopolitical limitations.
Chechnya	Chechnya claimed independence in 1991. After a humiliating military defeat against Chechen separatists in 1996, Russia withdrew all forces and signed a peace agreement, but the conflict re-ignited in 1998 and recently there has been a marked increase in both violence by Russian troops and terrorist actions by thef Chechens.[3]	The Chechen conflict is one that the international community has assiduously avoided.[4] Nevertheless, the European Parliament has at times condemned Russia's military campaign there,[5] as has NATO.[6] Chris Patten, as a Member of the European Commission, condemned the "disproportionate military force,	

[1] BBC "Indonesia Launches Aceh Offensive" (19 May 2003) www.bbc.co.uk.

[2] General Affairs and External Relations Council: Indonesia (19 May 2003).

[3] Human Rights Watch *World Report* eg hostages taken by Chechen rebels in October 2002 in Moscow theatre.

[4] BBC Monitoring Trans Caucasus Unit "Chechen Rebel Leader Accuses G7 Of Indifference To Russian Atrocities" (20 July 2001) web.lexis-nexis.com/executive/.

[5] See *Project Ploughshares Armed Conflict Report, Russia* (2002) www.ploughshares.ca. The EU parliament called for an immediate ceasefire in Chechnya and asked Moscow to look into allegations of war crimes committed by both sides in the conflict. Agence France Presse "Europe Living In 'Virtual Reality' About Chechnya: Moscow" (20 February 2001) web.lexis-nexis.com/executive/. The EU parliament also condemned the conflict in 2002. Global News Wire—Asia Africa Intelligence Wire "Russia Dismisses European Parliament's resolution on Chechnya" (12 April 2002) web.lexis-nexis.com/executive/.

[6] In 1999 at their year-end meeting, the NATO foreign ministers condemned Russia for its bloody assault on Chechnya. The Associated Press "NATO Warily Watches Development Of EU Defense Arm" (15 December 1999) web.lexis-nexis.com/executive/.

APPENDIX 3: RATIONALE FOR NON-INTERVENTION IN CONFLICTS *(continued)*

Country	Situation	Response	Possible explanation
		disregard for the need to seek a political solution, and equal disregard for the tragic human consequences", he emphasised that there was no alternative to a negotiated settlement, and also that the EU had condemned "the indiscriminate use of force in Chechnya and urged the Russian government to observe its commitments under humanitarian law".[7] The EU recently reiterated that it rejected "any kind of violence, in particular terrorist acts, which could endanger the prospects for a political solution".[8]	None given. Likely geopolitical limitations
Nepal	Civil war broke out in 2002	This conflict, between an unpopular government and a Maoist insurgency, has seemingly not attracted international attention other than an EC Conflict Prevention Assessment Mission that recommended	None given.

[7] Commission of the European Communities "The Rt Hon Christopher Patten Member of the European Commission responsible for External Relations Declaration on Chechnya European Parliament Strasbourg, 17 November 1999" (17 November 1999) web.lexis-nexis.com/executive/.

[8] Agence France Presse "Main Points From Russia-EU Summit Statement" (31 May 2003) web.lexis-nexis.com/executive/.

APPENDIX 3: RATIONALE FOR NON-INTERVENTION IN CONFLICTS *(continued)*

Country	Situation	Response	Possible explanation
		containment action, but no direct action, on the basis that it would not be effective in resolving the conflict at that stage.[9]	
Colombia	The conflict intensified again in 2002 following the collapse of three years of formal talks between the government and Colombia's largest guerrilla group.	There is indirect US involvement in this conflict, which has been played out though its War on Drugs Campaign.[10] In addition, the EU has been minimally involved, supporting a negotiated solution to the conflict and offering to assist the government in reaching this situation.[11]	None given. Likely geopolitical limitations

9 Nepal: Report of the EC Conflict Prevention Assessment Mission (2002) //europa.eu.int/comm/external_relations/cpcm/mission/nepal02.htm.

10 The US has given $2.5 billion in the past three years to battle drugs and the rebel insurgency. Associated Press Worldstream "Colombian President Denounces U.S. Decision To Cut Off Military Aid" (3 July 2003) web.lexis-nexis.com/executive/.

11 EU— General Affairs and External Affairs "Colombia Council Conclusions" (10 December 2002) europaeuint/comm/external_relations/.

APPENDIX 3: RATIONALE FOR NON-INTERVENTION IN CONFLICTS *(continued)*

NON-INTERVENTION BY THE SECURITY COUNCIL

Country	Situation	Response	Possible explanation
Ireland	Ireland's struggle for independence from the United Kingdom can be traced back to 1916. By 1921, 26 southern counties obtained independence from the UK, although the 6 northern counties remained part of Great Britain. This has sparked decades of civil conflict, both within Northern Ireland with violent clashes between loyalists and republicans, and in London through terrorist actions.	Despite significant violence and bloodshed, the Council has not intervened or even called on parties to resolve their differences by non-violent means.	The United Kingdom's involvement must be acknowledged to be a major reason for this lack of intervention. An attempt to place the question on the Council agenda in 1969 was strongly rejected by the British Representative on the Council. The matter was not even put on the agenda, but would have undoubtedly faced a UK veto. Nonetheless, the formal justifications given were that Article 2(7) prevented such intervention and that the conflict in Northern Ireland was in no sense a threat to international peace and security.[12]
Spain	Civil war	No intervention	The failure to intervene in the civil war in Spain was based on an argument that it was a domestic matter. The debate in the Council in 1946 assumed that Article 2(7) prohibits intervention into civil conflicts unless these constitute a threat to international peace and security. No resolution was passed, and no intervention permitted. Poland and Russia suggested that there was a threat to international peace and security, but this was rejected by the UK and the US.[13]

12 UN doc S/9394 1969, SC Meeting 24 UN SCOR 1969.

13 S/32 and S/34 SCOR, 1.1 Supp 2 at 54-55, Security Council, April 17, 1946, SCOR 1.1 N2, 167.

APPENDIX 3: RATIONALE FOR NON-INTERVENTION IN CONFLICTS *(continued)*

Country	Situation	Response	Possible explanation
Chechnya	Chechnya's attempt to obtain independence from Russia in 1991 resulted in a vicious civil conflict between Russian troops and Chechen rebels. In 1996 the Khasavyurt Peace Accords were signed according to which Russia agreed to withdraw from Chechnya and discuss its independence after five years. In 1997 the Chechens chose a president and a parliament in democratic elections. In May 1997 the new president, Maskhadov, signed a peace treaty with President Yeltsin in Moscow. However, by 1999 Dagestan had become a serious destabilising force, and Chechen militants led by warlord Shamil Basayev were staging violent attacks. This led to Russian forces invading Chechnya for a second time in 1999.	No action	The conflict has been repeatedly claimed to be a domestic matter.[14] This conflict involves many factors that have in other cases led to intervention,[15] and yet, unsurprisingly given Russia's veto power, no action has been taken. The conflicts in Algeria[16] and Tibet also involve veto powers, and have not been subject to Council action.
El Salvador, Colombia, Chile, Nigeria.	Various civil conflicts	No action	None given. Likely cold war politics. Kenney-Pipe and Jones suggest that were proxy wars influenced by ideology but also marked by domestic concerns.[17]

14 See comments of US and French Ministers reported in Dipaola "A Noble Sacrifice? Jus Ad Bellum and the International Community's Gamble in Chechnya" (1997) 4 Ind J Global Leg Stud 435 at 435.

15 Particularly the overthrow of the democratically elected president and parliament in 1997 and the repeated breaching of the Peace Accords.

16 The most recent conflict in Algeria is a low-grade civil conflict sparked by the success of the fundamentalist FIS (Islamic Salvation Front) party in first round ballots in December 1991, which caused the army to intervene, crack down on the FIS, and postpone the elections.

17 See Kennedy-Pipe and Jones "An Introduction to Civil Wars" (1998) Civil Wars Vol 1(1), 1. For a review of the conflicts in Nigeria and Pakistan, where there was also no action other than humanitarian assistance, see Andemicael *Peaceful Settlement among African States—Roles of the United Nations and the Organization of African Unity* (UNITAR Study, 1972) at Pt D para 3.

APPENDIX 3: RATIONALE FOR NON-INTERVENTION IN CONFLICTS *(continued)*

Country	Situation	Response	Possible explanation
Guatemala	The Guatemala civil war began in 1954 when the Guatemalan military led a CIA-backed coup against the democratically elected President. In 1966 right wing death squads were blamed for killing 30 000 civilians over the following years. In 1981, the army initiated a massive, scorched-earth counter-insurgency campaign against potential guerrilla supporters.	Civil war raged from 1954 after the democratically elected government was overthrown by a coup, but the Council did not intervene until 1996. It did so then pursuant to the 1994 Framework Agreement for the Resumption of the Negotiating Process,[18] which requested the United Nations carry out international verification of the peace accords, and even then the Council did not condemn the violence or comment on the conflict.	None given. Likely cold war politics.
Nicaragua	The two decade long struggle by the Sandinista rebels against the dictatorship of Somoza was formally a civil conflict, despite external intervention, particularly by the United States and Cuba. In 1984, Ortega was elected president although the conflict with the Contra rebels continued until 1989.	The Council has not acknowledged the civil aspect of this conflict and only intervened in 1983 in response to an overt intervention by the United States. Even then, its primary response was to call on the United States and Nicaragua to resume their dialogue.[19]	None given. Likely cold war politics.

[18] S/1994/53, annex.

[19] SC Res 562 (1985) para 4.

APPENDIX 3: RATIONALE FOR NON-INTERVENTION IN CONFLICTS *(continued)*

Country	Situation	Response	Possible explanation
Cambodia	Extreme violence towards civilians in civil conflict, which began in the early 1970's, and is believed to have caused over 1 million deaths from executions and starvation.	The Council only passed a first resolution dealing with Cambodia in 1991 in the run-up to United Nations sponsored elections. Ironically, this resolution stated that the Council was "Convinced of the need to find an early, just and lasting peaceful solution of the Cambodia conflict".[20]	None given.
Sudan	It has been torn by a series of vicious civil wars since at least 1962, aggravated by the discovery of oil in 1978. The latest conflict broke out in 1983 as the government in the North imposed Shari'ah law, and has continued unabated through serious famine.	There have been international attempts to find a peaceful solution, and many broken peace accords. Moreover, individual States, including the United States, have imposed sanctions against Sudan. However, although the Council has passed a series of resolutions dealing with the harbouring of terrorists,[21] it has not addressed the civil conflict.	None given.
Sri Lanka	Internal disruption begun in 1976 with the emergence of separatist tensions and the formation of Liberation Tigers of Tamil Eelam rebel group. The 1985 Peace Agreement, which provided for an Indian	Despite substantial international involvement by individual States[22] and pressure to bring the matter to the UN,[23] it has not been the subject of any Council resolutions.	None given.

20 SC Res 668 (1991) preamble.

21 See SC Res 1044 (1996), SC Res 1054 (1996), SC Res 1070 (1996).

22 Norway had taken forward the latest peace agreement initiative.

23 The European parliament adopted a resolution on 19 May 2000 urging the Sri Lanka issue to be taken up at the UN.

APPENDIX 3: RATIONALE FOR NON-INTERVENTION IN CONFLICTS *(continued)*

Country	Situation	Response	Possible explanation
	peacekeeping force, failed. Violence between the Sri Lankan army and separatists continued		
Burma	in 1990 when the ruling military junta refused to hand over power after multi-party elections led to the main opposition party winning a decisive victory	The Security Council did not act.	None given.
Fiji	military coup in May 2000 after democratic elections in 1999	Security Council did not intervene	None given.
The Gambia	A coup in 1981 followed weeks of violence, with a second coup also taking place in 1994.	Security Council did not intervene	None given.
Chad	Civil conflict practically since its independence from France in 1960. Democratic elections were held in 1996 but heavy fighting restarted in 1998.	France, Libya and the OAU have at times intervened to support one or other side. Other than a statement in 1982 "taking note" of the decision of the OAU to establish a peacekeeping force to maintain peace and security in Chad,[24] the Council has not intervened in or commented on the civil aspect of this conflict, even after the start of the rebellion against the democratic government in 1998.	None given.

24 SC Res 504 (1982).

BIBLIOGRAPHY

2005 World Summit Outcome: Final Document, U.N. Doc. A/60/L.1 (Sept. 20, 2005).

Abass, Ademola, *The New Collective Security Mechanism of ECOWAS: Innovations and Problems*, 5 J. CONFLICT & SECURITY L. 211, 211–12 (2000).

Abbott, Kenneth W., *Modern International Relations Theory: A Prospectus for International Lawyers*, 14 YALE J. INT'L L. 338 (1989).

AKEHURST, MICHAEL, A MODERN INTRODUCTION TO INTERNATIONAL LAW (6th ed. 1992).

———. *Custom as a Source of International Law*, 47 BRIT. Y.B. INT'L L. 1 (1974–75).

American Society of International Law, *The End of Sovereignty?*, 88 PROC. ANN. MEETING OF THE ASIL (1995).

ALLOTT, PHILIP ET AL., THEORY AND INTERNATIONAL LAW: AN INTRODUCTION (1991).

Alvarez, Jose E., *Judging the Security Council*, 90 AM. J. INT'L L. 1 (1996).

———. *Positivism Regained, Nihilism Postponed*, 15 MICH. J. INT'L L. 747 (1994) (reviewing GENNADY M. DANILENKO, LAW-MAKING IN THE INTERNATIONAL COMMUNITY (1993)).

ANDEMICAEL, BERHANYKUN, PEACEFUL SETTLEMENT AMONG AFRICAN STATES: ROLES OF THE UNITED NATIONS AND THE ORGANISATION OF AFRICAN UNITY, pt. D (1972).

Annan, Kofi, *Two Concepts of Sovereignty*, ECONOMIST, Sept. 18, 1999.

Arangio-Ruiz, Gaetano, *The Normative Role of the General Assembly of the United Nations and the Development of Principles of Friendly Relations*, 137 RECUEIL DES COURS 431 (1972).

AREND, ANTHONY C., AND ROBERT J. BECK, INTERNATIONAL LAW AND THE USE OF FORCE: BEYOND THE UN CHARTER PARADIGM (1993).

BAILEY, SYDNEY, AND SAM DAWS, THE PROCEDURE OF THE UN SECURITY COUNCIL (3d ed. 1998).

BEDJAOUI, MOHAMMED, THE NEW WORLD ORDER AND THE SECURITY COUNCIL: TESTING THE LEGALITY OF ITS ACTS (1994).

Bierzanek, Remigiusz, *Reprisals as a Means of Enforcing the Laws of Warfare: The Old and the New Law*, *in* THE NEW HUMANITARIAN LAW OF ARMED CONFLICT 232 (Antonio Cassese ed., 1979).

Bodansky, Daniel, *Customary (and Not So Customary) International Environmental Law*, 3 IND. J. GLOBAL LEGAL STUD. 105 (1995).

Bowett, Derek, *The Impact of Security Council Decisions on Dispute Settlement Procedures,* 5 EUR. J. INT'L L. 89 (1994).

———. *The Interrelation of Theories of Intervention and Self-Defense, in* LAW AND CIVIL WAR IN THE MODERN WORLD (John Norton Moore ed., 1974).

———. *Reprisals Involving Recourse to Armed Force,* 66 AM. J. INT'L L. 1, 2 (1972).

BOWETT, DEREK ET AL., BOWETT'S LAW OF INTERNATIONAL INSTITUTIONS (5th ed. 2001).

BROWNLIE, IAN, INTERNATIONAL LAW AND THE USE OF FORCE BY STATES (1963).

———. PRINCIPLES OF PUBLIC INTERNATIONAL LAW (5th ed. 1998).

———. THE RULE OF LAW IN INTERNATIONAL AFFAIRS (1998).

Boyle, Francis A., *The Irrelevance of International Law: The Schism Between International Law and International Politics,* 10 CAL. W. INT'L L.J. 198 (1980).

BYERS, MICHAEL, CUSTOM, POWER AND THE POWER OF RULES: INTERNATIONAL RELATIONS AND CUSTOMARY INTERNATIONAL LAW (1999).

Bureau of Democracy, Human Rights, and Labor, *U.S. Department of State, Sierra Leone Country Report on Human Rights Practices for 1997* (Jan. 30 1998), *available at* http://www.sierra-leone.org/usds013098.html.

Burke, William T., *The Legal Regulation of Minor International Coercion: A Framework of Inquiry, in* THE VIETNAM WAR AND INTERNATIONAL LAW 79 (Richard Falk ed., 1972).

CARNEGIE COMMISSION ON PREVENTING DEADLY CONFLICT, PREVENTING DEADLY CONFLICT: FINAL REPORT (1997).

Caron, David D., *The Legitimacy of the Collective Authority of the Security Council,* 87 AM. J. INT'L L. 552 (1993).

Carothers, Thomas, *Empirical Perspectives on the Emerging Norm of Democracy in International Law,* 86 PROC. ANN. MEETING OF THE ASIL 261 (1992)

CASANOVAS, ORIOL, UNITY AND PLURALISM IN PUBLIC INTERNATIONAL LAW 85 (2001)

CASSESE, ANTONIO, INTERNATIONAL LAW (2001)

———. *Le Droit International Et La Question De L'assistance Aux Mouvements De Libération Nationale,* 19 REVUE BELGE DE DROIT INTERNATIONAL 307 (1986).

Charlesworth, Hilary C.M., *Customary International Law and the Nicaragua Case,* 11 AUSTL. Y.B. INT'L L. 1 (1984–87).

CHESTERMAN, SIMON, JUST WAR OR JUST PEACE?: HUMANITARIAN INTERVENTION AND INTERNATIONAL LAW (2001).

CHIGARA, BEN, LEGITIMACY DEFICIT IN CUSTOM: A DECONSTRUCTIONIST CRITIQUE (2001).

Chip, William, *A United Nations Role in Ending Civil War,* 19 COLUM. J. TRANSNAT'L L. 15 (1981).

COLLIER, PAUL ET AL., BREAKING THE CONFLICT TRAP: CIVIL WAR AND DEVELOPMENT POLICY SOURCE (2003).

Committee of Enquiry into Breaches of International Law, *Report and Findings of Committee of Enquiry into Breaches of International Law Relating to Intervention in Spain,* S/32 and S/34 SCOR (1936), 1.1 Supp 2 at 54–55, Security Council, Apr. 17, 1946, SCOR 1.1 N2, 167.

Commission of Jurists, *Aaland Islands Situation,* LEAGUE OF NATIONS O. J., Spec. Supp. No. 3 (1920).

Cornell, Michael L., *A Decade of Failure: The Legality and Efficacy of United Nations Actions in the Elimination of Iraqi Weapons of Mass Destruction,* 16 CONN. J. INT'L L. 325 (2001).

COT, JEAN-PIERRE ET AL., LA CHARTE DES NATIONS UNIES: COMMENTAIRE ARTICLE PAR ARTICLE (1985).

Crawford, James, *State Practice and International Law in Relation to Secession,* 69 BRIT. Y.B. INT'L L. 85 (1999).

D'AMATO, ANTHONY, THE CONCEPT OF CUSTOM IN INTERNATIONAL LAW (1971).

———. *The Invasion of Panama Was a Lawful Response to Tyranny,* 4 AM. J. INT'L L. 516 (1990).

Damrosch, Lori F., *Changing Conceptions of Intervention in International Law, in* EMERGING NORMS OF JUSTIFIED INTERVENTION: A COLLECTION OF ESSAYS FROM A PROJECT OF THE AMERICAN ACADEMY OF ARTS AND SCIENCES 105 (Laura W. Reed et al. eds., 1993).

———. *Concluding Reflections in Enforcing Restraint: Collective Intervention, in* INTERNAL CONFLICTS 364 (Lori F. Damrosch ed., 1993).

———. ENFORCING RESTRAINT: COLLECTIVE INTERVENTION IN INTERNAL CONFLICTS (1993).

DANILENKO, GENNADY M., LAW-MAKING IN THE INTERNATIONAL COMMUNITY (1993).

DETTER, INGRID, THE LAW OF WAR 3–25 (2d ed. 2000).

de Vattel, Emerich, *The Law of Nations or the Principles of Natural Law, Originally Printed in 1758, in* THE VIETNAM WAR AND INTERNATIONAL LAW 1 (Richard Falk ed., 1972).

Diamond, Larry, and Leonardo Morlino, *The Quality of Democracy: An Overview,* 15 J. DEMOCRACY 19 (2004).

DICEY, ALBERT V., INTRODUCTION TO THE STUDY OF THE LAW OF THE CONSTITUTION (10th ed. 1959).

DICEY AND MORRIS ON THE CONFLICT OF LAWS (Collins et al. eds., 2002).

DiPaola, Peter D., *A Noble Sacrifice? Jus Ad Bellum and the International Community's Gamble in Chechnya,* 4 IND. J. GLOBAL LEGAL STUD. 435, 435 (1997).

DIXON, MARTIN, AND ROBERT MCCORQUODALE, CASES AND MATERIALS ON INTERNATIONAL LAW (3d ed. 2000).

DRAPER, GERALD I.A.D., THE RED CROSS CONVENTIONS (1958).

DULLES, JOHN FOSTER, WAR OR PEACE 194 (1950).

DWORKIN, RONALD, LAW'S EMPIRE 245 (1998).

Falk, Richard, *Janus Tormented: The International Law of Internal Law, in* INTERNATIONAL ASPECTS OF CIVIL STRIFE 185, 208 (James Rosenau ed., 1964).

———. *Introduction, in* 1 THE INTERNATIONAL LAW OF CIVIL WAR 1 (Richard Falk ed., 1971).

———. *Preface, in* 1 THE INTERNATIONAL LAW OF CIVIL WAR xi (Richard Falk ed., 1971).

Farer, Tom J., *Intervention in Civil Wars: A Modest Proposal,* 67 COLUM. L. REV. 266 (1967).

———. *Harnessing Rogue Elephants: A Short Discussion on Foreign Intervention in Civil Strife,* 82. HARV. L. REV. 511 (1969).

Fielding, Lois E., *Taking the Next Step in the Development of New Human Rights: The Emerging Right of Humanitarian Assistance to Restore Democracy,* 5 DUKE J. COMP. & INT'L L. 329 (1995).

———. *Taking a Closer Look at Threats to Peace: The Power of the Security Council to Address Humanitarian Crises,* 73 U. DET. MERCY L. REV. 551 (1996).

FINN, JOHN E., CONSTITUTIONS IN CRISIS; POLITICAL VIOLENCE AND THE RULE OF LAW (1991).

FINNIS, JOHN, NATURAL LAW AND NATURAL RIGHTS (1980).

Fitzmaurice, Gerald, *Law and Procedure of the International Court of Justice: General Principles and Sources of Law,* 30 BRIT. Y.B. INT'L L. 1 (1953)

Fox, Gregory H., *The Right to Political Participation in International Law,* 17 YALE J. INT'L L. 359 (1992).

———. *International Law and Civil Wars,* 26 N.Y.U. J. INT'L L. & POL. 633 (1994).

FOX, GREGORY H., AND BRAD R. ROTH, DEMOCRATIC GOVERNANCE AND INTERNATIONAL LAW (2000).

Franck, Thomas F., *Multiple Tiers of Sovereignty: The Future of International Governance,* 88 PROC. ANN. MEETING OF THE ASIL 51 (1994).

Franck, Thomas M., *United Nations Law in Africa: The Congo Operation as a Case Study,* 27 LAW & CONTEMP. PROBS. 632 (1962).

———. *Intervention Against Illegitimate Regimes, in* LAW AND FORCE IN THE NEW INTERNATIONAL ORDER 159 (Lori F. Damrosch and David J. Scheffer eds., 1991).

———. *The 'Powers of Appreciation': Who Is the Ultimate Guardian of UN Legality?*, 86 AM. J. INT'L L. 519 (1992).

———. *The Emerging Right to Democratic Governance*, 86 AM. J. INT'L L. 46 (1992).

———. FAIRNESS IN INTERNATIONAL LAW AND INSTITUTIONS (1995).

Franck, Thomas M., and Nigel Rodley, *Legitimacy and Legal Rights of Revolutionary Movements with Special Reference to the People's Revolutionary Government of South Viet Nam, in* THE VIETNAM WAR AND INTERNATIONAL LAW 723 (Richard Falk ed., 1972).

FREEMAN, M.D.A., LLOYD'S INTRODUCTION TO JURISPRUDENCE (7th ed. 2001).

Friedmann, Wolfgang, *Intervention, Civil War and the Role of International Law*, 59 PROC. ANN. MEETING OF THE ASIL 67 (1965).

FUND FOR PEACE, CONFLICT PREVENTION AND RECOVERY PROGRAM (2000).

Gilmour, D.R., *The Meaning of Intervene Within Article 2(7) of the United Nations Charter*, 16 INT'L & COMP. L.Q. 330 (1967)

Gilpin, Robert G., *The Richness of the Tradition of Political Realism*, 38 INT'L ORG. 290 (1984).

Goldsmith, Jack L., and Eric A. Posner, *A Theory of Customary International Law*, 66 U. CHI. L. REV. 1113 (1999).

GOLDSTEIN, ANNE T., RECOGNIZING FORCED IMPREGNATION AS A WAR CRIME UNDER INTERNATIONAL LAW (1993).

GOODRICH, LELAND M. ET AL., CHARTER OF THE UNITED NATIONS: COMMENTARY AND DOCUMENTS (3d ed. 1969).

Gordon, Ruth, *United Nations Intervention in Internal Conflicts: Iraq, Somalia, and Beyond*, 15 MICH. J. INT'L L. 519 (1994).

Gowlland-Debbas, Vera, *The Relationship Between the International Court of Justice and the Security Council in the Light of the Lockerbie Case*, 88 AM. J. INT'L L. 643 (1994).

———. *Security Council Enforcement Action and Issues of State Responsibility*, 43 INT'L & COMP. L.Q. 55 (1994).

GRAY, CHRISTINE, INTERNATIONAL LAW AND THE USE OF FORCE (2000).

GROTIUS, HUGO, DE JURE BELLI ET PACIS LIBRI TRES 88.

Gunning, Isabelle, *Modernizing Customary International Law: The Challenge of Human Rights*, 31 VA. J. INT'L L. 212 (1991).

Hall, Stephen, *The Persistent Spectre: Natural Law, International Order and the Limits of Legal Positivism*, 12 EUR. J. INT'L L. 269 (2001).

Harper, Keith, *Does the United Nations Security Council Have the Competence to Act as Court and Legislature?*, 27 N.Y.U. J. INT'L L. & POL. 103 (1994).

Henckaerts, Jean-Marie, and Louise Doswald-Beck eds., *Study on Customary International Humanitarian Law: A Contribution to the Understanding and Respect for the Rule of Law in Armed Conflict*, 87 INT'L REV. RED CROSS 175 (2005).

Henkin, Louis, *The Mythology of Sovereignty*, 21 PROC. ANN. CONF. OF THE CAN. COUNCIL INT'L L. 5 (1992).

HENSEL, PAUL R. ET AL., THE COLONIAL LEGACY AND BORDER STABILITY: UTI POSSIDETIS AND TERRITORIAL CLAIMS IN THE AMERICA (2004).

Herman, Lawrence L., *The Legal Status of Namibia and of the United Nations Council for Namibia*, 13 CAN. Y.B. INT'L L. 306 (1975).

Higgins, Rosalyn, THE DEVELOPMENT OF INTERNATIONAL LAW THROUGH THE POLITICAL ORGANS OF THE UNITED NATIONS (1963).

———. *Internal War and International Law, in* 3 THE FUTURE OF THE INTERNATIONAL LEGAL ORDER: CONFLICT MANAGEMENT 81 (Cyril E. Black and Richard A. Falk eds., 1969).

———. *The Place of International Law in the Settlement of Disputes by the Security Council*, 64 AM. J. INT'L L. 1, 5 (1970).

———. *The Advisory Opinion on Namibia: Which UN Resolutions Are Binding under Article 25 of the Charter?*, 21 INT'L & COMP. L.Q. 270 (1972).

———. *International Law and Civil Conflict, in* THE INTERNATIONAL REGULATION OF CIVIL WARS (Evan Luard ed., 1972).

———. *Integration of Authority and Control: Trends in the Literature of International Law and International Relations; in* TOWARD WORLD ORDER AND HUMAN DIGNITY 80 (W. Michael Riseman and Burns Weston eds., 1976).

———. PROBLEMS AND PROCESS: INTERNATIONAL LAW AND HOW WE USE IT (1994).

Human Rights Watch, *Getting Away with Murder, Mutilation, Rape: New Testimony from Sierra Leone*, 11(3A) AFR. RTS. WATCH (1999), *available at* http://www.hrw.org/reports/1999/sierra/.

———. CÔTE D'I VOIRE: GOVERNMENT ABUSES IN RESPONSE TO ARMY REVOLT (Nov. 2002).

INTERNATIONAL CRISIS GROUP. KOSOVO: LETS LEARN FROM BOSNIA: MODELS AND METHODS OF INTERNATIONAL ADMINISTRATION (1999).

———. *Current Legal Status of the Federal Republic of Yugoslavia and of Serbia and Montenegro, ICG Balkans Report N° 101* (2000).

———. *Sierra Leone: Time for a New Military and Political Strategy*, Africa Report No. 28 (Apr. 11, 2001).

Institut De Droit International, *Resolution*, 56 ANNUAIRE DE L'INSTITUT DE DROIT INTERNATIONAL 544 (1975).

INTERNATIONAL COMMISSION ON INTERVENTION AND STATE SOVEREIGNTY, RESPONSIBILITY TO PROTECT (2001).

INTERNATIONAL IDEA, DEMOCRACY AND DEEP-ROOTED CONFLICT: OPTIONS FOR NEGOTIATORS (1998).

INTERVENTION IN WORLD POLITICS (Hedley Bull ed., 1984).

International Law Association, *Final Report of the Committee on Formation of Customary General International Law* 742 (2000).

INTERNATIONAL LAW, CASES AND MATERIALS (Louis Henkin and Wolfgang Friedmann eds., 1980).

Itano, Nicole, *Liberating Liberia: Charles Taylor and the Rebels Who Unseated Him*, ISS Paper 82 (2003).

JENNINGS, ROBERT, AND ARTHUR WATTS, OPPENHEIM'S INTERNATIONAL LAW (9th ed. 1992).

JESSUP, PHILIP C., TRANSNATIONAL LAW (1956).

JOHNSON, JAMES TURNER, JUST WAR TRADITION AND THE RESTRAINT OF WAR: A MORAL AND HISTORICAL INQUIRY (1981).

Juss, Satvinder, *Nationality Law, Sovereignty, and the Doctrine of Exclusive Domestic Jurisdiction*, 9 FLA. J. INT'L L. 219 (1994).

KAHNG, TAE JIN, LAW, POLITICS, AND THE SECURITY COUNCIL: AN INQUIRY INTO THE HANDLING OF LEGAL QUESTIONS INVOLVED IN INTERNATIONAL DISPUTES AND SITUATIONS (1964).

Kelsen, Hans, The Law of the United Nations: A Critical Analysis of Its Fundamental Problems (1st ed. 1950).

———. PRINCIPLES OF INTERNATIONAL LAW (Robert W. Tucker rev. ed., 2d ed. 1966).

KEOHANE, ROBERT O., NEOREALISM AND ITS CRITICS (1986).

Kirgis, Jr., Frederic L., *Custom on a Sliding Scale*, 81 AM. J. INT'L L. 146 (1987).

———. *The United Nations at Fifty: The Security Council's First Fifty Years*, 89 AM. J. INT'L L. 506 (1995).

———. *Enforcing International Law*, ASIL INSIGHTS, Jan. 1996, *at* http://www.asil.org/insights/insight1.htm.

Komarnicki, Titus, *L'Intervention en Droit International Moderne*, REVUE GENERALE DE DROIT INTERNATIONAL PUBLIC 521 (1956).

Kooijmans, Peter H., *The Enlargement of the Concept 'Threat to the Peace,' in* PEACE-KEEPING AND PEACE-BUILDING, THE DEVELOPMENT OF THE ROLE OF THE SECURITY COUNCIL 111 (René-Jean Dupuy ed., 1992)

Koskenniemi, Martti, Book Review, 88 MICH. L. REV. 1946 (1990) (reviewing THEODOR MERON, HUMAN RIGHTS AND HUMANITARIAN NORMS AS CUSTOMARY LAW (1989)).

———. FROM APOLOGY TO UTOPIA (1989).

LAW AND CIVIL WAR IN THE MODERN WORLD (John Norton Moore ed., 1974).

Lillich, Richard B., *The Growing Importance of Customary International Human Rights Law*, 25 GA. J. INT'L & COMP. L. 1, 9–10 (1996).

Luard, Evan, *Civil Conflicts in Modern International Relations*, *in* THE INTERNATIONAL REGULATION OF CIVIL WARS 7 (Evan Luard ed., 1972).

MACCORMICK, NEIL, QUESTIONING SOVEREIGNTY: LAW, STATE, AND NATION IN THE EUROPEAN COMMONWEALTH (1999).

Magliveras, Konstantinos D., and Gino Naldi, *The African Union: A New Dawn for Africa?*, 51 INT'L & COMP. L.Q. 415 (2002).

MAYALL, JAMES, THE NEW INTERVENTIONISM 1991–1994: UNITED NATIONS EXPERIENCE IN CAMBODIA, FORMER YUGOSLAVIA AND SOMALIA (1996).

McDougal, Myres S., *International Law, Power and Policy: A Contemporary Conception*, 82 RECUEIL DES COURS 133 (1953).

MCDOUGAL, MYRES S., AND FLORENTINO P. FELICIANO, LAW AND MINIMUM WORLD PUBLIC ORDER: THE LEGAL REGULATION OF INTERNATIONAL COERCION (1961).

MCDOUGAL, MYRES S., AND W. MICHAEL REISMAN, INTERNATIONAL LAW ESSAYS: A SUPPLEMENT TO INTERNATIONAL LAW IN CONTEMPORARY PERSPECTIVE (1981).

Mendelson, Maurice H., *The Formation of Customary International Law*, 272 HAGUE ACADEMY OF INTERNATIONAL LAW, RECUEIL DES COURS 155 (1998).

MERON, THEODOR, HUMAN RIGHTS AND HUMANITARIAN NORMS AS CUSTOMARY LAW (1989).

———. *War Crimes in Yugoslavia and the Development of International Law*, 88 AM. J. INT'L L. 78 (1994).

———. *Editorial Comment: The Continuing Role of Custom in the Formation of International Humanitarian Law*, 90 AM. J. INT'L L. 238 (1996).

MOIR, LINDSAY, THE LAW OF INTERNAL ARMED CONFLICT (2002).

Morgenthau, Hans, *Positivism, Functionalism, and International Law*, *in* THE NATURE OF INTERNATIONAL LAW 159, 172 (Gerry Simpson ed., 2001).

Mori, Tadashi, *Namibia Opinion Revisited: A Gap in the Current Arguments on the Power of the Security Council*, 4 ILSA J. INT'L & COMP. L. 121 (1997).

Nafziger, James A.R., and Edward M. Wise, *The Status in United States Law of Security Council Resolutions Under Chapter VII of the United Nations Charter*, 46 AM. J. COMP. L. SUPP. 421 (1998)

Norton Moore, John, *Introduction*, *in* LAW AND CIVIL WAR IN THE MODERN WORLD I (John Norton Moore ed., 1974).

———. *Toward an Applied Theory for the Regulation of Intervention*, *in* LAW AND CIVIL WAR IN THE MODERN WORLD (John Norton Moore ed., 1974).

Nurick, Lester, and Roger W. Barrett, *Legality of Guerrilla Forces Under the Laws of War*, 40 AM. J. INT'L L. 563 (1946).

O'Brien, William V., *Reprisals, Deterrence and Self-Defense in Counterterror Operations*, 30 VA. J. INT'L L. 421 (1990).

O'Connell, D. P., *Mid-Ocean Archipelagos in International Law*, 45 BRIT. Y.B. INT'L L. 1 (1971).

O'Connell, Mary Ellen, *Continuing Limits on UN Intervention in Civil War*, 67 IND. L.J. 903 (1992).

———. *Regulating the Use of Force in the 21st Century: The Continuing Importance of State Autonomy*, *in* POLITICS, VALUES AND FUNCTIONS: INTERNATIONAL LAW IN THE 21ST CENTURY 443, 448 (Jonathan I. Charney et al. eds., 1998).

Ofodile, Anthony Chukwuka, *The Legality of ECOWAS Intervention in Liberia*, 32 COLUM. J. TRANSNAT'L L. 381 (1994)

O'NEILL, WILLIAM G., KOSOVO AN UNFINISHED PEACE (2002).

OPPENHEIM, L., INTERNATIONAL LAW, VOL II DISPUTES, WAR AND NEUTRALITY (Hersch Lauterpacht ed., 7th ed. 1963).

Packer, Corinne, and Donald Rukare, *The New African Union and Its Constitutive Act*, 96 AM. J. INT'L L. 365 (2002).

Paust, Jordan J., *Applicability of International Criminal Law to Events in the Former Yugoslavia*, 9 AM. U. J. INT'L L. & POL'Y 499 (1994).

Posner, Theodore R., "Kadic v Karadzic," 90 AM. J. INT'L L. 658 (1996).

Pratt, David, *Sierra Leone: The Forgotten Crisis*, Report to the Minister of Foreign Affairs (Apr. 23, 1999), *available at* http://www.globalsecurity.org/military/library/report/1999/crisis-e.htm.

President Bush Outlines His Agenda for U.S.-African Relations, AFR. J., June 26, 2003, *available at* http://www.africacncl.org/AfricaJournal/003_AfricaJournal_AugSept.pdf.

President of the Security Council, *The Situation Relating to Nagorny Karabakh*, Statement, U.N. Doc. S/PRST/1995/21 (Apr. 26, 1995).

———. *The Situation in Sierra Leone*, Statement, U.N. Doc. S/PRST/1997/29 (May 27, 1997).

———. *The situation in Sierra Leone*, Statement, S/PRST/1997/36 (July 11, 1997)

———. *The Situation in Sierra Leone*, Statement, U.N. Doc. S/PRST/1997/42 (Aug. 6, 1997).

———. Statement, U.N. Doc. S/PRST/1997/43 (Aug. 13, 1997).

———. Statement, U.N. Doc. S/PRST/1997/47 (Oct. 16, 1997).

———. Statement, U.N. Doc. S/PRST/1999/7 (Feb. 18, 1999).

———. Statement, U.N. Doc. S/PRST/2001/7 (Mar. 12, 2001).

———. *The Situation in the Central African Republic*, Statement, U.N. Doc. S/PRST/2001/18 (July 17, 2001).

———.Press Release, Security Council Condemns Attempts at Force to Influence Political Situation, Overthrow Elected Government in Côte d'Ivoire, U.N. Doc. AFR/506, SC/7558 (Oct. 31, 2002).

———. *Côte d'Ivoire,* Statement, U.N. Doc. S/PRST/2002/42 (Dec. 20, 2002).

———. Statement on Liberia, U.N. Doc. SC/7787, AFR/644 (Nov. 6, 2003).

RAMSBOTHAM, OLIVER, AND TOM WOODHOUSE, HUMANITARIAN INTERVENTION IN CONTEMPORARY CONFLICT: A RECONCEPTUALIZATION (1996).

Ratner, Steven R., *The Security Council and International Law: Deciphering the Normative Messages of a Political Organ, in* THE UNITED NATIONS SECURITY COUNCIL AFTER THE COLD WAR (David Malone ed., 2004).

Reisman, W. Michael, *Coercion and Self-Determination Construing Charter Article 2(4),* 78 AM. J. INT'L L. 642 (1984).

———. *Sovereignty and Human Rights in Contemporary International Law,* 84 AM. J. INT'L L. 866 (1990).

———. *Comment, Summing Up, in* THE DEVELOPMENT OF THE ROLE OF THE SECURITY COUNCIL: PEACE-KEEPING AND PEACE-BUILDING (René-Jean Dupuy ed., 1992).

———. *Editorial Comment: Assessing Claims to Revise the Laws of War,* 97 AM. J. INT'L L. 82, 83 (2003).

Report of the Conference Held at San Francisco by the Rt Hon Frazer, NZ Dept. of External Affairs Publication, No. 11, 28.

Report of the Panel of Experts Appointed Pursuant to U.N. Security Council Resolution 1306 (2000), *available at* http://www.sierra-leone.org/panelreport.html.

Riphagen, Willem, *The Legal Consequence of Illegal Acts Under Public International Law,* 20 NETH. INT'L L. REV. 27 (1973).

Roberts, Elizabeth A., *Traditional and Modern Approaches to Customary International Law: A Reconciliation,* 95 AM. J. INT'L L. 757 (2001).

ROBERTS, ADAM, AND RICHARD GUELFF, DOCUMENTS ON THE LAWS OF WAR (3d ed. 2000).

ROSENAU, JAMES N., INTERNATIONAL ASPECTS OF CIVIL STRIFE (1964).

ROTH, BRAD R., GOVERNMENTAL ILLEGITIMACY IN INTERNATIONAL LAW (1999).

Schachter, Oscar, *The Quasi-Judicial Role of the Security Council and the General Assembly,* 58 AM. J. INT'L L. 960 (1964).

———. *The United Nations and Internal Conflict, in* LAW AND CIVIL WAR IN THE MODERN WORLD (John Norton Moore ed., 1974).

———. *International Law in Theory and Practice,* 178 RECUEIL DES COURS 13 (1982).

———. *The Legality of Pro-Democratic Invasion,* 78 AM. J. INT'L L. 645 (1984).

———. *Entangled Treaty and Custom, in* INTERNATIONAL LAW AT A TIME OF PERPLEXITY: ESSAYS IN HONOUR OF SHABTAI ROSENNE 717 (Yoram Dinstein ed., 1989).

———. *Authorized Uses of Force by the United Nations and Regional Organisations, in* LAW AND FORCE IN THE NEW INTERNATIONAL ORDER 86 (Lori F. Damrosch and David J. Scheffer eds., 1991).

———. INTERNATIONAL LAW IN THEORY AND PRACTICE (1991).

———. *United Nations Law,* 88 AM. J. INT'L L. 1, 12 (1994).

Schrijver, Nico, *The Changing Nature of State Sovereignty,* 70 BRIT. Y.B. INT'L L. 65 (1999).

SCHWARZENBERGER, GEORG, THE INDUCTIVE APPROACH TO INTERNATIONAL LAW (1965).

Schwebel, Stephen M., *The Effect of Resolutions of the United Nations General Assembly on Customary International Law,* 73 PROC. ANN. MEETING OF THE ASIL 301 (1979).

———. *United Nations Resolutions, Recent Arbitral Awards and Customary International Law, in* REALISM IN LAW-MAKING: ESSAYS ON INTERNATIONAL LAW IN HONOUR OF WILLEM RIPHAGEN (Adriaan Bos and Hugo Siblesz eds., 1986).

Schwelb, Egon, *Crimes Against Humanity,* 23 BRIT. Y.B. INT'L L. 178 (1949).

Scott, Shirley V., *International Law as Ideology: Theorizing the Relationship Between International Law and International Politics,* 5 EUR. J. INT'L L. 313 (1994).

Secretary-General, *Report Submitted to the Security Council in Accordance with Resolution 605(1987),* U.N. Doc. S/19443 (Jan. 21, 1988).

———. *Annual Report of the Secretary-General on the Work of the Organization,* U.N. Doc. A/46/1 (Sept. 16, 1991).

———. *An Agenda for Peace: Preventive Diplomacy, Peacemaking and Peace-Keeping,* U.N. Doc. A/47/277, S/24111 (June 17, 1992).

———. *Report of the Secretary-General on Human Rights Questions: Enhancing the Effectiveness of the Principle of Periodic and Genuine Elections,* U.N. Doc. A/49/675 (Nov. 17, 1994).

———. *Report of the Secretary-General on the Work of the Organization: Supplement to an Agenda for Peace,* U.N. Doc. A/50/60*, S/1995/1* (Jan. 25, 1995).

———. *Report of the Secretary-General on Human Rights Questions: Enhancing the Effectiveness of the Principle of Periodic and Genuine Elections,* U.N. Doc. A/50/736 (Nov. 8, 1995).

———. *Report of the Secretary-General on the Situation in Sierra Leone,* U.N. Doc. S/1995/975 (Nov. 21, 1995).

———. *Report of the Secretary-General on Support by the United Nations System of the Efforts of Governments to Promote and Consolidate New or Restored Democracies,* U.N. Doc. A/51/512 (Oct. 18, 1996).

———. *An Agenda for Democratization, delivered to the General Assembly,* U.N. Doc. A/51/761 (Dec. 20, 1996)

———. *Annual Report of the Secretary-General on the Work of the Organization,* U.N. Doc. A/52/1 (Sept. 3, 1997).

———. *Human Rights Questions: Enhancing the Effectiveness of the Principle of Periodic and Genuine Elections,* U.N. Doc. A/52/474 (Oct. 16, 1997).

———. *Report of the Secretary-General on Support by the UN System of the Efforts of Governments to Promote and Consolidate New or Restored Democracies,* U.N. Doc. A/52/513 (Oct. 21, 1997).

———. *Report of the Secretary-General into the Causes of Conflict and the Promotion of Durable Peace and Sustainable Development in Africa, delivered to the Security Council,* UN Doc. A/52/871, S/1998/318 (Apr. 16, 1998), *available at* www.un.org/ecosocdev/geninfo/afrec/sgreport/index.html.

———. *Report of the Secretary-General on the United Nations Transitional Administration in East Timor,* U.N. Doc. S/2000/738 (July 26, 2000).

SELLERS, MORTIMER THE NEW WORLD ORDER: SOVEREIGNTY, HUMAN RIGHTS, AND THE SELF-DETERMINATION OF PEOPLES (1996).

SHAW, MALCOLM N., INTERNATIONAL LAW (4th ed. 1997).

SHEARER, IVAN A., STARKE'S INTERNATIONAL LAW (11th ed. 1994).

Simma, Bruno, and Andreas Paulus, *Symposium on Method in International Law: The Responsibility of Individuals for Human Rights Abuses in Internal Conflicts: A Positivist View,* 93 AM. J. INT'L L. 302 (1999).

SIMMA, BRUNO, AND HERMANN MOSLER, THE CHARTER OF THE UNITED NATIONS: A COMMENTARY (2d ed. 2002).

Simma, Bruno, and Philip Alston, *The Sources of Human Rights Law: Custom, Jus Cogens, and General Principles,* 12 AUSTL. Y.B. INT'L L. 82, 96 (1989).

Sivakumar, Sandesh, *Binding Armed Opposition Groups,* 55 INT'L & COMP. L.Q. 369 (2006).

Smillie, Ian et al., *The Heart of the Matter: Sierra Leone, Diamonds, and Human Security,* PARTNERSHIP AFR. CAN. INSIGHTS (Jan. 2000), *available at* http://www.sierra-leone.org/heartmatter.html.

SONNENFELD, RENATA, RESOLUTIONS OF THE UNITED NATIONS SECURITY COUNCIL (1988).

STARKE, JOSEPH G., INTRODUCTION TO INTERNATIONAL LAW (10th ed. 1989).

SUNGA, LYAL S., INDIVIDUAL RESPONSIBILITY IN INTERNATIONAL LAW FOR SERIOUS HUMAN RIGHTS VIOLATIONS (1992).

Szasz, Paul, *Role of the United Nations in Internal Conflicts*, 13 GA. J. INT'L & COMP. L. 345 (1983).

———. *Centralized and Decentralized Law Enforcement: The Security Council and the General Assembly Acting Under Chapters VII and VIII*, paper presented to the International Symposium on Allocation of Law Enforcement Authority (Kiel, Germany, Mar. 23–25, 1994).

———. *The Security Council Starts Legislating*, 96 AM. J. INT'L L. 901 (2002).

Taulbee, James L., *Governing the Use of Force: Does the UN Charter Matter Anymore?*, 4 CIVIL WARS 1 (2001).

Tejan-Cole, Abdul, *Human Rights Under the Armed Forces Revolutionary Council in Sierra Leone: A Catalogue of Abuse*, 10 AFR. J. INT'L & COMP. L. 407 (1998).

Tesón, Fernando R., *A Symposium on Re-Envisioning the Security Council: Collective Humanitarian Intervention*, 17 MICH. J. INT'L L. 323 (1996).

———. HUMANITARIAN INTERVENTION: AN INQUIRY INTO LAW AND MORALITY (2d ed. 1997).

Trainin, Iosee, *Questions of Guerrilla Warfare in the Law of War*, 40 AM. J. INT'L L. 534 (1946).

TUNKIN, GRIGORII I., THEORY OF INTERNATIONAL LAW 187 (2d ed. 2003).

UNITED NATIONS, THE BLUE HELMETS: A REVIEW OF UNITED NATIONS PEACE-KEEPING (3d ed. 1996).

U.S. Department of State, Press Release, Yugoslavia: Croatian and Slovenian Unilateral Assertions of Independence (June 26, 1991).

———. "Statement by the Honorable James A. Baker III to the OAS Meeting of Foreign Ministers on the Situation in Haiti" (Oct. 2, 1991).

VAN HOOF, G.J.H., RETHINKING THE SOURCES OF INTERNATIONAL LAW 34 (1983).

VILLIGER, MARK E., CUSTOMARY INTERNATIONAL LAW AND TREATIES: A MANUAL ON THE THEORY AND PRACTICE OF THE INTERRELATION OF SOURCES (2d ed. 1997).

Warbrick, Colin, *The Theory of International Law: Is There an English Contribution?*, *in* THE UNITED NATIONS AND THE PRINCIPLES OF INTERNATIONAL LAW: ESSAYS IN MEMORY OF MICHAEL AKEHURST 49 (Vaughan Lowe and Colin Warbrick eds., 1994).

———. *Brownlie's Principles of Public International Law: An Assessment*, 11 EUR. J. INT'L L. 621, 627 (2000).

Wedgwood, Ruth, *The Use of Force in Civil Disputes*, 26 ISR. Y.B. HUM. RTS. 239 (1996).

Weisburd, Arthur M., *The Significance and Determination of Customary International Human Rights Law*, 25 GA. J. INT'L & COMP. L. 99 (1996).

Wheatley, Steven, *Democracy in International Law: A European Perspective*, 51 INT'L & COMP. L.Q. 225 (2002).

WHITE, NIGEL D., KEEPING THE PEACE: THE UNITED NATIONS AND THE MAINTENANCE OF INTERNATIONAL PEACE AND SECURITY (2d ed. 1997).

WILSON, HEATHER A., INTERNATIONAL LAW AND THE USE OF FORCE BY NATIONAL LIBERATION MOVEMENTS (1988).

Wippman, David, *Treaty-Based Intervention: Who Can Say No?*, 62 U. CHI. L. REV. 607 (1995).

WOLFKE, KAROL, CUSTOM IN PRESENT INTERNATIONAL LAW (2d ed. 1993).

Wood, Michael C., *The Interpretation of Security Council Resolutions*, 2 MAX PLANK Y.B. U.N. L. 73 (1998).

YEMIN, EDWARD, LEGISLATIVE POWERS IN THE UNITED NATIONS AND SPECIALIZED AGENCIES (1969).

CASES, RESTATEMENTS

Advisory Opinion on the Legality of the Threat or Use of Nuclear Weapons, 1996 I.C.J. 226 (July 8).

Certain Expenses of the United Nations (U.N. Charter, art. 17, para. 2), 1962 I.C.J. 151 (July 20).

Conference on Yugoslavia Arbitration Commission Opinions, 31 I.L.M. 1488 (1992).

Fisheries (U.K. v. Nor.), 1951 I.C.J. 116 (Dec. 18).

Frontier Dispute (Burk. Faso/Mali), 1986 I.C.J. 554, 565 (Dec. 22).

Kadic v. Karadzic, 70 F.3d 232 (2d Cir. 1995).

Legal Consequences for States of the Continued Presence of South Africa in Namibia (South West Africa) Notwithstanding Security Council Resolution 276 (1970), Advisory Opinion, 1971 I.C.J. 16 (June 21).

Legality of the Threat or Use of Nuclear Weapons, Advisory Opinion, 1996 I.C.J. 226 (July 8).

Military and Paramilitary Activities in and Against Nicaragua (Nicar. v. U.S.), Merits, 1986 I.C.J. 14 (June 27).

Nationality Decrees Issued in Tunis and Morocco (French Zone) on November 8th, 1921, Advisory Opinion, 1923 P.C.I.J. (ser. B) No. 4 (Feb. 7).

North Sea Continental Shelf Cases, 1969 I.C.J. 3, 44 (Feb. 20).
Prosecutor v. Kupreskic, Case No. IT-95-16-T, Judgment (Jan. 4, 2000).
Prosecutor v. Morris Kallon, Brima Bazzy Kamara, SCSL 2004-15-AR72(E), SCSL-2004-16-AR72(E), Decision on Challenge to Jurisdiction: Lomé Accord Amnesty, Mar. 13, 2004.
Prosecutor v. Tadic, Case No. IT-94-1-A, Judgment of the Appeals Chamber (July 15, 1999).
Prosecutor v. Tadic, Case No. IT-94-1-AR72, Appeal on Jurisdiction (Oct. 2, 1995).
Provisional Measures Decision, United States Diplomatic and Consular Staff in Teheran, Provisional Measures, 1979 I.C.J. 7 (Dec. 15).
Questions of Interpretation and Application of the 1971 Montreal Convention Arising from the Aerial Incident at Lockerbie, (Libya v U.K.), Provisional Measures, 1992 I.C.J. 114 (Apr. 14).
Reference Re Secession of Quebec [1998] 2 S.C.R. 217, para. 112 (Can.).
Reference to Reparations for Injuries Suffered in the Service of the United Nations, 1949 I.C.J. 174, Advisory Opinion (Apr. 11).
RESTATEMENT (THIRD) OF FOREIGN RELATIONS LAW OF THE UNITED STATES 161 (1987).
United States Diplomatic and Consular Staff in Teheran, Judgment, 1980 I.C.J. 3 (May 24).
Yugoslavia Arbitration Commission Opinion 2, 31 I.L.M. 1497 (1992).

TREATIES AND INTERNATIONAL AGREEMENTS

Agreement on Ceasefire and Cessation of Hostilities Between the Government of the Republic of Liberia and Liberians United for Reconciliation and Democracy and the Movement for Democracy in Liberia (Aug 18, 2003).
Charter of the Organization of American States (Apr. 30, 1948), *available at* http://www.oas.org/juridico/English/charter.html.
Constitutive Act of the African Union, July 11, 2000, 2000 AFR. Y.B. INT'L L. 479, *available at* http://www.au2002.gov.za/docs/key_oau/au_act.htm.
Draft Code of Crimes Against the Peace and Security of Mankind (1996), *at* untreaty.un.org/ilc/texts/instruments/english/draft%20articles/7_4_1996.pdf.
ECOWAS Protocol on Democracy and Good Governance, Dec. 2001, A/SP1/12/01, *available at* http://www.issafrica.org/AF/RegOrg/unity_to_union/pdfs/ecowas/12ProtDemocGood.pdf.
ECOWAS, Protocol Relating to Mutual Assistance of Defence (1981), *available at* http://www.iss.co.za/af/RegOrg/unity_to_union/pdfs/ecowas/13ProtMutualDefAss.pdf.

The General Framework Agreement for Peace in Bosnia and Herzegovina (Dayton Peace Accords) (Nov. 21, 1995), ANNEX 1A: Agreement on the Military Aspects of the Peace Settlement, *available at* http://www.state.gov/www/regions/eur/bosnia/bosagree.html.

Inter-American Democratic Charter, September 11, 2001, OEA/Ser.G CP-1, *available at* http://www.oas.org/OASpage/esp/Publicaciones/CartaDemocratica_spa.pdf

International Law Commission, *Draft Articles on State Responsibility*, [1980] 2 Y.B. Int'l L. Comm'n, pt. 2, UN Doc. A/CN.4/SER.A/1980/Add.1 (81.V.4).

Linas-Marcoussis Accord, Jan. 24, 2003.

Lomé Declaration on the Framework for an OAU Response to Unconstitutional Changes of Government (2000) AHG/Decl.5 (XXXVI), *available at* http://www.africanreview.org/docs/govern/govchange.pdf.

Peace Accords for Angola, *available at* http://www.cmi.no/angola/literature/Bicesse_agreement.pdf.

Peace Agreement Between the Government of Sierra Leone and the Revolutionary United Front of Sierra Leone, U.N. Doc. S/1996/1034 (Nov. 30, 1996).

Protocol Additional to the Geneva Conventions of 12 August 1949, Relating to the Protection of Victims of Non-International Armed Conflicts, 16 I.L.M. 1442 (1977).

Protocol Relating to the Establishment of the Peace and Security Council of the African Union, *available at* http://www.africa-union.org/root/au/organs/psc/Protocol_peace%20and%20security.pdf.

Protocol Relating to the Mechanism for Conflict Prevention, Management, Resolution, Peace-Keeping and Security (Dec. 10, 1999), 5 J. CONFLICT & SECURITY L. 231 (2000), *available at* http://www.chr.up.ac.za/hr_docs/african/docs/other/ecowas4.doc.

Rome Statute of the International Criminal Court, U.N. Doc. No. A/CONF.183/9 (July 17, 1998).

Statute of the International Criminal Tribunal for Rwanda, *available at* http://www.ohchr.org/english/law/itr.htm.

Statute of the International Court of Justice, June 26, 1945, *available at* http://www.icj-cij.org/icjwww/ibasicdocuments/ibasictext/ibasicstatute.htm.

DECLARATIONS, LETTERS, PRESS RELEASES

Annex of Letter from the Permanent Representative of Poland to the United Nations Addressed to the President of the Security Council (Mar. 17, 1998), U.N. Doc. S/1998/246.

African Union, Communiqué de l'Union Africaine: Erythrée, Soudan, Côte d'Ivoire (Oct. 12, 2002), *available at* wwwnotes.reliefweb.int/w/rwb.nsf/d2fc8ae9db883867852567cb0083a028/d4ca80cd5deab9b8c1256c520058c898?OpenDocument.

African Union, First Extraordinary Session of the Executive Council: Decision on the Situation in Côte d'Ivoire (Dec. 16, 2002), *available at* wwwnotes.reliefweb.int/w/rwb.nsf/d2fc8ae9db883867852567cb0083a028/6d5ee11b6d5a1a6d85256c93006b6101?OpenDocument.

African Union, Le Conseil Exécutif de l'Union Africaine: Décision sur la situation en Côte d'Ivoire (Dec. 23, 2002), *available at* wwwnotes.reliefweb.int/w/rwb.nsf/d2fc8ae9db883867852567cb0083a028/351eb821cd25638bc1256c9c005c6e58?OpenDocument.

Council of the European Union, Liberia, Bulletin EU 5-2002, Common Foreign and Security Policy 23/29 (2002), *available at* www.europa.eu/bulletin/en/200205/p106023.htm.

Declaration by the Presidency on Behalf of the European Union on the Peace Process in Liberia, 11832/1/03 REV 1, P 92/03 (July 28, 2003).

Déclaration du porte-parole du Quai d'Orsay (Dec. 13, 2002).

Déclaration d'une porte-parole du Quai d'Orsay, (Dec. 12, 2002).

Declaration of the Assembly of Heads of State and Government on the Establishment, Within the OAU of a Mechanism for Conflict Prevention, Management and Resolution, Cairo, Egypt, June 1993, Provision 15.

Declaration on the Formation of the Federal Republic of Yugoslavia (Apr. 27, 1992).

Declaration on the Inadmissibility of Intervention in the Domestic Affairs of States and the Protection of Their Independence and Sovereignty, G.A. Res. 2131(XX), U.N. Doc. A/RES/20/2131 (Dec. 21, 1965).

ECOWAS, Final Communique (Conakry, June 26, 1997).

ECOWAS Six Month Peace Plan for Sierra Leone, U.N. Doc. S/1997/824 (Oct. 23, 1997).

Electoral Assistance Division of the Department of Peace-Keeping Operations of the Secretariat and Department for Development Support and Management Services and Non-Governmental Organisations Colloquium on African Election Administration (Zimbabwe, 1994)

Enhancing the Effectiveness of the Principle of Periodic and Genuine Elections, G.A. Res. 48/131, U.N. Doc. A/RES/48/131 (Feb. 15, 1994)

Entretien du Ministre des Affaires Etrangeres, M. Dominique de Villepin, avec L'Agence Algérienne de Presse, *Situation en Côte d'Ivoire: rôle de la France Dernière mise à jour* (Oct. 31, 2002).

European Community Declaration on Yugoslavia (Dec. 16, 1991)

European Community Declaration on Yugoslavia (Apr. 6, 1992).

European Guidelines on Recognition of New States in Eastern Europe and the Soviet Union, Adopted by the European Community and Its Member States, 92 INT'L L. REV. 174 (1991).

EU Presidency Declaration on Côte d'Ivoire Situation (May 19, 2005), *available at* http://www.europa-eu-un.org/articles/en/article_4707_en.htm.

EU Presidency Declaration on the Peace Process in Liberia (July 21, 2003), *available at* http://www.europa-eu-un.org/articles/en/article_2585_en.htm.

EU Presidency Declaration on Liberia's Peace Process (July 28, 2003), *available at* http://www.europa-eu-un.org/articles/en/article_2618_en.htm.

European Union, European Parliament Resolution on the Situation in Côte d'Ivoire, P5_TA-PROV(2002)0467 (10 Oct 2002), *at* http://www.reliefweb.int/.

International Commission of Inquiry on Darfur, *Report of the International Commission of Inquiry on Darfur to the United Nations Secretary-General,* (Jan. 25, 2005), *available at* http://www.un.org/News/dh/sudan/com_inq_darfur.pdf.

Letter from the Secretary-General to the President of the Security Council (June 28, 2003), U.N. Doc. S/2003/678.

Letter from the Secretary-General Addressed to the President of the Security Council (July 29, 2003), U.N. Doc. S/2003/769.

Letter from the Secretary-General to the Security Council 2 (Oct. 7, 1997), U.N. Doc. S/1997/776.

Proces-Verbaux Du Comité Consultatif Des Juristes, 16 Juin/24 Juillet, 306 (1920).

Press Release, African Union, Côte d'Ivoire: Communiqué of the 84th Ordinary Session (Sept. 24, 2002), *available at* http://www.reliefweb.int/rw/rwb.nsf/AllDocsByUNID/097ed0bcfa9001a2c1256c4500578c09.

Press Release, European Union, Declaration by the EU Presidency Concerning the Situation in Côte d'Ivoire (Dec. 17, 2002), *available at* http://www.reliefweb.int/rw/rwb.nsf/AllDocsByUNID/c2d93086084cde80c1256c980052b8bd.

Press Release, International Crisis Group, Liberia: ICG Urges U.S. to Lead a Robust Multinational Force (July 16, 2003).

Press Release, President of Security Council, Situation in Liberia, U.N. Doc. SC/7824, AFR/674 (July 24, 2003).

Press Release, The Secretary-General, Secretary-General Affirms UN Support for Subregional Efforts to Resolve Côte d'Ivoire Crisis, U.N. Doc. SG/SM/8408, AFR/489 (Oct. 1, 2002).

Press Release, The Secretary-General, Secretary-General Alarmed at Impact of Fighting in Liberia, U.N. Doc. SG/SM/8740, AFR/638 (June 10, 2003).

Press Release, The Secretary-General, Secretary-General Condemns Armed Attacks in Côte d'Ivoire, U.N. Doc. SG/SM/8395, AFR/485 (Sept. 20, 2002).

Press Release, President of Security Council, Security Council Condemns Attempts at Force to Influence Political Situation, Overthrow Elected Government in Côte d'Ivoire, U.N. Doc. AFR/506, SC/7558 (Oct. 31, 2002).

Press Release, The Secretary-General, Secretary-General Condemns Resumption of Hostilities in Liberia; Renews Call for Force Deployment to Restore Calm, U.N. Doc. SG/SM/8787, AFR/670 (July 21, 2003).

Press Release, The Secretary-General, Secretary-General Deeply Concerned at Renewed Fighting in Liberia, Calls for Immediate Cessation of Hostilities, U.N. Doc. SG/SM/8761, AFR/650 (June 26, 2003).

Press Release, The Secretary-General, Secretary-General, in Statement to Security Council, Demands Unconditional Release of United Nations Peacekeepers in Sierra Leone, SG/SM/7390, AFR/226 (May 11, 2000).

Press Release, The Secretary-General, Secretary-General Expresses Concern over Coup in Sierra Leone; Condemns Treatment of UN Staff, Looting of UN Offices, U.N. Doc. SG/SM/6241 (May 27, 1997)

Press Release, Secretary-General, Statement at Memorial Ceremony in New York, U.N. Doc. SG/SM/9223 (Mar. 26, 2004).

Press Release, Secretary-General, Secretary-General Stresses Need for Niger's Return to Democracy and Rule of Law, U.N. Doc. SG/SM/5889 (Feb. 2, 1996)

Press Release, Security Council, Security Council Calls on Sierra Leone Military Junta to Fulfil Obligations Under 23 October Agreement, U.N. Doc. SC/6444 (Nov. 14, 1997).

Resolution of the Institut de Droit International (Apr. 29, 1954).

Strengthening the Role of the United Nations in Enhancing the Effectiveness of the Principle of Periodic and Genuine Elections and the Promotion of Democratization, G.A. Res. 50/185, U.N. Doc. A/RES/50/185 (Mar. 6, 1996).

Strengthening the Role of the United Nations in Enhancing the Effectiveness of the Principle of Periodic and Genuine Elections and the Promotion of Democratization, G.A. Res. 49/190, U.N. Doc. A/RES/49/190 (Mar. 9, 1995).

Statement by Foreign Secretary, Robin Cook (House of Commons, 8 May 2000), *at* http://www.fco.gov.uk.

Speech by Foreign Secretary, Robin Cook (October 2000), *at* http://www.fco.gov.uk.

Speech by Foreign Commonwealth Office Minister of State, Brian Wilson, (Westminster Hall, London, 28 Feb 2001), *at* http://www.fco.gov.uk.

Statement by Defence Secretary on Sierra Leone (15 May 2000), *at* http://www.fco.gov.uk/news.

Statement by former Secretary-General Boutros Boutros-Ghali, United Nations Security Council Meeting on the Responsibility of the Security Council in the Maintenance of International Peace and Security, S.C. Mtg. 3046, U.N. Doc. S/PV.3046 (Jan. 31, 1992).

UN Mission in Liberia (UNMIL), National Transitional Government inaugurated in Liberia, UNMIL/PIO/PR/6 (Oct 15, 2003).

NEWS ARTICLES

Agence France-Presse, *Coast Rebels Gain Ground, But French Say 'No Entry' to Evacuation Zone* (Oct. 1, 2002).

———. *ECOWAS Statement: Liberian Peace Deal to Be Signed After Last-Minute Talks* (Aug. 18, 2003).

———. *First West African Peacekeeping Troops Arrive in Ivory Coast, www.reliefweb.int/.*

———. *Ivory Coast: A Crisis of Many Dimensions* (Sept. 27, 2002).

———. *Ivory Coast Belligerents Attend West African Summit to Defuse Crisis* (Dec. 16, 2002).

———. *Ivory Coast Government, Rebels Pledge to End 'Aggressive Acts'* (Oct. 31, 2002).

———. *Liberian Rebels Declare Truce to Prevent Humanitarian Disaster in Monrovia* (June 27, 2003).

———. *Liberia's Taylor, Rebels to Meet in Ghana for Landmark Peace Talks* (June 2, 2003).

———. *Senegalese Mediator in Bid to Stave off Ivory Coast Civil War* (Oct. 11, 2002).

———. *Statement of the Delta State Governor: Nigerian Troops Ready to "Enforce" Peace in Liberia* (July 30, 2003).

———. *West African Leaders Sending Peacekeepers to Ivory Coast* (Sept. 29, 2002).

AllAfrica, *International Indecision as Crisis Deepens in Liberia* (July 21, 2003), *available at* http://allafrica.com/stories/200307210520.html.

BBC, *US Approves Burma Sanctions* (July 16, 2003), *at* http:.//news.bbc.co.uk/2/hi/asia-pacific/3069841.stm.

———. *Burma Told to Release Suu Kyi* (July 24, 2003), *at* http://news.bbc.co.uk/2/hi/asia-pacific/3091941.stm.

———. *Burma Under Further Pressure* (July 17, 2003), *at* http://news.bbc.co.uk/2/hi/asia-pacific/3073357.stm.

Carribean Net News, *Aristide Departure Is a 'Dangerous Precedent': CARICOM President* (March 4, 2004), *at* http://www.caribbeannetnews.com/2004/03/04/aristide.htm.

CNN, *African Leaders Pledge to Oppose Coups, Support Democracy* (June 4, 1997), *at* http://www.cnn.com/WORLD/9706/04/zimbabwe.new.africa/index.html?eref=sitesearch.

———. *More West African Soldiers Join Nigerians in Sierra Leone* (May 31, 1997), *available at* http://www.cnn.com/WORLD/9705/31/sierra.leone/index.html?eref=sitesearch.

———. *Mutinous Soldiers Scrap Sierra Leone Constitution* (May 28, 1997), *at* www.cnn.com/WORLD/9705/28/sierra.leone/index.html.

———. *Nigerians Launch Attack on Sierra Leone Mutineers* (June 2, 1997), at http://www.cnn.com/WORLD/9706/02/sierra.leone/index.html?eref=sitesearch.

———. *Sierra Leone Fighting Eases, Allowing More Evacuations* (June 3, 1997), *available at* http://www.cnn.com/WORLD/9706/03/sierra.leone/index.html.

Deutsche Presse Agentur, *African, ECOWAS, Leaders Warn Liberian Rebels: No Recognition* (July 27, 2003).

Global News Wire, *Asia Africa Intelligence Wire "European Union condemns violence in Liberia* (June 16, 2003), *at* web.lexis-nexis.com/executive/.

L'Agence Algérienne de Presse, *Entretien du Ministre des Affaires Etrangeres, M Dominique de Villepin: Situation en Côte d'Ivoire: Rôle de la France* (Oct. 31, 2002).

Le Quotidien La Croix, *Entretien du Ministre des Affaires Etrangeres, M Dominique de Villepin* (Dec. 16, 2002), *at* http:// www.diplomatie.gouv.fr/actu/actu.asp.

Nevill, Hugh, *Ivory Coast Prepares to Strike Rebels as Foreigners Pull Out*, Agence France-Press, Sept. 27, 2002.

Pan African News Agency, *Ivorian Rebel Movement Urges France to Be Neutral* (Dec. 12, 2002).

Reuters, *Exodus from Ivory Coast City Under French Guard* (Sept. 26, 2002).

———. *Liberia's Blah Urges Peacekeepers to Halt Killings* (Aug. 25, 2003).

———. *Liberia's President Charles Taylor Resigns* (Aug. 11, 2003).
———. *Ivory Coast Rebels Reject Draft Peace Plan* (Nov. 14, 2002).
———. *Ivory Coast Rebels Sign Ceasefire to End War* (Oct. 17, 2002).
———. *Ivory Coast Urges West to Help Resolve Conflict* (Dec. 10, 2002).
South African Weekly Mail and Guardian, *Africa: Littered With The Debris Of Democracy* (May 30, 1997).
The Times, *Annan Hints at Use of Force to Topple Sierra Leone Coup* (June 5, 1997), *at* http://www.thetimes.co.uk.
U.N. News Centre, *Liberian Rebel Group "Disqualifying" Itself from Future Leadership Role—Annan* (July 28, 2003), *available at* http://www.un.org/apps/news/story.asp?NewsID=7846&Cr=Liberia&Cr1=.
U.N. News Centre, *UN-Backed Sierra Leone Court indicts Liberian President Charles Taylor* (June 4, 2003), *available at* http://www.un.org/apps/news/storyAr.asp?NewsID=7305&Cr=Sierra&Cr1=Leone.
UN OCHA Integrated Regional Information Network, *Côte d'Ivoire: ECOWAS Sets up Mediation Group* (Sept. 30, 2002), *at* http://www.reliefweb.int/.
———. *Côte d'Ivoire: France to Provide Interim Buffer Force* (Oct. 18, 2002), *at* http://www.reliefweb.int/.
———. *Instability in Côte d'Ivoire Situation Report* (Sept. 27, 2002), *at* http://www.reliefweb.int/.
———. *Liberia: Ceasefire Brokered, ECOWAS Military Chiefs to Meet* (June 27, 2003), *at* http://www.reliefweb.int/.
———. *Liberia: Disarmament of Combatants to Start in January* (Oct. 29, 2003), *at* http://www.reliefweb.int/.
———. *Liberia: ECOWAS and MODEL Call on LURD to Stop Fighting* (July 21, 2003), *at* http://www.reliefweb.int/.
———. *Liberia: Mediator Threatens to End Peace Talks, Bush Tells Taylor to Quit* (June 26, 2003), *at* http://www.reliefweb.int/.
———. *Liberia: Taylor Rejects Transition Government Within 30 Days* (June 20, 2003), *at* http://www.reliefweb.int/.

TABLE OF SECURITY COUNCIL RESOLUTIONS

Afghanistan

Concern, comments, acknowledgments
1076 (1996)
1193 (1998)
1214 (1998)
1378 (2001)
Condemnation
1193 (1998)
Calling for particular actions
1076 (1996)
1193 (1998)
1214 (1998)
1267 (1999)
1333 (2000)
1378 (2001)
Sanctions
1267 (1999)
1333 (2000)
1390 (2002)
Observer or peacekeeping forces
1386 (2001)
Use of force
1368 (2001)
Third party actions
622 (1988)
647 (1990)
1378 (2001)
1386 (2001)
Humanitarian laws of war
1193 (1998)
1214 (1998)
1267 (1999)

Sovereignty
1214 (1998)
1267 (1999)
Threats to international peace and security
1267 (1999)

Albania

Concern, comments, acknowledgments
1101 (1997)
Calling for particular actions
1101 (1997)
1114 (1997)
Use of force
1101 (1997)
Sovereignty
1101 (1997)
1114 (1997)
Threats to international peace and security
1101 (1997)

Angola

Concern, comments, acknowledgments
785 (1992)
811 (1993)
864 (1993)
1173 (1998)
Condemnation
785 (1992)
811 (1993)
834 (1993)
864 (1993)
Calling for particular actions
747 (1992)
785 (1992)
793 (1992)
811 (1993)
834 (1993)
864 (1993)
1173 (1998)
Sanctions
864 (1993)
1127 (1997)
1173 (1998)

Observer or peacekeeping forces
626 (1988)
696 (1991)
747 (1992)
1118 (1997)
1229 (1999)
Third party actions
864 (1993)
Humanitarian laws of war
811 (1993)
864 (1993)
696 (1991)
834 (1993)
864 (1993)
Threats to international peace and security
864 (1993)
1221 (1999)
1237 (1999)
1127 (1997)
1130 (1997)
1135 (1997)
1173 (1998)
1176 (1998)

Armenia

Concern, comments, acknowledgments
S/PRST/1995/21 (Statement of the President)
Calling for particular actions
S/PRST/1995/21 (Statement of the President)
Third party actions
S/PRST/1995/21 (Statement of the President)
S/1995/249, appendix

The Former Yugoslavia

Concern, comments, acknowledgments
713 (1991)
721 (1991)
727 (1992)
771 (1992)
777 (1992)
821 (1993)
943 (1994)
1022 (1995)
1031 (1995)
Condemnation
771 (1992)
847 (1993)
Calling for particular actions
713 (1991)
721 (1991)
740 (1992)
749 (1992)
771 (1992)
Sanctions
713 (1991)
757 (1992)
808 (1993)
1022 (1995)
Observer or peacekeeping forces
721 (1991)
740 (1992)
743 (1992)
749 (1992)
Third party actions
713 (1991)
943 (1994)
Humanitarian laws of war
771 (1992)
1034 (1995)
Threats to international peace and security
713 (1991)
724 (1991)
757 (1992)
760 (1992)
771 (1992)
787 (1992)
808 (1993)
827 (1993)
908 (1994)
914 (1994)
947 (1994)
967 (1994)
992 (1995)
1074 (1996)

Federal Republic of Yugoslavia and Kosovo

Croatia

Burundi

Concern, comments, acknowledgments
1012 (1995)
1040 (1996)
1049 (1996)
1072 (1996)
Condemnation
1040 (1996)
1049 (1996)
1072 (1996)
1286 (2000)
Calling for particular actions
1040 (1996)
1049 (1996)
1072 (1996)
Third party actions
1049 (1996)
1072 (1996)

Cambodia

Concern, comments, acknowledgments
668 (1991)
745 (1992)
810 (1993)
Condemnation
766 (1992)
Calling for particular actions
810 (1993)
880 (1993)
Observer or peacekeeping forces
717 (1992)
745 (1992)
Third party actions
668 (1990)
Humanitarian laws of war
880 (1993)
Sovereignty
880 (1993)

Central African Republic (CAR)

Concern, comments, acknowledgments
1125 (1997)
1271 (1999)
S/PRST/1999/7 (Statement of the President)
Condemnation
S/PRST/2001/18 (Statement of the President)
Calling for particular actions
1152 (1998)
S/PRST/2001/18 (Statement of the President)
S/PRST/2001/7 (Statement of the President)
Observer or peacekeeping forces
1159 (1998)
Third party actions
1125 (1997)
1159 (1998)
Sovereignty
1271 (1999)
Threats to international peace and security
1125 (1997)
1136 (1997)
1152 (1998)
1155 (1998)
1159 (1998)
1125 (1997)

Chad

Observer or peacekeeping forces
915 (1994)
Third party actions
504 (1982)

The Republic of the Congo (Brazzaville)

Concern, comments, acknowledgments
161 (1961)
169 (1961)
Calling for particular actions
161 (1961)
169 (1961)
S/PRST/1997/43 (Statement of the President)
S/PRST/1997/47 (Statement of the President)

Observer or peacekeeping forces
143 (1960)
146 (1960)
169 (1961)
S/PRST/1997/43 (Statement of the President)
Use of force
169 (1961)
Sovereignty
169 (161)
Threats to international peace and security
S/PRST/1997/43 (Statement of the President)

Democratic Republic of the Congo (DRC)

Concern, comments, acknowledgments
1078 (1996)
1080 (1996)
1097 (1997)
S/PRST/1997/11 (Statement of the President)
S/PRST/1997/19 (Statement of the President)
S/PRST/1997/31 (Statement of the President)
1234 (1999)
1258 (1999)
1279 (1999)
1484 (2003)
Condemnation
1078 (1996)
S/PRST/1997/11 (Statement of the President)
1234 (1999)
1279 (1999)
1304 (2000)
1399 (2002)
Calling for particular actions
1078 (1996)
1080 (1996)
1234 (1999)
1258 (1999)
1279 (1999)
1304 (2000)
1484 (2003)
Observer or peacekeeping forces
1080 (1996)
1258 (1999)
1279 (1999)
1291 (2000)
Use of force
1484 (2003)
Third party actions
S/PRST/1997/11 (Statement of the President)
1234 (1999)
1258 (1999)
1484 (2003)
1501 (2003)
Humanitarian laws of war
1080 (1996)
1234 (1999)
1304 (2000)
Sovereignty
1080 (1996)
1234 (1999)
1291 (2000)
Threats to international peace and security
1078 (1996)
1234 (1999)
1291 (2000)
1304 (2002)
1399 (2002)
1484 (2003)

Côte d'Ivoire

Concern, Comments, Acknowledgements
1464 (2003)
Calling for particular actions
S/PRST/2002/42 (Statement of the President)
1464 (2003)
Observer or peacekeeping forces
1479 (2003)

Israel and Palestine

Lebanon

INDEX

www.ingramcontent.com/pod-product-compliance
Lightning Source LLC
LaVergne TN
LVHW021038011026
849160LV00008BA/271
9781571053749